The Tathāgata Store

Selected Mahāyāna Sūtras

Translated by Rulu

AuthorHouse™
1663 Liberty Drive
Bloomington, IN 47403
www.authorhouse.com
Phone: 1 (800) 839-8640

Published by AuthorHouse 02/17/2017
Library of Congress Control Number: 2016917697

ISBN: 978-1-5246-4637-0 (sc)
ISBN: 978-1-5246-4636-3 (e)

Print information available on the last page.

This book is printed on acid-free paper.

To those who read and recite sūtras
pronounced by the Buddha

Contents

Preface

The aim of Mahāyāna teachings is for everyone, out of compassion for all sentient beings, to attain Buddhahood. The reason one can attain Buddhahood is that one possesses the Tathāgata store (tathāgata-garbha), which is one's inherent pure mind or Buddha nature. Therefore, the spiritual journey of whoever rides the One Vehicle to go from the Cause Ground to the Result Ground is to go from his belief that he is a Tathāgata in storage to his realization that he is a Tathāgata in splendor. Upon attaining Buddhahood, he truly sees that his fully enlightened mind is none other than his inherent pure mind. Hence there is no attainment.

The Introduction chapter of this book explores the origin of the concept of the Tathāgata store, and discusses how teachings on the Tathāgata store have come to be accepted in China as the mainstream of Mahāyāna teachings and a distinct school of thought, standing apart from and along with the Mādhyamaka School and the Yogācāra School. Highlights of teachings on the Tathāgata store presented in this chapter are based only on texts in the Chinese Buddhist Canon, avoiding scholarly publications that approach Buddhist teachings from the perspective of philosophy or other religions. These highlights include why all sentient beings possess the Tathāgata store, meanings of the dharma body and its four virtues, a comparison between the self claimed by those on non-Buddhist paths and a true self taught by the Buddha, meanings of one's Buddha nature, and how one's Tathāgata store and ālaya consciousness (ālaya-vijñāna) are unified.

For readers to receive teachings on the Tathāgata store as originally given, this book presents the English translations of six sūtras selected from the Chinese Buddhist Canon. Sūtra 1, the *Mahāvaipulya Sūtra of the Tathāgata Store,* gives a basic teaching and describes by nine analogies that one's Tathāgata store is shrouded by one's afflictions. Sūtra 2, the *Sūtra of Neither Increase Nor Decrease,* reveals that the Tathāgata store is a Tathāgata's dharma body, and that the realm of sentient beings neither increases nor decreases. Sūtra 3, the *Sūtra of Śrīmālā's Lion's Roar,* gives teachings on one's afflictions that shroud one's Tathāgata store and inspires all sentient beings to ride the One Vehicle to attain Buddhahood. Sūtra 4, the Mahāyāna version of the *Sūtra of Aṅgulimālika,* reveals that as one's Tathāgata store transcends all dharmas, all dharmas are one's Tathāgata store. Sūtra 5, the *Sūtra of the Unsurpassed Reliance,* teaches one to rely on one's Tathāgata store in order to walk the bodhi path to Buddhahood. Sūtra 6, the *Sūtra of the Vajra Samādhi,* reveals that one's inherent awareness, the pure awareness of one's true mind, has a mass of benefits.

Sūtras 4 and 5 have never before been translated into English. Sūtra 2 is a revised version of the English translation initially published in *Teachings of the Buddha* (Rulu 2012a, 97–102).

Preface

All texts used in the book are contained in the digital Chinese Canon on a DVD-ROM, 2014 version, produced by the Chinese Buddhist Electronic Text Association (CBETA) in Taiwan. Any cited text is identified by its volume and text numbers according to the CBETA system. For example, a text cited as T16n0666 is text 666 in volume 16 of the Chinese Canon (the Taishō Tripiṭaka); a text cited as X63n1217 is text 1217 in volume 63 of the Extension of the Chinese Canon (the Shinsan Zokuzōkyō). Any passage in a text can be located by its page, column, and line numbers. For example, a passage cited as 0458c19–23 is on page 458, column c, lines 19 to 23.

Following the rules of translation stated in "Translator's Note" in my first book, *Teachings of the Buddha,* I have done my best to render the English translation as faithful to the Chinese text, yet as clear as possible. As the Buddha teaches with one tone, all sentient beings receive benefits according to their needs and preferences. This book will benefit readers at all levels and can serve as a basis for scholarly research.

For the generous help I have received, I thank the following beneficent learned friends: Stephen Colley, who edited all my translations and the entire manuscript of this book; Avinash Sathaye, who with infinite patience helped me with a Sanskrit passage related to Sūtra 2; Nicholas Weeks, who captured typos on my webpages and asked questions that prompted me to revise my translations of several phrases; the Chua Lien Hoe Temple, Garden Grove, CA, which provided a picture of its Buddha statue for the cover of this book; visitors to my website, who appreciate the teachings of the Buddha; and earlier translators, who have benefited readers and inspired later translators.

Any flaws in my translations are my sole responsibility. May the merit of all contributors be transferred to all sentient beings for their rebirth in the Western Pure Land of Ultimate Bliss and for their eventual attainment of Buddhahood.

Rulu (如露)
February 14, 2017

Translator's Introduction

I see that as sentient beings with various afflictions transmigrate through countless births and deaths in the long night, the wondrous Tathāgata store in their bodies is stately and pure, no different from me. Therefore, I, the Buddha, expound the Dharma to sentient beings, to enable them to end their afflictions, acquire the pure Tathāgata wisdom, and then transform and guide all others in the world.

—*Mahāvaipulya Sūtra of the Tathāgata Store*
Translated from the Chinese Canon (T16n0666, 0458c19–23)

Meanings of Relevant Terms

Tathāgata

The Sanskrit word *tathāgata* is the compound "tathā-gata" or "tathā-āgata." As *tathā* means thusness or suchness, "tathā-gata" means thus gone; "tathā-āgata," thus come. The term "thus gone" means that a Tathāgata, taking the path of suchness, has gone into nirvāṇa; "thus come" means that a Tathāgata, knowing the suchness of dharmas, has come from suchness. Tathāgata is the first of the ten epithets of a Buddha because His nature is thusness, or suchness. A Tathāgata is the Thus-Gone One, who has finished His Buddha work and gone into nirvāṇa; He is the Thus-Come One, who has come to teach the suchness of dharmas to sentient beings and deliver them from their ignorance and suffering. In text 235, one of the six Chinese versions of the *Diamond Sūtra,* the Buddha says, "A Tathāgata comes from nowhere and goes to nowhere" (T08n0235, 0752b4–5). As a manifestation of suchness, a Tathāgata is beyond coming and going. Nevertheless, He appears in the world as if He has come, and enters parinirvāṇa as if He has gone, in the same way as did past Buddhas.

Master Zhiyi (智顗, 538–97), the founding patriarch of the Tiantai School of China, in fascicle 9 of text 1718 (in 10 fascicles), his commentary on the *Lotus Sūtra,* said that suchness pervades everywhere and never changes, and that when suchness comes without moving, it means a Tathāgata's dharma body (dharmakāya); when suchness comes from merit and wisdom, it means a Tathāgata's reward body (saṁbhogakāya); when suchness comes to display the eight scenes of attaining Buddhahood and to turn the Dharma wheel, it means a Tathāgata's response body (nirmāṇakāya) (T34n1718, 0128a7–16). As the dharma body is invisible, the other two bodies are the appearances of the dharma body (see "three bodies of a Buddha" in the glossary).

Garbha

The Sanskrit word *garbha* means embryo or womb. This word probably originated from the *Garbha Upaniṣad,* an ancient Indian text that describes the formation and development of a human embryo in its mother's womb. In

Chinese texts, this Sanskrit word *garbha* is translated as *zang* 藏, which means stored or hidden, and is an interpretation of the word *womb*. Here, the Chinese word *zang* is translated into English as store. While *womb* means a nurturing and protective container, *store* means either a storehouse or what is stored and hence hidden. For example, space store (ākāśa-garbha) can mean one's true mind or a Bodhisattva's store of merit and wisdom, which is as immeasurable as space; vajra store (vajra-garbha) can mean one's true mind, which is as indestructible as vajra (an adamantine substance, usually translated as diamond); earth store (kṣiti-garbha) means the secret store of all treasures hidden in the earth; precept store (śīla-garbha) means the collection of all precepts; Dharma store (dharma-garbha) means the store of all teachings in the Buddha Dharma.

Tathāgata-Garbha

Given that *garbha* means embryo or womb, scholars have translated "tathāgata-garbha" as the embryo of a Tathāgata, the germ of a Tathāgata, the womb of a Tathāgata, or the matrix of a Tathāgata. In Chinese texts, "tathāgata-garbha" is translated as *rulai zang* 如來藏. Here, these Chinese words are translated into English as Tathāgata store, which means a Tathāgata in storage or hidden.

"Tathāgata store" works well in all texts that use it. For example, in text 666 (T16n0666), one of the two extant Chinese versions of the *Mahāvaipulya Sūtra of the Tathāgata Store,* the Buddha reveals that all sentient beings have the Tathāgata store within them, and describes it by nine analogies, including a Buddha inside a lotus flower bud, who is revealed after the flower has withered; a chunk of gold fallen into a filthy place; the treasure store under a poor family's house. These analogies indicate that all sentient beings are a Tathāgata in storage, who is to be revealed, not developed or transformed from an embryo or a germ.

Does the Tathāgata store ever do anything or change? The answer is given in text 273 (in 2 fascicles), the Chinese version of the *Sūtra of the Vajra Samādhi.* In fascicle 1, the Buddha says, "Although one's Tathāgata store is hidden by the appearances of birth and death of one's thoughts and concerns, it is by nature quiet and motionless" (T09n0273, 0366c17–18).

In fascicle 3 of text 1610 (in 4 fascicles), the Chinese version of *A Treatise on Buddha Nature* (Buddhagotra-śāstra), the meaning of the Tathāgata store is explained in terms of (1) what is encompassed, (2) what is hidden, and (3) what it encompasses. According to this treatise, the Tathāgata store means that (1) all sentient beings are encompassed in a Tathāgata's wisdom-knowledge [jñāna], (2) a Tathāgata's dharma body is hidden because it is sheathed in one's afflictions, and (3) one's Tathāgata store fully encompasses all virtues of a Tathāgata (T31n1610, 0795c23–0796a28).

Moreover, in text 668 (in one fascicle), the Chinese version of the *Sūtra of Neither Increase Nor Decrease* (Anūnatva-apūrṇatva-nirdeśa-parivarta), the Buddha equates one's Tathāgata store to a Tathāgata's dharma body. He says, "The realm of sentient beings is the Tathāgata store, and the Tathāgata store is the dharma body" (T16n0668, 0467a18–19). In text 353, the earlier of the two extant Chinese versions of the *Vaipulya Sūtra of Śrīmālā's Lion's Roar* (Śrīmālādevī-siṁhanāda-sūtra), Śrīmālā explains the connection between the dharma body and one's Tathāgata store. She says, "When a Tathāgata's dharma body is not free from one's store of afflictions, it is called the Tathāgata store" (T12n0353, 0221c10–11). What are the other meanings of the Tathāgata store? Śrīmālā equates the Tathāgata store to four other stores. She says, "One's Tathāgata store is the store of the dharma realm [dharma-dhātu], the store of the dharma body, the store of supra-worldly dharmas, and the store of one's inherent pure nature [Buddha nature]" (Ibid., 0222b22–23).

Moreover, several Mahāyāna texts equate one's Tathāgata store to one's inherent pure mind (prakṛti-pariśuddha-citta) or Buddha nature (buddha-dhātu or buddha-gotra). For example, in fascicle 2 of text 839 (in 2 fascicles), the Chinese version of the *Sūtra of Detecting Good or Evil Karma and Requital,* Earth Store (Kṣitigarbha) Bodhisattva says, "One's inherent pure mind is profound and perfect because it does not differentiate objects. Because it does not differentiate, it is universal. As it is universal, all dharmas rely on it to establish themselves. Furthermore, this mind is called the Tathāgata store, which encompasses immeasurable, boundless, inconceivable, affliction-free, pure, meritorious karmas" (T17n0839, 0907c7–11; Rulu 2012a, 110). Also, in fascicle 4 of text 120 (in 4 fascicles), the Chinese version of the Mahāyāna version of the *Sūtra of Aṅgulimālika,* the Buddha says, "The Tathāgata store means one's inherent pure mind. As one's Tathāgata store transcends all dharmas, all dharmas are one's Tathāgata store" (T02n0120, 0540a3–5). Also, in the *Sūtra of Neither Increase Nor Decrease,* the Buddha pronounces that the Tathāgata store in accord with purity and true suchness (bhūta-tathātā) is one's inherent pure mind (T16n0668, 0467b28–29). Another example is found in text 272 (in 10 fascicles), the Chinese version of the *Sūtra Pronounced by Mahāsatya, a Nirgranthaputra Master* (Bodhisattva-gocaropāya-viṣaya-vikurvaṇa-nirdeśa). In fascicle 9, the Buddha says, "Know that in one's store of filthy afflictions, one's Tathāgata nature is clearly perfect" (T09n0272, 0359a28–29).

The teachings in these texts indicate that "tathāgata-garbha" does not mean an embryo or a germ that will grow and transform into a Tathāgata, but means a Tathāgata in storage, with all His virtues. Whether equated to a Tathāgata's dharma body or to one's inherent pure mind or Buddha nature, the Tathāgata store, though sheathed in one's afflictions, is pure and changeless.

The Second Meaning of the Tathāgata Store

The first meaning of the Tathāgata store as explained in the preceding section is based on the word *store* (zang 藏), translated from the Sanskrit word *garbha* (womb). However, in some Chinese texts, the word *store* is translated from the Sanskrit word *piṭaka* (basket). For example, the Sanskrit word Tripiṭaka is translated into Chinese as Triple Store (san zang 三藏), which means the three collections of texts in the Buddhist Canon: (1) the Sūtra-piṭaka, discourses of the Buddha; (2) the Vinaya-piṭaka, rules of conduct; and (3) the Abhidharma-piṭaka, treatises on the Dharma.

As an example of the second meaning of the word *store,* a stanza in fascicle 1 of text 125 (in 51 fascicles), the Chinese version of the Ekottarika Āgama (Numbered Discourses), is cited as follows: "Whoever intently upholds the

Ekottarika Āgama / Retains the Tathāgata store. / Even if he cannot end his afflictions in his current life, / He will acquire higher wisdom-knowledge in his next life" (T02n0125, 0550c3–4). Here, the Tathāgata store means a Tathāgata's store of teachings.

As another example, fascicle 3 of text 291 (in 4 fascicles), the Chinese version of the *Sūtra of a Tathāgata's Appearance in the World,* states: ". . . use these four [gems of great wisdom] to seek the Tathāgata store" (T10n0291, 0605c12). The meaning of the Tathāgata store in that passage is clarified by a corresponding passage in fascicle 35 of text 278, the 60-fascicle Chinese version of the *Mahāvaipulya Sūtra of Buddha Adornment* (Buddhāvataṁsaka-mahāvaipulya-sūtra). This passage states that "these four gems of great wisdom are kept in a Tathāgata's secret store of the Dharma jewel[1]" (T09n0278, 0622c19–20).

Then the meaning of a Tathāgata's secret store is clarified in text 374, the 40-fascicle Chinese version of the *Mahāparinirvāṇa Sūtra.* In fascicle 7, the Buddha says, "Good man, if one does not study a Tathāgata's profound secret store, how can one know that one possesses Buddha nature? What is meant by the secret store? It means Mahāyāna vaipulya sūtras" (T12n0374, 0405b4–6).

Therefore, depending upon the context, "Tathāgata store" in a Chinese text can mean either the Tathāgata store discussed in the preceding section or a Tathāgata's store of teachings. Readers and translators of Chinese texts should take care to distinguish between these two meanings.

The Origin of the Thought of the Tathāgata Store

One's Inherent Luminous Mind in Voice-Hearer Teachings

The concept of the Tathāgata store can be traced to that of one's inherent luminous mind (prakṛti-prabhāsvara-citta) mentioned in voice-hearer teachings. For example, in a chapter in volume 19 of the Aṅguttara Nikāya (Numbered Discourses) in the 70-volume Chinese version of the Pāli Canon,[2] the Buddha says, "Bhikṣus, one's mind is luminous and pure, but tainted by one's visitor-like afflictions [āgantuka kleśa].[3] Bhikṣus, one's mind is luminous and pure, and can be freed from one's visitor-like afflictions" (N19n0007, 0012a4–5 // PTS.A.1.10).

This teaching in the Aṅguttara Nikāya is repeated in text 1548 (in 30 fascicles), the Chinese version of the *Śāriputrābhidharma-śāstra.* Fascicle 27 states: "One's mind is inherently pure but tainted by one's visitor-like afflictions. Ordinary beings have not heard about it, and cannot truly know and see it, nor do they cultivate their minds. Sages have heard about it, can truly know and see it, and do cultivate their minds. One's mind is inherently pure and can be freed from one's visitor-like afflictions. Ordinary beings have not heard about it, and cannot truly know and see it, nor do they cultivate their minds. Sages have heard about it, can truly know and see it, and do cultivate their minds" (T28n1548, 0697b18–22). This treatise is attributed to Śāriputra, one of the Buddha's principal disciples, and its tenets accord with the doctrine of the Mahāsaṅghika sects, which laid the foundation for the rise of the Mahāyāna.

Both the Vibhajyavāda sect and the Mahāsaṅghika sects of early Buddhism held that one's mind is inherently pure. According to fascicle 27 of text 1545, the Chinese version of the *Abhidharma-mahāvibhāṣā-śāstra,* the Vibhajyavāda sect, whose members differentiated different doctrines, held that "one's mind is inherently pure but tainted by visitor-like afflictions. Hence it has an impure appearance" (T27n1545, 0140b25–26). According to text 2033, the Chinese version of a short treatise that summarizes the different doctrines of the twenty sects of early Buddhism, the common beliefs of the four Mahāsaṅghika sects included "one's mind is inherently pure but tainted by one's visitor-like afflictions" (T49n2033, 0021a1).

Such voice-hearer teachings indicate that one should train in meditation in order to realize one's inherent luminous mind, though no explanation of this mind is given. As Mahāyāna texts related to the Tathāgata store appeared in India between the second and third centuries CE, "inherent luminous mind" in voice-hearer texts has evolved into "inherent pure mind" (prakṛti-pariśuddha-citta), which is equated to Tathāgata store, dharma body, or Buddha nature.

Teachings on the Tathāgata Store Implied in Early Mahāyāna Sūtras

Although "inherent luminous mind" in voice-hearer texts looks similar to "inherent pure mind" in Mahāyāna texts, the doctrine of the Tathāgata store did not arise from voice-hearer teachings. Instead, it arose from early Mahāyāna teachings, given in prajñā-pāramitā sūtras and the *Buddha Adornment Sūtra.*

For example, in the chapter "Dharma Nature," in fascicle 569 of text 220 (in 600 fascicles), the Chinese version of the *Large Sūtra of Prajñā-Pāramitā,* the Buddha says, "As an analogy, a priceless wish-fulfilling jewel is lustrous, pure, and lovely. Its body is perfectly pure, without taints. However, it is left in mud for a long time. Then someone picks it up, washes it, and protects it from falling [into mud].[4] Likewise, although dharma nature [dharmatā] is shrouded by one's afflictions, it is not tainted by them and can be revealed. . . . Buddhas know that the nature of a sentient being has always been pure but is shrouded by his visitor-like afflictions" (T07n0220, 0936c27–0937a3). Then He explains, "When dharma nature, measureless and boundless, is sheathed in one's afflictions, follows the flow of birth and death, and transmigrates through the six life-paths in the long night, it is called the nature of sentient beings" (Ibid., 0937a24–26). In this passage, the priceless wish-fulfilling jewel is an analogy of the Tathāgata store; dharma nature is true suchness or emptiness (śūnyatā). Here, it means the dharma body or one's Buddha nature or Tathāgata store.

Moreover, "Tathāgata store" appears in the chapter "Meanings of Prajñā," in fascicle 578, in which the Buddha says, "All sentient beings are Tathāgata stores because Samantabhadra Bodhisattva's nature pervades them; all sentient beings are vajra stores because Vajra Store Bodhisattva sprinkles on them the water [of empowerment]; all sentient beings are true Dharma stores because they follow the words of truth; all sentient beings are wondrous karma stores because they do karmas after preparatory training" (Ibid., 0990b3–7).

In a subtle way, teachings on the Tathāgata store appear in the *Buddha Adornment Sūtra,* text 278 in 60 fascicles and text 279 in 80 fascicles. For example, in fascicle 10 of text 278, a stanza states: "The mind, a Buddha, and a sentient being / Are the three things with no difference" (T09n0278, 0465c28–20). In fascicle 37 of text 279, Vajra Store Bodhisattva says, "As all things in the Three Realms of Existence are encompassed in the mind, so too are the Twelve Links of Dependent Arising expounded by the Tathāgata. They are based in and arise from the mind" (T10n0279, 0194a14–15; Rulu 2013, 178). It is conceivable that "the mind" in these two passages means one's inherent pure mind. Then, in fascicle 38 of text 279, Vajra Store Bodhisattva says, "Moreover, good man, whether or not a Buddha appears in the world, dharma nature ever abides, without change" (Ibid., 0199b9–10; Rulu 2013, 199).

However, a teaching on one's Tathāgata store is evident in a passage in fascicle 51 of text 279. It indicates that all sentient beings possess Tathāgata wisdom, which implies that all sentient beings have the Tathāgata store in them. That passage parallels this Introduction chapter's epigraph, excerpted from the *Mahāvaipulya Sūtra of the Tathāgata Store*. For comparison, the passage is given below.[5]

> Then a Tathāgata observes all sentient beings in the dharma realm with His hindrance-free pure wisdom-eye and speaks these words: "Amazing! Amazing! Why do these sentient beings, deluded and confused, not know and not see that they have a Tathāgata's wisdom? I will teach them the holy path, enabling them to discard forever their attachments and deluded perceptions. Then they will be able to see within them vast Tathāgata wisdom, no different from a Buddha's." Then He teaches sentient beings to train on the holy path, enabling them to discard their deluded perceptions. After discarding their deluded perceptions, they realize their immeasurable Tathāgata wisdom, benefit all others, and bring them peace and joy. (T10n0279, 0272c25–0273a3; Rulu 2014, 236)

Texts Related to the Tathāgata Store

Appearance of Sanskrit Texts Related to the Tathāgata Store

Sanskrit texts related to the Tathāgata store appeared in India between the second and third centuries CE, earlier than those of the Yogācāra doctrine. According to the Buddha's prophecies, such texts would first appear in southern India. In fascicle 2 of text 270 (in 2 fascicles), the Chinese version of the *Sūtra of the Great Dharma Drum* (Mahābherī-hāraka-parivarta), the Buddha says, "When eighty years still remain for the true Dharma [saddharma] as it perishes, he [the Licchavi youth called Entire World Is Delighted to See] will be reborn in the south, in the kingdom of Madras [present-day Chennai] . . . . First, he will pronounce this *Sūtra of the Great Dharma Drum*. Second, he will pronounce Mahāyāna sūtras on the emptiness of dharmas. Third, he will pronounce the eternal abiding of a Tathāgata and the realm of sentient beings, in accordance with this *Sūtra of the Great Dharma Drum*" (T09n0270, 0299a15–22; Rulu 2012a, 181–82). The name of this youth reborn in the south is revealed in text 672, the 7-fascicle Chinese version of the *Laṅkāvatāra Sūtra*. In fascicle 6, the Buddha says, "Mahāmati, know that after the Sugata's parinirvāṇa, in times to come, in southern India there will be a bhikṣu of great virtue, called Nāgārjuna.[6] He will be able to shatter the views of existence and nonexistence [of dharmas], and reveal to the world my Dharma, the unsurpassed Mahāyāna teachings. He will ascend to the Joyful Ground [first Bodhisattva ground] and be reborn in the Land of Peace and Bliss" (T16n0672, 0627c17–22).

The Buddha also mentions the south in the *Sūtra of Aṅgulimālika*. In fascicle 4 of text 120, He says, "In the south, there will be those who, free from the eight evil ways, walk the firm path, train in a Tathāgata's actions, and expound that a Tathāgata is eternal and changeless, in accordance with a Tathāgata's store of teachings" (T02n0120, 0542a2–4). Then He says, "The Kophen Kingdom [in present-day Kashmir] will preserve my remaining Dharma, and my Dharma will not perish in the Bharukaccha Kingdom [present-day Bharuch, in northwestern India], nor in the kingdom of the Vindhya mountain range [in central India]" (Ibid., 0541c29–0542a1). Therefore, texts related to the Tathāgata store must have first appeared in southern India, then spread to central and northern India.

A List of Texts Related to the Tathāgata Store

Texts related to the Tathāgata store can be classified into two categories: (i) early Mahāyāna texts that imply the doctrine of the Tathāgata store, and (ii) sūtras and śāstras (treatises) on the Tathāgata store. Texts in each category are listed below.

I. Texts that imply the doctrine of the Tathāgata store

- (a) Prajñā-pāramitā sūtras, such as the *Large Sūtra of Prajñā-Pāramitā*
- (b) *Mahāvaipulya Sūtra of Buddha Adornment* (Buddhāvataṁsaka-mahāvaipulya-sūtra), especially the chapter "A Tathāgata's Appearance in the World"

II. Sūtras and śāstras on the Tathāgata store

A. Sūtras

- (1) *Mahāvaipulya Sūtra of the Tathāgata Store*
- (2) *Sūtra of Neither Increase Nor Decrease* (Anūnatva-apūrṇatva-nirdeśa-parivarta)
- (3) *Sūtra of Śrīmālā's Lion's Roar* (Śrīmālādevī-siṁhanāda-sūtra)
- (4) *Sūtra of Aṅgulimālika* (the Mahāyāna version)
- (5) *Sūtra of the Unsurpassed Reliance* (Anuttarāśraya-sūtra)
- (6) *Sūtra of the Vajra Samādhi*
- (7) *Sūtra of the Great Dharma Drum* (Mahābherī-hāraka-parivarta)
- (8) *Sūtra of the Great Cloud* (Mahāmegha-sūtra)
- (9) *Mahāparinirvāṇa Sūtra*
- (10) *Laṅkāvatāra Sūtra*
- (11) *Ghanavyūha Sūtra*

B. Śāstras

(12) *A Treatise on the Jewel Nature* (Ratnagotravibhāga Mahāyānottaratantra-śāstra [Discerning the jewel nature: A Mahāyāna treatise on higher tantra])

(13) *A Treatise on Buddha Nature* (Buddhagotra-śāstra)

(14) *A Mahāyāna Treatise on No Differences in the Dharma Realm* (Mahāyāna-dharma-dhātu-nirviśeṣa-śāstra)

(15) *A Treatise on Eliciting Faith in the Mahāyāna* (Mahāyāna-śraddhotpāda-śāstra)

Most scholars do not include texts (6) and (15) in the collection of texts related to the Tathāgata store because both are suspected of apocryphal origin. However, they are included here because their teachings on the Tathāgata store are considered correct, and are highly valued in China.

Sūtras 1 through 6 in this book are English versions of the first six of the eleven sūtras, each translated from its Chinese version in the Chinese Buddhist Canon. Sūtra 2 is a revised version of the English translation initially published in *Teachings of the Buddha* (Rulu 2012a, 97–102).

Arrival and Translation of Sanskrit Texts in China

Through the support of China's emperors and tremendous efforts of illustrious Buddhist masters from India, China, and kingdoms along the Silk Road, translation of the Sanskrit texts taken to China began in the first century CE, during the Eastern Han Dynasty (24–220), and continued for the following nine hundred years, finishing in the Song Dynasty (960–1279). The *Mahāvaipulya Sūtra of the Tathāgata Store* was the earliest arrival of a number of Sanskrit texts that give teachings on the Tathāgata store. The Sanskrit text of this sūtra first arrived in the Western Jin Dynasty (265–316), but its two Chinese versions have been lost. The earlier of the two extant Chinese versions of this sūtra was translated from Sanskrit in the Eastern Jin Dynasty (317–420). Translation of such texts continued through dynasties and ended in the Tang Dynasty (618–907). To show the arrival of Mahāyāna texts and how teachings on the Tathāgata store were gradually instilled into Chinese Buddhists' minds, a brief history of translation work is given below.

Before the Eastern Jin Dynasty

It was a historical event in the Eastern Han Dynasty that in 67, the tenth year of the Yongping (永平) years of Emperor Ming (漢明帝), the two Indian monks Dharmaratna (竺法蘭, circa first century) and Kāśyapamātaṅga (迦葉摩騰, ?–73) arrived in Luoyang (洛陽), Eastern Han's capital. Staying at the White Horse Temple, they jointly translated the *Sūtra in Forty-two Sections* (T17n0784) from Sanskrit into Chinese. However, voice-hearer sūtras translated by Dharmaratna alone have been lost. Then in 148, An Shigao (安世高, 2nd century) from the kingdom of Anxi (安西, the Arsacid Empire, in present-day northeastern Iran) arrived in Luoyang. Between 148 and 170, he translated into Chinese many Sanskrit texts on voice-hearer teachings.

Also in the Eastern Han Dynasty, Mahāyāna texts began to arrive in China. Their teachings laid the foundation of the Mahāyāna in China. A few important texts and their translators are given below.

Lokakṣema (支婁迦讖 or 支讖, 147–?) from Gandhāra was the first Indian master who went to China to propagate Mahāyāna teachings. He arrived in Luoyang in 167. During the last eleven years (178–89) of Emperor Ling (漢靈帝), he translated from Sanskrit into Chinese over twenty sūtras, of which twelve are extant. For example, text 224 (T08n0224) in 10 fascicles is the Chinese version of the *Sūtra of the Practice of Prajñā-Pāramitā,* the earliest in a series of prajñā-pāramitā sūtras that arrived in China; text 361 (T12n0361) in 4 fascicles is the earliest of the five Chinese versions of the *Sūtra of Amitāyus Buddha;* text 417 (T13n0417) in one fascicle and text 418 (T13n0418) in 3 fascicles are two Chinese versions of the *Sūtra of Pratyutpanna Buddha Sammukhāvasthita Samādhi,* which prescribes visualizing a Buddha in order to realize the Buddha within one.

The Eastern Han Dynasty was followed by the Three Kingdoms period (220–80), during which a few other illustrious masters successively went to China. For example, Saṅghavarman (康僧鎧, 3rd century) arrived in Luoyang in 252. He is the best known translator of this period because, of the five Chinese versions of the *Sūtra of Amitāyus Buddha,* text 360 (T12n0360) in 2 fascicles, translated from Sanskrit by him, is used as the principal text of the Pure Land School of China.

During the Western Jin Dynasty (265–316), in 265, Dharmarakṣa (竺法護, ?–313 or 316) from Dunhuang (敦煌, a major stop on the ancient Silk Road, in present-day Gansu Province, China) arrived in China and translated from Sanskrit into Chinese 154 texts in 309 fascicles, including texts 285, 291, and 398. Text 285 (T10n0285) in 5 fascicles is the earliest of the three Chinese versions of the *Sūtra of the Ten Grounds* (Daśa-bhūmika-sūtra), each of which is comparable to a corresponding chapter of the *Buddha Adornment Sūtra*—chapter 22 in fascicles 23–27 of texts 278 (T09n0278), and chapter 26 in fascicles 34–39 of text 279 (T10n0279). Text 291 (T10n0291) in 4 fascicles is the Chinese version of the *Sūtra of a Tathāgata's Appearance in the World*, which is comparable to a corresponding chapter of the *Buddha Adornment Sūtra*—chapter 32 in fascicles 33–36 of text 278, and chapter 37 in fascicles 50–52 of text 279. Text 398 (T13n0398) in 8 fascicles is the Chinese version of the *Sūtra of Great Compassion* (Tathāgata-mahākaruṇā-nirdeśa). Fascicle 6 mentions that a skilled jeweler cleans a stainless precious jewel to reveal its luster. This jewel is an analogy of one's Tathāgata store.

During the reign of Emperor Hui (晉惠帝), sometime between 290 and 306, Fajü (法炬) and Fali (法立) jointly translated the *Mahāvaipulya Sūtra of the Tathāgata Store* from Sanskrit into Chinese. However, their translation has been lost. Also lost is another Chinese version of this sūtra, translated by Bai Fazu (白法祖) during the same period.

The Eastern Jin Dynasty

In 415, Buddhabhadra (佛馱跋陀羅, 359–429) from northern India arrived in Jiankang (建康, present-day Nanjing, Jiangsu Province, China), Eastern Jin's capital. He translated from Sanskrit into Chinese thirteen texts in 125 fascicles, including texts 376, 278, and 666. Text 376 (T12n0376) in 6 fascicles, translated jointly by him and Faxian (法顯, circa 337–422), is the earliest of the three

Chinese versions of the *Mahāparinirvāṇa Sūtra.* Texts 278 and 666 were translated by him alone, probably between 418 and 421. Text 278 (T09n0278) is the 60-fascicle Chinese version of the *Buddha Adornment Sūtra.* Text 666 (T16n0666) in one fascicle is the earlier of the two extant Chinese versions of the *Mahāvaipulya Sūtra of the Tathāgata Store,* an English translation of which is Sūtra 1 in this book.

The Northern Liang Dynasty

During the Northern Liang Dynasty (397–439), one of the Sixteen Kingdoms (304–439), in 412, Dharmakṣema (曇無讖, 385–433) from central India arrived in China and stayed at Guzang (姑臧, present-day Wuwei (武威), in Gansu Province, China). He translated from Sanskrit into Chinese a few important sūtras, including texts 374 and 387. Text 374 (T12n0374) comprising thirteen chapters in 40 fascicles is the second of the three Chinese versions of the *Mahāparinirvāṇa Sūtra.* It is referred to as the northern version. Its first five chapters in fascicles 1–10 are comparable to the whole of text 376, translated by Buddhabhadra and Faxian. Text 387 (T12n0387) in 6 fascicles is the Chinese version of the *Sūtra of the Great Cloud* (Mahāmegha-sūtra). This sūtra gives teachings on Buddha nature. In fascicle 5, the Buddha explains, "This sūtra has three titles: (1) *Great Cloud,* (2) *Mahāparinirvāṇa,* and (3) *No Thoughts.* It is called *Great Cloud* because it was requested by Great Cloud Secret Store Bodhisattva. It is called *Mahāparinirvāṇa* because a Tathāgata ever abides and never enters parinirvāṇa [extinction], and because all sentient beings have Buddha nature. It is called *No Thoughts* because to accept, uphold, and recite this sūtra is to stop all thoughts" (T12n0387, 1099a26–b2). Then He affirms, "This sūtra bears the seal of Buddhas, which sanctifies that all sentient beings have Buddha nature, and that a Tathāgata is ever abiding and changeless" (Ibid., 1100a26–27). He says that the Licchavi youth called All Sentient Beings Are Delighted to See [who is featured in the *Sūtra of the Great Dharma Drum*] will be reborn in southern India, take the same name, praise Mahāyāna sūtras, and uphold the true Dharma (Ibid., 1100a2–11).

Also during the Northern Liang Dynasty, an unknown person translated from Sanskrit into Chinese the *Sūtra of the Vajra Samādhi* (T09n0273) in 2 fascicles, an English translation of which is Sūtra 6 in this book.

The Liu Song Dynasty

Huiyan (慧嚴, 363–443) and others in southern China under the rule of the Liu Song Dynasty (420–79), the first of the four successive Southern Dynasties (420–589), edited texts 374 and 376 into text 375 (T12n0375) comprising twenty-five chapters in 36 fascicles. This text is the latest of the three Chinese versions of the *Mahāparinirvāṇa Sūtra* and is referred to as the southern version. These three texts, which sparked the Nirvāṇa School of China, give teachings on the eternity of a Tathāgata and one's Tathāgata store and Buddha nature.

In 435, Guṇabhadra (求那跋陀羅, 394–468) from central India arrived in China and stayed in Jiankang. Around 440, he translated fifty-two sūtras in 134 fascicles from Sanskrit into Chinese. For example, text 120 (T02n0120) in 4 fascicles is the Chinese version of the Mahāyāna version of the *Sūtra of Aṅgulimālika,* an English translation of which is Sūtra 4 in this book; text 270 (T09n0270) in 2 fascicles is the Chinese version of the *Sūtra of the Great Dharma*

Drum, an English translation of which appears in *Teachings of the Buddha* (Rulu 2012a, 154–83); text 353 (T12n0353) in one fascicle is the earlier of the two extant Chinese versions of the *Vaipulya Sūtra of Śrīmālā's Lion's Roar,* an English translation of which is Sūtra 3 in this book; text 670 (T16n0670) is the 4-fascicle Chinese version of the *Laṅkāvatāra Sūtra.* At this point, the thought of the Tathāgata store became well instilled into Chinese Buddhists' minds.

The Northern Wei Dynasty

During the Northern Wei Dynasty (386–534), in 508, both Ratnamati (勒那摩提, 5th–6th centuries) from central India and Bodhiruci (菩提留支, 5th–6th centuries) from northern India arrived in Luoyang, Northern Wei's capital. Among the texts Ratnamati translated from Sanskrit into Chinese are texts 1522 and 1611. Text 1522 (T26n1522) in 12 fascicles is the Chinese version of Vasubandhu's (世親, circa 320–80) *A Treatise on the Sūtra of the Ten Grounds* (Daśabhūmika-sūtra-śāstra), jointly translated by him and Bodhiruci. Text 1611 (T31n1611) in 4 fascicles was translated by Ratnamati alone, which is the Chinese version of *A Treatise on the Jewel Nature* (Ratnagotravibhāga Mahāyānottaratantra-śāstra), attributed to Sāramati. This text is the most important treatise on the Tathāgata store.

Bodhiruci translated from Sanskrit into Chinese thirty-nine texts in 127 fascicles, including texts 272, 668, and 671. Text 272 (T09n0272) in 10 fascicles is the Chinese version of the *Sūtra Pronounced by Mahāsatya, a Nirgranthaputra Master* (Bodhisattva-gocaropāya-viṣaya-vikurvaṇa-nirdeśa). In fascicle 9, the Buddha says that one's body is the Tathāgata store, and uses ten analogies to describe how it is sheathed in one's afflictions (T09n0272, 0359a28–b3). Text 668 (T16n0668) in one fascicle is the Chinese version of the *Sūtra of Neither Increase Nor Decrease,* an English translation of which is Sūtra 2 in this book; text 671 (T16n0671) is the 10-fascicle Chinese version of the *Laṅkāvatāra Sūtra.*

The Southern Liang Dynasty

Then Paramārtha (真諦, 499–569) from northwestern India went to China. In the twenty-three years between his arrival in China in 546 during the Southern Liang Dynasty (502–57) and his death in 569 during the Southern Chen Dynasty (557–89), Paramārtha translated sixty-four texts in 278 fascicles from Sanskrit into Chinese. Among the thirty extant translations are texts 669, 1593, 1595, 1610, and 1666. Text 669 (T16n0669) in 2 fascicles is the Chinese version of the *Sūtra of the Unsurpassed Reliance,* an English translation of which is Sūtra 5 in this book. Text 1593 (T31n1593) in 3 fascicles is one of the three Chinese versions of Asaṅga's (無著, circa 310–90) *A Treatise on Adopting the Mahāyāna* (Mahāyāna-saṁparigraha-śāstra); text 1595 (T31n1595) in 15 fascicles is one of the three Chinese versions of Vasubandhu's *Mahāyāna-saṅgraha-bhāṣya,* his commentary on Asaṅga's treatise. Text 1610 (T31n1610) in 4 fascicles is the Chinese version of Vasubandhu's *A Treatise on Buddha Nature* (Buddhagotra-śāstra); text 1666 (T32n1666) in one fascicle is the earlier of the two Chinese versions of *A Treatise on Eliciting Faith in the Mahāyāna* (Mahāyāna-śraddhotpāda-śāstra), attributed to Aśvaghoṣa (馬鳴, circa 100–60) from central India. Texts 1610 and 1666 discuss Buddha nature, true mind, inherent awareness, ālaya consciousness (ālaya-vijñāna), and the Tathāgata store.

The Tang Dynasty

The Tang Dynasty was a boom time for Buddhism, and teachings on the Tathāgata store became well established as several important Sanskrit texts were translated into Chinese by a new wave of illustrious translators. For example, Xuanzang (玄奘, 600– or 602–64), who returned from India to China in 645, translated from Sanskrit into Chinese many texts, including the *Heart Sūtra* (T08n0251) in one fascicle, the *Large Sūtra of Prajñā-Pāramitā* (T05–07n0220) in 600 fascicles, the *Buddhabhūmi-sūtra-śāstra* (T26n1530) in 7 fascicles, and the *Yogācāra-bhūmi-śāstra* (T30n1579) in 100 fascicles. In 676, Divākara (地婆訶羅, 613–87) from central India arrived in Chang-an (長安), Tang's capital. In six years, he translated from Sanskrit into Chinese eighteen texts in 34 fascicles, including text 681 (T16n0681) in 3 fascicles, which is the earlier of the two Chinese versions of the *Ghanavyūha Sūtra.* In 689, Devaprajñā (提雲般若, dates unknown) from Yütian (于闐), or Khotan (和闐), present-day Hetian (和田), in Xinjiang, China, arrived in Luoyang, Tang's eastern capital. Among the texts he translated from Sanskrit into Chinese are texts 1626 (T31n1626) and 1627 (T31n1627), each in one fascicle. They are the two Chinese versions of *A Mahāyāna Treatise on No Differences in the Dharma Realm* (Mahāyāna-dharma-dhātu-nirviśeṣa-śāstra). Text 1627 has another title, *A Treatise on the Tathāgata store.* In 693, Buddhatrāta (佛陀多羅, 7th–8th centuries) from Kophen (罽賓, in present-day Kashmir, northern Pakistan, and eastern Afghanistan area) arrived in Luoyang. He translated from Sanskrit into Chinese the *Mahāvaipulya Sūtra of Perfect Enlightenment* (T17n0842) in one fascicle, an English translation of which appears in *Transcending the World* (Rulu 2015, 233–65). Another title of this sūtra is *Diversities Arising from the Nature of the Tathāgata Store.* In this sūtra, the Tathāgata store is equated to one's pure awareness (T17n0842, 0913c5-8; Rulu 2015, 234). Also in 693, Bodhiruci (菩提流志, 562–727) from southern India arrived in Chang-an. He translated from Sanskrit into Chinese fifty-three texts in 111 fascicles, including twenty-six sūtras in 39 fascicles in text 310 (T11n0310), the Chinese version of the *Great Treasure Pile Sūtra* (Mahā-ratnakūṭa-sūtra) comprising forty-nine sūtras in 120 fascicles. Among the twenty-six sūtras he translated is sūtra 48 in fascicle 119, which is the later of the two extant Chinese versions of the *Vaipulya Sūtra of Śrīmālā's Lion's Roar.* In 695, Śikṣānanda (實叉難陀, 652–710) from Yütian arrived in Luoyang. He translated from Sanskrit into Chinese the 80-fascicle version of the *Buddha Adornment Sūtra* (T10n0279), the 7-fascicle version of *Laṅkāvatāra Sūtra* (T16n0672), and the 2-fascicle version of *A Treatise on Eliciting Faith in the Mahāyāna* (T32n1667). In 720, Amoghavajra (不空金剛, 705–74) from southern India was taken by his uncle to Luoyang, where he studied under Vajrabodhi (金剛智). After Vajrabodhi died, he traveled extensively across the five regions of India and received esoteric teachings and many Sanskrit texts, then returned to Luoyang. In 771, he presented to Emperor Daizong (唐代宗) his Chinese translations of seventy-seven texts in 101 fascicles, including texts 667 and 682. Text 667 (T16n0667) in one fascicle is the later of the two extant Chinese versions of the *Mahāvaipulya Sūtra of the Tathāgata Store;* text 682 (T16n0682) in 3 fascicles is the later of the two Chinese versions of the *Ghanavyūha Sūtra*. In 781, Prajñā (般若, 734–?) from Kophen arrived in Guangzhou (廣州). Then he went to Chang-an and translated from Sanskrit into Chinese several important sūtras, including texts 261 and 291. Text 261 (T08n0261) in 10 fascicles is the Chinese version of the *Sūtra of the*

Six Pāramitās in the Tenets of the Mahāyāna, translated in 788. Text 293 (T10n0293) is the 40-fascicle Chinese version of the *Buddha Adornment Sūtra,* translated in 798.

As Buddhism thrived through the middle of the Tang Dynasty, teachings on the Tathāgata store were incorporated into the doctrines of major Chinese Buddhist schools, such as the Tiantai School, the Huayan School, the Chán (dhyāna) School, and the Esoteric School. Then in 845, Emperor Wuzong (唐武宗), in favor of Daoism, destroyed Buddhist temples and forced Buddhist monks and nuns to return to secular life. Although these schools, except the Southern Chán School, declined, their influence has spread far and wide in China and to Korea and Japan.

Works on the Tathāgata Store since the Early Twentieth Century

Although sūtras and treatises on the Tathāgata store have long been translated from Sanskrit into Chinese and/or Tibetan, English translations of these texts were not available in the early 20th century, and Western scholars were mainly interested in Hīnayāna, Mādhyamaka, or Yogācāra teachings. Then in 1931, E. Obermiller published "The sublime science of the great vehicle to salvation: Being a manual of Buddhist monism," his English translation of the Tibetan version of the *Ratnagotravibhāga Mahāyānottaratantra-śāstra* [Discerning the jewel nature: A Mahāyāna treatise on higher tantra]. In 1950, E. H. Johnston (1885–1942) edited and published the Sanskrit text of this treatise. These two publications drew Western scholars' attention to teachings on the Tathāgata store. In 1961, using Johnston's Sanskrit text, Zuiryū Nakamura (中村瑞隆, 1915–2003) published in Japanese a book that compares Johnston's Sanskrit text with the Chinese text (Nakamura 1988). In 1966, Jikido Takasaki (高崎直道, 1926–2013) published *A Study on the Ratnagotravibhāga (Uttaratantra),* his English translation of Johnston's Sanskrit text (Takasaki 2014a), a translation that takes into consideration the differences from the Sanskrit text found in the Chinese and Tibetan texts. His book sparked across continents a great deal of interest in study and research in the doctrine of the Tathāgata store.

Many studies have been published in Japan and China in the 20th century. For example, in 1930, Tokiwa Daijō (常盤大定, 1870–1945) published in Japanese his study of Buddha nature. In 1955, Yinshun (印順, 1906–2005) published in Chinese his study of the Tathāgata store, which has served as a guidebook for other Chinese scholars. In 1974, Takasaki published in Japanese a voluminous book on the formation of the thought of the Tathāgata store. His book is a compendium of scriptural texts and studies published up to 1974, and covers the development of this thought in India, China, and Japan.

Since the 1970s, Western scholars have published many articles and books. Their works range from translations of a few selected sūtras from Chinese into English, to studies of specific texts and subjects, such as Buddha nature, the Tathāgata store, and the relationship between the Tathāgata store and ālaya consciousness. They relate the view of cessation of dharmas to nihilism, the view of perpetuity of dharmas to eternalism, the three bodies of a Buddha to docetism, and the universal Tathāgata store to monism, injecting several isms into Buddhist teachings. Some works cite Sanskrit passages without translating them into English. Obviously, they are of academic interest to fellow scholars, at a safe distance from the general public and Buddhists who are not versed in Sanskrit. For a comprehensive reference of contemporary works in Chinese, English, and Japanese, one can consult Du Zhengmin's (杜正民) two-part article (Du 1997) or the reference in a scholarly book.

Teachings on the Tathāgata Store as the Third Mahāyāna School of Thought

It is generally held that the Mādhyamaka and the Yogācāra are the only two schools of Mahāyāna Buddhism originated in India. For example, according to fascicle 4 of text 2053 (in 10 fascicles), a biography of Xuanzang, while studying in India at the Nālandā Monastery, Xuanzang wrote "Meeting of the two schools," a treatise in three thousand stanzas, to reconcile the arguments between the Mādhyamaka and the Yogācāra (T50n2053, 0244c8–10). Then Yijing (義淨, 635–713), another Chinese master in the Tang Dynasty, who also studied at the Nālandā Monastery, confirmed Xuanzang's understanding. In fascicle 1 of text 2125 (in 4 fascicles), his account of Buddhist religions practiced in India and the South Sea Archipelago, Yijing wrote: "Mahāyāna teachings are of but two kinds, the Middle View [Mādhyamaka] and the Yoga Practice [Yogācāra]. The Middle View holds that all things are illusory and empty. The Yoga Practice holds that all things perceived as external are nonexistent, but one's consciousness, which is internal, is existent" (T54n2125, 0205c13–15).

Even to this day, most scholars hold that there are only those two Mahāyāna schools of thought. Some disregard teachings on the Tathāgata store, and others claim that such teachings have been absorbed into the Yogācāra doctrine and failed to become an independent school of thought (Takasaki 2014a, 60). Nevertheless, after texts on the Tathāgata store began to arrive in China, Chinese Buddhists earnestly studied their tenets and regarded their teachings as the third Mahāyāna school of thought. For comparison, the developments of these three schools are summarized below.

The Mādhyamaka School

The Sanskrit word *mādhyamaka* means middle way. Ācārya Nāgārjuna (龍樹菩薩, circa 150–250) from southern India is revered as the founding patriarch of the Mādhyamaka School. In China, this school is called the Emptiness School because Nāgārjuna wrote treatises that expound on the emptiness of dharmas, which is an essential tenet of prajñā-pāramitā sūtras. These sūtras teach the relative truth that dharmas arise through causes and conditions in accordance with the principle of dependent arising (pratītya-samutpāda). Hence dharmas have no autonomous self (ātman) and are empty. They also teach the absolute truth that dharmas are false names of illusory appearances arising through illusory causes and conditions, and that dharma nature is emptiness, which, as a concept, is also empty.

This school is founded on prajñā-pāramitā sūtras and Nāgārjuna's most important treatise, the *Mūla-madhyamaka-kārikā* [Fundamental verses on the Middle Way], whose Chinese version is text 1564 (T30n1564) in 4 fascicles. The opening stanza in fascicle 1 states the middle view: "Dharmas have neither birth nor death; they are neither perpetual nor ceasing, neither the same nor different, neither coming nor going" (T30n1564, 0001b14–16). These eight negations in four pairs of opposites are the Middle Way, or the Middle View, which rises above the plane of polar opposites. The emptiness of dharmas lies in the first pair of negations, neither birth nor death, with the other three pairs of negations as its corollaries. Further simplified, the principal thesis of the Middle Way is that dharmas have no birth because without birth there cannot be death. Nāgārjuna's work was continued by his student Āryadeva (提婆, 3rd century), then by Āryadeva's student Rāhulabhadra (羅睺羅跋陀羅, 3rd century), and then by Piṅgalanetra (青目, 4th century) and other masters. They wrote commentaries on Nāgārjuna's treatises and expounded the Middle Way.

In the sixth century, Buddhapālita (佛護, circa 470–550) and Bhāvaviveka (清辨, circa 500–578) wrote commentaries on the works of Nāgārjuna and Āryadeva. Because their views differed, the Mādhyamaka split into two philosophical camps, the Prāsaṅgika (具緣派 or 應成派) and the Svātantrika (依自起派 or 自續派). The Prāsaṅgika founded by Buddhapālita refutes other views without stating its own view; the Svātantrika founded by Bhāvaviveka states its own view in order to refute other views. Then Candrakīrti (月稱, circa 600–50) severely criticized the Svātantrika and supported the Prāsaṅgika. Candrakīrti was succeeded by Śāntideva (寂天, 8th century), whose *Bodhisattva-caryāvatāra* [A guide to a Bodhisattva's way of life] is highly regarded in Tibet. The Gelug sect of Tibet rules that the Prāsaṅgika teachings and polemic methods reflect a definitive understanding of the Mādhyamaka. In the eighth century, Śāntarakṣita (寂護, 700–60) and his student Kamalaśīla (蓮華戒, 8th century) followed the Mādhyamaka-svātantrika's view of the absolute truth and accepted the Yogācāra's teachings of the relative truth. He founded the Yogācāra-mādhyamaka-svātantrika, thus sycretizing the Yogācāra and the Mādhyamaka. Starting from the tenth century, Buddhism in India began to decline. It was eliminated by Muslims in the eleventh century.

In China, the Three Treatises School was the Chinese counterpart of the Mādhyamaka School. It was founded on three treatises: (1) Nāgārjuna's *A Middle Treatise* (Mūla-madhyamaka-kārikā), whose Chinese version with explanations by Piṅgalanetra is text 1564 (T30n1564) in 4 fascicles; (2) his *A Treatise on the Twelve Entrances* (Dvādaśa-mukha-śāstra), whose Chinese version is text 1568 (T30n1568) in one fascicle; (3) Āryadeva's *A Treatise in One Hundred Stanzas* (Śataka-śāstra), whose Chinese version is text 1569 (T30n1569) in 2 fascicles. Branched out of this school was the Four Treatises School, which added to its scope of study a fourth treatise, Nāgārjuna's *A Treatise on the Sūtra of Mahā-Prajñā-Pāramitā,* whose Chinese version is text 1509 (T25n1509) in 100 fascicles. These two schools used Nāgārjuna's eight negations to expound the two truths in order to reveal that there is no attainment, and that "there is attainment" is the wrong view. Although these two schools declined after the middle of the Tang Dynasty, the Middle View has spread to Korea and Japan, and been accepted as the basic view in the doctrines of major Chinese Buddhist schools.

The Yogācāra School

The Sanskrit word *yogācāra* means yoga practice. Maitreya-nātha (彌勒, circa 270–350) is the originating patriarch of the Yogācāra (or Yogacāra) School, because its foundation was laid by Maitreya-nātha's works, including the *Yogācāra-bhūmi-śāstra*[7,8] (T30n1579) in 100 fascicles and the *Madhyānta-vibhāga-kārikā* (T31n1601) in one fascicle. Then the two brothers Asaṅga (無著, circa 310–90) and Vasubandhu (世親, circa 320–80) wrote many treatises and officially established the Yogācāra School.

The Yogācāra School is founded on six sūtras and eleven treatises. Of the six sūtras, the principal ones are the *Buddha Adornment Sūtra,* of which there are three Chinese versions (T09n278 in 60 fascicles, T10n0279 in 80 fascicles, and T10n0293 in 40 fascicles), the *Saṁdhinirmocana Sūtra,* of which there are two Chinese versions (T16n0675 and T16n0676, each in 5 fascicles), and the *Laṅkāvatāra Sūtra,* of which there are three Chinese versions (T16n0670 in 4 fascicles, T16n0671 in 10 fascicles, and T16n0672 in 7 fascicles). Of the eleven treatises, the principal ones are Maitreya's *Yogācāra-bhūmi-śāstra* (T30n1579) in 100 fascicles, Asaṅga's *Mahāyāna-sūtrālaṅkāra-śāstra* (T31n1604) in 13 fascicles, and Vasubandhu's *Daśa-bhūmika-sūtra-śāstra* (T26n1522) in 12 fascicles and *Viṁśatikā-vijñapti-mātratā-siddhi* (T31n1590) in one fascicle.

Although the word *yogācāra* means yoga practice, the doctrine of this school is called vijñānavāda (doctrine of consciousness) or vijñapti-mātratā (consciousness only). It holds that all dharmas in one's mental or physical world are projections of one's eight consciousnesses. All dharmas arise from the seeds (bīja) in ālaya consciousness, one's eighth consciousness, have three natures: (1) the imagined [parikalpita], (2) the other-dependent [paratantra], and (3) the perfectly completed [pariniṣpanna],[9] and are encompassed in five dharmas: (1) name, (2) appearance, (3) differentiation, (4) true wisdom-knowledge, and (5) true suchness.[10]

In China, the Dharma-Appearance School, also called the Consciousness-Only School, is the Chinese counterpart of the Yogācāra School. Its founding patriarch is Master Xuanzang (玄奘, 600– or 602–64). After studying in India for seventeen years, in 645 he brought 657 Sanskrit texts back to China. Xuanzang translated from Sanskrit into Chinese many texts, including important Yogācāra texts such as the *Yogācāra-bhūmi-śāstra.* His definitive work is text 1585 (T31n1585) in 10 fascicles, which is the Chinese version of the *Vijñapti-mātratā-siddhi-śāstra* [A treatise on establishing consciousness-only]. Xuanzang took ten Yogācāra masters' commentaries (each in 10 fascicles) on Vasubandhu's *Triṁśikā-vijñapti-mātratā-siddhi* [Thirty stanzas on consciousness-only] and edited them into text 1585, placing emphasis on Dharmapāla's (護法, circa 6th century) commentary. This treatise accords with the Middle View, as fascicle 7 states: "A self and dharmas are nonexistent, but their emptiness and one's consciousness are existent. Holding neither the view of existence nor the view of nonexistence [of anything] accords with the Middle Way" (T31n1585, 0039b1–2). Xuanzang's foremost student, Kuiji (窺基, 632–82), who is honored as the first patriarch of the Dharma-Appearance School, wrote many commentaries on the doctrine of consciousness-only, including text 1829

(T43n1829) in 16 fascicles, which is a summary of the *Yogācāra-bhūmi-śāstra,* text 1830 (T43n1830) in 10 fascicles, which is a commentary on Xuanzang's treatise, and more. His student Huizhao (慧沼, 651–714) was the second patriarch, and Huizhao's student Zhizhou (智周, 668–723) was the third patriarch. Zhizhou had many students, including those from Korea and Japan, who propagated his teachings in their own countries. After Zhizhou's death, this school declined and its lineage ceased. However, interest in its doctrine revived after the Song Dynasty, and contemporary scholars still study its doctrine and publish their works.

The Tathāgata-Store School

As the Mādhyamaka and the Yogācāra are the two widely known schools of Mahāyāna Buddhism, each school boasted a large following and was promoted by illustrious ancient masters who wrote important treatises and expounded its doctrine. By contrast, although teachings on the Tathāgata store have long been available in sūtras, in India they were not regarded as a school of thought. Possible reasons are that there were no principal exponents of these teachings, and that there are few treatises on the doctrine.

Nevertheless, in China, teachings on the Tathāgata store have been earnestly embraced and have come to be accepted as the mainstream of Mahāyāna teachings. The Ground Treatise School[11] established in the Northern Wei Dynasty (386–534) by Ratnamati's students in southern China was the first Chinese Buddhist school that recognized the significance of the Tathāgata store. This school was founded on text 1522, the Chinese version of Vasubandhu's *A Treatise on the Sūtra of the Ten Grounds,* in which the terms "Tathāgata store" and "ālaya consciousness" are mentioned. This school viewed ālaya consciousness as one's inherent pure mind, or one's Tathāgata store, and upheld dependent arising of dharmas from dharma nature, which is true suchness.

In the Tang Dynasty, Master Dushun (杜順, 557–640), the first patriarch of the Huayan School, classified the Buddha's teachings into five levels: (1) Hīnayāna teachings, which include the Four Noble Truths and dependent arising of dharmas from karmic response as explained by the Twelve Links of Dependent Arising; (2) beginning Mahāyāna teachings, which include the emptiness of dharmas, and dependent arising of dharmas from ālaya consciousness; (3) concluding Mahāyāna teachings, which include dependent arising of dharmas from the Tathāgata store, or true suchness; (4) immediate-realization teachings, as given in the *Vimalakīrti Nirdeśa Sūtra;* (5) all-embracing teachings, which include dependent arising of dharmas from the dharma realm because all dharmas are interdependent. Dushun's classification means that Mādhyamaka and Yogācāra teachings are beginning Mahāyāna teachings, and that teachings on the Tathāgata store are concluding Mahāyāna teachings.

In the Tang Dynasty, three masters—Kuiji, Fazang, and Zongmi—regarded teachings on the Tathāgata store as a distinct Mahāyāna school of thought. Kuiji, the first patriarch of the Dharma-Appearance School, in fascicle 1 of text 1861 (in 7 fascicles), his exposition of the meanings of Mahāyāna teachings, said, "Taking all dharmas as asaṁskṛta is saying that they are [manifestations of] true suchness. Taking all dharmas as saṁskṛta is saying that that they are merely [projections of] one's consciousness. Subjecting all dharmas to critical examination is saying that they are penetrated by one's prajñā [wisdom]" (T45n1861, 0260b7–9). Kuiji's first sentence implies the True-Suchness School (the Tathāgata-Store School); his second sentence refers to the Yogācāra School; his third sentence refers to the Mādhyamaka School.

Fazang (法藏, 643–712), the third patriarch of the Huayan School, in fascicle 1 of text 1846 (in 3 fascicles), his commentary on the *Mahāyāna-śraddhotpāda-śāstra* [A treatise on eliciting faith in the Mahāyāna], said, "Mahāyāna and Hīnayāna teachings can be classified into four schools. The first is the school that holds dharma appearances to be existent, founded on the Āgamas and treatises such as the *Abhidharma-mahāvibhāṣā-śāstra*. The second is the school of the emptiness and no appearance of dharmas, founded on prajñā-pāramitā sūtras, and treatises such as *A Middle Treatise*. The third is the school of dharma appearance and consciousness only, founded on the *Saṁdhinirmocana Sūtra* and treatises such as the *Yogācāra-bhūmi-śāstra*. The fourth is the school of dependent arising of dharmas from one's Tathāgata store [true suchness], founded on the *Laṅkāvatāra Sūtra*, the *Ghanavyūha Sūtra*, and treatises such as the *Ratnagotravibhāga-śāstra* and the *Mahāyāna-śraddhotpāda-śāstra*. . . . This fourth school unifies the principle and matters because, as the principle pervades matters, this school endorses that the Tathāgata store, through causes and conditions, appears as ālaya consciousness, and because, as matters contain the principle, this school endorses dependent arising of dharmas from the Tathāgata store" (T44n1846, 0243b22–c8). Fazang's first school corresponds to the Hīnayāna School. His second school corresponds to the Mādhyamaka School; his third school corresponds to the Yogācāra School; his fourth school implies the Tathāgata-Store School.

Zongmi (宗密, 780–841), the fifth patriarch of the Huayan School, classified Mahāyāna teachings into three schools. In fascicle 1 of his large commentary on the *Sūtra of Perfect Enlightenment*, text 243 in the Extension of the Chinese Canon, he said, "Mahāyāna teachings come under three schools [of thought]: (1) the Dharma-Appearance School, (2) the Appearance-Negation School, and (3) the Dharma-Nature School" (X09n0243, 0329b10–11). The Dharma-Appearance School holds that all pure and impure dharmas arise from seeds stored in ālaya consciousness according to their own natures, unrelated to true suchness. This school establishes names for dharmas. The Appearance-Negation School holds that all pure and impure dharmas are empty, and that even attaining nirvāṇa is an illusion. This school accepts neither appearances nor names of dharmas. The Dharma-Nature School holds that all dharmas arise through causes and conditions from true suchness, which is changeless, and that one's Tathāgata store is the dharma body that transmigrates through different life-paths until one attains Buddhahood. This school equates dharma nature to one's true mind. Zongmi's first school corresponds to the Yogācāra School; his second school corresponds to the Mādhyamaka School; his third school implies the Tathāgata-Store School.

In the twentieth century, Taixü and Yinshun, two renowned Chinese masters, affirmed that teachings on the Tathāgata store are a distinct Mahāyāna school of thought. Taixü (太虛, 1890-1947), a scholar monk who advocated reform of Chinese Buddhist organizations to revitalize Chinese Buddhism and bring about a pure land on earth, classified Mahāyāna teachings in line with

Kuiji's ideas. In his 1922 article "A summary critical examination of Buddhist teachings," Taixü grouped six Chinese Buddhist schools into three: (1) the Prajñā School, which corresponds to the Three Treatises School; (2) the Consciousness-Only School, which corresponds to the Dharma-Appearance School; (3) the True-Suchness School, which encompasses the Tiantai School, the Huayan School, the Chán School, and the Esoteric School. He explained that dharmas depend on the Tathāgata store because one's Tathāgata store is the resident that accords with true suchness and never departs or perishes, while one's ignorance of the truth is the visitor that disaccords with true suchness and can be removed. In his view, the first school emphasizes practice, the second school emphasizes understanding, and the third school emphasizes faith, but all three schools are equal in providing the One Vehicle (Ekayāna) to Buddhahood.

Congruent with Taixü's classification, Yinshun classified Mahāyāna thoughts into three systems: (1) dharmas are empty by nature and exist as mere names; (2) dharmas are false for they are mere projections of one's consciousness; (3) only one's true mind is eternal (Yinshun 1985, 374). Yinshun's first system corresponds to the Mādhyamaka School, his second system corresponds to the Yogācāra School, and his third system corresponds to Taixü's True-Suchness School, or the Tathāgata-Store School.

From the Tang Dynasty to this day, Chinese masters have always recognized three Mahāyāna schools of thought. Whether teachings on the Tathāgata store and Buddha nature are referred to as the Tathāgata-Store school, the Dharma-Nature School, the True-Suchness School, or the True-Mind School, they stand apart from and along with the Mādhyamaka School and the Yogācāra School. Regarded by Chinese Buddhists as the culmination of Mahāyāna teachings, they have become the core tenet in the doctrines of well-established Chinese Buddhist schools. In other words, according to Taixü's classification, the Tathāgata-Store School of thought, though not formalized as a school, is an integral part of the Tiantai School, the Huayan School, the Chán School, and the Esoteric School.

Highlights of Teachings on the Tathāgata Store

All Sentient Beings Possess the Tathāgata Store

In Mahāyāna teachings, the Three Vehicles—the Voice-Hearer Vehicle, the Pratyekabuddha Vehicle, and the Bodhisattva Vehicle (the Mahāyāna)—are established to take riders to their chosen destinations according to their aspirations and capacities. Although the destination of the Bodhisattva Vehicle is Buddhahood, its riders are Bodhisattvas only. The One Vehicle, the Buddha Vehicle, introduced in the *Buddha Adornment Sūtra,* the *Lotus Sūtra,* and the *Śrīmālā Sūtra,* is established for all to ride it, because the aim of Mahāyāna teachings is for all to attain Buddhahood. That is why it is introduced in the *Lotus Sūtra* as a fourth vehicle that supersedes the Three Vehicles. Even Arhats and Pratyekabuddhas, who have achieved liberation from karmic rebirth, will someday board the One Vehicle and train to attain Buddhahood.

The reason all sentient beings can attain Buddhahood is that they possess the Tathāgata store, like gold to be extracted from ore through causes and conditions. This teaching is given in the *Mahāvaipulya Sūtra of the Tathāgata Store,* in which the Buddha says, "Whether or not a Buddha appears in the world, the Tathāgata store in all sentient beings is ever abiding and changeless. However, sentient beings are shrouded by their afflictions. Therefore, a Tathāgata appears in the world to widely expound the Dharma, to enable them to remove their fatiguing afflictions and acquire the pure overall wisdom-knowledge [sarvajña]. Good man, if a Bodhisattva believes and delights in this teaching and intently practices and learns, he will achieve liberation, become a Samyak-Saṁbuddha, and do Buddha work in the world" (T16n0666, 0457c7–12). Therefore, the spiritual journey of whoever rides the One Vehicle to go from the Cause Ground to the Result Ground is to go from his belief that he is a Tathāgata in storage to his realization that he is a Tathāgata in splendor. Upon attaining Buddhahood, he truly sees that his fully enlightened mind is none other than his inherent pure mind. Hence there is no attainment.

To describe the Tathāgata store shrouded by one's afflictions, the Buddha uses analogies. For example, nine analogies are given in the *Mahāvaipulya Sūtra of the Tathāgata Store,* and ten analogies are given in the *Sūtra Pronounced by Mahāsatya, a Nirgranthaputra Master.* In fascicle 9 of the latter sūtra, the Buddha says, "One's body is the Tathāgata store. . . . Know that in one's store of filthy afflictions, one's Tathāgata nature is clearly perfect, like gold in ore, water under the ground, oil in a sesame seed, treasure in a treasury, the sun behind clouds, . . . That is why I say that in one's affliction-laden body there is the Tathāgata store" (T09n0272, 0359a28–b3).

All sentient beings possess the Tathāgata store because they and Buddhas have the same nature. This reason is given in text 261 (in 10 fascicles), the Chinese version of the *Sūtra of the Six Pāramitās in the Tenets of the Mahāyāna.* In fascicle 1, the Buddha speaks in verse: "All sentient beings possess the Tathāgata store, / Hence the Three Jewels appear in the world. / All sentient beings enter a Buddha's wisdom / Because their nature is pure beyond exception. / Buddhas and sentient beings are no different in their nature. / While ordinary beings perceive differences, holy ones do not. / Tathāgatas in the three time frames expound that / All sentient beings have always been pure" (T08n0261, 0868a7–10).

Teachings on the equality of sentient beings and Buddhas are also given in text 1489 (in one fascicle), the Chinese version of the *Vaipulya Sūtra of the Pure Vinaya,* in which the Buddha says, "Just as different vessels [made of clay, wood, silver, or gold] contain the same kind of space, likewise they are the same in dharma nature, true suchness, and true reality. Similarly, sentient beings assume various shapes and forms . . . , becoming hell-dwellers, hungry ghosts, animals, humans, gods, voice-hearers, Pratyekabuddhas, Bodhisattvas, or Buddhas. These forms are equal in true suchness and emptiness" (T24n1489, 1080c21–1081a1; Rulu 2012c, 79).

According to fascicle 3 of text 1611 (in 4 fascicles), the Chinese version of *A Treatise on the Jewel Nature,* the statement that all sentient beings possess the Tathāgata store has three meanings: (1) a Buddha's dharma body pervades all sentient beings' bodies; (2) true suchness never varies; (3) all sentient beings have Buddha nature (T31n1611, 0828b1–6). These three meanings are then explained by a stanza: "The realm of all sentient beings is not separate from the wisdom of Buddhas, / Because sentient beings and Buddhas are no different in their pure and taint-free nature. / As all Buddhas equally possess the body of dharma nature [dharma body], / All sentient beings possess the Tathāgata store" (Ibid., 0828b8–12). In fascicle 4, a stanza affirms that all sentient beings equally possess the Tathāgata store because the pure dharma of true suchness is the essence of a Tathāgata (Ibid., 0838c25–28).

One should avoid the misunderstanding that Buddhas possess the dharma body while sentient beings possess the Tathāgata store, as if they were two different things. One should note that the first of the three meanings stated in the preceding paragraph provides the premise that a Buddha's dharma body pervades all sentient beings' bodies. Therefore, sentient beings and Buddhas are equal in possessing the dharma body. The difference is that while Buddhas have realized the dharma body, sentient beings have not, because it is hidden in their store of afflictions. The connection between a Buddha's dharma body and a sentient being's Tathāgata store is explained in the *Śrīmālā Sūtra,* in which Śrīmālā says, "When a Tathāgata's dharma body is not free from one's store of afflictions, it is called the Tathāgata store" (T12n0353, 0221c10--11).

Therefore, in fascicle 1 of text 669 (in 2 fascicles), the Chinese version of the *Sūtra of the Unsurpassed Reliance,* the Buddha advises one to turn to and rely on one's Tathāgata store, because "one's reliance on it is the condition for (1) the arising of the bodhi path, (2) ending one's afflictions, (3) acquiring the Dharma fruit through intense pondering, and (4) realizing the body of the purest dharma realm" (T16n0669, 0470c22–26).

Moreover, the knowledge that one possesses the Tathāgata store motivates one to ride the One Vehicle and gives one the confidence that one will reach the desired destination, as stated in the *Sūtra of Aṅgulimālika.* In fascicle 4 of text 120, the Buddha says, "Mañjuśrī, because one knows that milk contains butter, one churns milk to get butter; because water contains no butter, one does not churn it. Likewise, Mañjuśrī, because one knows that one possesses the Tathāgata store, one diligently observes the pure precepts and practices the Brahma way of life. Moreover, because one knows that a mountain contains gold, one excavates the mountain to get gold; because a tree contains no gold, one does not excavate it. Likewise, Mañjuśrī, because one knows that one possesses the Tathāgata store, one diligently observes the pure precepts and practices the Brahma way of life, and declares, 'I will definitely attain Buddha bodhi.' Moreover, Mañjuśrī, if one had no Tathāgata store, practicing the Brahma way of life would be futile, like churning water for a kalpa but never getting butter" (T02n0120, 0540a18–25).

Also, in the *Śrīmālā Sūtra,* Śrīmālā says, "If one has no doubts about the Tathāgata store being sheathed in one's store of immeasurable afflictions, one will have no doubts about a Tathāgata's dharma body leaving behind one's store of immeasurable afflictions" (T12n0353, 0221b17–18). Therefore, faith in one's Tathāgata store motivates one to embark on the spiritual journey to attain Buddhahood, a journey of self-verification that a Tathāgata fully realized is the Tathāgata initially in storage.

The Dharma Body

Important teachings on the dharma body are given in the *Sūtra of Neither Increase Nor Decrease,* in which the Buddha says, "Śāriputra, the dharma body . . . is not separate, not detached, not split, and not different from a Tathāgata's merit and wisdom, nor from the inconceivable Buddha Dharma [with teachings] more numerous than the sands of the Ganges" (T16n0668, 0467a19–21). Then He says, "Śāriputra, the dharma body is a dharma of no birth and no death, neither of the past nor of the future, because it is apart from the two opposites. Śāriputra, it is not of the past because it is apart from the time of birth; it is not of the future because it is apart from the time of death. Śāriputra, a Tathāgata's dharma body is permanent because it is a dharma of no change and a dharma of no end. Śāriputra, a Tathāgata's dharma body is eternal because it is an ever-available refuge and because it is equal [in all Buddhas and sentient beings] throughout all time" (Ibid., 0467a27–b3). The Buddha teaches that the dharma body takes different names when one's afflictions continue, diminish, or end. He says, "Śāriputra, when this dharma body, fettered by endless afflictions without a beginning, follows the world, drifts along with [its ocean] waves, and shuttles between birth and death, it is called a sentient being. Śāriputra, when this dharma body, tired of the suffering of repeated birth and death in the world, abandons all desires and pursuits, and trains to attain bodhi by practicing the ten pāramitās and going through the 84,000 Dharma Doors [dharma-paryāya], it is called a Bodhisattva. Śāriputra, when this dharma body has passed all suffering in the world and left behind the fetters and filth of all one's afflictions, it reveals its purity and abides in pure dharma nature [dharmatā] on the opposite shore, . . . [and] is called a Tathāgata, Arhat, Samyak-Saṁbuddha" (Ibid., 0467b6–16).

Moreover, the dharma body is the truth body, as described in text 673 (in 2 fascicles), one of the two Chinese versions of the *Sūtra of Achieving a Clearing Understanding of the Mahāyāna* (Mahāyānābhisamaya-sūtra). In fascicle 2, the Buddha says, "Good man, a Tathāgata's truth body is invisible. It has no form, no appearance, no hindrance, no indication, no dependency, no grasping, no birth, no death, and no analogy, and abides nowhere. Thus, good man, a Tathāgata's ineffable body, dharma body, wisdom body, unequaled body, peerless body, Vairocana body, sky body, endless body, indestructible body, boundless body, ultimate reality body, no-falsity body, and no-analogy body are called His truth body. . . . [A] Tathāgata's truth body is neither nonexistent nor existent. Yet it does Buddha work for all sentient beings' sake" (T16n0673, 0651c16–0652a9; Rulu 2015, 225–26).

Moreover, in fascicle 3 of the *Sūtra of Aṅgulimālika,* the Buddha gives seventy-three reasons for, and descriptions of, the dharma body that He has realized (T02n0120, 0536a1–0537c9).

The Four Virtues of the Dharma Body

The four virtues of the dharma body are revealed in the *Śrīmālā Sūtra,* in which Śrīmālā says, "If a sentient being, because of his belief in a Buddha's words, perceives a Tathāgata as eternity, bliss, a [true] self, and purity, this is not an inverted view, but the right view. Why? Because a Tathāgata's dharma body is the eternity pāramitā, the bliss pāramitā, the true-self pāramitā, and the purity pāramitā" (T12n0353, 0222a23–24). Here, the Sanskrit word *pāramitā* means transcendental virtue. A simple explanation of these four virtues is given in the *Mahāparinirvāṇa Sūtra,* of which there are three Chinese versions: texts 374, 375, and 376. In fascicle 2 of text 374, the Buddha says, "A [true] self means a Buddha; eternity means the dharma body [of a Buddha]; bliss means nirvāṇa; purity means the Dharma" (T12n0374, 0377b21–22).

A detailed description of these four virtues is given in the *Sūtra of the Unsurpassed Reliance.* In fascicle 1, the Buddha says, "Ānanda, a Tathāgata's dharma body has the great purity pāramitā with two appearances: (1) purity by nature as its general appearance [in all sentient beings], and (2) purity free from taints as its particular appearance [in Buddhas]. His dharma body has the great true-self pāramitā for two reasons: (1) He stays far away from the fixation of those on non-Buddhist paths [tīrthika] because He has transcended their imagination that one has a self, and (2) He stays far away from the fixation of riders of the Two Vehicles because He has transcended their limited understanding that one has no self. His dharma body has the great bliss pāramitā because He has achieved cessation of all His suffering in two ways: (1) ending His accumulation of afflictions and continuation of habits, and (2) eliminating His mind-created bodies [manomaya-kāya]. His dharma body has the great eternity pāramitā for two reasons: (1) He does not denounce impermanent processes [in saṁsāra] because He has transcended the view of cessation [uccheda-dṛṣṭi], and (2) He does not grasp the ever-abiding nirvāṇa because he has transcended the view of perpetuity [śaśvata-dṛṣṭi]. Seeing that impermanent processes cease is called the view of cessation, while seeing that nirvāṇa ever abides is called the view of perpetuity. Because He has eliminated the four affliction hindrances and corrected the four inversions, He harvests the perfect fruits of bodhi—eternity, bliss, a true self, and purity" (T16n0669, 0472b24–c5).

No Self versus a True Self

In the days of the Buddha, most Hindus believed, as they still do today, that they have a self (ātman), an individual soul, "who is the inner controller, the immortal" (Olivelle 2008, 41–45), whether distinct or indistinct from Brahman, the universal spirit. By contrast, the Buddha teaches that dharmas, including sentient beings, are processes that arise, change, and end through causes and conditions in accordance with the principle of dependent arising. Thus they have no self-essence (svabhāva) or inherent existence, and are empty and without a self, an autonomous self. For example, a sentient being composed of the five aggregates, twelve fields, and eighteen spheres is a mental-physical process without "a self" that controls his transmigration through the six life-paths. He is a process characterized by impermanence, suffering, no self (anātman), and impurity. Therefore, Buddhist doctrine is summarized in the Four Dharma Seals (dharma-mudrā): (1) processes are impermanent; (2) experiences boil down to suffering; (3) dharmas have no self;[12] (4) nirvāṇa is silence and stillness.

The first three of the Four Dharma Seals seem to call into question the truth of the four virtues of a Tathāgata's dharma body. However, one should note that these three seals describe saṁskṛta dharmas, dharmas subject to causes and conditions, while a Tathāgata as a manifestation of true suchness, and His dharma body as described in the preceding section, are asaṁskṛta dharmas, dharmas free from causes and conditions. In the *Mahāparinirvāṇa Sūtra,* the Buddha uses examples to contrast the four virtues with their opposites. In fascicle 2 of text 374, He says, "While no self means [anyone undergoing] birth and death, a [true] self means a Tathāgata; while impermanence means [the body of] a voice-hearer or Pratyekabuddha, eternity means the dharma body of a Tathāgata; while suffering means those on non-Buddhist paths, bliss means nirvāṇa; while impurity means saṁskṛta dharmas, purity means the true Dharma of Buddhas and Bodhisattvas. . . . To stay far away from the four inversions, one should know in this way [the meanings of] eternity, bliss, a [true] self, and purity" (T12n0374, 0377c9–14). To broaden these meanings, one can add that impermanence means saṁskṛta dharmas such as the body of a sentient being, that suffering means sentient beings on any life-paths, and that purity means a Tathāgata or His dharma body.

In different fascicles of the *Mahāparinirvāṇa Sūtra,* these four virtues variously belong to nirvāṇa, Buddha nature, a Tathāgata, or His dharma body. For example, in fascicle 22 of text 374, the Buddha says, "Where does one find eternity, bliss, a [true] self, and purity? In nirvāṇa" (T12n0374, 0494a29–b1). This teaching reveals that nirvāṇa is not merely silence and stillness after cessation of all one's suffering, as defined in the fourth Dharma Seal, but is a realization of eternity, bliss, a true self, and purity. Also, this teaching eliminates the possible misunderstanding that nirvāṇa means extinction. Confirmation is found in the *Sūtra of the Great Dharma Drum.* In fascicle 2, the Buddha says, "If [a Tathāgata's parinirvāṇa] does not mean extinction, then it means eternal peace and bliss. To be in eternal peace and bliss, there must be a [true] self, just as to have smoke, there must be fire" (T09n0270, 0296c23–26).

Then what is the meaning of a true self? For sentient beings, who are on the Cause Ground, in the *Mahāparinirvāṇa Sūtra,* a true self means one's Tathāgata store or Buddha nature. For example, in fascicle 7 of text 374, the Buddha says, "Good man, a [true] self means one's Tathāgata store. All sentient beings have Buddha nature, which means a [true] self. However, it has always been shrouded by their countless afflictions. That is why they cannot see it" (T12n0374, 0407b9–11). It follows that until a sentient being attains Buddhahood, he does not see his true self, nor its eternity, bliss, and purity.

For Buddhas, who are on the Result Ground, in the *Mahāparinirvāṇa Sūtra,* a true self means a Tathāgata or His dharma body. For example, in fascicle 32 of text 374, the Buddha says, "Good man, because a Tathāgata ever abides, He is a [true] self. Because a Tathāgata's dharma body is boundless and hindrance free, has neither birth nor death, and has command of eight great displays,[13] it is a [true] self" (Ibid., 0556c11–13).

In the *Mahāparinirvāṇa Sūtra,* the Buddha uses an analogy to explain why He first teaches sentient beings that one has no self, then teaches them that one has a true self. In fascicle 7 of text 374, He tells the story of an ill baby boy, who is forbidden by his physician to drink milk soon after taking medicine. So the mother smears bitter flavor on her nipples to keep her son from suckling. After the medicine is spent, she cleanses her nipples and calls her son to suckle. Like the mother who smears her nipples with bitter flavor, the Tathāgata teaches that dharmas have no self, in order to eliminate sentient beings' wrong views and purify their minds. Then, like the mother who cleanses her nipples and calls her son to suckle, the Tathāgata teaches that all sentient beings possess the Tathāgata store (Ibid., 0407b29–c18).

Denouncing the Claim That One Has an Autonomous Self

However, a true self, whether symbolizing a Tathāgata or His dharma body, or symbolizing a sentient being's Tathāgata store or Buddha nature, seems to carry the flavor of the autonomous self claimed by those on non-Buddhist paths. This issue is raised in the *Laṅkāvatāra Sūtra,* of which there are three Chinese versions: texts 670, 671, and 672. In fascicle 3 of text 671, Mahāmati Bodhisattva asks the Buddha, "As those on non-Buddhist paths claim that one possesses a divine self [ātman], which is ever abiding and changeless, likewise the Tathāgata teaches that one possesses the Tathāgata store, which is ever abiding and changeless. . . . Then the Tathāgata's and non-Buddhists' teachings are no different" (T16n0671, 0529b22–26)?

In answer to this question, the Buddha says, "The Tathāgata store taught by me is different from the divine self claimed by those on non-Buddhist paths. To describe the Tathāgata store, I use terms such as emptiness, true reality, nirvāṇa, no birth, no death, no appearance, and no wish. Mahāmati, a Tathāgata, Arhat, Samyak-Saṁbuddha, knows that stupid and deluded ordinary beings are shocked and terrified when they hear that one has no self. Therefore, I say that one possesses the Tathāgata store, which makes no differentiation, has no appearances, and is quiet. Mahāmati, present and future Bodhisattvas should not hold the [wrong] view that one has a self. Mahāmati, as an analogy, to make various vessels, a potter transforms a lump of clay by means of manual skill, water, a wheel, and a rope. Mahāmati, a Tathāgata-Bhagavān does the same. . . . Using wisdom and skillful means, He expounds that one has no self or that one possesses the Tathāgata store, or expounds on true reality or nirvāṇa. He expresses his meaning through various names and phrases, like a potter making various vessels. Therefore, Mahāmati, the Tathāgata store taught by me is different from the self claimed by those on non-Buddhist paths. Mahāmati, I expound the Tathāgata store to draw in those on non-Buddhist paths, enabling them to discard their fixation that one has a divine self and to enter the Three Liberation Doors [emptiness, no appearance, and no wish], so that they will quickly attain anuttara-samyak-saṁbodhi. For this reason, as [other] Tathāgatas expound the Tathāgata store, I too expound it, which is different from the divine self claimed by those on non-Buddhist paths. Therefore, Mahāmati, to reject the view of those on non-Buddhist paths, you should, as Buddha-Tathāgatas advise, study the teaching that a Tathāgata does not have the appearances of a self" (Ibid., 0529b26–c18).

This teaching is confirmed in the *Śrīmālā Sūtra.* Affirming that one's Tathāgata store is free from a person's four false self-images,[14] Śrīmālā says, "One's Tathāgata store is not a self, not a person, not a sentient being, and not an everlasting soul. It is incomprehensible to those who hold the wrong view that one has a self, those who hold inverted views, and those who misunderstand the emptiness of dharmas" (T12n0353, 0222b19–21).

In the *Mahāparinirvāṇa Sūtra,* the Buddha affirms that the self claimed by those on non-Buddhist paths does not exist. In fascicle 30 of text 374, He says, "If a self were a doer, how could it be said to be permanent? If it were permanent, why would it sometimes do good and sometimes do evil? If they claim that it sometimes does good and sometimes does evil, how could it be said to be boundless? If a self were a doer, why would it practice doing evil? . . . Because of this meaning, the self in the teachings of those on non-Buddhist paths definitely does not exist" (T12n0374, 0544c11–15).

Then the Buddha explains the meaning of a true self. He says, "Speaking of a self, it must be a Tathāgata. Why? Because His body is boundless, without doubts. He is eternity because He neither does nor experiences anything. He is bliss because He has neither birth nor death. He is purity because He has no afflictions. He is emptiness because He does not have the ten appearances. Therefore, a Tathāgata is eternity, bliss, a [true] self, and purity, free from appearances. When those on non-Buddhist paths hear that a Tathāgata with the four virtues is described as emptiness only because He is free from appearances, they are convinced that the Buddha's teaching is not about nothingness, and decide to accept and uphold it with the highest reverence" (T12n0374, 0544c15–22). This teaching reveals that although the Tathāgata store, equated to emptiness, true reality, or inherent nirvāṇa, is not the self claimed by those on non-Buddhist paths, its seeming resemblance has drawn them into the Dharma.

Based on the teachings in preceding paragraphs, one can reach the understanding that a Tathāgata's eternity is beyond the view of perpetuity opposite that of cessation; His bliss is beyond the experience of joy opposite that of suffering; His true self is beyond the imagination that one has a self and the teaching that one has no self, but does not invalidate this teaching; His purity is beyond the perception of purity opposite that of impurity.

Although a Tathāgata's dharma body fully reveals its four virtues, they are hidden in a sentient being's Tathāgata store. The reason is that a Tathāgata is on the Result Ground while a sentient being is on the Cause Ground. Until he has attained Buddhahood, he does not see these four virtues.

Buddha Nature

The term "Buddha nature" is translated from the Sanskrit compound word "buddha-dhātu" or "buddha-gotra." The word *dhātu* (界) means element, realm, or sphere; the word *gotra* (種姓 or 種性) means family name or inborn character-type. In fascicle 2 of text 1530 (in 7 fascicles), the Chinese version of *A Treatise on the Sūtra of the Buddha Ground* (Buddhabhūmi-sūtra-śāstra), its author Bandhuprabha (親光, 6th century) classified all sentient beings into five character-types (pañca-gotra): (1) the voice-hearer character-type, (2) the Pratyekabuddha character-type, (3) the Tathāgata character-type, (4) the unfixed character-type, and (5) the character-type with no virtue to transcend the world (T26n1530, 0298a12–15). Except for the fourth one, character-types are fixed in their nature. The first three character-types will train to become an Arhat, a Pratyekabuddha, or a Buddha, respectively. The fourth character-type may become one of these three holy beings through causes and conditions. The fifth character-type, also called the no-nature type (agotra), is interested only in rebirth as a human or god and will never transcend the world. According to this treatise, although some sūtras state that all sentient beings have Buddha nature, it is merely a skillful means to persuade those of the unfixed character-type to train to attain Buddhahood (Ibid., 0298a24–28). The Consciousness-Only School upholds this five-type classification because its exponents believe that the original seeds in ālaya consciousness, one's eighth consciousness, determine one's character-type, which does not change. However, teachings of the Consciousness-Only School are classified by the Huayan School as beginning Mahāyāna teachings, which are provisional teachings.

Extensive teachings on Buddha Nature are given in the *Mahāparinirvāṇa Sūtra,* whose essential tenet is that a Tathāgata ever abides, and that all sentient beings have Buddha nature and will eventually attain Buddhahood. These teachings are classified as concluding Mahāyāna teachings, which are definitive teachings. The 40-fascicle Chinese version of this sūtra is text 374. This text was translated from Sanskrit by Dharmakṣema from central India, who arrived in China in 412. He first translated into Chinese the first five chapters in fascicles 1–10 from the Sanskrit text that he had brought with him. Then he went to Yütian, acquired the Sanskrit text of chapters 6–13, and translated them into Chinese. It is interesting that while the term "Tathāgata store" appears only in fascicles 7 and 8, the term "Buddha nature" appears in fascicles 2 through 38. This shows a shift in theme, from one's Tathāgata store to Buddha nature, and there is no telling whether this shift has to do with the Sanskrit texts coming from two different sources. Although in the doctrine of the Tathāgata store, "Buddha nature" and "Tathāgata store" are synonyms, teachings on Buddha nature provide further insight into one's potential to attain Buddhahood.

In fascicle 14 of text 374, the Buddha describes one's Buddha nature. He says, "Good man, Buddha nature has neither birth nor death, neither comes nor goes, is of neither the past nor the future, nor the present, is neither made nor not made by a cause, neither doing nor a doer, has neither appearances nor no appearances, neither names nor no names, and is neither mental nor physical, neither long nor short. It is not sustained by one's five aggregates, twelve fields, or eighteen spheres, so it is permanent. Good man, Buddha nature is a Tathāgata. . . . Good man, all saṁskṛta dharmas are impermanent. . . . As Buddha nature is an asaṁskṛta dharma, it is permanent. Likewise, as a Tathāgata is an asaṁskṛta dharma, He is permanent" (T12n0374, 0445b29–c15).

Moreover, in fascicle 27, the Buddha defines Buddha nature as emptiness in the highest sense (paramārtha-śūnyatā), the Middle Way, and the seed of anuttara-samyak-saṁbodhi, the unsurpassed perfect enlightenment. He says, "Good man, Buddha nature means emptiness in the highest sense, which is wisdom [prajñā]. . . . The wise see what is empty and what is not empty, what is impermanent and what is permanent, what is suffering and what is joy, what is no self and what is a [true] self. While emptiness is saṁsāra, not-emptiness is the great nirvāṇa. While no self is [anyone undergoing] birth and death, a [true] self is the great nirvāṇa. Seeing emptiness in everything but not seeing what is not empty is not the Middle Way.[15] Seeing no self in everything but not seeing a [true] self is not the Middle Way. The Middle Way is called Buddha nature.[16] One's Buddha nature is eternal and changeless. However, shrouded by their ignorance [of the truth], sentient beings cannot see their Buddha nature. A voice-hearer or Pratyekabuddha sees emptiness in everything but does not see what is not empty. He sees no self in everything but does not see a [true] self. Therefore, he does not realize emptiness in the highest sense. Not realizing emptiness in the highest sense, he does not walk the Middle Way. Not walking the Middle Way, he does not see his Buddha nature" (Ibid., 0523b12–23). Then the Buddha says, "Good man, Buddha nature, or the Middle Way, is the seed of all Buddhas' anuttara-samyak-saṁbodhi" (Ibid., 0523c1–2).

Moreover, in fascicle 27, the Buddha explains that observing the dependent arising of dharmas reveals one's Buddha nature. He says, "Good man, sentient beings hold either of the two views, the view of perpetuity and the view of cessation. Neither of these two views is the Middle Way, because [seeing dharmas as] neither perpetual nor ceasing is the Middle Way. . . . The wisdom-knowledge that arises from observing the Twelve Links of Dependent Arising is the seed of anuttara-samyak-saṁbodhi. Therefore, the Twelve Links of Dependent Arising are called Buddha nature" (Ibid., 0523c24–0524a3).

Moreover, in fascicle 32, the Buddha describes Buddha nature as a Tathāgata's virtues—great lovingkindness, great compassion, great sympathetic joy, great relinquishment, great faith, the ground of [equality of all sentient beings as] one son, the fourth power of a Buddha's Ten Powers,[17] the Twelve Links of Dependent Arising, the four kinds of unimpeded wisdom-knowledge, and the top samādhi (Ibid., 0556c14–0557a16). Here, the top samādhi refers to the Śūraṅgama Samādhi, which according to fascicle 27 has five names: (1) Śūraṅgama Samādhi, (2) Prajñā-Pāramitā, (3) Vajra Samādhi, (4) Lion's Roar Samādhi, and (5) Buddha Nature (Ibid., 0524c18–25).

Text 1610 (in 4 fascicles), the Chinese version of *A Treatise on Buddha Nature,* provides further insight into Buddha nature. Fascicle 4 states that one's Buddha nature is of two kinds that tie in with the three bodies of a Buddha. The first kind is the self-abiding Buddha nature, and the second kind is the drawn-forth Buddha nature.[18] Self-abiding Buddha nature means a Tathāgata's dharma body, like gold wrapped in filthy rags, available to anyone who removes the rags. Drawn-forth Buddha nature manifests as a Tathāgata's reward body and response body. The reward body arises from achieving the Thirty-seven Elements of Bodhi and personifies a Buddha's immeasurable merit. The response body has a physical form like the moon in the water and displays its birth and death (T31n1610, 0808c8–28). The dharma body has five virtues: (1) immeasurability, (2) uncountability, (3) inconceivability, (4) supremacy, and (5) absolute purity. The reward body has three virtues: (1) great wisdom [prajñā] (2) great meditation [dhyāna], and (3) great compassion [karuṇā]. The response body has great compassion as its root, uses meditation to produce manifestations, and does Buddha work with wisdom. In summary, the virtue of the dharma body is profundity, the virtue of the reward body is vastness, and the virtue of the response body is benevolence. These three bodies are said to be ever abiding because they constantly benefit the world" (Ibid., 0810c8–0811a11).

Even Icchantikas Have Buddha Nature

According to fascicle 2 of text 671, the 10-fascicle Chinese version of the *Laṅkāvatāra Sūtra,* there are two kinds of icchantika. Icchantikas of the first kind cannot attain nirvāṇa because they malign the Bodhisattva store of teachings (Bodhisattva-piṭaka) and burn away their roots of goodness. Icchantikas of the second kind do not enter nirvāṇa because they are Bodhisattvas who, out of compassion, vow not to enter nirvāṇa until all sentient beings have entered it (T16n0671, 0527b2–10).

In most sūtras, the Buddha denounces icchantikas of the first kind. For example, in fascicle 1 of the *Sūtra of the Unsurpassed Reliance,* the Buddha says, "Ānanda, whoever maligns the Mahāyāna and is attached to existence and greedy for lingering in the Three Realms of Existence is called an icchantika. He falls into the group that definitely is on the wrong path" (T16n0669, 0471b20–21).

Nevertheless, a saving grace is provided by a teaching in the *Mahāparinirvāṇa Sūtra.* In fascicle 22 of text 374, Pervasive Radiance Noble Virtue King Bodhisattva asks the Buddha whether an icchantika's Buddha nature is destroyed when he destroys his roots of goodness (T12n0374, 0493b26–27). In answer to this question, the Buddha says, "There are two kinds of roots of goodness, internal and external. Because Buddha nature is neither internal nor external, it never ends. There are another two kinds of roots of goodness, with afflictions and without afflictions. Because Buddha nature is neither with nor without afflictions, it never ends. There are another two kinds of roots of goodness, permanent and impermanent. Because Buddha nature is neither permanent nor impermanent, it never ends" (Ibid., 0493c27–0494a2).

In fascicle 27 of text 374, the Buddha says, "I often declare that all sentient beings, even icchantikas, have Buddha nature. . . . Why? Because even an icchantika will definitely attain anuttara-samyak-saṁbodhi. . . . All sentient beings have minds. Whoever has a mind will definitely attain anuttara-samyak-saṁbodhi. For this reason, I often declare that all sentient beings have Buddha nature" (T12n0374, 0524c1–10).

An icchantika can attain Buddhahood because he will not remain an icchantika forever. The issue is addressed in the *Laṅkāvatāra Sūtra.* In fascicle 2 of text 671, the Buddha says, "Mahāmati, if an icchantika, who has abandoned his roots of goodness, encounters a Buddha or beneficent learned friend, he will activate the bodhi mind, replant his roots of goodness, and attain nirvāṇa. Why? Because Buddha-Tathāgatas never abandon any sentient beings" (T16n0671, 0527b16–19).

Ālaya Consciousness and the Tathāgata Store Unified

Ālaya consciousness (ālaya-vijñāna), one's eighth consciousness, is also called root consciousness (mūla-vijñāna), because it is the source of all dharmas and one's first seven consciousnesses. It is also called existence-grasping consciousness (ādāna-vijñāna) and karma-ripening consciousness (vipāka-vijñāna), because it maintains one's life and carries seeds to one's karmic rebirth. It is also called storehouse consciousness and seeds consciousness, because it stores all the pure, impure, and neutral seeds of one's experience without a beginning. When one attains Buddhahood, all seeds stored in ālaya consciousness become pure seeds that will neither change nor manifest any karmic rebirth. Then it sheds its name "ālaya-vijñāna" and takes a new name "amala-vijñāna," stainless consciousness, which is one's inherent pure awareness and possesses the great mirror-like wisdom-knowledge.

According to fascicle 2 of text 1585 (in 10 fascicles), the Chinese version of *A Treatise on Establishing Consciousness-Only,* ālaya consciousness means (1) a storehouse of seeds of all dharmas, (2) the stored seeds, and (3) something mistaken for a self by manas consciousness (manas-vijñāna), one's seventh consciousness (T31n1585, 0007c20–21). The Consciousness-Only School holds that one's seventh consciousness has four defilements: (1) self-delusion, (2) self-love, (3) self-view, and (4) self-arrogance. One's instinctive sense of self and self-preservation is attributed to its mistaking one's eighth consciousness for a self. In fascicle 1 of text 676 (in 5 fascicles), the later of the two Chinese versions of the *Saṁdhinirmocana Sūtra,* the Buddha speaks in verse: "Ādāna consciousness is profound and imperceptible, / And its seeds churn like raging rapids. / I do not reveal it to the ordinary and the foolish / For I worry that they would perceive and grasp it as a self" (T16n0676, 0692c22–23). Although one's Tathāgata store is one's true self, it appears as ālaya consciousness, which can be mistaken for a self as a controller or an entity.

In the *Laṅkāvatāra Sūtra,* ālaya consciousness is equated to the Tathāgata store. In fascicle 7 of text 671, the Buddha says, "Mahāmati, ālaya consciousness is called the Tathāgata store. It is accompanied by one's ground-abiding ignorance [avidyāvāsa-bhūmi] and first seven consciousnesses, like the ocean with its waves, and continues without end. Pure by nature, it is free from the faults of impermanence and a self, whereas one's first seven consciousnesses arise and perish thought after thought" (T16n0671, 0556b22–c4). Then, in fascicle 8, He says, "Ālaya consciousness is called the Tathāgata store. It is empty because it is not tainted by one's first seven consciousnesses; it is not empty because it encompasses affliction-free dharmas" (Ibid., 0559c2–4). This accords with teachings in the *Śrīmālā Sūtra,* that the empty Tathāgata store is separate from one's afflictions, and that the not-empty Tathāgata store is not separate from countless virtues (T12n0353, 0221c16–18).

The purity of ālaya consciousness is affirmed in text 681 (in 3 fascicles), the earlier of the two Chinese versions of the *Ghanavyūha Sūtra.* In fascicle 1, Vajra Store Bodhisattva says, "Although ālaya consciousness stays together with one's first seven consciousnesses, their mental functions, and all pure and impure seeds, it is not tainted by them, because it is by nature luminous and pure" (T16n0681, 0727b15–17). In fascicle 2, he says, "A sentient being's ālaya consciousness has always been existent, perfect, and pure, the same as nirvāṇa. . . . As the moon behind clouds is always luminous and pure, likewise one's storehouse consciousness, in the midst of one's first seven consciousnesses, mental objects, and habits, is always luminous and pure (Ibid., 0737c24–0738a2). In fascicle 3, he describes the connection between one's ālaya consciousness and Tathāgata store in verse: "The pure Tathāgata store and the worldly ālaya consciousness / Are like gold and a gold ring. / One turns into the other with no change [in essence]" (Ibid., 0747a19–20).

The connection between one's ālaya consciousness and Tathāgata store is explained in text 1666, the one-fascicle Chinese version of *A Treatise on Eliciting Faith in the Mahāyāna.* According to this text, one's mind comprises the true-suchness [Tathāgata-store] mind and the birth-and-death mind (T32n1666, 0576a5–7). The true-suchness mind has neither birth nor death, and is changeless. It is empty because it is always incoherent with impure dharmas, and not empty because it is always coherent with pure dharmas. The birth-and-death mind relies on the Tathāgata store to manifest dharmas with birth and death. When the mind with neither birth nor death and the mind with birth and death are united, it is called ālaya consciousness, which encompasses and manifests all dharmas (Ibid., 0576a24–b10).

Beginning Mahāyāna teachings, such as those of Consciousness-Only School, uphold dependent arising of dharmas from the original and changing seeds stored in ālaya consciousness, while concluding Mahāyāna teachings, such as those on the Tathāgata store, uphold dependent arising of dharmas from the Tathāgata store, or true suchness. Based on the teachings in the *Laṅkāvatāra Sūtra* and the *Ghanavyūha Sūtra,* and the explanation in *A Treatise on Eliciting Faith in the Mahāyāna,* ālaya consciousness and the Tathāgata store are unified. The theory is that the Tathāgata store, likened to gold, is the pure and changeless essence of ālaya consciousness, liken to a gold ring, and that the Tathāgata store appears as ālaya consciousness, which manifests myriad dharmas.

The Spiritual Journey from Potential to Fulfillment

A teaching in the *Mahāparinirvāṇa Sūtra* equates Buddha nature to the One Vehicle. In fascicle 27 of text 374, the Buddha says, "The One Vehicle is called Buddha nature. Therefore, I say that as all sentient beings have Buddha nature, they possess the One Vehicle. However, shrouded by their ignorance [of the truth], they cannot see it" (T12n0374, 0524c14–16). This teaching means that one's Buddha nature is not only one's potential to attain Buddhahood, but one's vehicle to fulfill this potential. However, one should take action driving oneself to one's destination because, unlike a magnet attracting metal, one's Buddha nature does not automatically bring one bodhi. In fascicle 32, the Buddha says, "Through the power of one's Buddha nature, one attains anuttara-samyak-saṁbodhi. However, it does not mean that one does not need to walk the holy path. Good man, as an analogy, a man travels across a wilderness. Tired and thirsty, he stumbles upon a well. Although he cannot see the water in the deep well, he knows that it is there. Then he finds himself a pail and a rope, and uses them as skillful means to draw water from the well. Once the water is fetched, he sees it. Likewise, although all sentient beings have Buddha nature, they must train by walking the affliction-free holy path. Then they will come to see it" (Ibid., 0555b6–13).

Are skillful means the cause for one to fully reveal one's Buddha nature? In fascicle 21 of text 374, the Buddha uses examples to distinguish between a producing cause and a revealing cause. He says, "A potter and his equipment are called the producing cause [of ceramic pots]. Lamplight and candlelight are called the revealing cause of things in the dark. Good man, the great nirvāṇa is attained not through producing causes, but through revealing causes, such as the Thirty-seven Elements of Bodhi and the six pāramitās" (Ibid., 0492c2–7). Therefore, one's Buddha nature, one's inherent nirvāṇa, is revealed through one's spiritual training as its revealing cause.

The basis of a Bodhisattva's spiritual journey is his compassion for all sentient beings, his belief in the Buddha's words, and his faith in his Buddha nature. Training on the Bodhisattva Way to Buddhahood, a Bodhisattva must accomplish four things: (1) faith, (3) understanding, (3) action, and (4) verification. Through hearing and pondering the Dharma, he elicits faith and acquires understanding. His understanding of the Dharma contained in the sūtras gives him the right views, which provide the essential foundation for his action. His action means carrying out the teachings in the sūtras through the Three Learnings: precepts (śīla), meditation (dhyāna), and wisdom (prajñā). For a Bodhisattva to develop wisdom, he must practice the ten pāramitās on the Bodhisattva Way. Through the power of his wisdom, he progressively verifies by self-realization the ultimate truth as taught by Buddhas. Adorned with fully accumulated merit and perfect wisdom, he attains Buddhahood. Having fulfilled his potential to attain Buddhahood, he sees that his fully revealed Buddha nature is his initially hidden Buddha nature.

Notes

1. The Dharma jewel is the second of the Three Jewels: the Buddha, the Dharma, and the Saṅgha. See Three Jewels in the glossary.

2. The Aṅguttara Nikāya (Numbered Discourses) in volumes 19–25 is the seventh of thirty-eight collections of texts in the 70-volume Chinese version of the Pāli Canon (漢譯南傳大藏經), the whole of which was translated from its Japanese version between 1990 and 1998 by a team of translators commissioned by the Yuanheng Temple (元亨寺), in Kaohsiung, Taiwan. Volume 19 of the Aṅguttara Nikāya was translated by Ye Qingchun (葉慶春).

3. The literal translation of the Sanskrit term "āgantuka kleśa" is adventitious afflictions, which is widely used by scholars. However, adventitious means coming from outside or occurring by chance. As explained in chapter 5 of the *Vaipulya Sūtra of Śrīmālā's Lion's Roar,* underlying one's ground-abiding afflictions and their ensuring afflictions is one's root affliction, one's ground-abiding ignorance. Therefore, there is nothing external or accidental about one's afflictions, though they are illusory. Here, this term is translated from Chinese as visitor-like afflictions. In text 844 in the Extension of the Chinese Canon (the Shinsan Zokuzōkyō), Kuiji (窺基, 632–82), the first patriarch of the Consciousness-Only School of China, gave an explanation. To the question of why one's afflictions are called visitors if one's inherent pure

mind has always been tainted by one's afflictions, Kuiji answered, "As one trains to attain bodhi, one's afflictions end but one's pure nature remains. That is why one's afflictions are called visitors" (X53n0844, 0860c10–12). Therefore, one's afflictions are visitor-like only to the extent that they can be removed through spiritual training and awakening, like visitors being removed.

4. This analogy also appears in fascicle 1 of text 669, the Chinese version of the *Sūtra of the Unsurpassed Reliance* (T16n0669, 0469b19–23).

5. A similar passage appears in fascicle 35 of text 278 (T09n0278, 0624a15–22), and a corresponding passage, though in obscure wording, appears in fascicle 3 of text 291, (T10n0291, 0607c24–0608a2).

6. However, a note in text 672 states that this bhikṣu was Nāgāhvāya, not Nāgārjuna (龍樹菩薩, circa 150–250), who is revered in China as the distant founding patriarch of eight Mahāyāna schools. According to *Tāranātha's History of Buddhism in India,* Nāgāhvāya, whose real name was Tathāgatabhadra, was a contemporary of Āryadeva, a student of Nāgārjuna (Tāranātha 1970, 126). While Nāgārjuna mainly expounded on the emptiness of dharmas, it is possible that Nāgāhvāya, often confused with Nāgārjuna, expounded on the Tathāgata store.

7. According to text 8888 in Taiwan's National Central Library's collection of intact ancient Buddhist texts, at the request of Asaṅga, Maitreya Bodhisattva, the next Buddha to come, descended from Tuṣita Heaven, the fourth desire heaven, to a lecture hall in the kingdom of Ayodhyā in central India every night for four months, and recited five Mahāyāna treatises, among which the *Yogācāra-bhūmi-śāstra* is of foremost importance (D29n8888, 0001b2–5). Also, in fascicle 1 of text 824 in the Extension of the Chinese Canon, Master Zhixü (智旭, 1599–1655), the ninth patriarch of the Pure Land School, told a similar story. According to his account, Asaṅga, through his transcendental power, often went up to Tuṣita Heaven and received from Maitreya Bodhisattva teachings on the Mahāyāna view of emptiness. In response to Asaṅga's prayer, Maitreya Bodhisattva descended to this world every night for four months, and recited the *Yogācāra-bhūmi-śāstra* in a lecture hall in Ayodhyā (X51n0824, 0298b8–19). Therefore, Chinese tradition identifies Maitreya-nātha, a Yogācāra master, with Maitreya Bodhisattva, while some scholars hold that works attributed to Maitreya-nātha are actually Asaṅga's works inspired by Maitreya Bodhisattva.

8. The Chinese title of this treatise is *A Treatise on the Ground of the Yoga Teacher* 瑜伽師地論, which can be translated into Sanskrit as *Yogacārya-bhūmi-śāstra,* as listed in *A Dictionary of Chinese Buddhist Terms* (Soothill and Hodous 1962, 407). However, in Sanskrit texts, the term "yoga practice" (yogācāra or yogacāra) is used, not "yoga teacher" (yogācārya).

9. See "three natures of dharmas" in fascicle 4 of text 676, the later of the two Chinese versions of the *Saṁdhinirmocana Sūtra* [Sūtra of the profound secret unraveled] (T16n0676, 0706c14–15).

10. See "five dharmas" in fascicle 5 of text 672, the 7-fascicle Chinese version of the *Laṅkāvatāra Sūtra* (T16n0672, 0620a22–26).

11. See the Ground Treatise School introduced in Bodhiruci's biography in this book.

12. Riders of the Two Vehicles train to realize that a person has no self, while riders of the Mahāyāna train to realize not only that a person has no self and is empty, but that a dharma (a thing, such as a component of a person) has

no self and is empty. Here, dharmas in this third seal include both persons and things.

13. See "command of eight great displays" in the glossary.

14. See "four appearances" in the glossary.

15. In several prajñā-pāramitā sūtras, Mañjuśrī Bodhisattva is the principal exponent of the absolute emptiness of everything. Such teachings are classified by the Huayan School as beginning Mahāyāna teachings. In fascicle 2 of text 120 (in 4 fascicles), the Chinese version of the Mahāyāna version of the *Aṅgulimālika Sūtra,* Aṅgulimāla criticizes Mañjuśrī, saying that he trains to see the utter emptiness of dharmas and constantly ponders their emptiness to destroy his perception of all dharmas. Although liberation is actually not empty, he thinks that it is utterly empty (T02n0120, 0527b22–25). Then Aṅgulimāla gives concluding Mahāyāna teachings. He says that one's afflictions are empty and can be eradicated, like hailstones melting. However, a Tathāgata's true liberation is not empty. Because liberation is free from all faults, it is said to be empty. Likewise a Tathāgata is actually not empty. Because He has left behind all afflictions and the form of a god or human, He is said to be empty (Ibid., 0527b28–c13). Also, in the *Śrīmālā Sūtra,* Śrīmālā says that "there are two kinds of wisdom-knowledge of the emptiness of one's Tathāgata store. The first kind is the wisdom-knowledge of the empty Tathāgata store, which is separate, detached, or different from one's store of all afflictions. The second kind is the wisdom-knowledge of the not-empty Tathāgata store, which is not separate, detached, or different from the inconceivable Buddha Dharma [with teachings] more numerous than the sands of the Ganges" (T12n0353, 0221c16–18).

16. The Middle Way is called Buddha nature because its eight negations aptly describe Buddha nature, and because walking the Middle Way reveals one's Buddha nature, for the last sentence in this passage states that "not walking the Middle Way, he does not see his Buddha nature."

17. The fourth power of a Buddha's Ten Powers is perfect wisdom-knowledge of the capacity of every sentient being. See Ten Powers in the glossary.

18. Self-abiding Buddha nature means one's inherent Buddha nature, and drawn-forth Buddha nature means one's Buddha nature gradually revealed through one's spiritual training. According to fascicle 4 of text 1611 (in 4 fascicles), the Chinese version of *A Treatise on the Jewel Nature,* the first kind of Buddha nature is like something stored under the ground, and the second kind of Buddha nature is like fruit on a tree. If one uses one's inherent pure mind to train to attain the unsurpassed bodhi, these two kinds of Buddha nature reveal the three bodies of a Buddha (T31n1611, 0839a1–5).

PART I

Sūtras on the Tathāgata store

About Sūtra 1

Records in the Chinese Canon mention four Chinese versions of the *Mahāvaipulya Sūtra of the Tathāgata Store,* but only two are extant. Text 666 (T16n0666) in one fascicle was translated from Sanskrit in 420, the second year of the Yuanxi (元熙) years of the Eastern Jin Dynasty (317–420), by Buddhabhadra (佛馱跋陀羅, 359–429) from northern India. Text 667 (T16n0667) in one fascicle was translated from Sanskrit between 746 and 771 during the Tang Dynasty (618–907) by Amoghavajra (不空金剛, 705–74) from present-day Sri Lanka. Text 666 is the concise and more popular version.

Text 2154 (T55n2154), a catalog of texts compiled in 730, the eighteenth year of the Kaiyuan (開元) years of Emperor Xuanzong (唐玄宗) of the Tang Dynasty, mentions two earlier Chinese versions of this sūtra, but both have been lost. The first was translated between 290 and 307 during the reign of Emperor Hui (晉惠帝) of the Western Jin Dynasty (266–316), by Fajü (法炬) and Fali (法立). The second was translated by Bai Fazu (白法祖), also during Emperor Hui's reign. This means that texts on the Tathāgata store (tathāgata-garbha) arrived in China as early as the third century.

In 1995, William H. Grosnick was the first to translate text 666 into English. Sūtra 1 in the present book is also an English translation of text 666. For the convenience of the reader, headings are added to this translation.

This sūtra describes the Tathāgata store and mentions Tathāgata nature and Buddha nature as its synonyms, but does not mention its relationship to ālaya consciousness. It reveals that all sentient beings have the Tathāgata store within them, which is forever pure and changeless, and encourages them to train diligently in order to become fully revealed Tathāgatas. To describe the Tathāgata store, it gives nine analogies: (1) a Buddha inside a lotus flower bud, (2) honey guarded by bees, (3) rice before its husk is removed, (4) a chunk of gold fallen into a filthy place, (5) the treasure store under a poor family's house, (6) a viable seed in a fruit's pit, (7) a gold statue wrapped in filthy rags, (8) a noble son carried by a poor and ugly pregnant woman, and (9) a gold statue inside a filthy mold.

While seven of these nine analogies are fitting analogies of the Tathāgata store, which is forever pure and changeless, the sixth and eighth analogies seem to miss the mark, because as a viable seed in a fruit's pit needs to grow into a huge tree through causes and conditions, so does a noble son carried by an poor and ugly pregnant woman need to grow into a great king. A possible interpretation is that the Tathāgata store in the sixth analogy is the life force of a viable seed in a fruit's pit, not the seed itself, and in the eighth analogy is the royal blood of an unborn king, not the fetus itself. The seed and fetus are analogies of a sentient being who needs to walk the Bodhisattva Way to attain Buddhahood, leaving behind his afflictions, likened to a fruit's pit and the womb of an ugly woman.

An explanation of these nine analogies is given in text 1610 (in 4 fascicles), the Chinese version of Vasubandhu's (世親, circa 320–80) *A Treatise on Buddha Nature* (Buddhagotra-śāstra), translated from Sanskrit in the Southern Chen

Dynasty (557–89) by Paramārtha (真諦, 499–569). The explanation in fascicle 4 is summarized as follows.

(1) The flower's petals are one's greed; (2) the bees are one's anger; (3) the husk is one's ignorance; (4) the filthy place is the preceding three afflictions; (5) the poor family is one's ground-abiding ignorance; (6) A fruit's pit is one's view confusions; (7) the filthy rags are one's thinking confusions;* (8) the poor pregnant woman is one's impure confusions; (9) the mold is one's pure confusions. The first three analogies reveal the dharma body, the fourth reveals true suchness, and the last five reveal Buddha nature (T31n1610, 0807c9–0808a25).

———

* See "view confusions" and "thinking confusions" defined in the glossary's "afflictions."

1 大方等如來藏經
Mahāvaipulya Sūtra of the Tathāgata Store

Translated from Sanskrit into Chinese in the the Eastern Jin Dynasty
by
The Tripiṭaka Master Buddhabhadra from India

The Assembly

Thus I have heard:

At one time the Buddha was staying on the Gṛdhrakūṭa Mountain, near the city of Rājagṛha, in the Treasure Moon Lecture Hall in a great sandalwood tower. He had attained Buddhahood ten years ago. He was accompanied by 100,000 great bhikṣus, and Bodhisattva-Mahāsattvas as numerous as the sands of sixty Ganges Rivers. These Bodhisattvas had acquired the power of great energetic progress[1] and made offerings to 100,000 koṭi nayuta Buddhas. All of them could turn the no-regress Dharma wheel. Whoever heard any of their names would not regress from the unsurpassed bodhi mind.

[These Bodhisattvas included] Dharma Wisdom Bodhisattva, Lion Wisdom Bodhisattva, Vajra Wisdom [Vajramati] Bodhisattva, Attuned Wisdom Bodhisattva, Wondrous Wisdom Bodhisattva, Moonlight Bodhisattva, Treasure Moon Bodhisattva, Full Moon Bodhisattva, Valor Bodhisattva, Immeasurable Valor Bodhisattva, Boundless Valor Bodhisattva, Transcending the Three Realms of Existence Bodhisattva, Avalokiteśvara Bodhisattva, Great Might Arrived [Mahāsthāmaprāpta] Bodhisattva, Fragrant Elephant Bodhisattva, Superior Fragrance Bodhisattva, Foremost Fragrance Bodhisattva, Foremost Store Bodhisattva, Sun Store Bodhisattva, Banner Appearance Bodhisattva, Great Banner Appearance Bodhisattva, Taint-Free Banner Bodhisattva, Boundless Light Bodhisattva, Emitting Light Bodhisattva, Taint-Free Light Bodhisattva, Joy King Bodhisattva, Constant Joy Bodhisattva, Jewel Hand [Ratnapāṇi] Bodhisattva, Space Store [Ākāśa-garbha] Bodhisattva, Arrogance-Free Bodhisattva, Sumeru Bodhisattva, Radiant Virtue King Bodhisattva, Dhāraṇī Commanding King Bodhisattva, Dhāraṇī Bodhisattva, Ending Faults Bodhisattva, Curing All Sentient Beings' Diseases Bodhisattva, Joyful Mind Bodhisattva, Contented Mind Bodhisattva, Constant Contentment Bodhisattva, Universal Illumination Bodhisattva, Moonshine Bodhisattva, Treasure Wisdom Bodhisattva, Able to Change a Female Body Bodhisattva, Great Thunder Bodhisattva, Guiding Teacher Bodhisattva, No False Views Bodhisattva, Mastering All Dharmas Bodhisattva, Maitreya Bodhisattva, and Mañjuśrī Bodhisattva.

From countless Buddha Lands, Bodhisattva-Mahāsattvas as numerous as the sands of sixty Ganges Rivers, and innumerable gods, dragons, yakṣas, gandharvas, asuras, garuḍas, kiṁnaras, and mahoragas gathered there to pay respects and make offerings.

A Miraculous Manifestation

At that time, in the great sandalwood tower, the World-Honored One was properly seated and in samādhi. Using His spiritual power, he produced a miraculous manifestation. There appeared countless thousand-petaled lotus flowers in various colors and with various fragrances. Although not yet unfurled, each bud was as large as a carriage wheel. Inside each was a conjured Buddha. Then all flowers rose up into the open sky and covered the world, like a jeweled canopy. Each and every lotus flower emitted immeasurable radiance, and all of them simultaneously unfurled. Then, through the Buddha's spiritual power, they withered in an instant, revealing the conjured Buddhas seated crossed-legged [on lotus seed cups], each Buddha emitting countless hundreds and thousands of beams of light. Seeing this extraordinary adornment of the world, all in this assembly rejoiced exuberantly. However, they were perplexed by this unprecedented display and wondered why these countless wonderful flowers suddenly withered and became black, stinky, and loathsome.

Then the World-Honored One, knowing the perplexity of the multitude of Bodhisattvas, told Vajra Wisdom Bodhisattva, "Good man, if you have any doubts about the Buddha Dharma, you may ask questions as you please."

Then Vajra Wisdom Bodhisattva, who knew the perplexity of the multitude, asked the Buddha, "World-Honored One, why did these countless lotus flowers contain conjured Buddhas, rise up into the open sky to cover the world, and wither in an instant to reveal all conjured Buddhas seated cross-legged, each emitting countless hundreds and thousands of beams of light? All in this assembly witnessed this and joined their palms in reverence."

Then Vajra Wisdom Bodhisattva spoke in verse:

> Never before have I seen
> Such a miraculous manifestation as displayed today.
> Conjured Buddhas by the hundreds of thousands of koṭis
> Are seated in the lotus flower stores [puṇḍarīka-garbha],
> Each Buddha emitting countless beams of light
> That pervade all Buddha Lands.
> These taint-free guiding teachers
> Adorn all worlds.
>
> When these lotus flowers suddenly withered,
> They became loathsome to all.
> For what reason
> Do you display this miraculous manifestation?
> I have seen Buddhas as numerous as the sands of the Ganges
> And Their countless miraculous manifestations.
> Never before have I seen such a manifestation as displayed today.
> I pray that You will explain to us in detail.

Nine Analogies

Then the World-Honored One said to Vajra Wisdom Bodhisattva and other Bodhisattvas, "Good men, there is a mahāvaipulya sūtra called *Tathāgata Store* [tathāgata-garbha].[2] It is because I will expound this sūtra that I display this auspicious sign. You all should hearken and ponder well the teachings in this sūtra."

They all said, "Very good! We will be delighted to hear it."

1. The Buddha said, "Good men, in my manifestation, when countless lotus flowers suddenly withered and turned into something loathsome, innumerable conjured Buddhas are revealed, who have majestic appearances, are seated cross-legged, and emit vast radiance. Witnessing this rare miraculous manifestation, all in this multitude paid respects. Indeed, good men, I use the Buddha eye to observe all sentient beings, and see that, in the midst of their afflictions, such as greed, anger, and delusion, they have the Tathāgata wisdom, the Tathāgata eye,[3] and a Tathāgata's body seated cross-legged and solemnly motionless. Good men, although all sentient beings transmigrate through various life-paths, in their affliction-laden bodies is the Tathāgata store, which is free from taints and bears marks of virtue, no different from me.

"Moreover, good men, just as someone with the god eye sees that the unfurled flowers contain Tathāgatas' bodies seated cross-legged, which will be revealed when the withered flowers are removed, likewise a Buddha sees the Tathāgata store in sentient beings. Wanting to reveal it, He expounds to them the Dharma in sūtras, to enable them to remove their afflictions and reveal their Buddha nature.

"Good men, such is the way of Buddhas. Whether or not a Buddha appears in the world, the Tathāgata store in all sentient beings is ever abiding and changeless. However, sentient beings are shrouded by their afflictions. Therefore, a Tathāgata appears in the world to widely expound the Dharma, to enable them to remove their fatiguing afflictions and acquire the pure overall wisdom-knowledge [sarvajña].[4] Good men, if a Bodhisattva believes and delights in this teaching and intently practices and learns, he will achieve liberation, become a Samyak-Saṁbuddha, and do Buddha work in the world."

Then the World-Honored One spoke in verse:

In the analogy of flowers that wither,
Before they have unfurled,
Someone with the god eye can see that inside each
Is a Tathāgata's body free from taints.

After a withered flower is removed,
A guiding teacher with unimpeded wisdom-knowledge[5] is fully revealed.
To end sentient beings' afflictions,
The most victorious one[6] appears in the world.

A Buddha sees that all sentient beings
Have the Tathāgata store within them,
Which is shrouded by countless afflictions,

Like being fettered by filthy flower petals.

For all sentient beings
To remove their afflictions,
I expound the true Dharma [saddharma]
To enable them to quickly attain Buddha bodhi.

Using the Buddha eye,
I see that the Buddha store steadily abides
In all sentient beings' bodies.
So I expound the Dharma to reveal it.

2. "Moreover, good men, as an analogy, pure honey is stored in a tree on a cliff, guarded by countless bees. An intelligent man removes the bees by skillful means and takes the honey. Then he eats the honey at will and benefits others near and far. Similarly, good men, all sentient beings possess the Tathāgata store, like that pure honey in the tree on a cliff. It is shrouded by afflictions, as if guarded by bees. I use the Buddha eye to observe sentient beings as they truly are, and use skillful means to expound the Dharma according to their capacities, for them to remove their afflictions, acquire a Buddha's knowledge and views, and do Buddha work in the world."

Then the World-Honored One spoke in verse:

As an analogy, the honey in a tree on a cliff
Is surrounded by countless bees.
A honey collector
First removes the bees by skillful means.

A sentient being's Tathāgata store
Is like the honey in a tree on a cliff.
It is fettered by fatiguing afflictions,
As if guarded by bees.

I expound the true Dharma to sentient beings
By skillful means,
To enable them to remove their bee-like afflictions,
Open their Tathāgata store,
Acquire unimpeded eloquence,
Expound the Dharma like showering down sweet dew,
Attain true enlightenment and,
With great compassion, benefit sentient beings.

3. "Moreover, good men, as an analogy, before the husk of rice is removed, even the poor loathe it and say that it should be discarded. However, after its husk is removed, rice is a food for royalty. Indeed, good men, I use the Buddha eye to observe sentient beings, and see that their husk-like afflictions sheathe a Tathāgata's immeasurable knowledge and views. Therefore, I expound the Dharma by skillful means according to their capacities, to enable them to

remove their afflictions, acquire the pure overall wisdom-knowledge, and attain true enlightenment in the world."

Then the World-Honored One spoke in verse:

As an analogy, before the husk of
Rice is removed,
Even the poor loathe it
And say that it should be discarded.

Although it seems useless because of its outside,
Its inside is unspoiled.
After its husk is removed,
Rice becomes a food fit for a king.

Seeing that sentient beings' afflictions
Conceal their Buddha store,
I teach them how to remove their afflictions
And acquire the overall wisdom-knowledge.

As I have Tathāgata nature,
So too do sentient beings.
I teach them to achieve purity
And quickly attain the unsurpassed bodhi.

4. "Moreover, good men, as an analogy, [a chunk of] pure gold has fallen into a filthy place, and for years is hidden from view. Although pure gold is indestructible, no one knows about it. Then someone with the god eye says to the multitude, 'In this filth lies a treasure of pure gold, and you can excavate it and enjoy it at will.' Good men, the filthy place is [a sentient being's] countless afflictions; the treasure of pure gold is his Tathāgata store. The one with the god eye is a Tathāgata. Therefore, a Tathāgata widely expounds the Dharma, to enable sentient beings to remove their afflictions, attain true enlightenment, and do Buddha work."

Then the World-Honored One spoke in verse:

As an analogy, [a chunk of] pure gold buried in filth
Is hidden from view.
Only someone with the god eye can see it,
And he tells others
To remove it from filth
And cleanse it to reveal its purity.
Then they can enjoy it at will
And benefit their kin and friends.

Likewise the Sugata[7] uses the Buddha eye
To observe sentient beings,
And sees that their Tathāgata nature in the mire of their afflictions
Is indestructible.

He expounds the Dharma according to their capacities,
To enable them to do the right things
To remove their afflictions that shroud their Buddha nature,
And to reveal its purity.

5. "Moreover, good men, as an analogy, a poor family has a treasure store buried under the floor of their house,[8] but the treasure cannot announce, 'I am here.' It neither knows itself nor has speech. Then no one can open this treasure store. Likewise all sentient beings have in their bodies a great treasure store, which includes a Tathāgata's knowledge and views, Ten Powers, and Four Fearlessnesses. However, they neither know it nor hear about it, as they follow their afflictions and five desires to transmigrate through their cycles of birth and death, undergoing immeasurable suffering. Therefore, Buddhas appear in worlds to reveal the Tathāgata store in their bodies and enable them to open it, acquire the pure overall wisdom-knowledge and unimpeded eloquence, and become great almsgivers. Indeed, good men, I use the Buddha eye to see that all sentient beings possess the Tathāgata store. Hence I give this teaching to Bodhisattvas."

Then the World-Honored One spoke in verse:

As an analogy, a poor family
Has a treasure store under the floor of their house.
The owner neither sees nor knows it,
And his treasure cannot speak.

For years, no one tells him about it,
And he remains in the darkness of ignorance.
Because he does not know his own treasure,
He remains in poverty.

I use the Buddha eye to see that
Although sentient beings transmigrate through the five life-paths,
The great treasure in their bodies
Is always there, changeless.

Having made this observation,
I tell sentient beings
And let them know about their treasure store,
So that they will become hugely wealthy and widely benefit others.

Whoever believes in my statement that
All possess the treasure store
And diligently trains by skillful means
Will quickly attain the unsurpassed bodhi.

6. "Moreover, good men, as an analogy, the pit of an āmra [mango] contains an unspoiled seed. Once planted in the ground, it grows into a huge tree. Indeed, good men, I use the Buddha eye to observe sentient beings, and see that the precious Tathāgata store inside the shell of their ignorance is like a seed in

an āmra's pit. Good men, the Tathāgata store is cool, free from the heat of burning afflictions, an aggregate of great wisdom, and quietly in nirvāṇa. It is called a Tathāgata, Arhat, Samyak-Saṁbuddha. Good men, after a Tathāgata has observed sentient beings, to enable Bodhisattva-Mahāsattvas to acquire a Buddha's pure wisdom-knowledge [jñāna], He reveals this meaning."

Then the World-Honored One spoke in verse:

As an analogy, a seed in
An āmra's pit is unspoiled.
Once planted in the great earth,
It grows into the king of trees.

A Tathāgata uses the affliction-free eye
To observe all sentient beings,
In whose bodies the Tathāgata store
Is like a seed in a fruit's pit.

You all should believe and know that
One's ignorance shrouds one's Buddha store,
Which abides in samādhi and wisdom
That nothing can destroy.

Therefore, I expound the Dharma
To reveal their Tathāgata store,
So that they can quickly attain the unsurpassed bodhi,
Like a seed becoming the king of trees.

7. "Moreover, good men, as an analogy, a man carries a holy statue in pure gold as he travels to another country. Traveling perilous roads, for fear of bandits, he wraps it in filthy rags to hide it. Then he dies on his way, and his gold statue is discarded in a wilderness. Travelers trample it and say that it is fifth. However, someone with the god eye sees that within the filthy rags is a holy statue in pure gold. He takes it out, and all salute it. Likewise, good men, I see that as sentient beings with various afflictions transmigrate through countless births and deaths in the long night, the wondrous Tathāgata store in their bodies is stately and pure, no different from me. Therefore, I, the Buddha, expound the Dharma to sentient beings, to enable them to end their afflictions, acquire the pure Tathāgata wisdom, and then transform and guide all others in the world."

Then the World-Honored One spoke in verse:

As an analogy, a man carries a gold statue
As he travels to another country.
Wrapped in filthy rags,
It is discarded in a wilderness.

Someone with the god eye sees it
And tells the multitude
To remove the filthy rags to reveal the gold statue.

Then all greatly rejoice.

Likewise I use the Buddha eye
To observe sentient beings, and see that,
Fettered by afflictions and evil karmas,
They undergo suffering through repeated birth and death.

I also see that, in the midst of
Their dirt-like ignorance and afflictions,
Their Tathāgata nature remains motionless
And indestructible.

Having seen this,
I, the Buddha, tell Bodhisattvas that
Their afflictions and evil karmas
Shroud a Tathāgata's supreme body [dharma body].

They should diligently remove them
To reveal the Tathāgata wisdom,
And to be revered by all,
Such as gods, humans, dragons, and ghosts.

8. "Moreover, good men, as an analogy, a poor and ugly woman is loathed by all. However, she is pregnant with a noble son, who will become a holy king to rule the four continents.[9] She does not know this, and for a long time thinks, as do others, that a lowly woman gives birth to a lowly child. Indeed, good men, a Tathāgata observes all sentient beings, and sees that they transmigrate through repeated birth and death, undergoing suffering, though the precious Tathāgata store is in their bodies. Like that woman, they do not know this. Therefore, a Tathāgata expounds the Dharma to all, saying, 'Good men, do not belittle yourselves. Buddha nature is in your bodies. If you diligently make energetic progress and end your evils, you will be called a Bodhisattva, then a World-Honored One, and will transform and deliver innumerable sentient beings."

Then the World-Honored One spoke in verse:

As an analogy, a poor woman
With ugly features
Is pregnant with a noble son
Who will become a Wheel-Turning King
To possess virtues and the seven treasures[10]
And to rule the four continents.
However, she does not know this
And regards herself as lowly.

I observe sentient beings in suffering,
And see that they are like that woman.
They do not know that
They carry the Tathāgata store in their bodies.

Therefore, I tell Bodhisattvas,
'Do not belittle yourselves,
Because the Tathāgata store in your bodies
Will bring [wisdom] light to relieve the world.

If you diligently make energetic progress,
You will soon sit in a bodhimaṇḍa,
Attain the supreme bodhi,
And deliver innumerable multitudes.'

9. "Moreover, good men, as an analogy, a foundryman casts a statue in pure gold. After casting is finished, he places the mold on the ground. Although its outside is scorched and blackened, the statue inside is unchanged. When the mold is removed, the golden color is dazzling. Indeed, good men, a Tathāgata observes all sentient beings, and sees that the Buddha store in their bodies is replete with all excellent marks. Having made this observation, He widely expounds the Dharma to bring sentient beings tranquility and teach them how to use vajra wisdom to destroy their afflictions and reveal a Buddha's pure body, like taking the gold statue out of the mold."

Then the World-Honored One spoke in verse:

As an analogy, a master foundryman
Casts countless statues in pure gold.
Fools see only a blackened mold outside,
Which is scorched clay.

The foundryman waits for the mold to cool,
Then opens it to reveal what is inside.
After the filthy mold is removed,
The gold statue with excellent features is fully revealed.

I use the Buddha eye
To observe sentient beings,
And see that, in the mire of their afflictions,
There is Tathāgata nature.

I teach them to use vajra wisdom
To destroy their afflictions, like removing the mold,
And to open the Tathāgata store,
Like uncovering the gold statue.

Having made this observation,
I tell Bodhisattvas,
'You all should accept and uphold [my teachings],
And transform sentient beings.'

Merit Acquired by Upholding This Sūtra

Then the World-Honored One said to Vajra Wisdom Bodhisattva-Mahāsattva, "Whether a monastic or a householder, if a good man or woman accepts and upholds this *Sūtra of the Tathāgata Store,* reads, recites, or copies it, makes offering to it, or widely expounds it to others, the merit acquired will be immeasurable.

"Vajra Wisdom, suppose that a Bodhisattva who aspires to attain Buddha bodhi diligently trains, makes energetic progress, learns and practices transcendental powers, and enters various samādhis. To plant roots of goodness, he makes offerings to present Buddhas more numerous than the sands of the Ganges and uses the seven treasures to build towers more numerous than the sands of the Ganges. Each tower is ten yojanas tall and one yojana in length and width. Inside each tower are couches made of the seven treasures and spread with celestial silks. For each and every Buddha, every day he uses the seven treasures to build towers more numerous than the sands of the Ganges and offers these towers to Buddhas, Bodhisattvas, and voice-hearers. As he makes such offerings to all present Buddhas more numerous than the sands of the Ganges, so too for countless billions of kalpas he builds treasure towers more numerous than the sands of fifty Ganges Rivers and offers these towers to present Buddhas, Bodhisattvas, and voice-hearers, all of whom are more numerous than the sands of fifty Ganges Rivers.

"However, Vajra Wisdom, that Bodhisattva cannot compare with someone who, aspiring to attain bodhi, accepts and upholds this *Sūtra of the Tathāgata Store,* reads, recites, or copies it, makes offerings to it, or uses only one of its analogies. Vajra Wisdom, although that Bodhisattva has planted various roots of goodness under innumerable Buddhas and acquired immeasurable merit, his merit is less than one hundredth or one thousandth of the merit acquired by whoever accepts and upholds this sūtra, reads, recites, or copies it, or expounds it to others. The disparity is beyond calculation or analogy."

Then the World-Honored One spoke in verse:

Suppose that someone who seeks bodhi
Hears and upholds this sūtra,
Copies it, and makes offerings to it,
Even if for only one stanza.

If he expresses sympathetic joy
Over hearing its teachings
On the wondrous Tathāgata store,
His merit acquired is immeasurable.

Suppose that a Bodhisattva who seeks bodhi
Abides in great transcendental powers
For inconceivable koṭis of kalpas
To make offerings to Buddhas, Bodhisattvas,
And voice-hearers in worlds in the ten directions,
All of whom are more numerous than the sands of the Ganges.

For each and every Buddha,
He builds wonderful treasure towers,
Each ten yojanas tall
And one yojana in length and width.

Inside each tower are couches made of the seven treasures,
Adorned with wonderful things
And spread with celestial silks and cushions,
Different from couch to couch.

He offers such towers,
More numerous than the sands of the Ganges,
To Buddhas and Their multitudes,
Day and night without rest
For a billion kalpas,
And receives corresponding merit.

If someone hears this sūtra
And explains to others,
Even if only one of its analogies,
His merit acquired
Surpasses the merit of that Bodhisattva,
Beyond measure or analogy.
He will be the reliance of all sentient beings
And quickly attain the unsurpassed bodhi.

If a Bodhisattva intently ponders
The profound Tathāgata store
Possessed by all sentient beings,
He will quickly attain the unsurpassed bodhi.

Vajra Wisdom Bodhisattva Received This Teaching in a Past Life

Then the World-Honored One told Vajra Wisdom Bodhisattva, "Before inconceivable asaṁkhyeya kalpas in the distant past, there was a Buddha called Constantly Emitting Radiance King Tathāgata, Arhat, Samyak-Saṁbuddha, Knowledge and Conduct Perfected, Sugata, Understanding the World, Unsurpassed One, Tamer of men, Teacher of Gods and Men, Buddha-Bhagavān. Vajra Wisdom, why was He called Constantly Emitting Radiance King? Because when that Buddha was still walking the Bodhisattva Way, after His consciousness descended into His mother's womb, He constantly emitted radiance, illuminating everywhere in worlds in the ten directions, worlds as numerous as the dust particles in a thousand Buddha Lands. If sentient beings saw His radiance, they would rejoice, and their afflictions would end. They would acquire bodies with good appearances and strength, become accomplished in meditation, possess wisdom, and acquire unimpeded eloquence. If King Yama, hell-dwellers, hungry ghosts, animals, or asuras saw His radiance, they would quit their evil life-paths and be reborn as humans or gods. If humans or gods saw His radiance, they would not regress from the unsurpassed bodhi mind but would acquire the five transcendental powers. Those who would never regress on the Bodhisattva Way would acquire endurance in their realization that dharmas have no birth, and acquire the turn-around dhāraṇī[11] with fifty virtues.

"Vajra Wisdom, the ground of the worlds illuminated by His radiance became pure, like celestial aquamarine [vaiḍūrya]. Golden cords on the ground marked eight boulevards.[12] Each was lined with various jeweled trees, whose abundant flowers and fruits gave off profuse fragrance. When breezes blew, these trees rustled with wonderful tones, expounding the virtues of the Three Jewels and Bodhisattvas, the Five Roots, the Five Powers,[13] the Seven Bodhi Factors, the Eightfold Right Path, meditation, and liberation. Those who heard [this music] acquired Dharma delight and firm faith, and were forever free from taking evil life-paths. Vajra Wisdom, all sentient beings in worlds in the ten directions, because they were touched by His radiance, in the six periods of day and night joined their palms in reverence.

"Vajra Wisdom, that Bodhisattva, from His staying in his mother's womb, to His birth, to His attaining Buddhahood, and to His entering nirvāṇa without remnants,[14] constantly emitted radiance. After His parinirvāṇa, His relics enshrined in pagodas constantly emit radiance as well. For this reason, gods and humans call Him Constantly Emitting Radiance King.

"Vajra Wisdom, when Constantly Emitting Radiance Tathāgata, Arhat, Samyak-Saṁbuddha, first attained Buddhahood, with twenty koṭi Bodhisattvas in his retinue, in His Dharma [assembly] there was a Bodhisattva called Infinite Light. Infinite Light Bodhisattva-Mahāsattva asked that Buddha to expound the *Sūtra of the Tathāgata Store.* That Buddha sat in His seat for fifty large kalpas,[15] expounding this sūtra in detail. To protect and support all Bodhisattvas, His voice reached worlds as numerous as the dust particles in ten Buddha Lands. Through countless causes and conditions, He used 100,000 analogies to expound to Bodhisattvas this *Mahāyāna Sūtra of the Tathāgata Store.* Those who heard it accepted and upheld it, read and recited it, and trained accordingly. They all have attained Buddhahood, except for four Bodhisattvas.

"Vajra Wisdom, do not think otherwise. Is Infinite Light Bodhisattva then a different person now? He is none other than yourself. The four Bodhisattvas who have not yet attained Buddhahood are Mañjuśrī, Avalokiteśvara, Great Might Arrived [Mahāsthāmaprāpta], and you, Vajra Wisdom. Vajra wisdom, this *Sūtra of the Tathāgata Store* can benefit all. Whoever hears it will attain Buddha bodhi."

Then the World-Honored One spoke in verse:

> Before countless kalpas in the past,
> There was a Buddha called Radiance King,
> Who constantly emitted vast radiance,
> Illuminating [everywhere in] countless worlds.

When that Buddha first attained Buddhahood,
Infinite Light Bodhisattva
Asked Him about this sūtra,
And He immediately expounded it.

Those who encountered that most victorious one
And heard this sūtra
Have attained Buddhahood,
Except for four Bodhisattvas:
Mañjuśrī, Avalokiteśvara,
Great Might Arrived, and Vajra Wisdom.

Of these four Bodhisattvas, who
Heard this sūtra,
Vajra Wisdom was a Buddha-son
Foremost in transcendental powers.
When you were called Infinite Light,
You heard this sūtra.

When I was seeking bodhi,
I received this sūtra
From Lion Banner Buddha
And trained in accordance with its teachings as heard.
Because of these roots of goodness,
I quickly attained Buddha bodhi.

Therefore, all Bodhisattvas
Should uphold this sūtra,
Listen to its teachings, and train accordingly.
Then they will attain Buddhahood as I have.

Whoever upholds this sūtra
Should be saluted as a World-Honored One.
Whoever has acquired this sūtra
Is called a Master of the Buddha Dharma.
He is protected by the world
And praised by Buddhas.
Whoever upholds this sūtra
Is called a Dharma King.
He is the eye of the world
And should be praised as a World-Honored One.

After the World-Honored One pronounced this sūtra, Vajra Wisdom and other Bodhisattvas, His retinues and four groups of disciples, gods, gandharvas, asuras, and all others heard the Buddha's words and joyfully carried out His teachings.

Notes

1. The power of energetic progress is the second of the Five Powers listed in the glossary's Thirty-seven Elements of Bodhi.

2. See "store" defined in the glossary.

3. The "Tathāgata eye" is the "Buddha eye" defined in the glossary's "five eyes."

4. See "overall wisdom-knowledge" defined in the glossary's "three kinds of wisdom-knowledge."

5. See "four kinds of unimpeded wisdom-knowledge" in the glossary.

6. The "most victorious one" means a Buddha.

7. Sugata, Well-Gone One, is the fifth of a Buddha's ten epithets.

8. Text 666 does not indicate where the poor family's treasure store is. Text 667, another Chinese version of this sūtra, states that it is buried under the floor of their house (T16n0667, 0462c15–16). Text 667 was translated from Sankrit in the Tang Dynasty (618–907) by Amoghavajra (不空金剛, 705–74) from Sri Lanka, in southern India.

9. A holy king who rules the four continents in this world is a Wheel-Turning King with a gold wheel. See Wheel-Turning King in the glossary.

10. According to text 456, the Chinese version of the *Sūtra of Maitreya Bodhisattva's Attainment of Buddhahood,* a Wheel-Turning King with a gold wheel possesses seven precious things: (1) the gold wheel, (2) the white elephant, (3) the blue horse, (4) the divine jewel, (5) exquisite maidens, (6) the treasure minister, and (7) the military minister (T14n0456, 0429c27–0430a6; Rulu 2012a, 82).

11. The turn-around dhāraṇī (dhāraṇyāvartā, 旋陀羅尼) turns ordinary beings attached to dharma appearances around to seeing dharmas in the one appearance of no appearance, i.e., emptiness. It is one of the three dhāraṇīs mentioned in chapter 28 of the *Lotus Sutra* (T09n0262, 0061b6–9).

12. One can interpret the eight boulevards as the Eightfold Right Path.

13. See Five Roots and Five Powers defined in the glossary's Thirty-seven Elements of Bodhi.

14. See "nirvāṇa without remnants" defined in the glossary's "nirvāṇa."

15. See "large kalpa" and "small kalpa" defined in the glossary's "kalpa."

About Sūtra 2

Text 668 (T16n0668) in one fascicle is the Chinese version of the *Sūtra of Neither Increase Nor Decrease,* translated from Sanskrit in the Northern Wei Dynasty (386–534) by Bodhiruci (菩提留支, 5th–6th centuries) from northern India, who arrived in Luoyang (洛陽) in 508, the first year of the Yongping (永平) years of Emperor Xuanwu (宣武帝). As listed in fascicle 9 of the 30-fascicle text 2157 (T55n2157), the Zhenyuan (貞元) catalog compiled by Yuanzhao (圓照) in 799 during the Tang Dynasty (618–907), text 668 was translated from Sanskrit by Bodhiruci in 525, the sixth year of the Zhenguang (正光) years of Emperor Xiaoming (孝明帝).

The Sanskrit title of text 688 is *Anūnatva-apūrṇatva-nirdeśa-parivarta,* as cited in *The Ratnagotravibhāga Mahāyānottaratantraśāstra* [Discerning the jewel nature: A Mahāyāna treatise on higher tantra],* a Sanskrit text edited and published in 1950 by E. H. (Edward Hamilton) Johnston (1885–1942). The "jewel nature" refers the nature of the Three Jewels: the Buddha, the Dharma, and the Saṅgha. The Chinese version of this treatise is text 1611 (T31n1611) in 4 fascicles, translated from Sanskrit in the Northern Wei Dynasty by Ratnamati (勒那摩提, 5–6th centuries) from central India, who also arrived in Luoyang in 508. The Chinese title of text 1611 is abbreviated as *A Treatise on the Jewel Nature.* This treatise expounds on the Tathāgata store (tathāgata-garbha) and cites passages from many texts, including text 668. Because the Sanskrit title of text 668 uses the word *parivarta* (chapter), it is generally accepted that text 688 is a chapter of a large sūtra, whose Sanskrit text is unavailable.

Text 2183 (T55n2183) in one fascicle, a catalog compiled in 1095 by the Japanese monk Yongchao (永超) when he was eighty-one years old, lists a commentary on text 668, dictated by the Korean scholar Yuanxiao (元曉, 617–86), or Wŏnhyo, and another commentary by Rongye (榮業). However, these two commentaries are not extant. Text 668 gives important teachings on the Tathāgata store. Its words are cited in many treatises and commentaries. For example, texts 1512 (T25n1512), 1611 (T31n1611), 1626 (T31n1626), and 1627 (T31n1627) are Chinese versions of treatises originated in India; texts 1709 (T33n1709), 1733 (T35n1733), 1735 (T35n1735), 1747 (T37n1747), 1757 (T37n1757), and 1838 (T44n1838) are commentaries written by Chinese masters.

In 2015, Jonathan A. Silk published his English translation, with annotation, of text 668. Sūtra 2 in the present book is also an English translation of text 668. It is a revised version of the translation initially published in *Teachings of the Buddha* (Rulu 2012a, 97–102).

In this sūtra, the Buddha tells Śāriputra that because foolish ordinary beings neither know nor see the one realm in accord with true reality, they entertain extremely evil, enormously wrong views in their minds, saying that the realm of sentient beings increases or that the realm of sentient beings decreases. From the view of increase or decrease, sentient beings derive other wrong views. For example, from the view of decrease arise the view of cessation, the view of extinction, and the view that nirvāṇa is a void. From these three views arise the view of no desire to attain nirvāṇa and the view that ultimately there is no nirvāṇa. From the view of no desire arises the view in favor of observing useless precepts and the inverted view, such as taking impurity as purity. From the view that ultimately there is no nirvāṇa arise six more wrong views. Furthermore, from the view of increase arise the view that nirvāṇa originates births of sentient beings and the view that sentient beings suddenly come into existence without causes or conditions. From these two views arise all other wrong views.

Then the Buddha explains that the profound meaning of the one realm is the highest truth (paramārtha), and the highest truth is the realm of sentient beings. The realm of sentient beings is the Tathāgata store, and the Tathāgata store is the dharma body (dharmakāya), which is not separate, detached, split, or different from a Tathāgata's merit and wisdom, nor from the teachings of the inconceivable Buddha Dharma.

The dharma body is a dharma of no birth and no death, a dharma of no change, and a dharma of no end. It is eternal because it is an ever-available refuge and because it is equal in all Buddhas and sentient beings throughout all time. The realm of sentient beings is the dharma body; the dharma body is the realm of sentient beings.

When the dharma body, fettered by endless afflictions, drifts in the ocean of birth and death, it is called a sentient being. When the dharma body, tired of the suffering of repeated birth and death, trains to attain bodhi by practicing the ten pāramitās and going through the 84,000 Dharma Doors, it is called a Bodhisattva. Finally, when the dharma body leaves behind all suffering in the world and is freed from the fetters and filth of all one's afflictions, it reveals its purity and abides in pure dharma nature (dharmatā) on the opposite shore. Because it has achieved the unsurpassed understanding of all states of realization, is free from all hindrances and obstructions, and has acquired the power of freedom in the midst of all dharmas, it is called a Tathāgata, Arhat, Samyak-Saṁbuddha. Therefore, the realm of sentient beings is the dharma body; the dharma body is the realm of sentient beings.

Then Buddha expounds three dharmas that describe the nature of the Tathāgata store. These three dharmas are (1) the Tathāgata store's pure dharma nature (dharmatā), which is innately coherent (sambaddha) with the Tathāgata store's original state; (2) one's afflictions that sheathe one's Tathāgata store, which are innately incoherent (asambaddha) with one's Tathāgata store's original state; (3) the Tathāgata store's existence, which has the nature of being changeless throughout all time.

Based on the first dharma, the Buddha pronounces this inconceivable dharma of the inherent pure mind. Based on the second dharma, He pronounces this inconceivable dharma of one's inherent pure mind, tainted by one's visitor-like afflictions (āgantuka kleśa). Based on the third dharma, He pronounces that the dharma realm is the realm of sentient beings. Whoever relies on these three dharmas, which are true suchness, with no difference or distinction, never elicits the wrong view that the realm of sentient beings increases or decreases, because he sees dharmas in accord with true reality.

The teachings that the dharma realm neither increases nor decreases also appear in other sūtras. For example, in text 680, the Chinese version of the *Sūtra of the Buddha Ground,* the Buddha says, ". . . although the open sky displays increases and decreases of various appearances of forms, it neither increases nor decreases. Likewise, although a Tathāgata's pure dharma realm displays increases and decreases of the sweet dew of a Tathāgata's holy teachings, it neither increases nor decreases" (T16n0680, 0721a19–20; Rulu 2015, 155). Also, in fascicle 51 of text 279 (in 80 fascicles), one of the three Chinese versions of the *Mahāvaipulya Sūtra of Buddha Adornment* (Buddhāvataṁsaka-mahāvaipulya-sūtra), Samantabhadra Bodhisattva says, "Buddha-Sons, the dharma realm sees the liberation of voice-hearers, Pratyekabuddhas, and Bodhisattvas, but the dharma realm neither increases nor decreases" (T10n0279, 0271a29–b1; Rulu 2014, 231).

The teachings that the realm of sentient beings neither increases nor decreases also appear in other sūtras. For example, in fascicle 1 of text 232 (in 2 fascicles), one of the two Chinese versions of the *Sūtra of Mahā-Prajñā-Pāramitā Pronounced by Mañjuśrī Bodhisattva,* Mañjuśrī Bodhisattva says, "Suppose that every Buddha delivers as many sentient beings as the innumerable sands of the Ganges, enabling them to enter nirvāṇa. Yet the realm of sentient beings neither increases nor decreases. Why not? Because the definite appearances of sentient beings can never be captured. Hence, the realm of sentient beings neither increases nor decreases" (T08n0232, 0726c2–9; Rulu 2012b, 154). Then he says, "The appearance of the realm of sentient beings is just like that of the realm of Buddhas. . . . The measure for the realm of sentient beings is just like that for the realm of Buddhas" (Ibid., 0726c16–18; Rulu 2012b, 154). Moreover, in fascicle 1 of text 673 (in 2 fascicles), one of the two Chinese versions of the *Sūtra of Achieving a Clear Understanding of the Mahāyāna* (Mahāyānābhisamaya-sūtra), the Buddha says, "King of Laṅkā, because the realm of sentient beings is indescribable, we know that it neither increases nor decreases. Thus, in the ocean of the Three Realms of Existence, although some sentient beings have crossed it and some will cross it, the realm of sentient beings neither increases nor decreases. King of Laṅkā, one can never find the beginning, middle, or end of the realm of sentient beings" (T16n0673, 0643b1–7; Rulu 2015, 201).

———

* Tibetan tradition attributes this treatise's stanzas to Maitreya-nātha (彌勒, circa 270–350) or Maitreya Bodhisattva, the next Buddha to come, and its prose commentary (vyākhyā) to Asaṅga (無著, circa 310–90). Chinese tradition attributes this treatise to Sthiramati (安慧, circa 475–555), then to Sāramati (堅慧). According to a commentary of Fazang (法藏, 643–712), the third patriarch of the Huayan School, Sāramati was a Bodhisattva on the first Bodhisattva ground, belonged to the kṣatriya caste, and lived in central India seven hundred years after the death of the Buddha (T44n1838, 0063c5–21). As most historians in the early 20th century dated the Buddha's lifetime as circa 563 to 483 BCE (Wikipedia), Sāramati's lifetime might be circa 3rd to 4th centuries CE. In 1931, E. Obermiller published his English translation of the Tibetan version of this treatise (Prasad 1991, 209–406). In 1966, Jikido Takasaki (1926–2013) published his English translation of Johnston's Sanskrit text (Takasaki 2014a). These two translations are the earliest English versions of this treatise.

2 佛說不增不減經
Buddha Pronounces the Sūtra of Neither Increase Nor Decrease

Translated from Sanskrit into Chinese in the Northern Wei Dynasty
by
The Tripiṭaka Master Bodhirucii from India

Thus I have heard:

At one time the Bhagavān [World-Honored One] was staying on the Gṛdhrakūṭa Mountain, near the city of Rājagṛha, together with 1,250 great bhikṣus and a boundless multitude of Bodhisattva-Mahāsattvas, in numbers beyond reckoning. In the huge multitude, Śāriputra the Wise rose from his seat, came to the Buddha, and bowed down at His feet. He then stepped back and sat on one side. Joining his palms, he said to the Buddha, "World-Honored One, for ages without a beginning, sentient beings have been transmigrating, through the four modes of birth in saṁsāra, along the six life-paths in the Three Realms of Existence, suffering endlessly. World-Honored One, does this mass of sentient beings, or ocean of sentient beings, increase and decrease? I cannot understand this profound meaning. If someone asks me about this, how should I answer?"

The World-Honored One told Śāriputra, "Very good! Very good! You can ask me about this profound meaning because you want to bring stability to all sentient beings, to bring peace and joy to all sentient beings, to pity all sentient beings, to help all sentient beings, and to bring comfort and benefits to all sentient beings, such as gods and humans. Śāriputra, if you did not ask the Tathāgata, Arhat, Samyak-Saṁbuddha, about this meaning, there would be many faults. Why? Because, in present and future times, gods, humans, and all other sentient beings would long undergo distress and harm, and lose forever all benefits, peace, and joy.

"Śāriputra, the enormously wrong view means seeing the realm of sentient beings [sattva-dhātu] increase or seeing the realm of sentient beings decrease. Śāriputra, sentient beings who hold this enormously wrong view are born as if without eyes and willfully walk the evil way in the long night. For this reason, they go down the evil life-paths in their current lives. Śāriputra, the enormously perilous tribulation means one's obstinate adherence to [the wrong view] that the realm of sentient beings increases or decreases. Śāriputra, those who are obstinate in their wrong adherence willfully walk the evil way in the long night. For this reason, they will go down the evil life-paths in their future lives.

"Śāriputra, foolish ordinary beings do not know the one dharma realm [dharma-dhātu] in accord with true reality.[1] Because they do not see the one dharma realm in accord with true reality, they elicit wrong views in their minds, saying that the realm of sentient beings increases or decreases.

Śāriputra, when the Tathāgata is in the world, my disciples will not elicit these wrong views. However, over five hundred years after my entering nirvāṇa,[2] there will be many sentient beings who are foolish and senseless. Although they will remove their hair and beards, and don the three Dharma robes to appear as śramaṇas in the Buddha Dharma, they will not have within them the virtues of a śramaṇa. Such people are not śramaṇas, but will claim to be śramaṇas. They are not disciples of the Buddha though they will claim to be disciples of the Buddha, saying, 'I am a śramaṇa, a true disciple of the Buddha.'

"Such people hold the wrong view of increase or decrease. Why? Because these sentient beings follow the Tathāgata's sūtras of provisional meaning and do not have the wisdom eye; because they are far from the view of emptiness [of dharmas], which is in accord with true reality; because they do not know in accord with true reality what the Tathāgata has realized since His initial resolve [to attain Buddhahood]; because they do not know in accord with true reality how to train in countless virtuous ways and accumulate merit in order to attain bodhi; because they do not know in accord with true reality the innumerable dharmas acquired by the Tathāgata; because they do not know in accord with true reality the Tathāgata's immeasurable power; because they do not know in accord with true reality the Tathāgata's immeasurable attainments; because they do not believe in the Tathāgata's immeasurable action range; because they do not know in accord with true reality the Tathāgata's inconceivable, immeasurable command of dharmas; because they do not know in accord with true reality the Tathāgata's countless inconceivable skillful means; because they cannot differentiate in accord with true reality the Tathāgata's immeasurable, different attainments; because they cannot enter into the Tathāgata's inconceivable great compassion; because they do not know in accord with true reality the Tathāgata's great nirvāṇa.

"Śāriputra, foolish ordinary beings do not have the wisdom that comes from hearing the Dharma. When they hear about a Tathāgata's entering nirvāṇa, they take the wrong view of cessation or extinction. Because of their perception of cessation or extinction, they claim that the realm of sentient beings decreases. Their claim constitutes an enormously wrong view and an extremely grave, evil karma.

"Furthermore, Śāriputra, from the wrong view of decrease, these sentient beings derive three more wrong views. These three views and the view of decrease, like a net,[3] are inseparable from each other. What are these three views? They are (1) the view of cessation, which means the ultimate end; (2) the view of extinction, which is equated to nirvāṇa; (3) the view that nirvāṇa is a void, which means that nirvāṇa is the ultimate quiet nothingness. Śāriputra, in this way these three views fetter, hold, and impress [sentient beings].

"From the force of those three views successively arise two more wrong views. These two views and those three views, like a net, are inseparable from each other. What are these two views? One is the view of no desire [to attain nirvāṇa], and the other is the view that ultimately there is no nirvāṇa.

"Śāriputra, from the view of no desire arise two more wrong views. These two views and the view of no desire, like a net, are inseparable from each other. What are these two views? One is the view in favor of observing useless precepts [śīla-vrata-parāmarśa],[4] and the other is the inverted view,[5] such as taking impurity as purity.

"Śāriputra, from the view that ultimately there is no nirvāṇa arise six more wrong views. These six views and the view of no nirvāṇa, like a net, are inseparable from each other. What are these six views? They are the views that (1) the world has a beginning, (2) the world has an end, (3) sentient beings are created by an illusion, (4) there is neither pain nor pleasure, (5) there are no affairs of sentient beings,[6] and (6) there are no noble truths.[7]

"Furthermore, Śāriputra, from the wrong view of increase, these sentient beings elicit two more wrong views. These two views and the view of increase, like a net, are inseparable from each other. What are these two views? One is the view that nirvāṇa originates births [of sentient beings], and the other is the view that [sentient beings] suddenly come into existence without causes or conditions. Śāriputra, these two wrong views cause the minds of sentient beings to have no desire and no drive to make energetic progress in doing good dharmas. Śāriputra, because these sentient beings hold these two views, even if seven Buddha-Tathāgatas, Arhats, Samyak-Saṁbuddhas, successively appeared in the world to expound the Dharma to them, it would be impossible for them to generate the desire and drive to make energetic progress in doing good dharmas. Śāriputra, these two views—the view that nirvāṇa originates births [of sentient beings] and the view that [sentient beings] suddenly come into existence without causes and conditions—are the roots of afflictions arising from ignorance.

"Śāriputra, these two views are a dharma[8] of extremely evil, enormous fundamental troubles. Śāriputra, from these two views arise all other wrong views. All other wrong views and these two views, like a net, are inseparable from each other. All views include various kinds of views, whether internal or external, whether coarse, fine, or in between.

"Śāriputra, the two wrong views—the view of increase and the view of decrease—depend on the one realm, identify with the one realm, and unite with the one realm. Because foolish ordinary beings neither know nor see the one realm in accord with true reality, they entertain extremely evil, enormously wrong views in their minds, saying that the realm of sentient beings increases or that the realm of sentient beings decreases."

Then Śāriputra the Wise asked the Buddha, "World-Honored One, what is meant by 'the one realm,' which caused You to say, 'Because foolish ordinary beings neither know nor see the one realm in accord with true reality, they entertain extremely evil, enormously wrong views in their minds, saying that the realm of sentient beings increases or that the realm of sentient beings decreases.' Very good! World-Honored One, this meaning is too profound for me to comprehend. I pray that the Tathāgata will explain to me, to make me comprehend it."

Then the World-Honored One told Śāriputra the Wise, "This profound meaning is in the realm of a Tathāgata's wisdom, and in the action range of a Tathāgata's mind. Śāriputra, even using their wisdom, no voice-hearer or Pratyekabuddha can know, see, or observe such profound meaning. Much less can any foolish ordinary being fathom it. Only the wisdom of Buddha-Tathāgatas can know, see, and observe this meaning. Śāriputra, using their wisdom, all voice-hearers and Pratyekabuddhas can only believe this meaning out of respect, but they cannot know, see, or observe it in accord with true reality. Śāriputra, this profound meaning is the highest truth [paramārtha], and the highest truth is the realm of sentient beings. The realm of sentient beings is the Tathāgata store [tathāgata-garbha], and the Tathāgata store is the dharma body [dharmakāya].[9] Śāriputra, the dharma body, as I have explained its meaning, is not separate, not detached, not split, and not different from a Tathāgata's merit and wisdom, nor from the inconceivable Buddha Dharma [with teachings] more numerous than the sands of the Ganges.

"Śāriputra, as an analogy, a lamp is not separate or detached from its light, color, and touch. As another analogy, a precious jewel is not separate or detached from its luster, color, and shape. Śāriputra, likewise is the dharma body as the Tathāgata has explained its meaning. It is not separate, not detached, not split, and not different from a Tathāgata's merit and wisdom, nor from the inconceivable Buddha Dharma [with teachings] more numerous than the sands of the Ganges.

"Śāriputra, the dharma body is a dharma of no birth and no death, neither of the past nor of the future, because it is apart from the two opposites. Śāriputra, it is not of the past because it is apart from the time of birth; it is not of the future because it is apart from the time of death. Śāriputra, a Tathāgata's dharma body is permanent because it is a dharma of no change and a dharma of no end. Śāriputra, a Tathāgata's dharma body is eternal because it is an ever-available refuge and because it is equal [in all Buddhas and sentient beings][10] throughout all time. Śāriputra, a Tathāgata's dharma body is tranquil because it is a dharma free from duality and a dharma free from differentiation. Śāriputra, a Tathāgata's dharma body never changes because it is a dharma of no destruction and a dharma of no action.

"Śāriputra, when this dharma body, fettered by endless afflictions more numerous than the sands of the Ganges, for ages without a beginning follows the world, drifts along with [its ocean] waves, and shuttles between birth and death, it is called a sentient being.

"Śāriputra, when this dharma body, tired of the suffering of repeated birth and death in the world, abandons all desires and pursuits, and trains to attain bodhi by practicing the ten pāramitās and going through the 84,000 Dharma Doors [dharma-paryāya],[11] it is called a Bodhisattva.

"Furthermore, Śāriputra, when this dharma body has passed all suffering in the world and left behind the fetters and filth of all one's afflictions, it reveals its purity and abides in pure dharma nature [dharmatā] on the opposite shore,[12] arriving on the ground that all sentient beings wish for. Because it has achieved the unsurpassed understanding of all states of realization, is free from all hindrances[13] and obstructions, and has acquired the power of freedom in the midst of all dharmas, it is called a Tathāgata, Arhat, Samyak-Saṁbuddha. Therefore, Śāriputra, not apart from the realm of sentient beings is the dharma body; not apart from the dharma body is the realm of sentient beings. The realm of sentient beings is the dharma body; the dharma body is the realm of sentient beings. Śāriputra, these two dharmas with different names have the same meaning.

"Furthermore, Śāriputra, as I said before, there are three dharmas[14] in the realm of sentient beings. They are true suchness [bhūta-tathātā], with no difference or distinction. What are these three dharmas? They are (1) the Tathāgata store's pure dharma nature, which is innately coherent [sambaddha] with the Tathāgata store's original state; (2) one's afflictions that sheathe one's Tathāgata store, which are innately incoherent [asambaddha] with one's

Tathāgata store's original state; (3) the Tathāgata store's existence, which has the nature of being changeless throughout all time.[15,16]

"Śāriputra, know that the Tathāgata store's pure dharma nature being innately coherent with the Tathāgata store's original state is in accord with true reality and is not false. It is an inconceivable dharma, not separate or detached from the dharma realm of wisdom, purity, and true suchness. Since the origin without a beginning, this pure and coherent dharma nature has always been existent. Śāriputra, in accord with the dharma realm of purity and true suchness, I pronounce to sentient beings this inconceivable dharma of the inherent pure mind [prakṛti-pariśuddha-citta].

"Śāriputra, know that the impure dharma of one's afflictions that sheathe one's Tathāgata store has always been separate from, detached from, and incoherent with one's Tathāgata store's original state. It can be eradicated only by a Tathāgata's bodhi wisdom [when one becomes a Buddha]. Śāriputra, in accord with this inconceivable dharma realm of incoherent afflictions that sheathe the Tathāgata store, I pronounce to sentient beings this inconceivable dharma of one's inherent pure mind, tainted by one's visitor-like afflictions [āgantuka kleśa].[17]

"Śāriputra, know that the Tathāgata store, whose existence is changeless throughout all time, is the root of all dharmas, provides all dharmas, possesses all dharmas, and is not separate or detached from the true reality of all dharmas. It sustains all dharmas and encompasses all dharmas. Śāriputra, in accord with this permanent, tranquil, and changeless refuge with neither birth nor death, the inconceivable dharma realm, I say that it [the dharma realm] is called sentient beings. Why? Because 'sentient beings' is a different name for a permanent, tranquil, and changeless refuge with neither birth nor death, and for the inconceivable pure dharma realm. Based on this meaning, in accord with that dharma, I say that it is called sentient beings.[18]

"Śāriputra, these three dharmas are true suchness, with no difference or distinction. Relying on these three dharmas, which are true suchness, with no difference or distinction, one never elicits the two extremely evil, wrong views. Why not? Because one sees dharmas in accord with true reality. As for the view of increase and the view of decrease, Śāriputra, Buddha-Tathāgatas forever stay far away from these two wrong views. They are denounced by Buddha-Tathāgatas.

"Śāriputra, if, among bhikṣus, bhikṣuṇīs, upāsakas, and upāsikās, there are those who hold either or both of these two wrong views, Buddha-Tathāgatas are not their World-Honored Ones. These people are not my disciples. Śāriputra, by holding these two wrong views, they will go from gloom into gloom, from dark into dark. I say that they are called icchantikas. Therefore, Śāriputra, you now should study this teaching to transform sentient beings, enabling them to stay away from these two wrong views and stay on the right path.[19] Śāriputra, you should study other such teachings to stay away from these two wrong views and stay on the right path."

After the Buddha pronounced this sūtra, Śāriputra the Wise, bhikṣus, bhikṣuṇīs, upāsakas, and upāsikās, as well as Bodhisattva-Mahāsattvas and the eight classes of Dharma protectors—gods, dragons, yakṣas, gandharvas, asuras, garuḍas, kiṁnaras, and mahoragas—together with humans, nonhumans, and all others in the multitude greatly rejoiced. They all believed in, accepted, and reverently carried out His teachings.

Notes

1. See "true reality (bhūta-koṭi)" defined in the glossary's "true suchness."

2. Attaining nirvāṇa means attaining bodhi; entering nirvāṇa means entering parinirvāṇa. See "parinirvāṇa" in the glossary.

3. A net is used in different contexts as different analogies. It is well known that the god-king Indra's net (Indra-jāla), made of jewels, adorns his palace. In fascicle 2 of text 1484 (in 2 fascicles), the Chinese version of the *Sūtra of the Brahma Net,* after observing the jeweled nets adorning Brahma-kings' palaces, the Buddha says that countless worlds are like the eyes of a net (T24n1484, 1003c14–15). Moreover, the Huayan School of China holds that as manifestations of the one mind, all dharmas are like mutual reflections of the jewels of Indra's net, all reflections reflecting one another, forming endless reflections (Rulu 2014, 19). However, text 1484 should be distinguished from the *Brahmajāla-sutta* in the Pāli Canon, whose Chinese counterpart is text 21 (T01n0021) in the Chinese Canon. In text 21, the word *net* (jāla) means dragnet, a snare that catches all wrong views, and the Buddha discusses the sixty-two views held by non-Buddhists and praises the true Dharma (saddharma). Here, *net* means a dragnet made of wrong views.

4. See "the view in favor of observing useless precepts" in the glossary's "afflictions."

5. See "inversion" in the glossary.

6. The affairs of sentient beings are transmigration in the Three Realms of Existence.

7. See Four Noble Truths in the glossary.

8. See "dharma" in the glossary. As the word *dharma* means "anything" (mental, physical, or event), anything can be labeled as dharma, such as the dharma of drinking, the dharma of a river, and the dharma of a sentient being. Other examples in a later passage are "a dharma of no change and a dharma of no end." If *dharma* in certain contexts clearly means doctrine or teachings, it is translated as such or capitalized.

9. See "dharma body" in the glossary's "three bodies of a Buddha."

10. The term "equal dharma body" (pingdeng fashen 平等法身) means that all Buddhas and all sentient beings have "the same" dharma body throughout all time. This term appears in many texts. For example, text 962, the Chinese version of the *Sūtra of the Dhāraṇi of the Jewel Siddhi for Attaining Buddhahood,* states that "the one dharma that all sentient beings and all Tathāgatas have is the equal dharma body . . . because things and the principle are equal, like the

open sky that always abides in one appearance [the appearance of no appearance], without any differences" (T19n0962, 0335b21–23); text 1666, the earlier of the two Chinese versions of *A Treatise on Eliciting Faith in the Mahāyāna,* states that "the dharma realm in one appearance is a Tathāgata's equal dharma body" (T32n1666, 0576b13); text 1924, a Chinese treatise on śamatha and vipaśyanā, states that "all sentient beings and all Buddhas have the [same] one pure mind, which is the Tathāgata store, the equal dharma body" (T46n1924, 0649a1).

11. Dharma Door (dharma-paryāya) means the teachings of the Buddha. The Sanskrit word *paryāya* means course, and is translated into Chinese as door because teachings provide an entrance into attaining bodhi. As Dharma Door is the general term for all teachings of the Buddha, 84,000 different Dharma Doors, as a figure of speech, are available to serve the needs of sentient beings of different capacities.

12. The opposite shore is that shore of nirvāṇa, opposite this shore of saṁsāra.

13. See "three kinds of hindrances" in the glossary.

14. The three dharmas describe the nature of the Tathāgata store. From *The Ratnagotravibhāga Mahāyānottaratantraśāstra* [Discerning the jewel nature: A Mahāyāna treatise on higher tantra], a Sanskrit text edited and published by E. H. Johnston (1885–1942) in 1950, Jikido Takasaki 高崎直道 (1926–2013) cites in his book *A Study on the Ratnagotravibhāga (Uttaratantra)* these three dharmas (Takasaki 2014a, 39):

(1) anādi-sāṁnidhya-saṁbaddha-svabhāva-śubha-dharmatā;
(2) anādi-sāṁnidhya-asaṁbaddha-svabhāva-kleśa-kośatā;
(3) aparāntakoṭi-sama-dhruva-dharmatā-saṁvidya-mānatā.

15. The phrase "throughout all time" is an interpretation of the Sanskrit phrase "at both ends" (aparāntakoṭi). Takasaki translates this third dharma as ". . . the existence [saṁvidyamānatām] of the Essential Nature [dharmatā] as eternal and the ultimate limit of the world [aparāntakoṭi-sama], . . . " (Ibid., 268).

16. The first dharma means that the Tathāgata store is not empty because it is one's inherent pure mind; the second dharma means that the Tathāgata store is empty because one's afflictions that sheathe it are empty; the third dharma means that the Tathāgata store is existent and changeless throughout all time.

17. See note 39 in Sūtra 3 in the present book.

18. According to fascicle 2 of text 462, the Chinese version of the *Mahāvaipulya Sūtra of the Treasure Chest,* "the realm of sentient beings, the dharma realm, and the realm of space are the same, without any difference" (T14n0462, c13–14). According to text 470, the Chinese version of the *Sūtra of Mañjuśrī's Cruise,* "true suchness neither increases nor decreases; the dharma realm neither increases nor decreases; the realm of sentient beings neither increases nor decreases" (T14n0470, 0511c5–8). This is also the conclusion of this Sūtra 2.

19. See Eightfold Right Path in the glossary.

About Sūtra 3

The earliest Chinese version of the *Sūtra of Śrīmālā's Lion's Roar* (Śrīmālā-siṁha-nāda-sūtra) was translated from Sanskrit during the Xuanshi years (玄始年, 412–428) of the Northern Liang Dynasty (397–439) by Dharmakṣema (曇無讖, 385–433) from central India. However, this Chinese version has been lost. Text 353 (T12n0353) in one fascicle and sūtra 48 in text 310 (T11n0310) are the two extant Chinese versions of this sūtra, probably translated from the same Sanskrit text. Text 353 was translated from Sanskrit in the Liu Song Dynasty (420–79) by Guṇabhadra (求那跋陀羅, 394–468) from central India. Its long title, *Vaipulya Sūtra of Śrīmālā's Lion's Roar That Reveals the Great Skillful Means of the One Vehicle,* was probably created by a Chinese scholar involved with its translation. Text 310 in 120 fascicles is the Chinese version of the *Great Treasure Pile Sūtra* (Mahā-ratnakūṭa-sūtra), which comprises forty-nine sūtras, translated from Sanskrit by several translators in a long period from the Cao Wei Dynasty (220–265) through the Tang Dynasty (618–907). Of these forty-nine sūtras, twenty-six sūtras in 39 fascicles, including sūtra 48 in fascicle 119, were translated in the Tang Dynasty by Bodhiruci (菩提流志, 562–727) from southern India. Sūtra 48 is not divided into chapters, and its title is *Assembly of Queen Śrīmālā*. However, text 353 comprises fifteen chapters, probably laid out by a Chinese master. Of these two Chinese versions, text 353 is the more popular one.

This sūtra is highly valued in China as representative of sūtras that reveal one's Tathāgata store (tathāgata-garbha). Ancient Chinese masters wrote commentaries on it, and some have been preserved. For example, in the Chinese Canon (Taishō Tripiṭaka) are texts 1744 and 2762. Text 1744 (T37n1744) in 3 fascicles was written by Jizang (吉藏, 549–623) around 598, in the Sui Dynasty (581–619); text 2762 (T85n2762) in one fascicle was written by Zhaojiang (照江, dates unknown) in 515, in the Northern Wei Dynasty (386–534). In the Extension of the Chinese Canon (the Shinsan Zokuzōkyō) are texts 351–353. Text 351 (X19n0351) in 2 fascicles was written in the Sui Dynasty by Huiyuan (慧遠, 523–92); text 352 (X19n0352) in 2 fascicles was written in the Tang Dynasty by Kuiji (窺基, 632–82); text 353 (X19n0353) in 6 fascicles was written by the Japanese prince Shengde (聖德太子, dates unknown), whose manuscript arrived in China in 772, in the Tang Dynasty. Of these commentaries, text 1744, *Shengman Baoku* 勝鬘寶窟 [Śrīmālā's treasure grotto], written by Jizang, cites many other texts and is considered to be the most extensive one. Contemporary Chinese masters continue to study and expound this sūtra, and publish their commentaries in books.

In this sūtra, through the Buddha's spiritual power, Śrīmālā, a laywoman, gives Mahāyāna teachings that all sentient beings have within them the Tathāgata store, or Buddha nature, and inspires all sentient beings to accept the true Dharma and ride the One Vehicle to attain Buddhahood. Therefore, this sūtra has the same special status as that of the *Vimalakīrti-nirdeśa Sūtra,* in which Vimalakīrti, a layman, gives Mahāyāna teachings.

In 1974, two English translations of text 353 were published: one by Diana Mary Paul, and the other by Alex and Hideko Wayman. In 1983, an English translation of sūtra 48 in fascicle 119 of text 310 was published in *A Treasury of*

About Sūtra 3

Mahāyāna Sūtras: Selections from the Mahāratnakūṭa Sūtra, translated by the Buddhist Association of the United States (Chang 1983, 363–86). Sūtra 3 in the present book is also an English translation of text 353, which comprises fifteen chapters. Sūtra 3 follows the layout of the first six chapters, and presents chapters 7–15 under subheadings of chapter 6, "The Boundless Holy Truth." The teachings in this sūtra are summarized below.

An ordinary being undergoes karmic birth and death. An Arhat, a Pratyekabuddha, or a holy Bodhisattva undergoes the inconceivable changeable birth and death in his mind-created bodies (manomaya-kāya) until his eventual attainment of the unsurpassed bodhi. Although an Arhat or a Pratyekabuddha declares that he will not undergo a subsequent existence, he has not ended his changeable birth and death, because there are certain afflictions that he cannot end.

There are two kinds of afflictions: (1) the ground-abiding afflictions and (2) their ensuing afflictions. There are four kinds of ground-abiding afflictions: (1) ground-abiding views, (2) ground-abiding love of desire, (3) ground-abiding love of form, and (4) ground-abiding love of existence. From these four kinds of ground-abiding afflictions ensue all afflictions, which respond to one's mind from moment to moment. Underlying these four kinds of ground-abiding afflictions is ground-abiding ignorance (avidyāvāsa-bhūmi) without a beginning, the root affliction, which does not respond to one's mind. It can be ended only on the Buddha Ground by a Buddha's bodhi wisdom. Therefore, only a Buddha attains nirvāṇa. An Arhat or a Pratyekabuddha has ended his four kinds of ground-abiding afflictions, but his ground-abiding ignorance remains. Therefore, he attains lesser nirvāṇa, called toward the realm of nirvāṇa.

Both the Voice-Hearer Vehicle and the Pratyekabuddha Vehicle are encompassed in the Mahāyāna. The Mahāyāna is the Buddha Vehicle. Therefore, the Three Vehicles are the One Vehicle. Whoever rides the One Vehicle to seek bodhi will attain anuttara-samyak-saṁbodhi, which is the realm of nirvāṇa. The realm of nirvāṇa is a Tathāgata's dharma body. A Tathāgata is the dharma body. Therefore, realizing the ultimate dharma body is reaching the ultimate destination of the One Vehicle. What is not separate, detached, or different from the inconceivable Buddha Dharma with teachings more numerous than the sands of the Ganges is called a Tathāgata's dharma body. When a Tathāgata's dharma body is not free from one's store of afflictions, it is called the Tathāgata store.

As a Tathāgata's abiding has no limit, so too His compassion for the world has no limit. Therefore, for a world that has not been delivered and has no refuge, the one who serves as its endless, ever-abiding, and ultimate refuge throughout the endless future is a Tathāgata, Arhat, Samyak-Saṁbuddha. The two refuges, the Dharma and the Saṅgha, are not the ultimate refuge, but the lesser refuge.

The ultimate wisdom-knowledge that destroys one's store of all afflictions is called the wisdom-knowledge of the highest truth. This holy truth is first realized by a Tathāgata, Arhat, Samyak-Saṁbuddha, and then He reveals it to a world shrouded in the store of ignorance. It reveals the profound Tathāgata store, which is a Tathāgata's state, unknown to any voice-hearer or Pratyekabuddha. However, if one has no doubts about the Tathāgata store being sheathed in one's store of immeasurable afflictions, one will have no doubts about a Tathāgata's dharma body leaving behind one's store of immeasurable afflictions.

Not through an undertaking, a Tathāgata, Arhat, Samyak-Saṁbuddha, fully verifies the meaning of the Four Noble Truths. He fully knows all future suffering, ends all His accumulations of afflictions and their ensuing afflictions, eliminates all His mind-created bodies, and ends all His suffering upon attaining nirvāṇa. The noble truth of cessation of one's suffering upon attaining nirvāṇa does not destroy anything, but reveals one's ever-abiding inherent pure nature (Buddha nature), which has no beginning, no action, no arising, no end, and no expiring, and is apart from one's store of all afflictions. The noble truth of cessation of one's suffering upon attaining nirvāṇa is the one truth and the one reliance. The other three noble truths—suffering, accumulation of afflictions, and the path—are not the highest truth, because they are impermanent and are not a place of refuge.

There are two kinds of wisdom-knowledge of the emptiness of one's Tathāgata store. The first kind is the wisdom-knowledge of the empty Tathāgata store, which is not separate, detached, or different from one's store of all afflictions, which are empty. The second kind is the wisdom-knowledge of the not-empty Tathāgata store, which is not separate, detached, or different from the inconceivable Buddha Dharma with teachings more numerous than the sands of the Ganges.

One's birth and death depend on one's Tathāgata store, which has neither birth nor death. Not only the inconceivable Buddha Dharma, which is not separate, detached, split, or different from the wisdom-knowledge of liberation, depends on the Tathāgata store to establish itself, but all saṁskṛta dharmas, which are separate, detached, split, and different from the wisdom-knowledge of liberation, depend on the Tathāgata store to establish themselves.

One's Tathāgata store is not a self, not a person, not a sentient being, and not an everlasting soul. It is incomprehensible to those who hold the wrong view that one has a self, those who hold inverted views, and those who misunderstand the emptiness of dharmas. One's Tathāgata store is the store of the dharma realm, the store of the dharma body, the supreme store of supra-worldly dharmas, and the store of one's inherent pure nature (Buddha nature). How one's Tathāgata store, the store of one's inherent pure nature, is tainted by one's visitor-like afflictions (āgantuka kleśa) and their ensuing afflictions can be known only through a Tathāgata's inconceivable wisdom. There are two things that are hard to know: (1) one's inherent pure mind and (2) its being tainted by afflictions. Only Bodhisattva-Mahāsattvas with great attainments can hear and accept these two hard-to-know things. Voice-hearers can only believe in a Buddha's words.

3 勝鬘師子吼一乘大方便方廣經
Vaipulya Sūtra of Śrīmālā's Lion's Roar That Reveals the Great Skillful Means of the One Vehicle

Translated from Sanskrit into Chinese in the Liu Song Dynasty
by
The Tripiṭaka Master Guṇabhadra from India

Chapter 1 – A Tathāgata's Virtues

Thus I have heard:

At one time the Buddha was outside Śrāvastī [the capital city of Kauśala], staying in the Jetavana garden, which was purchased for the Buddha from Prince Jeta by Anāthapiṇḍika the Elder. At that time King Prasenajit and his queen Mallikā[1] had not been believers in the Dharma for long. He said to his queen, "Queen Śrīmālā [Superb Garland] is our daughter. She is kind, intelligent, and endowed with a keen capacity. If she sees the Buddha, she will quickly understand the Dharma without harboring doubts. We should send her a letter at the right time to inspire her to seek the Dharma."

The queen said, "Now is the time."

Then the king and queen wrote a letter, briefly praising the Tathāgata's immeasurable virtues. They ordered a palace attendant named Candra to deliver the letter to Śrīmālā. Upon arriving in the kingdom of Ayodhyā, Candra entered the palace and respectfully handed the letter to Queen Śrīmālā. She joyfully accepted it with the highest reverence by touching it to the crown of her head. After reading it, inspired by its rare information, Śrīmālā spoke to Candra in verse:

> I have heard that a Buddha's voice
> Is hard to encounter in the world.
> If this letter reveals the truth,
> I should make an offering to you [the messenger].[2]
>
> If that Buddha-Bhagavān
> Has appeared in the world to benefit all,
> He should pity me
> And enable me to see Him.

As soon as she had this thought, the Buddha appeared in the sky, in His unparalleled body, and emitted vast radiance. Śrīmālā and her retinue prostrated themselves at His feet. With a pure mind, they praised the Buddha's virtues as she spoke in verse:

The Tathāgata's sublime body
Is unequaled, unparalleled,
And inconceivable in the world.
So I now pay homage.

As the Tathāgata's physical form is endless,
So too is His wisdom,
And His Dharma is ever abiding.
So I now take refuge.

You have removed the faults of Your mind
And the four faults of Your body,[3]
And arrived on the inconceivable ground [the Buddha Ground].
So I now pay homage to the Dharma King.

You have learned jñeya [all there is to know],
And Your wisdom body is hindrance free
And encompasses all dharmas.
So I now pay homage.

I pay homage to Your immeasurable virtues.
I pay homage to Your unequaled virtues.
I pay homage to Your boundless Dharma.
I pay homage to Your inconceivable [state].

I pray that You will pity and protect me,
And enable the Dharma seeds to grow in me.
I pray that You will accept and support me
In this life and future lives.

I have performed meritorious works
And will continue in this life and future lives.
With these roots of goodness,
I pray that You will accept and support me.

After Śrīmālā spoke these stanzas, she and her retinue prostrated themselves at the Buddha's feet. Then the World-Honored One spoke to Śrīmālā in verse:[4]

I set you [in the Dharma] long ago,
And you came to realization [of the truth] in your previous life.
Again I accept and support you now
And in your future lives.

Then Śrīmālā and her retinue bowed down to the Buddha. In their midst, the Buddha bestowed upon her a prophecy, "Because of the roots of goodness you have acquired by praising the Tathāgata's virtues, you will be reborn as a commanding king of gods and humans for countless asaṁkhyeyas of kalpas. Wherever you will be reborn, you will always see me and praise me as you do now. You will make offerings to innumerable asaṁkhyeyas of Buddhas. After 20,000 asaṁkhyeya kalpas, you will become a Buddha called Universal Light, the Tathāgata, Arhat, Samyak-Saṁbuddha. In His Buddha Land, there will be no evil life-paths and no suffering, such as old age, illness, deterioration, distress, or unpleasant experiences, nor will there be evils or the names of evil karmas.[5] Sentient beings in that world will have good appearances and strength, live long lives, and enjoy the five desires. Their happiness will surpass that of gods in Paranirmita-vaśa-vartin Heaven [the sixth desire heaven in this world], and they will ride only the Mahāyāna [the Great Vehicle]. Those in the Three Realms of Existence who cultivate roots of goodness will gather there."

When Śrīmālā received this prophecy, innumerable sentient beings, such as gods and humans, aspired to be reborn in that world. Then the World-Honored One bestowed upon them the prophecy of their rebirth there.

Chapter 2 – Accepting Ten Precepts

After Śrīmālā received the prophecy, she stood respectfully and accepted ten vast precepts. She vowed:

(1) World-Honored One, from now on until I attain bodhi, I will never entertain the thought of violating the precepts I have accepted.

(2) World-Honored One, from now on until I attain bodhi, I will never harbor arrogance toward my teachers.

(3) World-Honored One, from now on until I attain bodhi, I will never harbor anger toward sentient beings.

(4) World-Honored One, from now on until I attain bodhi, I will never harbor jealousy of others' appearances or things.

(5) World-Honored One, from now on until I attain bodhi, I will never harbor stinginess about giving away internal or external things.

(6) World-Honored One, from now on until I attain bodhi, I will never accept or accumulate things for myself. Anything I accept will be for relieving sentient beings in need.

(7) World-Honored One, from now on until I attain bodhi, I will practice the Four Drawing-in Dharmas, never for receiving good requitals, but for benefiting all sentient beings. My mind free from greedy desire, complacency, and hindrances, I will draw in sentient beings.

(8) World-Honored One, from now on until I attain bodhi, when I see sentient beings in forlornness, confinement, shackles, sickness, tribulation, or hardship, I will not abandon them even for a short while, but will properly benefit them until they are free from suffering.

(9) World-Honored One, from now on until I attain bodhi, when I see those who make an evil livelihood, such as hunting or raising animals [for slaughter], or those who violate a Tathāgata's pure precepts, I will not abandon them. Wherever I see such sentient beings, if I have the power [of authority], I will

tame those who should be tamed and draw in those who should be drawn in. Why? Because taming them and drawing them in will enable the Dharma to abide in the world for a long time. If the Dharma abides in the world for a long time, there will be more gods and humans, and fewer sentient beings taking the evil life-paths. Then all will be able to follow the Dharma wheel a Tathāgata turns. Because I see this benefit, I will draw them in, not abandoning them.

(10) World-Honored One, from now on until I attain bodhi, I will uphold the true Dharma [saddharma] and never forget or lose it. Why? Because forgetting or losing the Dharma means forgetting the Mahāyāna. Forgetting the Mahāyāna means forgetting the pāramitās.[6] Forgetting the pāramitās means not wanting to ride the Mahāyāna. If a Bodhisattva is indecisive about riding the Mahāyāna, he has no motivation to accept the true Dharma and enter it with delight. Then he will never be able to transcend the ground of ordinary beings. As I see this immeasurable loss, I also see the immeasurable benefits received by a Bodhisattva-Mahāsattva who accepts the true Dharma. Therefore, I accept these ten vast precepts.[7]

"May the Dharma King, the World-Honored One, be my present witness, because at present only the Buddha-Bhagavān knows [my truthfulness]. Sentient beings have small and weak roots of goodness. They form a web of doubts because these ten vows are hard to carry out, or they do evil karmas in the long night and suffer the dire consequences. To settle their minds, before the Buddha I now make a truthful vow: 'If I fully observe these ten vast precepts, this multitude will see a rain of celestial flowers and hear celestial sounds.'"

As soon as she spoke these words, the open sky rained down celestial flowers, and wonderful sounds were heard saying, "Indeed, indeed! What you say is true, not false."

Upon seeing the celestial flowers and hearing the celestial sounds, all in the assembly removed their doubts. They rejoiced exuberantly and said that they wished always to be with Śrīmālā and to do the same as she would. Then the World-Honored One bestowed upon the multitude the prophecy of the fulfillment of their wish.

Chapter 3 – The Three Vast Vows

Then Śrīmālā made three vast vows before the Buddha. She said, "I will benefit endless innumerable sentient beings through the power of these true vows:

(1) In all my lives, I will use my roots of goodness to acquire the wisdom-knowledge [jñāna] of the true Dharma. This is my first vast vow.

(2) After I have acquired the wisdom-knowledge of the true Dharma, I will tirelessly expound it to sentient beings. This is my second vast vow.

(3) I accept the true Dharma and will relinquish my body, life, and wealth to protect and uphold it. This is my third vast vow.

Then the Buddha said to Śrīmālā, "Your three vast vows are like the domain of space, which encompasses all dharmas. Hence a Bodhisattva's vows as numerous as the sands of Ganges are all encompassed in these three vast vows. These three vast vows are truly vast."

Chapter 4 – Accepting the True Dharma

Then Śrīmālā said to the Buddha, "Through the Buddha's awesome power, I would like to condense my vast vows into what they truly are."

The Buddha said, "You have my permission to speak."

Śrīmālā said to the Buddha, "All vows as numerous as the sands of the Ganges, which are made by a Bodhisattva, are encompassed in one vast vow, the vow of accepting the true Dharma. Accepting the true Dharma is truly a vast vow."

The Buddha praised Śrīmālā, "Very good, very good! Your wisdom and skill are profound and wonderful because you have planted roots of goodness in the long night. Among future sentient beings, only those who have long planted roots of goodness can understand your words. You can expound [the meaning of] accepting the true Dharma, just as past Buddhas expounded it, present Buddhas do expound it, and future Buddhas will expound it. As I now have attained the unsurpassed bodhi, I too often expound [the meaning of] accepting the true Dharma. Indeed, I say that as the merit acquired by accepting the true Dharma is boundless, so too a Tathāgata's wisdom and eloquence are boundless. Why? Because accepting the true Dharma has great virtues and great benefits."

The Vast Meaning of Accepting the True Dharma

Śrīmālā said to the Buddha, "Through the Buddha's spiritual power, I would like to expound the vast meaning of accepting the true Dharma."

The Buddha said, "Speak."

Śrīmālā said, "The vast meaning of accepting the true Dharma is immeasurable. Accepting the true Dharma means acquiring the entire Buddha Dharma and gathering 84,000 Dharma Doors [dharma-paryāya]. As an analogy, when a new kalpa begins, vast clouds form and send down colorful rains and various treasures. Likewise, accepting the true Dharma rains down immeasurable fortunate requitals and countless roots of goodness.

"World-Honored One, as another analogy, when a new kalpa begins, vast waters gather and form a Three-Thousand Large Thousandfold World with 400 koṭi continents of different kinds. Likewise, accepting the true Dharma gives rise to the Mahāyāna's store of immeasurable realms, the transcendental powers of all Bodhisattvas, worldly security, happiness, gratification, and ease, supra-worldly peace and joy, and even virtues that gods and humans have never before had.

"As another analogy, the great earth bears four heavy burdens. What are these four? They are (1) vast seas, (2) mountains, (3) grass and trees, and (4) sentient beings. Likewise a good man or woman who accepts the true Dharma can, like the great earth, perform four heavy tasks. What are these four? They are (1) giving a god's or human's roots of goodness to bring to [spiritual] maturity those who stay away from beneficent learned friends, do not hear the Dharma, or engage in non-dharmas [evil karmas]; (2) giving the Voice-Hearer Vehicle to those who seek it; (3) giving the Pratyekabuddha Vehicle to those who seek it; (4) giving the Mahāyāna to those who seek it. These are the four heavy tasks that a good man or woman who accepts the true Dharma can, like the great earth, perform. Indeed, World-Honored One, a good man or woman who accepts the true Dharma can, like the great earth, perform these four heavy tasks, befriend sentient beings unasked,[8] pity and comfort sentient beings with great compassion, and become a Dharma mother of the world.

"As another analogy, the great earth has four treasure stores. What are these four? They are treasures of (1) low price, (2) medium price, (3) high price, and (4) pricelessness. These are the great earth's four treasure stores. Likewise a good man or woman who accepts the true Dharma has, like the great earth, four supreme treasures. What are these four? They are (1) giving a god's or human's roots of goodness to those who do not hear the Dharma but engage in non-dharmas; (2) giving the Voice-Hearer Vehicle to those who seek it; (3) giving the Pratyekabuddha Vehicle to those who seek it; (4) giving the Mahāyāna to those who seek it. From a good man or woman who accepts the true Dharma, a sentient being can receive such great treasures, which are extraordinary and rare benefits.

"World-Honored One, producing great treasure stores is accepting the true Dharma. World-Honored One, what is meant by accepting the true Dharma? [The action of] accepting the true Dharma is no different from the true Dharma. The true Dharma is [the action of] accepting the true Dharma.

Practicing the Pāramitās Is Accepting the True Dharma

"World-Honored One, practicing the pāramitās is no different from accepting the true Dharma. Accepting the true Dharma means practicing the pāramitās. Why? Because a good man or woman who accepts the true Dharma practices the six pāramitās in the following way.

"For those who should be brought to [spiritual] maturity through almsgiving, he or she gives them alms, not even sparing his or her body parts, to bring them to [spiritual] maturity according to their mentalities and enable them to abide in the true Dharma. This is called dāna-pāramitā [the almsgiving pāramitā].

"For those who should be brought to [spiritual] maturity through observing the precepts, he or she protects his or her six faculties, purifies his or her body, voice, and mind karmas, and displays his or her four majestic deportments [walking, standing still, sitting, and lying down], to bring them to [spiritual] maturity according to their mentalities and enable them to abide in the true Dharma. This is called śīla-pāramitā [the precept pāramitā].

"For those who should be brought to [spiritual] maturity through enduring adversity, he or she endures their abusive words, insults, slanders, and threats with an altruistic mind and the foremost endurance, without anger or even changing color, to bring them to [spiritual] maturity according to their mentalities and enable them to abide in the true Dharma. This is called kṣānti-pāramitā [the endurance pāramitā].

"For those who should be brought to [spiritual] maturity through making energetic progress, he or she helps them with a tireless mind, makes the foremost energetic progress with great aspirations, and displays his or her four majestic deportments, to bring them to [spiritual] maturity according to their mentalities and enable them to abide in the true Dharma. This is called vīrya-pāramitā [the progress pāramitā].

"For those who should be brought to [spiritual] maturity through practicing meditation, he or she uses an undisturbed mind, an undistracted mind, and the foremost right mindfulness that never forgets what he or she did or said long ago, to bring them to [spiritual] maturity according to their mentalities and enable them to abide in the true Dharma. This is called dhyāna-pāramitā [the meditation pāramitā].

"For those who should be brought to [spiritual] maturity through developing wisdom, he or she uses a fearless mind to answer their questions about all meanings of the Dharma and expounds to them all doctrines, all studies,[9] and even various technical skills, to bring them to [spiritual] maturity according to their mentalities and enable them to abide in the true Dharma. This is called prajñā-pāramitā [the wisdom pāramitā].

"Therefore, World-Honored One, practicing the pāramitās is no different from accepting the true Dharma. Accepting the true Dharma means practicing the pāramitās.

Relinquishing Three Things to Accept the True Dharma

"World-Honored One, through the Buddha's awesome spiritual power, I would like to further expound the vast meaning [of accepting the true Dharma]."

The Buddha said, "Speak."

Śrīmālā said to the Buddha, "What is meant by accepting the true Dharma? [The action of] accepting the true Dharma is no different from the person who accepts the true Dharma. A good man or woman who accepts the true Dharma is [the action of] accepting the true Dharma.[10]

"Why? Because to accept the true Dharma, a good man or woman relinquishes three things. What are these three? They are (1) body, (2) life, and (3) wealth. He or she relinquishes his or her body throughout future births and deaths, leaving behind old age, illness, and death, to acquire a Tathāgata's indestructible, ever-abiding, and changeless dharma body [dharmakāya][11] with inconceivable virtues. He or she relinquishes his or her life throughout future births and deaths, to become absolutely free from death, acquire the limitless, ever-abiding, and inconceivable virtues, and fully understand the entire profound Buddha Dharma. He or she relinquishes his or her wealth to acquire the endless, never-diminishing, ever-abiding, and inconceivable virtues unavailable to other sentient beings, and to receive excellent offerings from other sentient beings. World-Honored One, a good man or woman who relinquishes these three things to accept the true Dharma is remembered by all Buddhas and respected by all sentient beings.

"World-Honored One, when the Dharma is ending, while bhikṣus, bhikṣuṇīs, upāsakas, and upāsikās will destroy the Saṅgha, split into factions, dispute, and disperse, a good man or woman who accepts the true Dharma without sycophancy, deceit, or falsity will delight in the true Dharma and join Dharma friends. Joining Dharma friends means that he or she will definitely receive a good prophecy from Buddhas.

"World-Honored One, I see the great power of accepting the true Dharma. I also know and see that the Buddha is the true eye, the one with true wisdom-knowledge, the root of the true Dharma, the imparter of the true Dharma, and the reliance of the true Dharma."

Immeasurable Virtues and Benefits of Accepting the True Dharma

Then the World-Honored One expressed sympathetic joy over Śrīmālā's words about the great awesome power of accepting the true Dharma. He said, "Indeed, Śrīmālā, indeed as you say, accepting the true Dharma has great awesome power. As an analogy, whoever is even lightly touched by a strong man feels a great deal of pain. Likewise, Śrīmālā, accepting even a little of the true Dharma can distress māras. Indeed, Śrīmālā, I do not see any other good dharmas that can worry māras as can accepting even a little of the true Dharma.

"As another analogy, the shape and color of the ox-king are unparalleled and surpass those of all other oxen. Likewise the roots of goodness of a rider of the Mahāyāna who accepts even a little of the true Dharma surpass those of riders of the Two Vehicles. Why? Because accepting the true Dharma has vast virtues.

"As another analogy, Mount Sumeru, king of mountains, surpasses all other mountains in size and majesty. Likewise the roots of goodness of a new rider of the Mahāyāna who accepts the true Dharma with an altruistic mind, not even sparing his life or wealth, surpass those of longtime riders of the Mahāyāna who are attached to their lives and wealth, not to mention those of riders of the Two Vehicles. Why? Because accepting the true Dharma has vast virtues.

"Therefore, Śrīmālā, you should expound [the vast meaning of] accepting the true Dharma to teach and establish sentient beings. Indeed, Śrīmālā, accepting the true Dharma brings such great benefits, such great blessings, and such great spiritual fruits. Śrīmālā, for countless asaṁkhyeyas of kalpas, I expounded the virtues and benefits of accepting the true Dharma but never reached their limit. Indeed, accepting the true Dharma has immeasurable and limitless virtues."

Chapter 5 – The One Vehicle

The Buddha told Śrīmālā, "You now should further expound [the meaning of] accepting the true Dharma, as expounded by all Buddhas."

Śrīmālā said to the Buddha, "Very good, World-Honored One, I gladly obey Your command."

Accepting the True Dharma Is Accepting the Mahāyāna

Then she said to the Buddha, "World-Honored One, accepting the true Dharma is accepting the Mahāyāna. Why? Because the Mahāyāna brings forth all voice-hearers, Pratyekabuddhas, and worldly and supra-worldly good dharmas. World-Honored One, as Lake Anavatapta [Heatless] issues eight great rivers,[12] likewise the Mahāyāna brings forth all voice-hearers, Pratyekabuddhas, and worldly and supra-worldly good dharmas. World-Honored One, as all seeds depend on the ground to grow, likewise all voice-hearers, Pratyekabuddhas, and worldly and supra-worldly good dharmas depend on the Mahāyāna to grow. Therefore, World-Honored One, abiding in and accepting the Mahāyāna are abiding in and accepting the Two Vehicles and all worldly and supra-worldly good dharmas.

"World-Honored One, You have expounded six things. What are these six? They are (1) abiding of the true Dharma, (2) end of the true Dharma, (3) prātimokṣa [liberation achieved severally by observing the precepts], (4) the Vinaya,[13] (5) renouncing family life [to take the spiritual path], and (6) accepting the complete monastic precepts. To expound the Mahāyāna, You have expounded these six things.

"To expound the Mahāyāna, You have expounded the abiding of the true Dharma because the abiding of the Mahāyāna is the abiding of the true Dharma. To expound the Mahāyāna, You have expounded the end of the true Dharma because the end of the Mahāyāna is the end of the true Dharma. Prātimokṣa and the Vinaya have the same meaning but have different names. The Vinaya is Mahāyāna teachings. Why? Because one relies on a Buddha to renounce family life and accept the complete monastic precepts. Therefore, Mahāyāna precepts encompass the Vinaya, renouncing family life, and accepting the complete monastic precepts. However, an Arhat has no need to renounce family life and accept the complete monastic precepts. Why? Because an Arhat has taken refuge in a Tathāgata to renounce family life and accept the complete monastic precepts.

Only a Tathāgata Has Attained Nirvāṇa

"An Arhat takes refuge in a Buddha because he has fear. Why? Because an Arhat has fear even as he abides in freedom from actions [i.e., nirvāṇa], as if someone would harm him with a sword. Therefore, an Arhat has no ultimate joy. Why? Because he relies on the one who never seeks refuge [i.e., a Buddha]. Just as sentient beings that have no reliance have various fears, and seek refuge because of their fears, likewise an Arhat has fear, and relies on a Tathāgata because of his fear.

"World-Honored One, an Arhat or a Pratyekabuddha has fear. Because his changeable birth and death are not ended, his rebirth continues. Because his Brahma way of life is not fully established, his training on the path is not entirely pure. Because his undertaking to attain nirvāṇa is not fully accomplished, he still has something to do [to end his suffering]. Because he has not fully crossed the ocean of birth and death, he still has something [his changeable birth and death] to end. Because he has not ended certain afflictions, he is still far from the realm of nirvāṇa.

"Only a Tathāgata, Arhat, Samyak-Saṁbuddha, has attained nirvāṇa[14] because He has acquired all merits, while an Arhat or a Pratyekabuddha has not acquired all merits. Saying that he has attained nirvāṇa is a Buddha's skillful means of expression. Only a Tathāgata, Arhat, Samyak-Saṁbuddha, has attained nirvāṇa because He has acquired immeasurable merits, while an Arhat or a Pratyekabuddha has acquired measurable merits. Saying that he has attained nirvāṇa is a Buddha's skillful means of expression. Only a Tathāgata, Arhat, Samyak-Saṁbuddha, has attained nirvāṇa because He has acquired inconceivable merits, while an Arhat or a Pratyekabuddha has acquired conceivable merits. Saying that he has attained nirvāṇa is a Buddha's skillful means of expression. Only a Tathāgata, Arhat, Samyak-Saṁbuddha, has attained nirvāṇa because He has removed all faults that should be removed and has achieved the foremost purity, while an Arhat or a Pratyekabuddha has remaining faults and has not achieved the foremost purity. Saying that he has attained nirvāṇa is a Buddha's skillful means of expression. Only a Tathāgata, Arhat, Samyak-Saṁbuddha, has attained nirvāṇa and is revered by all sentient beings, and His state surpasses that of any Arhat, Pratyekabuddha, or Bodhisattva. Therefore, an Arhat or a Pratyekabuddha is still far from the realm of nirvāṇa. Saying that an Arhat or a Pratyekabuddha observes his level of liberation, acquires the four kinds of wisdom-knowledge,[15] and arrives at the reviving rest place [nirvāṇa] is also a Tathāgata's skillful means of expression, which has something remaining unsaid, and is not definitive.

The Two Kinds of Birth and Death

"Why? Because there are two kinds of birth and death. What are these two? They are (1) karmic birth and death through successive lifespans; (2) changeable birth and death, which are inconceivable. An ordinary being undergoes karmic birth and death. An Arhat, a Pratyekabuddha, or a holy Bodhisattva[16] undergoes the inconceivable changeable birth and death in his mind-created bodies [manomaya-kāya] until his eventual attainment of the unsurpassed bodhi.

"Because an Arhat or a Pratyekabuddha has ended his karmic birth and death, he declares that his rebirth is ended. Because he has attained nirvāṇa with remnants,[17] he declares that his Brahma way of life is established. Because he has ended certain afflictions, which all ordinary beings cannot end and voice-hearers in the first seven ranks[18] have not yet completely ended, he declares that his undertaking is accomplished. Because has ended the afflictions that drive his karmic rebirths, he declares that he will not undergo a subsequent existence. However, although he declares that he will not undergo a subsequent existence, he has ended neither all afflictions nor all rebirths. Why? Because there are certain afflictions that an Arhat or a Pratyekabuddha cannot end.

The Ground-Abiding Afflictions and Their Ensuing Afflictions

"There are two kinds of afflictions. What are these two? They are (1) the ground-abiding afflictions and (2) their ensuing afflictions. There are four kinds of ground-abiding afflictions. What are these four? They are (1) ground-abiding views, (2) ground-abiding love of desire, (3) ground-abiding love of form, and (4) ground-abiding love of existence.[19] From these four kinds of ground-abiding afflictions ensue all afflictions, which respond to one's mind from moment to moment. [Underlying these four kinds of ground-abiding afflictions is] ground-abiding ignorance [avidyāvāsa-bhūmi] without a beginning,[20] the root affliction, which does not respond to one's mind. World-Honored One, the power of these four kinds of ground-abiding afflictions is the relied-upon seed for all ensuing afflictions to grow. However, it cannot compare with the power of ground-abiding ignorance by any measure or analogy.

"Indeed, World-Honored One, ground-abiding ignorance is far more powerful than the four ground-abiding afflictions.[21] As an analogy, the appearance, strength, lifespan, retinue, accouterments, and transcendental powers of the celestial māra-king Pāpīyān surpass those of gods in Paranirmita-vaśa-vartin Heaven [the sixth desire heaven]. Likewise the power of ground-abiding ignorance surpasses that of the four ground-abiding afflictions. Ensuing afflictions as numerous as the sands of the Ganges depend on ground-abiding ignorance to arise, and it enables the four ground-abiding afflictions to abide for a long time. The wisdom of an Arhat or a Pratyekabuddha cannot end it. Only a Tathāgata's bodhi wisdom can end it. Indeed, World-Honored One, ground-abiding ignorance is the strongest.

"World-Honored One, through grasping[22] as the condition, and affliction-driven karmas as the cause, an ordinary being transmigrates in different karmic bodies in the Three Realms of Existence. Likewise, through ground-abiding ignorance as the condition, and affliction-free karmas as the cause, an Arhat's, a Pratyekabuddha's, or a holy Bodhisattva's three kinds of mind-created body appear.[23] His affliction-free karmas and three kinds of mind-created body depend on his ground-abiding ignorance to arise, not without conditions. Indeed, World-Honored One, his ground-abiding ignorance is the condition for his affliction-free karmas and three kinds of mind-created body to arise.

Only a Tathāgata Can End His Ground-Abiding Ignorance

"Indeed, World-Honored One, the four ground-abiding afflictions and affliction-driven karmas are different from ground-abiding ignorance. Because ground-abiding ignorance is apart from the four ground-abiding afflictions, it can be ended only on the Buddha Ground by a Buddha's bodhi wisdom. Why? Because an Arhat or a Pratyekabuddha has ended his four kinds of ground-abiding afflictions but has not completely ended all his afflictions, has not acquired the power to end them, and has not attained nirvāṇa. That his afflictions are not completely ended means that his ground-abiding ignorance remains.

"World-Honored One, because an Arhat, a Pratyekabuddha, or a holy Bodhisattva in his final body [which is for attaining Buddhahood] is still hindered by his ground-abiding ignorance, he does not clearly know or see the truth of various dharmas. Because he does not clearly know or see it, he cannot completely end what should be ended. Therefore, he achieves liberation with remaining faults, not liberation free from all faults; he achieves purity with remnants, not total purity; he acquires merits with remnants, not all merits. Because he achieves liberation with remnants, achieves purity with remnants, and acquires merits with remnants, his knowledge of suffering has remnants [is incomplete], the end of his accumulation of afflictions has remnants, the cessation of his suffering upon attaining nirvāṇa has remnants, and the completion of his training on the path has remnants. Therefore, he attains lesser nirvāṇa, called toward the realm of nirvāṇa.

"If one knows all suffering, ends all one's accumulations of afflictions, ends all one's suffering upon attaining nirvāṇa, and completes one's training on all paths, one will attain the ever-abiding nirvāṇa in a world plagued by destruction through impermanence and by the disease of impermanence, and become the protection and refuge for a world without protection and refuge. Why? Because one attains nirvāṇa when one sees that dharmas are equal [in their emptiness], neither good nor bad; wisdom is equal [in all]; liberation is equal [for all]; purity is equal [in all]. Therefore, nirvāṇa has one flavor, the same flavor, called the liberation flavor.

"World-Honored One, if one's ground-abiding ignorance is not completely ended, one cannot attain nirvāṇa, which has one flavor, the same flavor, the liberation flavor. Why not? Because if one's ground-abiding ignorance is not completely ended, afflictions that should be ended, which are more numerous than the sands of the Ganges, cannot be completely ended. Because these afflictions that should be ended are not completely ended, one cannot acquire or attain virtuous dharmas that should be acquired or attained, which are more numerous than the sands of the Ganges.

"One's ground-abiding ignorance accumulates, and brings forth all afflictions and their ensuing afflictions, both of which should be ended through one's spiritual training. It brings forth afflictions that arise from one's mind, śamatha, vipaśyanā, meditation, samāpatti, skillful means, wisdom-knowledge, spiritual fruit, attainment, power, and fearlessness. Such ensuing afflictions more numerous than the sands of the Ganges can be ended only by a Tathāgata's bodhi wisdom [when one attains Buddhahood]. All ensuing afflictions are established on one's ground-abiding ignorance, arise from one's ground-abiding ignorance as their cause and condition, and respond to one's mind from moment to moment. World-Honored One, one's ground-abiding ignorance without a beginning does not respond to one's mind.

"World-Honored One, all one's afflictions, which are more numerous than the sands of the Ganges and can be ended only by a Tathāgata's bodhi wisdom [when one attains Buddhahood], are established on and sustained by one's ground-abiding ignorance. As an analogy, all seeds depend on the ground to arise, establish themselves, and grow. If the ground is destroyed, the seeds are destroyed as well. Likewise one's afflictions, which are more numerous than the sands of the Ganges and can be ended only by a Tathāgata's bodhi wisdom [when one attains Buddhahood], depend on one's ground-abiding ignorance to arise, establish themselves, and grow. If one's ground-abiding ignorance is ended, one's afflictions are ended as well. When all one's ground-abiding afflictions[24] and all their ensuing afflictions are ended, one acquires all virtuous dharmas acquired by a Tathāgata, which are as numerous as the sands of the Ganges, acquires hindrance-free transcendental powers, acquires all wisdom-knowledge and views, removes all faults, acquires all merits, becomes a Dharma King, a Dharma Master, masters all dharmas, and ascends to the ground where all dharmas are hindrance free. One roars the lion's roar of a Tathāgata, Arhat, Samyak-Saṁbuddha, declaring, 'My rebirth is ended; my Brahma way of life is established, my undertaking is accomplished; I will not undergo a subsequent existence.' Indeed, World-Honored One, this lion's roar based on the definitive meaning has always been remembered and expounded [by Buddhas].

Two Kinds of Wisdom-Knowledge of Freedom from a Subsequent Existence

"World-Honored One, there are two kinds of wisdom-knowledge that one will not undergo a subsequent existence. [The first kind belongs to] a Tathāgata, who uses an unsurpassed tamer's power to subjugate the four māras, transcends the world, and is revered by all sentient beings. He realizes the inconceivable dharma body, and acquires mastery of all dharmas on the jñeya [all-there-is-to-know] ground, above which there is nothing more to do or to attain. Equipped with the Ten Powers, He valiantly ascends to the foremost unsurpassed fearless ground [Buddha Ground], and uses His hindrance-free wisdom to observe all dharmas, without others' help. With the wisdom-knowledge that He will not undergo a subsequent existence, He roars a lion's roar.

"World-Honored One, [the second kind belongs to] an Arhat or a Pratyekabuddha, who overcomes his fear of birth and death and, step by step, comes to enjoy the happiness of liberation. He thinks, 'I have left behind my fear of repeated birth and death, and will no longer undergo the suffering of repeated birth and death.' World-Honored One, as he observes his freedom from a subsequent existence, he also observes the foremost reviving rest place, the nirvāṇa ground. World-Honored One, abiding on the ground he has reached before,[25] he is neither ignorant of the Dharma nor dependent on others. He knows that he has reached the ground with remnants but will definitely attain anuttara-samyak-saṁbodhi someday.

The One Vehicle

"Why? Because both the Voice-Hearer Vehicle and the Pratyekabuddha Vehicle are encompassed in the Mahāyāna. The Mahāyāna is the Buddha Vehicle. Therefore, the Three Vehicles are the One Vehicle. Whoever rides the One Vehicle to seek bodhi will attain anuttara-samyak-saṁbodhi. Anuttara-samyak-saṁbodhi is the realm of nirvāṇa. The realm of nirvāṇa is a Tathāgata's dharma body. Realizing the ultimate dharma body is reaching the ultimate destination of the One Vehicle. A Tathāgata is no different from the dharma body. A Tathāgata is the dharma body. [Therefore] realizing the ultimate dharma body is reaching the ultimate destination of the One Vehicle. 'Ultimate' means boundless and endless [across space and time].

The One Refuge in a Tathāgata

"World-Honored One, the abiding of a Tathāgata has no time limit because a Tathāgata, Arhat, Samyak-Saṁbuddha, abides throughout the endless future. As a Tathāgata's abiding has no limit, so too His compassion for the world has no limit. His limitless great compassion limitlessly comforts the world. These words are a good description of a Tathāgata. If someone says that a Tathāgata is the endless dharma, the ever-abiding dharma, and the refuge for the whole world, his words are also a good description of a Tathāgata. Therefore, for a world that has not been delivered and has no refuge, the one who serves as its endless, ever-abiding, and ultimate refuge throughout the endless future is a Tathāgata, Arhat, Samyak-Saṁbuddha.

"The Dharma is the path of the One Vehicle. The Saṅgha is the multitude that rides the Three Vehicles. The two refuges, the Dharma and the Saṅgha, are not the ultimate refuge. They are called the lesser refuge. Why? Because the Dharma, which is the path of the One Vehicle, leads to realization of the ultimate dharma body, which does not address the Dharma affairs of the One Vehicle [when one was riding it].[26] And the Saṅgha, which is the multitude that rides the Three Vehicles, has fear, takes refuge in a Tathāgata to seek liberation, and trains and learns to attain anuttara-samyak-saṁbodhi. Therefore these two refuges are not the ultimate refuge, but a limited refuge.

"Suppose that a sentient being tamed by a Tathāgata takes refuge in Him and tastes the Dharma flavor. Faith and delight arising in his mind, he takes refuge in the Dharma and the Saṅgha. His two refuges are not merely these two refuges, but the refuge in a Tathāgata. Taking refuge in the highest sense [paramārtha] is taking refuge in a Tathāgata. The two refuges in the highest sense are the ultimate refuge in a Tathāgata. Why? Because a Tathāgata is no different from the two refuges. The refuge in a Tathāgata is the Three Refuges.

"How is the path of the One Vehicle revealed? A Tathāgata, who has acquired the Four Fearlessnesses, reveals it in a lion's roar. If a Tathāgata gives provisional teachings by skillful means according to sentient beings' desires, they are in essence Mahāyāna teachings. There are no Three Vehicles because they are encompassed in the One Vehicle.[27] The One Vehicle is the vehicle in the highest sense.

Chapter 6 – The Boundless Holy Truth

"World-Honored One, when a voice-hearer or Pratyekabuddha first observes the holy truth, he does not use only one kind of wisdom-knowledge to end his four ground-abiding afflictions by meeting the four conditions[28]—knowing the suffering of repeated birth and death, completing his virtuous training on the path, ending his accumulation of afflictions, and attaining nirvāṇa to end all his suffering—although he knows well their meaning. World-Honored One, he does not have the highest supra-worldly wisdom-knowledge. While his four kinds of wisdom-knowledge come gradually as he gradually meets the four conditions, a Tathāgata's highest supra-worldly wisdom-knowledge comes immediately, not gradually.

"World-Honored One, the wisdom-knowledge of the highest truth is likened to vajra [an adamantine substance]. It is not the initial wisdom-knowledge of the holy truth acquired by a voice-hearer or Pratyekabuddha, who cannot end his ground-abiding ignorance. World-Honored One, only a Tathāgata's wisdom-knowledge of the non-dual holy truth can end all His ground-abiding afflictions. World-Honored One, a Tathāgata, Arhat, Samyak-Saṁbuddha, whose state is not that of a voice-hearer or Pratyekabuddha, uses His inconceivable wisdom-knowledge of the emptiness of dharmas to destroy His store of all afflictions. World-Honored One, the ultimate wisdom-knowledge that destroys one's store of all afflictions is called the wisdom-knowledge of the highest truth. The initial wisdom-knowledge of the holy truth is not the ultimate wisdom-knowledge, but is the wisdom-knowledge that leads to anuttara-samyak-saṁbodhi.

"World-Honored One, what is meant by holy? It does not describe a voice-hearer or Pratyekabuddha, though he is called a holy being, because of the measurable and meager virtue [of his attainment]. The holy truth is not the truth realized by a voice-hearer or Pratyekabuddha, nor is it founded on the meager virtue [of his attainment].[29] World-Honored One, the holy truth is first realized by a Tathāgata, Arhat, Samyak-Saṁbuddha, and then He reveals it to a world shrouded in the store of ignorance. That is why it is called the holy truth.

The Tathāgata Store

"The holy truth reveals the profound meaning of dharmas, which is subtle, hard to know, and beyond the thinking mind. Only a wise man [a Buddha] knows it, and the whole world cannot believe it. Why? Because it reveals the profound Tathāgata store [tathāgata-garbha]. The Tathāgata store is a Tathāgata's state, unknown to any voice-hearer or Pratyekabuddha. The Tathāgata store reveals the meaning of the holy truth. Because the Tathāgata store is profound, the holy truth revealed is also profound, subtle, hard to know, and beyond the thinking mind. Although a wise man knows it, the whole world cannot believe it.

A Tathāgata's Dharma Body

"If one has no doubts about the Tathāgata store being sheathed in one's store of immeasurable afflictions, one will have no doubts about a Tathāgata's dharma body leaving behind one's store of immeasurable afflictions [when one realizes that they are empty]. If one has no doubts about one's Tathāgata store, a Tathāgata's dharma body, a Buddha's inconceivable state, and a Buddha's provisional teachings by skillful means, one will believe in and understand the two ways to realize the holy truth, which are hard to know and hard to understand. What are these two? They are (1) through an undertaking and (2) not through an undertaking.

"The holy truth realized through an undertaking reveals the measurable meaning of the Four Noble Truths. Why? Because one relies on another [a Buddha] and fails to (1) know all suffering, (2) end all one's accumulations of afflictions, (3) end all one's suffering upon attaining nirvāṇa, and (4) complete one's training on all paths. One does not know that there are saṁskṛta birth and death versus asaṁskṛta birth and death, nor that there is nirvāṇa with remnants versus nirvāṇa without remnants.[30]

"The holy truth realized not through an undertaking reveals the immeasurable meaning of the Four Noble Truths. Why? Because one uses one's own power [as does a Buddha] to (1) know all suffering, (2) end of all one's accumulations of afflictions, (3) end all one's suffering upon attaining nirvāṇa, and (4) complete one's training on all paths.

"Of these two ways to realize the Four Noble Truths, a Tathāgata reveals only the first way because only a Tathāgata, Arhat, Samyak-Saṁbuddha, can fully verify the Four Noble Truths not through an undertaking, which is beyond the ability of an Arhat or a Pratyekabuddha. Why? Because nirvāṇa is not attained gradually through practicing low, middle, and high dharmas. Why? Because a Tathāgata, Arhat, Samyak-Saṁbuddha, fully verifies the meaning of the Four Noble Truth not through an undertaking. He fully knows all future suffering, ends all His accumulations of afflictions and their ensuing afflictions, eliminates all His mind-created bodies [because He has ended His changeable birth and death], and ends all His suffering upon attaining nirvāṇa.

"World-Honored One, cessation of one's suffering upon attaining nirvāṇa does not destroy anything, but reveals one's ever-abiding inherent pure nature [Buddha nature], which has no beginning, no action, no arising, no end, and no expiring, and is apart from one's store of all afflictions. World-Honored One, what is not separate, detached, or different from the inconceivable Buddha Dharma [with teachings] more numerous than the sands of the Ganges is called a Tathāgata's dharma body. World-Honored One, when a Tathāgata's dharma body is not free from one's store of afflictions, it is called the Tathāgata store.

A Limited Understanding of Emptiness Conceals the Truth

"World-Honored One, the wisdom-knowledge of the Tathāgata store is a Tathāgata's wisdom-knowledge of the emptiness of dharmas. World-Honored One, no Arhat, Pratyekabuddha, or holy Bodhisattva has ever seen his Tathāgata store or realized that he possesses it.

"World-Honored One, there are two kinds of wisdom-knowledge of the emptiness of one's Tathāgata store. The first kind is the wisdom-knowledge of the empty Tathāgata store, which is separate, detached, or different from one's store of all afflictions. The second kind is the wisdom-knowledge of the not-empty Tathāgata store, which is not separate, detached, or different from the inconceivable Buddha Dharma [with teachings] more numerous than the sands of the Ganges.

"World-Honored One, only great Arhats can believe in a Tathāgata's teachings on these two kinds of wisdom-knowledge of the emptiness of one's Tathāgata store. For all Arhats and Pratyekabuddhas, their wisdom-knowledge of emptiness revolves around the four inverted views.[31] Therefore, they have never known or realized [that they possess the Tathāgata store]. Only a Buddha has verified the cessation of all His suffering, destroyed His store of all afflictions, and completed His training on all paths to end all His suffering.

One of the Four Noble Truths Is the One Truth and the One Reliance

"World-Honored One, of the Four Noble Truths, three are impermanent, and one is permanent. Why? Because three noble truths have the appearances of a saṁskṛta dharma,[32] and anything with the appearances of a saṁskṛta dharma is impermanent. Impermanent dharmas are destructible, not a place of refuge. Therefore, the three noble truths—suffering, accumulation of afflictions, and the path—are not the highest truth, because they are impermanent and are not a place of refuge.

"The noble truth of cessation of one's suffering upon attaining nirvāṇa is free from the appearances of a saṁskṛta dharma, and anything free from the appearances of a saṁskṛta dharma is permanent. A permanent dharma is indestructible. This noble truth is permanent and a place of refuge. Therefore, it is the highest truth to rely on.

Wrong Views Invert the Truth

"The noble truth of cessation of one's suffering upon attaining nirvāṇa is inconceivable, beyond the capacity of all sentient beings' minds and beyond the wisdom of all Arhats and Pratyekabuddhas. As an analogy, the born-blind cannot see sights, and a seven-day-old infant cannot see the sun. Likewise the noble truth of cessation of one's suffering upon attaining nirvāṇa is not an object in an ordinary being's mind, nor is it an item in the wisdom-knowledge of riders of the Two Vehicles. An ordinary being's consciousness is dictated by two opposite views, while the [limited] wisdom-knowledge of all Arhats and Pratyekabuddhas is pure.

"An ordinary being holds the wrong view that there is a self [ātman] in the five aggregates that constitute a sentient being and, from that view, derives two opposite views, perpetuity and cessation. When he sees that all processes are impermanent, he holds the view of cessation [uccheda-dṛṣṭi], which is not the right view. When he seeks nirvāṇa, he holds the view of perpetuity [śāśvata-dṛṣṭi], which is not the right view. These two opposite views arise from deluded thinking. When he sees that the faculties of the body presently expire, he does not know that it will be succeeded by a new body [at rebirth]. His view of cessation is based on deluded perception. When he sees that his thinking continues, he does not know that each thought instantly expires. His view of perpetuity is based on deluded perception. Following deluded perception, he cannot see the truth because he shuttles between this view of perpetuity and that view of cessation, according to his differentiation. Thus a deluded sentient being entertains four inverted perceptions of the five aggregates, taking impermanence as permanence, suffering as joy, a nonexistent self as a self, and impurity as purity. The pure wisdom-knowledge of all Arhats and Pratyekabuddhas has never known a Tathāgata's wisdom state or dharma body.

"If a sentient being, because of his belief in a Buddha's words, perceives a Tathāgata as eternity, bliss, a [true] self, and purity,[33] this is not an inverted view, but the right view. Why? Because a Tathāgata's dharma body is the eternity pāramitā, the bliss pāramitā, the true-self pāramitā, and the purity pāramitā.[34] This view of a Buddha's dharma body is the right view. Whoever holds the right view is a Buddha's true son, born from His mouth [i.e., from hearing the Dharma], from pondering the Dharma, and from being transformed by the Dharma, who will acquire the remaining wealth of the Dharma.

"World-Honored One, what is meant by pure wisdom-knowledge? It is the wisdom-knowledge pāramitā [jñāna-pāramitā] of all Arhats and Pratyekabuddhas. However, their wisdom-knowledge, though called pure wisdom-knowledge, cannot know the true meaning of the noble truth of cessation of one's suffering upon attaining nirvāṇa,[35] much less can his four kinds of wisdom-knowledge that depend on [receiving teachings on] the Four Noble Truths. Why? Because if novice riders of the Three Vehicles were not ignorant of the Dharma, they would realize and acquire the true meaning of this noble truth. Therefore, the World-Honored One has expounded the Four Noble Truths for them to rely on. However, the Four Noble Truths [at their level] are worldly dharmas. The one reliance for all, the supreme supra-worldly reliance in the highest sense, is the noble truth of cessation of one's suffering upon attaining nirvāṇa.

One's Tathāgata Store and Inherent Pure Nature

"World-Honored One, one's birth and death depend on one's Tathāgata store, but the beginning of one's Tathāgata store is unknowable. World-Honored One, saying that one has birth and death because of one's Tathāgata store is a good explanation. World-Honored One, birth and death mean that one's faculties expire and one's new faculties have not arisen. World-Honored One, one's birth and death depend on one's Tathāgata store. According to worldly descriptions of death and rebirth, death means the expiring of one's old faculties; rebirth means the arising of one's new faculties. However, one's Tathāgata store has neither birth nor death. It does not have the appearances of a saṁskṛta dharma, and is ever abiding and changeless. Therefore, dharmas depend on the Tathāgata store to establish themselves, and are sustained by it. Not only the inconceivable Buddha Dharma, which is not separate, detached, split, or different from the wisdom-knowledge of liberation, depends on the Tathāgata store to establish itself, but all saṁskṛta dharmas, which are separate, detached, split, and different from the wisdom-knowledge of liberation, depend the Tathāgata store to establish themselves.

"World-Honored One, without one's Tathāgata store, one cannot come to tire of suffering and to delight in seeking nirvāṇa. Why not? Because, World-Honored One, one's seven dharmas—one's first six consciousnesses and their perceptions[36]—neither abide for a single moment nor retain one's experience of suffering. Then one cannot come to tire of suffering and to delight in seeking nirvāṇa. World-Honored One, one's Tathāgata store has no beginning, neither arising nor expiring, but retains one's experience of suffering.[37] Then one can come to tire of suffering and to delight in seeking nirvāṇa.

"One's Tathāgata store is not a self, not a person, not a sentient being, and not an everlasting soul.[38] It is incomprehensible to those who hold the wrong view that one has a self, those who hold inverted views, and those who misunderstand the emptiness of dharmas.

"World-Honored One, one's Tathāgata store is the store of the dharma realm [dharma-dhātu], the store of the dharma body, the supreme store of supra-worldly dharmas, and the store of one's inherent pure nature [Buddha nature]. How one's Tathāgata store, the store of one's inherent pure nature, is tainted by one's visitor-like afflictions [āgantuka kleśa][39] and their ensuing afflictions can be known only through a Tathāgata's inconceivable wisdom. Why? Because one's good or evil mind arising from moment to moment is not tainted by one's afflictions. One's afflictions do not touch one's mind, and one's mind does not touch one's afflictions. Then how can one's mind be tainted without touching anything? Yet, World-Honored One, one has afflictions, and one's mind is tainted by afflictions. It is hard to know why one's inherent pure mind can be tainted. Only a Buddha-Bhagavān, who has the true eye and true wisdom-knowledge, is the root and the reliance of the true Dharma, and has a full understanding of the Dharma, can truly know it."

After Śrīmālā raised this hard-to-answer question, the Buddha expressed His sympathetic joy, saying, "Indeed, indeed! The reason why one's inherent pure mind is tainted is hard to know. There are two things that are hard to know: (1) one's inherent pure mind and (2) its being tainted by afflictions. Only you and Bodhisattva-Mahāsattvas with great attainments can hear and accept these two hard-to-know things. Voice-hearers can only believe in a Buddha's words.

A Buddha's True Son

"If a disciple of mine follows his growing faith, he can rely on his right faith to follow the dharma wisdom-knowledge[40] to master it. Following the dharma wisdom-knowledge means that he makes five observations, which are observations of (1) his sense faculties, sense consciousnesses, and sense objects, (2) his karmic requitals, (3) an Arhat's lurking afflictions,[41] (4) the joy of his unconstrained mind and the joy of his meditation, and (5) the transcendental powers of an Arhat, a Pratyekabuddha, and a holy Bodhisattva. He should become accomplished in these five skillful observations [to be called my true son].

"After I have entered parinirvāṇa, if my disciples in the future follow their growing faith and rely on their right faith to follow the dharma wisdom-knowledge, they will fully understand that an ordinary being's inherent pure mind is tainted by his afflictions. This full understanding will be the cause of their entering the path of the Mahāyāna. Believing in a Tathāgata brings such great benefits that they will not malign the profound meaning of the Dharma."

Śrīmālā's Lion's Roar

Then Śrīmālā said to the Buddha, "There are other great benefits. I would like to expound them through the Buddha's awesome spiritual power."

The Buddha said, "Speak."

Śrīmālā said, "There are three kinds of good men and women who will never malign the profound meaning of the Dharma and, with this great merit, will enter the path of the Mahāyāna. Who are these three? They are (1) those who acquire the profound dharma wisdom-knowledge on their own, (2) those who are accomplished in following the dharma wisdom-knowledge, and (3) those who do not know the profound Dharma but rely on a World-Honored One. It is not my place to know how they rely on a Tathāgata, because only the Buddha knows. Aside from these good men and women, for other sentient beings who, like rotten seeds, obstinately misinterpret the profound Dharma, go against the true Dharma, and follow the wrong paths, they should be tamed by the power of the king and Dharma protectors, such as gods, dragons, and ghosts."

Then Śrīmālā and her retinue prostrated themselves at the Buddha's feet. The Buddha said, "Very good, very good! You protect and safeguard the profound Dharma by skillful means, and appropriately subjugate its enemies. You can expound this meaning because you have stayed close to 100,000 koṭi Buddhas."

Then the World-Honored One emitted vast radiance that illuminated the multitude. He rose into the open sky to the height of seven tāla [palm] trees and walked across the open sky back to Śrāvastī.

Meanwhile Śrīmālā and her retinue joined their palms and insatiably gazed at the Buddha, without moving their eyes even temporarily, until He was out of their sight. Then they exuberantly rejoiced and praised the Tathāgata's virtues.

Intently thinking of the Buddha, they entered the city of Ayodhyā and persuaded King Mitrayaśas to establish the Mahāyāna. He used the Mahāyāna to transform, in his kingdom, men and women over seven years of age. All subjects in his kingdom turned toward the Mahāyāna.

Chapter 7 – Entrusting This Sūtra with Fifteen Names

At that time the World-Honored One returned to the Jetavana garden. He summoned the venerable Ānanda and thought of the god-king Śakra. In response to His thought, Śakra and his retinue immediately arrived and stood before the Buddha. Then the World-Honored One broadly expounded this sūtra to the venerable Ānanda and the god-king Śakra.

After He finished expounding it, He told Śakra, "You should accept, uphold, and read and recite this sūtra. Kauśika,[42] suppose that a good man or woman trains to attain bodhi and practices the six pāramitās for kalpas as numerous as the sands of the Ganges. Then suppose that a good man or woman hears, accepts, reads and recites, and upholds this sūtra. The merit acquired by the latter surpasses that of the former, not to mention that the latter widely expounds it to others. Therefore, Kauśika, you should read and recite this sūtra, and widely expound it to gods in your Thirty-three Heavens [Trayastriṁśa Heaven]."

Then He told Ānanda, "You too should accept, uphold, and read and recite this sūtra, and widely expound it to my four groups of disciples."

Then the god-king Śakra asked the Buddha, "World-Honored One, what is the name of this sūtra? How should we uphold it?"

The Buddha said to him, "This sūtra has immeasurable boundless virtues. No voice-hearer or Pratyekabuddha can fully observe, know, or see them. Kauśika, know that this sūtra is an aggregate of profound wondrous great virtues. I now will reveal some of its names. Hearken, hearken. Ponder them well."

The god-king Śakra and the venerable Ānanda said to the Buddha, "World-Honored One, we gladly accept your instruction."

The Buddha said, "This sūtra praises a Tathāgata's virtues in the highest sense. Accept and uphold it as such. It reveals accepting ten vast precepts. Accept and uphold it as such. It reveals a great vow that encompasses all vows. Accept and uphold it as such. It reveals accepting the inconceivable true Dharma. Accept and uphold it as such. It reveals the One Vehicle. Accept and uphold it as such. It reveals the boundless holy truth. Accept and uphold it as such. It reveals one's Tathāgata store. Accept and uphold it as such. It reveals a Tathāgata's dharma body. Accept and uphold it as such. It reveals that a limited understanding of the emptiness of dharmas conceals the truth. Accept and uphold it as such. It reveals the one noble truth. Accept and uphold it as such. It reveals the one ever-abiding secure reliance. Accept and uphold it as such. It reveals that wrong views invert the truth. Accept and uphold it as such. It reveals that one's inherent pure mind is concealed by one's afflictions. Accept and uphold it as such. It reveals a Tathāgata's true son. Accept and uphold it as such. It reveals Queen Śrīmālā's lion's roar. Accept and uphold it as such.

"Moreover, Kauśika, the teachings in this sūtra end all doubts and reveal the definitive meaning of entering the path of the One Vehicle. Kauśika, I now entrust you with this *Sūtra of Queen Śrīmālā's Lion's Roar*. You should accept, uphold, and read and recite it as long as the Dharma abides in the world."

The god-king Śakra said to the Buddha, "Very good, World-Honored One, I accept your instruction with the highest reverence."

Then the god-king Śakra, the venerable Ānanda, and all others in this huge assembly, such as gods, humans, asuras, gandharvas, having heard the Buddha's words, rejoiced and carried out His teachings.

Notes

1. Queen Mallikā was from Kapilavastu, the city in which the Śākya clan resided. After her father died, she became a maid in Mahānāma's household, in Śrāvastī. She tended a mallikā (jasmine) garden and made garlands. Hence she was called Mallikā. When King Prasenajit, returning from a hunting trip, stopped by the garden, she led him to shade, prepared his seat, and served him attentively. The king married her, and she became his foremost wife. They had a daughter named Śrīmālā and a son named Virūḍhaka. Pincess Śrīmālā married Mitrayaśas, king of Ayodhyā, and propagated the Dharma. When Prince Virūḍhaka was eight, he and five hundred youths went to Kapilavastu to learn archery. At that time the Śākya clan built a new lecture hall for the Buddha. When Virūḍhaka entered it, he was driven away because he was the son of a maid. After King Prasenajit died, Virūḍhaka and his army massacred the Śākya clan. As predicted by the Buddha, seven days later he and his army rested by a river and were killed by a flood in a windstorm. Then he fell into Avīci Hell (Buddha's Light Dictionary 1988, 3853).

2. According to text 310, fascicle 119, sūtra 48, which is another Chinese version of this sūtra, she says, "I should bestow a robe upon you" (T11n0310, 0672c27). Text 310 in 120 fascicles is the Chinese version of the *Great Treasure Pile Sūtra* (Mahā-ratnakūṭa-sūtra), which comprises forty-nine sūtras, translated from Sanskrit by several translators in a long period from the Cao Wei Dynasty (220–265) through the Tang Dynasty (618–907). Of these forty-nine sūtras, twenty-six sūtras in 39 fascicles, including sūtra 48 in fascicle 119, were translated in the Tang Dynasty by Bodhiruci (菩提流志, 562–727) from central India.

3. The three faults of one's mind are greed, anger, and the wrong views. The four faults of one's body are killing, stealing, sexual misconduct, and false speech. See "ten evil karmas" in the glossary.

4. This paragraph is based on text 310, fascicle 119, sūtra 48 (T11n0310, 0673a19–20).

5. See "ten evil karmas" in the glossary.

6. See "six pāramitās" and "ten pāramitās" in the glossary.

7. These ten precepts are examples of Bodhisattva precepts in the three clusters. The first five precepts belong in the cluster of exercising self-restraint. The next four precepts belong in the cluster of benefiting sentient beings. The last belongs in the cluster of doing good dharmas. See "Bodhisattva precepts" in the glossary.

8. A Bodhisattva benefits sentient beings without being asked.

9. For "all studies," See "five studies" in the glossary.

10. In a preceding passage, Śrīmālā says that the action of accepting the true Dharma is no different from the true Dharma. Here, she says that the action of accepting the true Dharma is no different from the person who accepts the true Dharma. Therefore, she is revealing the truth that subject, object, and action are equal in their emptiness.

11. See "dharma body" defined in the glossary's "three bodies of a Buddha."

12. Lake Anavatapta (Heatless) and its four major rivers are described in fascicle 42 of text 279, the 80-fascicle Chinese version of the *Mahāvaipulya Sūtra*

of Buddha Adornment (Buddhāvataṁsaka-mahāvaipulya-sūtra). The English translation of this fascicle appears in *Two Holy Grounds* (Rulu 2014, 61–74). Here, the eight rivers issuing from this lake probably include four tributaries of some of the four major rivers.

13. See Vinaya in the glossary's "Tripiṭaka."

14. Text 353 uses the word "parinirvāṇa," while the corresponding word in text 310, fascicle 119, sūtra 48, is "nirvāṇa" (T11n0310, 0675a29–b1). Here, the latter is followed because a Buddha enters parinirvāṇa at death.

15. An Arhat has acquired four kinds of wisdom-knowledge, which are the wisdom-knowledge of (1) the end of his accumulation of afflictions, (2) the completion of his virtuous training on the path, (3) the cessation of his suffering upon attaining nirvāṇa, and (4) all his suffering through repeated birth and death. Hence he declares, "My rebirth is ended; my Brahma way of life is established; my undertaking is accomplished; I will not undergo a subsequent existence." See Four Noble Truths in the glossary.

16. A holy Bodhisattva is a Bodhisattva on the first Bodhisattva ground or above. See "stages of the Bodhisattva Way" in the glossary.

17. According to the definitions of "nirvāṇa" in the glossary, "nirvāṇa with remnants" means that an Arhat or a Pratyekabuddha, who has attained nirvāṇa, is still living in his body, the remnants of his karmic existence. Here, "nirvāṇa with remnants" means that his nirvāṇa is imperfect, whether he is still living in or has abandoned his body.

18. Voice-hearers in the first seven ranks are still learning (śaikṣa, 有學). See "eight holy ranks" defined in the glossary's "voice-hearer fruits."

19. Of the four ground-abiding afflictions, ground-abiding views are also called view confusions (見惑), which are ended at once when one sees bodhi, i.e., when a voice-hearer achieves the first fruit or a Bodhisattva enters the first Bodhisattva ground. The other three ground-abiding afflictions are also called thinking confusions (思惑), which are ended gradually through spiritual training. Ground-abiding love of desire pertains to love of sense objects in the desire realm; ground-abiding love of form pertains to love of one's body in the form realm; ground-abiding love of being pertains to love of one's existence in the formless realm.

20. Ground-abiding ignorance is the fifth ground-abiding affliction, the root of all afflictions.

21. Ground-abiding ignorance is the hindrance to wisdom-knowledge (jñeyāvaraṇa, 智障), and the four ground-abiding afflictions are the affliction hindrances (kleśāvaraṇa, 煩惱障). See "two kinds of hindrances" in the glossary.

22. Grasping [upādāna, 取] desire objects is the ninth of the glossary's Twelve Links of Dependent Arising, which generates the karmic force for being. In other contexts, *upādāna* means acceptance of worldly views, useless precepts, or theories that claim that one has an autonomous self.

23. According to fascicle 3 of text 670, the 4-fascicle Chinese version of the *Laṅkāvatāra Sūtra,* the three kinds of mind-created body (manomaya-kāya, 意生身) are (1) a body that arises from the joy of samādhi and samāpatti, (2) a body that arises from the realization of the illusory nature of dharmas and enters all Buddha Lands at will, and (3) a body that arises from the realization that all doctrines are the Buddha Dharma and instantly manifests, without action,

countless bodies of various kinds (T16n0670, 0497c20–22). A Bodhisattva on any of first five Bodhisattva grounds can create the first kind of body; a Bodhisattva on any of the next three grounds can create the second kind of body; a Bodhisattva on the ninth ground or above can create the third kind of body.

24. Here, "all one's ground-abiding afflictions" means one's five ground-abiding afflictions, i.e., one's ground-abiding ignorance and four ground-abiding afflictions.

25. One can interpret that this ground is the Cause Ground on which he activated the bodhi mind under past Buddhas. It implies that he has encountered Mahāyāna teachings and hence is not ignorant of the Dharma. However, the corresponding passage in text 310, fascicle 119, sūtra 48, states otherwise. It states, "As he observes his freedom from a subsequent existence, he does not attain the nirvāṇa ground, the foremost reviving rest place, because he has not encountered the Dharma to reach the ground he has not reached" (T11n0310, 0676b3–4). This statement implies that he has not encountered Mahāyāna teachings.

26. As stated in text 235, one of the six Chinese versions of the *Diamond Sūtra,* following the Dharma and training accordingly are like paddling a raft to cross the ocean of suffering to the shore of enlightenment. Upon arrival, the raft should be discarded (T08n0235, 0749b10–11).

27. In the *Lotus Sūtra,* fascicle 2, chapter 3, the Buddha likens the Voice-Hearer Vehicle, the Pratyekabuddha Vehicle, and the Mahāyāna respectively to a goat carriage, a deer carriage, and an ox carriage, all of which are then replaced by the One Vehicle, likened to a great jeweled carriage drawn by a giant white ox (T09n0262, 0012c16–24).

28. Text 353 states that he uses only one kind of wisdom-knowledge to end his four ground-abiding afflictions by meeting the four conditions. However, the corresponding passage in text 310, fascicle 119, sūtra 48, states that he does not use only one kind of wisdom-knowledge to end his four ground-abiding afflictions by meeting the four conditions (T11n0310, 0676c4–5). Here, the latter is followed because the last sentence of this paragraph states that he gradually acquires the four kinds of wisdom-knowledge, which are described in note 15.

29. The virtue of an Arhat's or a Pratyekabuddha's attainment is ending his karmic birth and death and acquiring certain wisdom-knowledge. See "ten kinds of wisdom-knowledge" in the glossary.

30. Saṁskṛta birth and death mean karmic birth and death, and asaṁskṛta birth and death mean changeable birth and death. An Arhat or a Pratyekabuddha has ended his saṁskṛta birth and death, not knowing that his asaṁskṛta birth and death remain. He has attained nirvāṇa with remnants, which is imperfect, not knowing that there is nirvāṇa without remnants, which is perfect. Although an earlier passage states that changeable birth and death have ground-abiding ignorance as their condition, and affliction-free karmas as their cause, they are free from affliction-driven karmas, hence they are called asaṁskṛta birth and death.

31. An Arhat's or a Pratyekabuddha's wisdom-knowledge of the emptiness of dharmas arises from his observation of impermanence, suffering, the nonexistence of a self in a person, and impurity. He does not have the wisdom-knowledge of the Tathāgata store, and can hold inverted views, taking (1) the eternity of a Tathāgata as impermanence, (2) the bliss of a Tathāgata as

suffering, (3) the true self, which symbolizes a Tathāgata, as no self, and (4) the purity of a Tathāgata as impurity. See "inversion" in the glossary.

32. A saṁskṛta dharma is anything subject to causes and conditions. Its appearances are arising, continuing, changing, and ending. See "four appearances" in the glossary.

33. The four virtues of a Tathāgata's dharma body are (1) eternity, (2) bliss, (3) a [true] self, and (4) purity. In fascicle 30 of text 374, the 40-fascicle Chinese version of the *Mahāparinirvāṇa Sūtra,* the Buddha says, "Speaking of a self, it must be a Tathāgata. Why? Because His body is boundless, without doubts. He is eternity because He neither does nor experiences anything. He is bliss because He has neither birth nor death. He is purity because He has no afflictions. He is emptiness because He does not have the ten appearances. Therefore, a Tathāgata is eternity, bliss, a [true] self, and purity, free from appearances" (T12n0374, 0544c15–19). In different fascicles of text 374, these four virtues variously belong to nirvāṇa, Buddha nature, a Tathāgata, or His dharma body.

34. The Sanskrit word *pāramitā* means gone across to that shore of bodhi (enlightenment), opposite this shore of birth and death. It also means transcendental virtue. One's ultimate destination is the realization of a Tathāgata's dharma body, with the four pāramitās (four virtues). They are mentioned in text 277, the Chinese version of the *Sūtra of the Dharma Procedure to Visualize Samantabhadra Bodhisattva,* in another way: "Śākyamuni Buddha is called Vairocana, who is everywhere, and whose abode is called eternal silent radiance. It is formed by the eternity pāramitā and established by the true-self pāramitā; it is where the purity pāramitā ends all appearances of existence, and where the bliss pāramitā never abides in the appearances of one's body and mind" (T09n0277, 0392c15–19).

35. The true meaning of the noble truth of cessation of one's suffering upon attaining nirvāṇa is that a Tathāgata, or a Tathāgata's dharma body, is revealed.

36. See "twelve fields" in the glossary.

37. According to the Consciousness-Only School, ālaya consciousness (ālaya-vijñāna), the storehouse consciousness, one's eighth consciousness, stores all pure, impure, and neutral seeds of one's experience without a beginning. Here, this sentence implicitly equates the Tathāgata store to ālaya consciousness.

38. See a sentient being's four self-images in the glossary's "four appearances."

39. The literal translation of the Sanskrit term "āgantuka kleśa" is adventitious afflictions, which is widely used by scholars. However, adventitious means coming from outside or occurring by chance. As explained in chapter 5 of this sūtra, underlying one's ground-abiding afflictions and their ensuring afflictions is one's root affliction, one's ground-abiding ignorance. Therefore, there is nothing external or accidental about one's afflictions, though they are illusory. Here, this term is translated from Chinese as visitor-like afflictions. In text 844 in the Extension of the Chinese Canon (the Shinsan Zokuzōkyō), Kuiji (窺基, 632–82), the first patriarch of the Consciousness-Only School of China, gave an explanation. To the question of why one's afflictions are called visitors if one's inherent pure mind has always been tainted by one's afflictions, Kuiji answered, "As one trains to attain bodhi, one's afflictions end but one's pure nature remains. That is why one's afflictions are called visitors" (X53n0844, 0860c10–12). Therefore, one's afflictions are visitor-like only to the

extent that they can be removed through spiritual training and awakening, like visitors being removed.

40. Dharma wisdom-knowledge (dharma-jñāna, 法智) is an Arhat's wisdom-knowledge that accords with the Four Noble Truths and ends his desire-realm afflictions. It is one of the glossary's "ten kinds of wisdom-knowledge."

41. "An Arhat's lurking afflictions" refers to his ground-abiding ignorance and subtle afflictions.

42. Kauśika is the god-king Śakra's family name. See Śakro-Devānām-Indra in the glossary.

About Sūtra 4

There are ten Chinese texts of the *Sūtra of Aṅgulimālika,* which are listed under the next section as texts A1–A10. The first text (A1) is in the Majjhima Nikāya (Middle-Length Discourses) in the 70-volume Chinese version of the Pāli Canon (漢譯南傳大藏經), the whole of which was translated from its Japanese version between 1990 and 1998 by a team of translators commissioned by the Yuanheng Temple (元亨寺), in Kaohsiung, Taiwan. The next six texts (A2–A7) are in the Āgamas[1] section of the Chinese Canon (Taishō Tripiṭaka). The last three texts (A8–A10) are in the Past Causes section of the Chinese Canon. While text A6 is a Mahāyāna sūtra, the other nine texts are Hīnayāna sūtras. Of these ten texts, text A1 is well known in Southeast Asia, and text A6 is the popular text in China. Also, in the Tibetan Canon there exists a text comparable to text A6.

Text A6 includes not only the story of Aṅgulimāla but also teachings on the Tathagata store, while the other nine texts include only the story of Aṅgulimāla. Because his story is given in all ten texts, each version is described below for comparison. The teachings in text A6 in 4 fascicles are then summarized.

The Story of Aṅgulimāla in Ten Chinese Texts

(A1) The 86th sūtra in volume 11 of the Majjhima Nikāya (N11n0005)

The Majjhima Nikāya is the fifth of thirty-eight collections of texts in the Chinese version of the Pāli Canon. This Nikāya in volumes 9–12 was translated from its Japanese version between 1990 and 1998 by Tongmiao (通妙, 1930–) when he was a monk at the Yuanheng Temple, who now teaches and writes as a layman under his secular name Wu Laoze (吳老擇).

In text A1, Aṅgulimāla is an atrocious bandit in the kingdom of Kauśala, who kills people and wears a garland made of their fingers. Against the admonition of cowherds, the Buddha walks toward Aṅgulimāla. When the Buddha walks away, Aṅgulimāla chases the Buddha but cannot catch up with Him. The Buddha gives him teachings, and he becomes a monk as soon as the Buddha says, "Come, bhikṣu."

Determined to eliminate Aṅgulimāla, King Prasenajit takes five hundred horsemen to visit the Buddha. When the Buddha points out Aṅgulimāla to him, the king is terrified. He asks Aṅgulimāla about his parents, and Aṅgulimāla answers that his father is Garga and his mother is Maitrāyaṇī. Seeing that Aṅgulimāla is now a noble monk, the king offers to give him, as alms, clothing, food, bedding, and medicine, but Aṅgulimāla says he is content with a monk's three robes. Then the king praises the Buddha and departs.

One day Aṅgulimāla enters the city of Śrāvastī to beg for food and sees a woman in obstructed labor. Following the Buddha's instruction, he says to the woman, "Since my noble birth as a monk, I have never intentionally taken any life. If my words are truthful, you will have a safe childbirth." Forthwith the woman safely gives birth to her child. Then Aṅgulimāla trains diligently and becomes an Arhat. One day he enters Śrāvastī to beg for food, and is stoned, clubbed, and stabbed by townspeople. Maimed and bleeding, he goes to the Buddha. The Buddha tells him to endure his pain because he has just received the requital for his evil karma, though this requital could have been suffering in hell for years, hundreds of years, or thousands of years. In his concluding verses, Aṅgulimāla says that although he killed many people before, he now never harms anyone, so Ahiṁsaka (Harmless) is his true name.

Aṅgulimāla's chasing the Buddha and receiving His teachings and his becoming a monk, then an Arhat, are covered in all ten texts. King Prasenajit's paying respects to him is covered in texts A1, A5, A6, A7, A8, and A9. His speaking truthful words to a woman in obstructed labor to bring about a safe childbirth is covered in texts A1, A4, A5, A7, and A8. His enduring his karmic requital of being stoned, clubbed, and stabbed is covered in texts A1, A4, A5, A7, and A10.

The original Pāli version of text A1 has been translated from Pāli into English. For example, Bikkhu Thanissaro's English translation (2003) and Hellmuth Hecker's English translation (2013) can be found on the Internet.

(A2) The 1077th sūtra in fascicle 38 of text 99 (T02n0099)

Text 99 in 50 fascicles is the Chinese version of the Saṁyukta Āgama (Connected Discourses), translated from Sanskrit in the Liu Song Dynasty (420–79) by Guṇabhadra (求那跋陀羅, 394–468) from central India.

Text A2 is very short. It covers only Aṅgulimāla's chasing the Buddha, receiving His teachings, and becoming a monk, then an Arhat. In his concluding verses, Aṅgulimāla says that although his given name is Ahiṁsaka, he killed innumerable people, and that he is now called Satya (Truth) and never harms anyone. These words appear in texts A2, A3, and A7.

(A3) The 16th sūtra in fascicle 1 of text 100 (T02n0100)

Text 100 in 16 fascicles is the Chinese version of a partial Saṁyukta Āgama, translated from Sanskrit by an unknown person. Scholars conjecture that it was translated earlier than was text 99.

Text A3 is as short as text A2, and their contents are virtually the same.

(A4) Text 118 (T02n0118)

Text 118 in one fascicle was translated from Sanskrit in the Western Jin Dynasty (265–316) by Dharmarakṣa (竺法護, dates unknown) from Dunhuang (敦煌, a major stop on the ancient Silk Road, in present-day Gansu Province, China), who arrived in China in 265.

In text A4, Aṅgulimāla is the foremost student of a Brahmin teacher in Śrāvastī. When his teacher is away, his teacher's wife tries to seduce him, but he rejects her. Then she lies to her husband that Aṅgulimāla tried to ravage her. Enraged, Aṅgulimāla's teacher gives him a sword and tells him that, to complete his training, he must kill at crossroads a hundred people and take a finger from each victim to make a garland. Then Aṅgulimāla kills ninety-nine people, short of a hundred by only one.

When Aṅgulimāla's mother goes to him to bring him food, Aṅgulimāla intends to kill her to make his quota. Then the Buddha walks toward Aṅgulimāla, diverting him from matricide. Aṅgulimāla chases the Buddha, who walks slowly, but cannot catch up with Him. The rest of the story in text A4 is the same as that in text A1.

His teacher's wife trying to seduce him and his rejecting her are covered in texts A4, A6, A8, A9, and A10. In texts A4 and A8, his teacher tells him to kill a hundred people, while in texts A6, A7, A9, and A10, his teacher tells him to kill a thousand people. His intending to kill his mother when she is bringing him food is covered in texts A4, A6, A7, A8, A9, and A10.

(A5) Text 119 (T02n0119)

Text 119 in one fascicle was translated from Sanskrit in the Western Jin Dynasty by Fajü (法炬, dates unknown) from Kucha (龜茲, or 庫車, in present-day Aksu Prefecture, Xinjiang, China).

The story of Aṅgulimāla in text A5 is similar to that in text A1. In text A1, Aṅgulimāla says that his father's name is Garga, while in text A5, he says that his own name is Garga. Text A7 clarifies that Garga is his family name.

(A6) Text 120 (T02n0120)

Text 120 in 4 fascicles was translated from Sanskrit in the in the Liu Song Dynasty (420–79) by Guṇabhadra (求那跋陀羅, 394–468) from central India. While the other nine texts are Hīnayāna sūtras, text A6 is a Mahāyāna sūtra. However, it is classified under the Āgamas section of the Chinese Canon to be with texts A2, A3, A4, A5, and A7, because they bear the same title.

The story of Aṅgulimāla in fascicle 1 of text A6 is similar to that in text A4, but omits his speaking truthful words to a woman in obstructed labor and his enduring his karmic requital of being stoned, clubbed, and stabbed. Teachings on the Tathāgata store (tathāgata-garbha) are given in fascicles 2, 3, and 4. In text A6, Aṅgulimāla's given name is World Appearance, not Ahiṁsaka as in texts A2, A3, and A7. Moreover, his mother's name is Bhadrā, not Maitrāyaṇī as in text A1.

(A7) The sixth sūtra in chapter 38 of fascicle 31 of text 125 (T02n0125)

Text 125 in 51 fascicles is the Chinese version of the Ekottarika Āgama (Numbered Discourses), translated from Sanskrit in the Eastern Jin Dynasty (317–420) by Gautama Saṅghadeva (瞿曇僧伽提婆, dates unknown) from Kophen (罽賓, an ancient kingdom, also called Gandhāra, in present-day Kashmir, northern Pakistan, and eastern Afghanistan area), who arrived in China in 383. It is possible that his contemporaries Dharmanandi (曇摩難提, dates unknown) and Zhu Fonian (竺佛念, dates unknown) were also involved in the translation.

The story of Aṅgulimāla in text A7 is similar to that in text A4, but omits his teacher's wife trying to seduce him and his rejecting her.

In text A7, the Buddha tells a story of a past life of Aṅgulimāla, which is also covered in texts A8 and A9. In this story, long before this Worthy Kalpa, there was a king called Great Fruit. He named his son Great Strength and expected him to enjoy the five desires. At twenty the crown prince refused to marry, so the king renamed him Purity. When Prince Purity approached thirty, the king made an announcement that he would reward with gold and treasures whoever could make the prince enjoy the five desires. Then a prostitute took up the task. She kept weeping outside the prince's bedchamber at night. When the prince asked why she was weeping, she answered that she was weak and fearful. The prince told her to sleep in his bed to become fearless. Then she undressed, and the prince succumbed to his desire.

When the king saw the prince next morning, he was delighted, and granted the prince's request that every maiden in the kingdom must come to his bed before her wedding night. Then people in the city took up arms to see the king. They said to the king, "If you wish to live, we will kill your son. If your son wishes to live, we will kill you. We cannot serve Prince Purity because he dishonors the law." They bound Prince Purity's hands and stoned him to death. Before dying, the prince said, "My father lets these people unjustly kill me, and I will not evade it. However, I vow that I will revenge this vendetta, and encounter a true Arhat to achieve liberation."

Then the Buddha reveals that King Great Fruit is none other than Aṅgulimāla's teacher, that the prostitute is none other than his teacher's wife, that those who killed Prince Purity are none other than those whom Aṅgulimāla has killed in his present life, and that Prince Purity is none other than Aṅgulimāla. Because of Prince Purity's vow of vengeance, Aṅgulimāla has killed innumerable people. Because of Prince Purity's vow to encounter a true Arhat, Aṅgulimāla has encountered the Buddha, become an Arhat, and achieved liberation.

(A8) The 41st sūtra in fascicle 4 of text 152 (T03n0152)

Text 152 in 8 fascicles is the Chinese version of the *Sūtra of the Six Pāramitās Gathered,* translated from Sanskrit during the Three Kingdoms period (220–80) by Kang Senghui (康僧會, ?–280) from Kangjü (康居, present-day northern Xinjiang, China), who arrived in China in 247. It is a collection of stories of the Buddha practicing the six pāramitās as a Bodhisattva in His past lives.

In text A8, the principal character is called Aqun (阿群), not Aṅgulimāla. Text A8 begins with two consecutive past lives of Aqun. In his earlier past life, Aqun was a man-eating king. After he was banished by his ministers to a forest, he decided to kill a hundred human kings as an offering to the tree gods, and captured ninety-nine kings. Then he captured King Universal Illumination (普明). Because King Universal Illumination had promised an offering to a Brahmin, he begged Aqun to let him keep his promise, so Aqun released him. Then King Universal Illumination went to see the Brahmin and received teachings on the impermanence of everything in the world. He offered the Brahmin 12,000 gold coins and, with a smile, returned to Aqun. When Aqun asked him how he could smile before his death, King Universal Illumination told him the stanza spoken by the Brahmin, and Aqun was overcome with awe. He set all the kings free and repented of his sins (a more elaborate version of this story is given in text A9).

After death, Aqun was reborn as a crown prince. In text A8, the story of Aqun as a crown prince is an abridged version of the story of Prince Purity in text A7. After the depraved crown prince was stoned to death by ninety-nine people, he was reborn many times.

Then he came to be reborn in Śrāvastī in the time of the Buddha. The rest of the story of Aqun is similar to that of Aṅgulimāla in text A4. In text A8, the Buddha reveals that King Universal Illumination, whose teaching to Aqun saved the lives of a hundred kings, is none other than the Buddha, that the ninety-nine people who stoned Aqun to death are none other than those whom Aṅgulimāla killed and whose fingers he made into a garland in his present life, and that the person who wanted to stone Aqun but arrived after his death is none other than Aṅgulimāla's mother, whom Aṅgulimāla wants to kill but is dissuaded by the Buddha.

(A9) Chapter 45 in fascicle 11 of text 202 (T04n0202)

Text 202 in 13 fascicles is the Chinese version of the *Sūtra of the Wise and the Foolish* (Damamūka-nidāna-sūtra), translated from Sanskrit around 445 in the Northern Wei Dynasty (386–534) by Huijue (慧覺, dates unknown) from the Liang region (涼州, present-day Gansu Province) in China.

The story of Aṅgulimāla in text A9 is similar to that in text A4. However, in texts A1, A4, A5, A7, and A8, Aṅgulimāla speaks truthful words to a woman in obstructed labor to bring about a safe childbirth, while in texts A9 and A10, he speaks truthful words to a female elephant to bring about a safe birth of her calf.

Text A9 also provides the stories of two past lives of Aṅgulimāla, which are similar to those in text A8, but whose characters' names differ. In one past life, Aṅgulimāla was King Kalmāṣapāda (Spotted Foot[2]), not Aqun as in text A8, who regularly made offerings to a ṛṣi. One day he unwittingly offended the ṛṣi and was cursed by the ṛṣi to eat flesh for twelve years. Because he had his kitchen manager kill children for his meals, his ministers led an army to kill him. However, using his merit acquired by making offerings to that ṛṣi, he turned himself into a rākṣasa. Hovering in the air, he announced that he would eat their beloved wives and children. Then other rākṣasas became his wingmen. They planned a banquet to eat a thousand human kings, and captured nine hundred ninety-nine kings. Then Kalmāṣapāda captured King Sutasoma (Presser of Soma[3]) to make the quota. King Sutasoma begged to have seven days to keep his promise of offering to a Brahmin, and promised that he would come back, so Kalmāṣapāda granted his request. After King Sutasoma made his offering, the Brahmin spoke a stanza that described the impermanence of everything in the world. Against the objections of his ministers, King Sutasoma returned as promised to Kalmāṣapāda. He told Kalmāṣapāda the stanza that he had heard from the Brahmin, and explained the merit of no killing, and the sin of killing and its inevitable requital. Then Kalmāṣapāda came to an awakening, set all the kings free, and returned to his own kingdom. Because the twelve-year curse on him expired, he never ate flesh again.[4]

In text A9, the Buddha reveals that Kalmāṣapāda is none other than Aṅgulimāla, and that King Sutasoma is none other than the Buddha. As King Sutasoma tamed Kalmāṣapāda, so too the Buddha tamed Aṅgulimāla. Those whom Kalmāṣapāda ate in twelve years are none other than those whom Aṅgulimāla has killed in his present life. Life after life, whenever Aṅgulimāla killed people, the Buddha used virtue to tame him.

In another past life, Aṅgulimāla was a prince who went into a mountain to train to become a ṛṣi. However, after he came to the throne, he became depraved. Like Prince Purity in text A7, before he was stoned to death he vowed that in his future lives he would, life after life, kill those who killed him. Therefore, those who stoned him to death are none other than those whom Aṅgulimāla has killed in his present life.[5]

(A10) Chapter 17 in fascicles 17 and 18 of text 212 (T04n0212)

Text 212 in 30 fascicles is the Chinese version of the *Sūtra of the Sunrise,* written by Dharmatrāta (法救, dates unknown), and translated from Sanskrit between 350 and 417 of the Eastern Jin Dynasty (317–420) by Zhu Fonian (竺佛念, dates unknown) from the Liang region in China.

The story of Aṅgulimāla in text A10 is similar to that in text A4. In texts A1, A4, A5, and A7, Aṅgulimāla is stoned, clubbed, and stabbed by townspeople after he has become an Arhat, while in text A10, this happens before he has become an Arhat. At the request of King Prasenajit, the Buddha explains that Aṅgulimāla, a killer of many people, can become an Arhat because his evil is ended by the Eightfold Right Path. Now he illuminates the world, like the moon after the clouds are gone.

Teachings in the Story

The common element in all versions of the story of Aṅgulimāla is that as Aṅgulimāla chases the Buddha, the Buddha gives him teachings and converts him from a killer to a monk, and that through diligent practice, he becomes an Arhat. Therefore, this story teaches that when the right causes and conditions converge, even a killer can become a holy being. However, he still has to answer to his evil karma. Texts A1, A4, A5, and A7 state that although Aṅgulimāla has become an Arhat, he is stoned, clubbed, and stabbed by townspeople, and that the Buddha tells him to endure his pain because the karma requital for his crimes could have been suffering in hell for countless years.

While texts A1, A2, A3, and A5 portray Aṅgulimāla simply as an atrocious killer, who for no reason kills people and takes a finger from each victim to make a garland, texts A4, A6, A7, A8, A9, and A10 portray him as the victim of his blind obedience to his teacher, who commands him to kill a hundred or a thousand people in order to complete his training, become a Brahmin, and be reborn in heaven. Then texts A8 and A9 connect his killing spree in his present life to the karmic events in two of his past lives (text A7 covers only the second past life). In one past life Aṅgulimāla was King Kalmāṣapāda, a man-eating king converted by King Sutasoma, who is none other than the Buddha. As King Sutasoma tamed Kalmāṣapāda, so too the Buddha tames Aṅgulimāla. In another past life Aṅgulimāla was Prince Purity, who became depraved and was stoned to death. The prostitute who seduced Prince Purity is none other than Aṅgulimāla's teacher's wife, who tries to seduce him. Prince Purity's father, who let people stone his son to death, is none other than Aṅgulimāla's teacher, who wants Aṅgulimāla to die by law.

These past-life stories teach that some people in one's past lives have significant impact on one's present life. They also reveal the power of one's vows. Before Prince Purity was stoned to death, he vowed that in his future lives he would kill those who killed him, and encounter a true Arhat to achieve liberation. His first vow reveals that the reason for Aṅgulimāla's killing spree in his present life goes deeper than his blind obedience to his teacher, and implies that, not just in his present life, he has repeatedly killed those who killed him. This vow does not justify atrocious killing but indicates the unfortunate fact that, life after life, enemies reciprocate their revenge. It is fortunate that Aṅgulimāla is able to end his karmic debts because he has encountered the Buddha, the true Arhat in his second vow, and achieved liberation, fulfilling his second vow.

Text A6 provides a different perspective on the story. It portrays Aṅgulimāla as an arrogant Bodhisattva who mocks god-kings and holy voice-hearers as puny mosquitoes. In fascicle 1, Aṅgulimāla righteously declares, without evidence, that those whom he killed and whose fingers he made into a garland were sentient beings that sabotaged the Dharma. Then, in fascicle 2, he says that all things done by Buddhas and Bodhisattvas are illusory, and claims that he manifested killing sentient beings to tame those who sabotage the Dharma, and did not actually harm anyone. In fascicle 4, the Buddha reveals that there is a world called Adorned with All Treasures, whose Buddha is called Superior Great Energetic Progress That the World Is Delighted to See, and that Aṅgulimāla is none other than that Buddha's self-manifestation.

The Mahāyāna Sūtra of Aṅgulimālika

Sūtra 4 in the present book is an English translation of text A6 (text 120 in 4 fascicles), which has never before been translated into English. This Mahāyāna sūtra comprises two topics, the story of Aṅgulimāla and teachings on the Tathāgata store. The former is covered in fascicle 1, the latter in fascicles 2 through 4. This sūtra teaches that the Mahāyāna is the One Vehicle that leads to a Tathāgata's hindrance-free wisdom-knowledge (jñāna). It is the only definitive vehicle, and all others are for convenience. A Tathāgata is eternal, and all sentient beings possess the Tathāgata store because they each are a Tathāgata in storage. A Tathāgata's true liberation is not empty. Because liberation is free from all faults, it is said to be empty. Likewise a Tathāgata is actually not empty, but is said to be empty because He has left behind all afflictions and the form of a god or human. Given below are summaries of the four fascicles.

Fascicle 1 (of 4)

A poor Brahmin woman named Bhadrā lives in a village not too far north of Śrāvastī, the capital city of Kauśala. Her son, World Appearance, who lost his father when he was young, studies under a Brahmin master named Maṇibhadra. When Maṇibhadra goes away on a trip, his wife tries to seduce World Appearance, but he rejects her. Angered, upon her husband's return she lies to him that World Appearance tried to ravage her. To have World Appearance die by law, Maṇibhadra tells him to kill a thousand people and take a finger from each victim to make a garland, so that he can become a Brahmin and be reborn in heaven.

Following his teacher's instruction, World Appearance kills nine hundred ninety-nine people and becomes known as Aṅgulimāla (Finger Garland). When he sees his mother coming to bring him food, he decides to kill her to make his quota and have her reborn in heaven.

The Buddha knows that Aṅgulimāla is about to kill his mother, and walks toward him. Then Aṅgulimāla decides to kill Him instead. As the Buddha walks away, Aṅgulimāla chases Him but cannot catch up with Him. As Aṅgulimāla keeps telling the Buddha to stand still because he wants to take a finger of His, the Buddha teaches him to abide in the pure precepts, and gives him the sword of wisdom and the water of the unsurpassed good Dharma.

Then Aṅgulimāla casts away his sword and his finger garland. At the Buddha's command, he repents of his sins to his mother and requests her permission to renounce family life.

When god-king Śakra offers Aṅgulimāla a celestial garment to use as his dharma robe, he rejects Śakra's offering because, as a śramaṇa, he has no need for a priceless robe and should practice asceticism. He declares that those whom he killed and whose fingers he made into a garland were sentient beings that sabotaged the Dharma. He calls Śakra an outsider to the true Dharma and mocks him as a puny mosquito.

Fascicle 2 (of 4)

When the Brahma-king offers Aṅgulimāla a celestial garment for him to practice the Brahma way of life, Aṅgulimāla rejects his offering and calls him a puny mosquito, because he does not know that good and evil are illusory. When the four world-protecting god-kings offer Aṅgulimāla a celestial bowl, he rejects their offering and calls them puny mosquitoes. He tells them to protect the Dharma, not the world. When the evil māra-king, Pāpīyān, advises Aṅgulimāla to renounce family life as a hoax and enter his city, Aṅgulimāla rejects his advice, calls him a thieving dog, and tells him to listen to the Dharma. When the Brahma-king Maheśvara praises that Aṅgulimāla has tamed the māra-king, though he abides on the ground of ordinary beings, Aṅgulimāla indicates that Maheśvara does not know even his own true nature, much less whether Aṅgulimāla abides on the ground of ordinary beings. When a tree goddess offers him a meal, Aṅgulimāla rejects her offering, and tells her to discard her attachment to male or female appearances, and train to realize the emptiness of dharmas.

Then great voice-hearers, one after another, come to see Aṅgulimāla. He mocks each of them as practicing the way of a mosquito. To Mahāmaudgalyāyana, who is foremost in transcendental powers, Aṅgulimāla says that benefiting oneself and others, and even sacrificing one's body to save and protect others, bring superior transcendental powers. To Śāriputra, who is foremost in wisdom, Aṅgulimāla says that praising that Tathāgatas are eternal brings great wisdom, which enables one to expound the Dharma. To Ānanda, who is foremost in hearing much of the Dharma, Aṅgulimāla says that praising that Tathāgatas are eternal is called hearing much of the Dharma. To Rāhula, who is foremost in respecting the precepts, Aṅgulimāla says that praising that Tathāgatas are eternal is called the highest way to respect the precepts. To Aniruddha, who possesses the foremost god eye, Aṅgulimāla says that expounding the Tathāgata's profound Dharma store by skillful means brings one the most excellent eye. To Dravya, Aṅgulimāla says that discarding arrogance and attachment to one's body and life, to widely expound the Tathāgata store is called enduring superior self-restraint in the world.

To Pūrṇa-Maitrāyaṇīputra, who is foremost in expounding the Dharma, Aṅgulimāla says that all past Buddha-Bhagavāns looked into all sentient beings by skillful means and did not find the absence of their Tathāgata store; that all present Buddha-Bhagavāns look into all sentient beings by skillful means and do not find the absence of their true self; that all future Buddhas will look into all sentient beings by skillful means and will not find the absence of their true nature. Moreover, all past, present, and future Buddha-Bhagavāns did not, do not, and will not find the action of one's Tathāgata store, because the Tathāgata in every sentient being by nature has no action, but has immeasurable purity and majesty and countless good characteristics. As oil does not mix with water, likewise one's Buddha nature never mixes with one's afflictions, though one's countless afflictions shroud one's Buddha nature. Hence one's Buddha nature (Tathāgata store) abides in one's afflictions, like a lamp contained in a bottle. When the bottle is broken, the lamp is revealed. As an analogy, when the sun or moon is covered by dense clouds, its light is obscured. When the clouds are removed, its radiance illuminates. It is the same with one's Tathāgata store. When it is covered by one's afflictions, it is unseen; when one's afflictions are removed, its radiance illuminates everywhere. One's Buddha nature is radiant and pure, like the sun or moon.

To Sundara-Nanda, who has the foremost respectable looks, Aṅgulimāla says that one's understanding of a Buddha's skillful means is the applied wisdom-knowledge that brings one's respectable looks. To Upāli, who is foremost in upholding the Vinaya, Aṅgulimāla says that taking away the things of an evil bhikṣu who sabotages the Dharma is called the foremost way to uphold the Vinaya, because the Brahma way of life precludes violation of the precepts.

To Mañjuśrī Bodhisattva, Aṅgulimāla says that Mañjuśrī trains to see the utter emptiness of dharmas, and thinks liberation is utterly empty, though it is actually not empty. Aṅgulimāla says that some dharmas are empty; some dharmas are not empty. All afflictions are like hailstones, and destroying all evil is like hailstones melting. He affirms that a Tathāgata's true liberation is not empty. Because liberation is free from all faults, it is said to be empty. Likewise a Tathāgata is actually not empty, but is said to be empty because He has left behind all afflictions and the form of a god or human. Aṅgulimāla says that there are two kinds of people who sabotage the true Dharma, those who declare that all dharmas are utterly empty and those who declare that dharmas have a self. He states that all things done by Buddhas and Bodhisattvas are illusory, and claims that he manifested killing sentient beings to tame those who sabotage the Dharma, and did not actually harm anyone.

Aṅgulimāla tells Mahāmaudgalyāyana that all Tathāgatas forever abide in the world to deliver those who renounce family life and accept the complete monastic precepts. Therefore, there are only two groups of sentient beings, one on the wrong path and the other on the right path. There is no group that is indecisive about its path. Those definitely on the wrong path are icchantikas; those definitely on the right path are Tathāgatas, holy Bodhisattvas, and riders of the Two Vehicles. While a Tathāgata is the highest, an icchantika the vilest.

When the Buddha tells Aṅgulimāla to take the Three Refuges, Aṅgulimāla indicates that while the Buddha is the refuge in the highest truth, the Dharma and the Saṅgha are the two refuges of convenience. Therefore, he takes refuge in the Tathāgata. When the Buddha tells him to accept the five precepts, Aṅgulimāla declares that he will always accept and observe the precept for ending sentient beings' lives, where sentient beings mean countless afflictions. He will reveal that the real truth is the Tathāgata store and that the eternal body in the highest truth is a Buddha's inconceivable dharma body. He will indulge in drinking the alcohol produced by the Mahāyāna and persuade sentient beings to do the same. He will take samādhi as his wife, the truth as his son, the loving-kind and compassionate mind as his daughter, the emptiness of dharmas as his house, and countless pāramitās as his high and wide bed. He will take bodhi, which no one can give him. He will always enjoy the pleasure of dancing and singing songs to proclaim the Tathāgata store and recite Mahāyāna sūtras.

Fascicle 3 (of 4)

Aṅgulimāla says that the one learning means that the Tathāgata store of all sentient beings constantly abides. The path of the Mahāyāna leads to the teaching that a Tathāgata forever abides because He is forever, eternal, supreme, changeless, pure, and extremely quiet. The one path, one vehicle, and one refuge all mean a Tathāgata. Therefore, the One Vehicle (Buddha Vehicle) is the only definitive vehicle. All others are for convenience.

When the Buddha says, "Come, bhikṣu," Aṅgulimāla immediately becomes a śramaṇa. He asks the Buddha why He, who abides in the state of no birth and on the ground of liberation, also abides here. Then the Buddha sends Aṅgulimāla and Mañjuśrī to ten worlds, in each of the ten directions, to ask their Buddhas this question. Each of those Buddhas tells them that He is one of the bodies of Śākyamuni Buddha and sends them back to Śākyamuni Buddha.

The Buddha tells them that eighty koṭi Buddhas are but one Buddha, Himself. As Buddha Lands are countless, so too are Tathāgatas. A Tathāgata's body is immeasurable and boundless because He has acquired immeasurable merit. A Tathāgata forever abides in His boundless body. Then He gives seventy-three reasons for, and descriptions of, the dharma body that He has realized. For countless asaṁkhyeyas of kalpas, He, who abides in all boundless places, also abides here.

Fascicle 4 (of 4)

The Buddha tells Aṅgulimāla that during the remaining eighty years as the true Dharma perishes, for a Bodhisattva-Mahāsattva who can abandon his body and life, to expound a Tathāgata's teaching on the eternal and changeless Tathāgata store will be very difficult. For those who have heard a Tathāgata's teaching on the eternal and changeless Tathāgata store, to elicit belief and delight will also be very difficult. All sentient beings possess the Tathāgata store. However, like a lamp in a bottle, it is shrouded by countless afflictions. Although sentient beings hear the Dharma, they abandon self-restraint. It is their own fault that they do not become Buddhas.

The Buddha tells Mañjuśrī that whoever hears the name Śākyamuni Tathāgata, even if he has not yet activated the bodhi mind, is already a Bodhisattva. Why? Because the Tathāgata made a great vow to deliver all in the world who have not yet been delivered, to transform them by using the true Dharma, and to enable them to come to realization of the truth. For those who have heard even a little of this sūtra, their countless asaṁkhyeyas of sins will be expunged.

There are two paths, the voice-hearer path and the Bodhisattva path. The voice-hearer path is the Eightfold Right Path. The Bodhisattva path is the understanding that all sentient beings possess the Tathāgata store, which is one's inherent pure mind. As one's Tathāgata store transcends all dharmas, all dharmas are one's Tathāgata store. One's realm and the realms of all sentient beings are one realm, and all flesh is one flesh. Therefore, Buddhas do not eat flesh.

Those who seek the supra-worldly truth do not know a Tathāgata's veiled teachings but claim that a Buddha has taught "no self" only. Therefore, a Tathāgata expounds the Middle Way of the One Vehicle (Buddha Vehicle), which is apart from the two opposites, and reveals that one's true self, the Buddha, the Dharma, and the Saṅgha are true. Therefore, the Middle Way is called the Mahāyāna. During the remaining eighty years as the true Dharma perishes, the Buddha Dharma will abide in the south. Mañjuśrī and other Bodhisattvas will bear and uphold the true Dharma in Jambudvīpa (the southern continent) and other continents.

The Buddha reveals that in the world called Adorned with Treasures, Aṅgulimāla is the Buddha called Superior Great Energetic Progress That the World Is Delighted to See; and that in the world called Constant Joy, Mañjuśrī is the Buddha called Joy Store Jewel Accumulation. If one reverently pays respects to Aṅgulimāla and Mañjuśrī and has heard their names, one will see the world Constant Joy as if seeing one's own home. Because one has heard their names, one can close the door to the four evil life-paths.

Notes

1. See Five Āgamas in the glossary.

2. The Sanskrit word *Kalmāṣa* means spotted; the Sanskrit word *pāda* means foot. Kalmāṣapāda's mother was a lioness and his father, a human king. He had a human body, but his feet were spotted.

3 The Sanskrit word *suta* means pressed; the Sanskrit word *soma* means the juice of the soma plant. Sutasoma means presser of soma, who presses the soma plant for its juice, to offer it to gods during sacrifice.

4 This story also appears in fascicle 1 of text 205 (T04n0205), fascicle 2 of text 245 (T08n0245), fascicle 2 of text 246 (T08n0246), and fascicle 4 of text 1509 (T25n1509). Text 205 in 2 fascicles is one of the four Chinese versions of the *Sūtra of Sundry Parables,* which was translated from Sanskrit in the Later Han Dynasty (947–51) by an unknown person. Text 245 in 2 fascicles and text 246 in 2 fascicles are the two Chinese versions of the *Sūtra of Prajñā-Pāramitā for Benevolent Kings to Protect Their Countries.* Text 245 was translated from Sanskrit in the Later Qin Dynasty (384–417) by Kumārajīva (鳩摩羅什, 344–413) from Kucha; text 246 was translated from Sanskrit in 765 during the Tang Dynasty (618–907) by Amoghavajra (不空金剛, 705–74) from Sri Lanka. Text 1509 in 100 fascicles is the Chinese version of the *Treatise on Mahāprajñā-Pāramitā*

(Mahāprajñā-pāramitā-śāstra), written by Ācārya Nāgārjuna (龍樹菩薩, circa 150–250) and translated from Sanskrit by Kumārajīva. Text 205 does not mention the names of the two kings and only states that the man-eating king is none other than Aṅgulimāla. In the other three texts, the man-eating king is Kalmāṣapāda as in text A9, but the king who kept his promise to a Brahmin and to Kalmāṣapāda is Universal Illumination as in text A8, not Sutasoma as in text A9.

5. One can conjecture that those who stoned the depraved prince to death were those whom he had eaten when he was the man-eating king.

4 央掘魔羅經
Sūtra of Aṅgulimālika

Translated from Sanskrit into Chinese in the Liu Song Dynasty
by
The Tripiṭaka Master Guṇabhadra from India

Fascicle 1 (of 4)

Thus I have heard:

At one time the Buddha was outside Śrāvastī [the capital city of Kauśala], staying in the Jetavana garden, which was purchased for the Buddha from Prince Jeta by Anāthapiṇḍika the Elder. He was accompanied by innumerable Bodhisattva-Mahāsattvas, His four groups of disciples, and innumerable gods, dragons, yakṣas, gandharvas, asuras, garuḍas, kiṁnaras, mahoragas, piśācas, and rākṣasas, as well as the god-son Sun-Moon, the four world-protecting god-kings, and celestial māras.

At that time the World-Honored One, to widely expound the wondrous Dharma to deliver sentient beings, pronounced a mahāvaipulya sūtra called *Wielding a Sword*. Good in the beginning, in the middle, and in the end, [its teaching was] completely pure and fully revealed good meaning, good flavor, and the appearance of the Brahma way of pure life.

Not too far north of Śrāvastī was a village called Sana. There lived a poor woman named Bhadrā, in the Brahmin caste.[1] Her son, World Appearance, lost his father when he was young. At age twenty,[2] his body, strength, and appearance were outstanding, and he was intelligent and eloquent. There was another village, called Prahasa. Having lived there for a long time was a Brahmin master named Maṇibhadra, who had mastered the four Vedas, and World Appearance studied under him. Humble, submissive, and respectful, World Appearance made offerings to him with total devotion.

One day, at the invitation of King Prasenajit [the king of Kauśala], Maṇibhadra left his house and told Worldly Appearance to stay there. Maṇibhadra's wife was a young and comely woman. Lusting for World Appearance, she disregarded all propriety and grabbed him by his clothes. World Appearance said to her, "You are virtually my mother. How can you do this wicked thing in your house?"

Ashamed and fearful, he abandoned his clothes and evaded her.

Driven by burning desire, she wept and thought, "He flatly refused to comply with my will. Because he disobeyed me, I want to end his life, so that he cannot marry."

Consumed by burning desire like a disease, she scratched her body with her fingernails. Then she suspended herself with a rope, her feet still on the floor. After Maṇibhadra finished his business, he came home and saw his wife suspended on a rope. He cut off the rope with a knife and loudly asked her, "Who did this?"

She answered, "World Appearance tried to ravage me and forced me to do this."

Maṇibhadra knew that World Appearance had the power of great virtue, as he thought to himself, "The day he was born, all those in the kṣatriya [warrior] caste were terrified because their sabers and swords unsheathed themselves, bent, and fell to the ground. So I know that he has the power of great virtue."

After pondering, he said to World Appearance, "You are shamefully honored by evil men and are not a true Brahmin. You should kill a thousand people to expunge your sin."

World Appearance was by nature humbly obedient. Respectful of his teacher's words, he said, "Alas, Preceptor, killing a thousand people is not something I should do."

His teacher asked him, "You are an evil man. Do you not aspire to become a Brahmin and be reborn in heaven?"

He answered, "Very well, Preceptor, at your command, I will kill a thousand people." Then he prostrated himself at his teacher's feet.

His teacher marveled at his obedience and said, "Because you are a hugely evil man, you will not be killed."

Then he thought, "I will let him die [by law]."

He told World Appearance, "From every person you have killed, take a finger. After you have killed a thousand people, use their fingers to make a garland, wear it, and come back. Then you can become a Brahmin."

World Appearance said to his teacher, "Very well, Preceptor, I will follow your instruction."

Then he killed nine hundred ninety-nine people, short of a thousand by only one, and became known as Aṅgulimāla [Finger Garland].

At that time Aṅgulimāla's mother thought that her son might be hungry. She took four kinds of fine food and went to give to him. When he saw his mother [in the distance], he thought, "I should enable my mother to be reborn in heaven."

He drew his sword and went to kill her.

At that time [the World-Honored One was sitting under] a tree called aśoka [carefree], ten yojanas less ten feet from Śrāvastī. Using his wisdom [He knew that Aṅgulimāla was about to kill his mother]. As elegant as a goose-king, He walked toward Aṅgulimāla. When Aṅgulimāla saw the World-Honored One approaching, he drew his sword and quickly charged forward. He thought, "I will kill this śramaṇa called Gautama."

When the World-Honored walked away, Aṅgulimāla spoke in verse:

> Stand still, stand still, great śramaṇa, the prince of King Śuddhodana.
> I am Aṅgulimāla, and must take a finger of Yours.
> Stand still, stand still, great śramaṇa, the one who has no greed and dons a dyed robe.
> I am Aṅgulimāla, and must take a finger of Yours.
>
> Stand still, stand still, great śramaṇa, the one who shaved off His hair to blemish his appearance.

I am Aṅgulimāla, and must take a finger of Yours.
Stand still, stand still, great śramaṇa, the one who is content and holds a begging bowl.
I am Aṅgulimāla, and must take a finger of Yours.

Stand still, stand still, great śramaṇa, the one who is fearless and roams like a lion.
I am Aṅgulimāla, and must take a finger of Yours.
Stand still, stand still, great śramaṇa, the one who is robust and walks like a ferocious tiger.
I am Aṅgulimāla, and must take a finger of Yours.

Stand still, stand still, great śramaṇa, the one who is elegant and walks like a goose-king.
I am Aṅgulimāla, and must take a finger of Yours.
Stand still, stand still, great śramaṇa, the one who is serene and walks like an elephant.
I am Aṅgulimāla, and must take a finger of Yours.

Stand still, stand still, great śramaṇa, the one who is radiant like the rising sun.
I am Aṅgulimāla, and must take a finger of Yours.
Stand still, stand still, great śramaṇa, the one who is radiant like the full moon.
I am Aṅgulimāla, and must take a finger of Yours.

Stand still, stand still, great śramaṇa, the one who is majestic like a mountain of gold.
I am Aṅgulimāla, and must take a finger of Yours.
Stand still, stand still, great śramaṇa, the one who is like the eye of a thousand-petaled lotus flower.
I am Aṅgulimāla, and must take a finger of Yours.

Stand still, stand still, great śramaṇa, the one whose teeth are like the petals of a white lotus flower.
I am Aṅgulimāla, and must take a finger of Yours.
Stand still, stand still, great śramaṇa, the one whose tongue speaks truthful words.
I am Aṅgulimāla, and must take a finger of Yours.

Stand still, stand still, great śramaṇa, the one who has a white hair between His eyebrows.
I am Aṅgulimāla, and must take a finger of Yours.
Stand still, stand still, great śramaṇa, the one who has lustrous purple hair.
I am Aṅgulimāla, and must take a finger of Yours.

Stand still, stand still, great śramaṇa, the one whose long arms reach below the knees.

I am Aṅgulimāla, and must take a finger of Yours.
Stand still, stand still, great śramaṇa, the one who is free from desire and whose male organ is hidden like that of the horse-king.
I am Aṅgulimāla, and must take a finger of Yours.

Stand still, stand still, great śramaṇa, the one whose kneecaps are inconspicuous.
I am Aṅgulimāla, and must take a finger of Yours.
Stand still, stand still, great śramaṇa, the one who has copper-colored fingernails and toenails.
I am Aṅgulimāla, and must take a finger of Yours.

Stand still, stand still, great śramaṇa, the one who takes light steps.
I am Aṅgulimāla, and must take a finger of Yours.
Stand still, stand still, great śramaṇa, the one whose voice is like that of a kalaviṅka bird.
I am Aṅgulimāla, and must take a finger of Yours.

Stand still, stand still, great śramaṇa, the one whose kākila [throat] emits wonderful tones.
I am Aṅgulimāla, and must take a finger of Yours.
Stand still, stand still, great śramaṇa, the one who emits 100 koṭi beams of radiant light.
I am Aṅgulimāla, and must take a finger of Yours.

Stand still, stand still, great śramaṇa, the one whose faculties excel in taming sentient beings.
I am Aṅgulimāla, and must take a finger of Yours.
Stand still, stand still, great śramaṇa, the one who possesses the Ten Powers.
I am Aṅgulimāla, and must take a finger of Yours.

Stand still, stand still, great śramaṇa, the one who upholds the Four Noble Truths.
I am Aṅgulimāla, and must take a finger of Yours.
Stand still, stand still, great śramaṇa, the one who reveals the Eightfold Right Path to benefit others.
I am Aṅgulimāla, and must take a finger of Yours.

Stand still, stand still, great śramaṇa, the one who possesses the thirty-two physical marks [of a great man].
I am Aṅgulimāla, and must take a finger of Yours.
Stand still, stand still, great śramaṇa, the one who possesses the eighty excellent physical characteristics.
I am Aṅgulimāla, and must take a finger of Yours.

Stand still, stand still, great śramaṇa, the one who has ended forever His love and desire.
I am Aṅgulimāla, and must take a finger of Yours.

Stand still, stand still, great śramaṇa, and do not anger me.
I am Aṅgulimāla, and must take a finger of Yours.

Stand still, stand still, great śramaṇa, the one who is extraordinary, never before seen.
I am Aṅgulimāla, and must take a finger of Yours.
Stand still, stand still, great śramaṇa, the one who conquers the arrogance of the god-king Indra, asuras, and rākṣasas.
Who are you, walking so fast?
Before I slay You with my sword, You should know that this is the time to stand still.

Stand still, stand still, great śramaṇa.
Have you not heard my name?
I am Aṅgulimāla, and You should quickly relinquish a finger of Yours.
Stand still, stand still, great śramaṇa.
All those who hear my name die from fear.
How can anyone survive after seeing me face to face?

Stand still, stand still, great śramaṇa.
Quickly tell me who You are.
Are You the sky or the wind
As You walk swiftly before me?

Stand still, stand still, great śramaṇa.
I am tired now
And cannot catch up with You,
But I must take a finger of Yours.

Stand still, stand still, great śramaṇa.
Because You observe well the pure precepts,
You should quickly relinquish a finger of Yours,
Not to cross me.

Then the World-Honored One, like a goose-king, walked seven steps and looked about like a lion. He spoke to Aṅgulimāla in verse:

Abide, abide, Aṅgulimāla, abide in the pure precepts.
I am a Samyak-Saṁbuddha, and give you the sword of wisdom.
I abide in [the truth that dharmas have] no birth,[3] which you do not know.
You are Aṅgulimāla, and I am a Samyak-Saṁbuddha.
I now give you the water of the unsurpassed good Dharma.
You should drink it quickly to end forever your thirst for birth and death.

Abide, abide, Aṅgulimāla, abide in the pure precepts.
I am a Samyak-Saṁbuddha, and give you the sword of wisdom.
I abide in the true reality [of dharmas], which you do not know.
You are Aṅgulimāla, and I am a Samyak-Saṁbuddha.

I now give you the water of the unsurpassed good Dharma.
You should drink it quickly to end forever your thirst for birth and death.

Abide, abide, Aṅgulimāla, abide in the pure precepts.
I am a Samyak-Saṁbuddha, and give you the sword of wisdom.
I abide in [the truth that dharmas have] no action,[4] which you do not know.
You are Aṅgulimāla, and I am a Samyak-Saṁbuddha.
I now give you the water of the unsurpassed good Dharma.
You should drink it quickly to end forever your thirst for birth and death.

Abide, abide, Aṅgulimāla, abide in the pure precepts.
I am a Samyak-Saṁbuddha, and give you the sword of wisdom.
I abide in what is asaṁskṛta [free from conditions], which you do not know.
You are Aṅgulimāla, and I am a Samyak-Saṁbuddha.
I now give you the water of the unsurpassed good Dharma.
You should drink it quickly to end forever your thirst for birth and death.

Abide, abide, Aṅgulimāla, abide in the pure precepts.
I am a Samyak-Saṁbuddha, and give you the sword of wisdom.
I abide in no aging, which you do not know.
You are Aṅgulimāla, and I am a Samyak-Saṁbuddha.
I now give you the water of the unsurpassed good Dharma.
You should drink it quickly to end forever your thirst for birth and death.

Abide, abide, Aṅgulimāla, abide in the pure precepts.
I am a Samyak-Saṁbuddha, and give you the sword of wisdom.
I abide in no illness, which you do not know.
You are Aṅgulimāla, and I am a Samyak-Saṁbuddha.
I now give you the water of the unsurpassed good Dharma.
You should drink it quickly to end forever your thirst for birth and death.

Abide, abide, Aṅgulimāla, abide in the pure precepts.
I am a Samyak-Saṁbuddha, and give you the sword of wisdom.
I abide in no death, which you do not know.
You are Aṅgulimāla, and I am a Samyak-Saṁbuddha.
I now give you the water of the unsurpassed good Dharma.
You should drink it quickly to end forever your thirst for birth and death.

Abide, abide, Aṅgulimāla, abide in the pure precepts.
I am a Samyak-Saṁbuddha, and give you the sword of wisdom.
I abide in no taints, which you do not know.
You are Aṅgulimāla, and I am a Samyak-Saṁbuddha.
I now give you the water of the unsurpassed good Dharma.
You should drink it quickly to end forever your thirst for birth and death.

Abide, abide, Aṅgulimāla, abide in the pure precepts.
I am a Samyak-Saṁbuddha, and give you the sword of wisdom.

I abide in no afflictions, which you do not know.
You are Aṅgulimāla, and I am a Samyak-Saṁbuddha.
I now give you the water of the unsurpassed good Dharma.
You should drink it quickly to end forever your thirst for birth and death.

Abide, abide, Aṅgulimāla, abide in the pure precepts.
I am a Samyak-Saṁbuddha, and give you the sword of wisdom.
I abide in no sins, which you do not know.
You are Aṅgulimāla, and I am a Samyak-Saṁbuddha.
I now give you the water of the unsurpassed good Dharma.
You should drink it quickly to end forever your thirst for birth and death.

Abide, abide, Aṅgulimāla, abide in the pure precepts.
I am a Samyak-Saṁbuddha, and give you the sword of wisdom.
I abide in the truth [of dharmas], which you do not know.
You are Aṅgulimāla, and I am a Samyak-Saṁbuddha.
I now give you the water of the unsurpassed good Dharma.
You should drink it quickly to end forever your thirst for birth and death.

Abide, abide, Aṅgulimāla, abide in the pure precepts.
I am a Samyak-Saṁbuddha, and give you the sword of wisdom.
I abide in the Dharma, which you do not know.
You are Aṅgulimāla, and I am a Samyak-Saṁbuddha.
I now give you the water of the unsurpassed good Dharma.
You should drink it quickly to end forever your thirst for birth and death.

Abide, abide, Aṅgulimāla, abide in the pure precepts.
I am a Samyak-Saṁbuddha, and give you the sword of wisdom.
I abide in accordance with the Dharma, which you do not know.
You are Aṅgulimāla, and I am a Samyak-Saṁbuddha.
I now give you the water of the unsurpassed good Dharma.
You should drink it quickly to end forever your thirst for birth and death.

Abide, abide, Aṅgulimāla, abide in the pure precepts.
I am a Samyak-Saṁbuddha, and give you the sword of wisdom.
I abide in quietness, which you do not know.
You are Aṅgulimāla, and I am a Samyak-Saṁbuddha.
I now give you the water of the unsurpassed good Dharma.
You should drink it quickly to end forever your thirst for birth and death.

Abide, abide, Aṅgulimāla, abide in the pure precepts.
I am a Samyak-Saṁbuddha, and give you the sword of wisdom.
I abide in stability, which you do not know.
You are Aṅgulimāla, and I am a Samyak-Saṁbuddha.
I now give you the water of the unsurpassed good Dharma.
You should drink it quickly to end forever your thirst for birth and death.

Abide, abide, Aṅgulimāla, abide in the pure precepts.
I am a Samyak-Saṁbuddha, and give you the sword of wisdom.

I abide in no worry, which you do not know.
You are Aṅgulimāla, and I am a Samyak-Saṁbuddha.
I now give you the water of the unsurpassed good Dharma.
You should drink it quickly to end forever your thirst for birth and death.

Abide, abide, Aṅgulimāla, abide in the pure precepts.
I am a Samyak-Saṁbuddha, and give you the sword of wisdom.
I abide in freedom from worry, which you do not know.
You are Aṅgulimāla, and I am a Samyak-Saṁbuddha.
I now give you the water of the unsurpassed good Dharma.
You should drink it quickly to end forever your thirst for birth and death.

Abide, abide, Aṅgulimāla, abide in the pure precepts.
I am a Samyak-Saṁbuddha, and give you the sword of wisdom.
I abide in no soil, which you do not know.
You are Aṅgulimāla, and I am a Samyak-Saṁbuddha.
I now give you the water of the unsurpassed good Dharma.
You should drink it quickly to end forever your thirst for birth and death.

Abide, abide, Aṅgulimāla, abide in the pure precepts.
I am a Samyak-Saṁbuddha, and give you the sword of wisdom.
I abide in freedom from soil, which you do not know.
You are Aṅgulimāla, and I am a Samyak-Saṁbuddha.
I now give you the water of the unsurpassed good Dharma.
You should drink it quickly to end forever your thirst for birth and death.

Abide, abide, Aṅgulimāla, abide in the pure precepts.
I am a Samyak-Saṁbuddha, and give you the sword of wisdom.
I abide in no weakness, which you do not know.
You are Aṅgulimāla, and I am a Samyak-Saṁbuddha.
I now give you the water of the unsurpassed good Dharma.
You should drink it quickly to end forever your thirst for birth and death.

Abide, abide, Aṅgulimāla, abide in the pure precepts.
I am a Samyak-Saṁbuddha, and give you the sword of wisdom.
I abide in no disaster, which you do not know.
You are Aṅgulimāla, and I am a Samyak-Saṁbuddha.
I now give you the water of the unsurpassed good Dharma.
You should drink it quickly to end forever your thirst for birth and death.

Abide, abide, Aṅgulimāla, abide in the pure precepts.
I am a Samyak-Saṁbuddha, and give you the sword of wisdom.
I abide in no distress, which you do not know.
You are Aṅgulimāla, and I am a Samyak-Saṁbuddha.
I now give you the water of the unsurpassed good Dharma.
You should drink it quickly to end forever your thirst for birth and death.

Abide, abide, Aṅgulimāla, abide in the pure precepts.
I am a Samyak-Saṁbuddha, and give you the sword of wisdom.

I abide in no trouble, which you do not know.
You are Aṅgulimāla, and I am a Samyak-Saṁbuddha.
I now give you the water of the unsurpassed good Dharma.
You should drink it quickly to end forever your thirst for birth and death.

Abide, abide, Aṅgulimāla, abide in the pure precepts.
I am a Samyak-Saṁbuddha, and give you the sword of wisdom.
I abide in freedom from trouble, which you do not know.
You are Aṅgulimāla, and I am a Samyak-Saṁbuddha.
I now give you the water of the unsurpassed good Dharma.
You should drink it quickly to end forever your thirst for birth and death.

Abide, abide, Aṅgulimāla, abide in the pure precepts.
I am a Samyak-Saṁbuddha, and give you the sword of wisdom.
I abide in nonexistence, which you do not know.
You are Aṅgulimāla, and I am a Samyak-Saṁbuddha.
I now give you the water of the unsurpassed good Dharma.
You should drink it quickly to end forever your thirst for birth and death.

Abide, abide, Aṅgulimāla, abide in the pure precepts.
I am a Samyak-Saṁbuddha, and give you the sword of wisdom.
I abide in the immeasurable, which you do not know.
You are Aṅgulimāla, and I am a Samyak-Saṁbuddha.
I now give you the water of the unsurpassed good Dharma.
You should drink it quickly to end forever your thirst for birth and death.

Abide, abide, Aṅgulimāla, abide in the pure precepts.
I am a Samyak-Saṁbuddha, and give you the sword of wisdom.
I abide in the unsurpassable, which you do not know.
You are Aṅgulimāla, and I am a Samyak-Saṁbuddha.
I now give you the water of the unsurpassed good Dharma.
You should drink it quickly to end forever your thirst for birth and death.

Abide, abide, Aṅgulimāla, abide in the pure precepts.
I am a Samyak-Saṁbuddha, and give you the sword of wisdom.
I abide in utmost excellence, which you do not know.
You are Aṅgulimāla, and I am a Samyak-Saṁbuddha.
I now give you the water of the unsurpassed good Dharma.
You should drink it quickly to end forever your thirst for birth and death.

Abide, abide, Aṅgulimāla, abide in the pure precepts.
I am a Samyak-Saṁbuddha, and give you the sword of wisdom.
I abide in eternity, which you do not know.
You are Aṅgulimāla, and I am a Samyak-Saṁbuddha.
I now give you the water of the unsurpassed good Dharma.
You should drink it quickly to end forever your thirst for birth and death.

Abide, abide, Aṅgulimāla, abide in the pure precepts.
I am a Samyak-Saṁbuddha, and give you the sword of wisdom.

I abide in exaltation, which you do not know.
You are Aṅgulimāla, and I am a Samyak-Saṁbuddha.
I now give you the water of the unsurpassed good Dharma.
You should drink it quickly to end forever your thirst for birth and death.

Abide, abide, Aṅgulimāla, abide in the pure precepts.
I am a Samyak-Saṁbuddha, and give you the sword of wisdom.
I abide in superiority, which you do not know.
You are Aṅgulimāla, and I am a Samyak-Saṁbuddha.
I now give you the water of the unsurpassed good Dharma.
You should drink it quickly to end forever your thirst for birth and death.

Abide, abide, Aṅgulimāla, abide in the pure precepts.
I am a Samyak-Saṁbuddha, and give you the sword of wisdom.
I abide in no destruction, which you do not know.
You are Aṅgulimāla, and I am a Samyak-Saṁbuddha.
I now give you the water of the unsurpassed good Dharma.
You should drink it quickly to end forever your thirst for birth and death.

Abide, abide, Aṅgulimāla, abide in the pure precepts.
I am a Samyak-Saṁbuddha, and give you the sword of wisdom.
I abide in no collapse, which you do not know.
You are Aṅgulimāla, and I am a Samyak-Saṁbuddha.
I now give you the water of the unsurpassed good Dharma.
You should drink it quickly to end forever your thirst for birth and death.

Abide, abide, Aṅgulimāla, abide in the pure precepts.
I am a Samyak-Saṁbuddha, and give you the sword of wisdom.
I abide in the boundless, which you do not know.
You are Aṅgulimāla, and I am a Samyak-Saṁbuddha.
I now give you the water of the unsurpassed good Dharma.
You should drink it quickly to end forever your thirst for birth and death.

Abide, abide, Aṅgulimāla, abide in the pure precepts.
I am a Samyak-Saṁbuddha, and give you the sword of wisdom.
I abide in the invisible, which you do not know.
You are Aṅgulimāla, and I am a Samyak-Saṁbuddha.
I now give you the water of the unsurpassed good Dharma.
You should drink it quickly to end forever your thirst for birth and death.

Abide, abide, Aṅgulimāla, abide in the pure precepts.
I am a Samyak-Saṁbuddha, and give you the sword of wisdom.
I abide in the profound Dharma, which you do not know.
You are Aṅgulimāla, and I am a Samyak-Saṁbuddha.
I now give you the water of the unsurpassed good Dharma.
You should drink it quickly to end forever your thirst for birth and death.

Abide, abide, Aṅgulimāla, abide in the pure precepts.
I am a Samyak-Saṁbuddha, and give you the sword of wisdom.

I abide in what is hard to see, which you do not know.
You are Aṅgulimāla, and I am a Samyak-Saṁbuddha.
I now give you the water of the unsurpassed good Dharma.
You should drink it quickly to end forever your thirst for birth and death.

Abide, abide, Aṅgulimāla, abide in the pure precepts.
I am a Samyak-Saṁbuddha, and give you the sword of wisdom.
I abide in what is subtle and tiny, which you do not know.
You are Aṅgulimāla, and I am a Samyak-Saṁbuddha.
I now give you the water of the unsurpassed good Dharma.
You should drink it quickly to end forever your thirst for birth and death.

Abide, abide, Aṅgulimāla, abide in the pure precepts.
I am a Samyak-Saṁbuddha, and give you the sword of wisdom.
I abide in the entire Dharma, which you do not know.
You are Aṅgulimāla, and I am a Samyak-Saṁbuddha.
I now give you the water of the unsurpassed good Dharma.
You should drink it quickly to end forever your thirst for birth and death.

Abide, abide, Aṅgulimāla, abide in the pure precepts.
I am a Samyak-Saṁbuddha, and give you the sword of wisdom.
I abide in what is extremely hard to see, which you do not know.
You are Aṅgulimāla, and I am a Samyak-Saṁbuddha.
I now give you the water of the unsurpassed good Dharma.
You should drink it quickly to end forever your thirst for birth and death.

Abide, abide, Aṅgulimāla, abide in the pure precepts.
I am a Samyak-Saṁbuddha, and give you the sword of wisdom.
I abide in no fixity, which you do not know.
You are Aṅgulimāla, and I am a Samyak-Saṁbuddha.
I now give you the water of the unsurpassed good Dharma.
You should drink it quickly to end forever your thirst for birth and death.

Abide, abide, Aṅgulimāla, abide in the pure precepts.
I am a Samyak-Saṁbuddha, and give you the sword of wisdom.
I abide in no dispute, which you do not know.
You are Aṅgulimāla, and I am a Samyak-Saṁbuddha.
I now give you the water of the unsurpassed good Dharma.
You should drink it quickly to end forever your thirst for birth and death.

Abide, abide, Aṅgulimāla, abide in the pure precepts.
I am a Samyak-Saṁbuddha, and give you the sword of wisdom.
I abide in no differentiation, which you do not know.
You are Aṅgulimāla, and I am a Samyak-Saṁbuddha.
I now give you the water of the unsurpassed good Dharma.
You should drink it quickly to end forever your thirst for birth and death.

Abide, abide, Aṅgulimāla, abide in the pure precepts.
I am a Samyak-Saṁbuddha, and give you the sword of wisdom.

I abide in nothing, which you do not know.
You are Aṅgulimāla, and I am a Samyak-Saṁbuddha.
I now give you the water of the unsurpassed good Dharma.
You should drink it quickly to end forever your thirst for birth and death.

Abide, abide, Aṅgulimāla, abide in the pure precepts.
I am a Samyak-Saṁbuddha, and give you the sword of wisdom.
I abide in liberation, which you do not know.
You are Aṅgulimāla, and I am a Samyak-Saṁbuddha.
I now give you the water of the unsurpassed good Dharma.
You should drink it quickly to end forever your thirst for birth and death.

Abide, abide, Aṅgulimāla, abide in the pure precepts.
I am a Samyak-Saṁbuddha, and give you the sword of wisdom.
I abide in silence, which you do not know.
You are Aṅgulimāla, and I am a Samyak-Saṁbuddha.
I now give you the water of the unsurpassed good Dharma.
You should drink it quickly to end forever your thirst for birth and death.

Abide, abide, Aṅgulimāla, abide in the pure precepts.
I am a Samyak-Saṁbuddha, and give you the sword of wisdom.
I abide in stillness, which you do not know.
You are Aṅgulimāla, and I am a Samyak-Saṁbuddha.
I now give you the water of the unsurpassed good Dharma.
You should drink it quickly to end forever your thirst for birth and death.

Abide, abide, Aṅgulimāla, abide in the pure precepts.
I am a Samyak-Saṁbuddha, and give you the sword of wisdom.
I abide in superior stillness, which you do not know.
You are Aṅgulimāla, and I am a Samyak-Saṁbuddha.
I now give you the water of the unsurpassed good Dharma.
You should drink it quickly to end forever your thirst for birth and death.

Abide, abide, Aṅgulimāla, abide in the pure precepts.
I am a Samyak-Saṁbuddha, and give you the sword of wisdom.
I abide in no cessation, which you do not know.
You are Aṅgulimāla, and I am a Samyak-Saṁbuddha.
I now give you the water of the unsurpassed good Dharma.
You should drink it quickly to end forever your thirst for birth and death.

Abide, abide, Aṅgulimāla, abide in the pure precepts.
I am a Samyak-Saṁbuddha, and give you the sword of wisdom.
I abide on that shore,[5] which you do not know.
You are Aṅgulimāla, and I am a Samyak-Saṁbuddha.
I now give you the water of the unsurpassed good Dharma.
You should drink it quickly to end forever your thirst for birth and death.

Abide, abide, Aṅgulimāla, abide in the pure precepts.
I am a Samyak-Saṁbuddha, and give you the sword of wisdom.

I abide in wondrousness, which you do not know.
You are Aṅgulimāla, and I am a Samyak-Saṁbuddha.
I now give you the water of the unsurpassed good Dharma.
You should drink it quickly to end forever your thirst for birth and death.

Abide, abide, Aṅgulimāla, abide in the pure precepts.
I am a Samyak-Saṁbuddha, and give you the sword of wisdom.
I abide in no falsity, which you do not know.
You are Aṅgulimāla, and I am a Samyak-Saṁbuddha.
I now give you the water of the unsurpassed good Dharma.
You should drink it quickly to end forever your thirst for birth and death.

Abide, abide, Aṅgulimāla, abide in the pure precepts.
I am a Samyak-Saṁbuddha, and give you the sword of wisdom.
I abide in no constraints, which you do not know.
You are Aṅgulimāla, and I am a Samyak-Saṁbuddha.
I now give you the water of the unsurpassed good Dharma.
You should drink it quickly to end forever your thirst for birth and death.

Abide, abide, Aṅgulimāla, abide in the pure precepts.
I am a Samyak-Saṁbuddha, and give you the sword of wisdom.
I abide in no arrogance, which you do not know.
You are Aṅgulimāla, and I am a Samyak-Saṁbuddha.
I now give you the water of the unsurpassed good Dharma.
You should drink it quickly to end forever your thirst for birth and death.

Abide, abide, Aṅgulimāla, abide in the pure precepts.
I am a Samyak-Saṁbuddha, and give you the sword of wisdom.
I abide in no illusion, which you do not know.
You are Aṅgulimāla, and I am a Samyak-Saṁbuddha.
I now give you the water of the unsurpassed good Dharma.
You should drink it quickly to end forever your thirst for birth and death.

Abide, abide, Aṅgulimāla, abide in the pure precepts.
I am a Samyak-Saṁbuddha, and give you the sword of wisdom.
I abide in no delusion, which you do not know.
You are Aṅgulimāla, and I am a Samyak-Saṁbuddha.
I now give you the water of the unsurpassed good Dharma.
You should drink it quickly to end forever your thirst for birth and death.

Abide, abide, Aṅgulimāla, abide in the pure precepts.
I am a Samyak-Saṁbuddha, and give you the sword of wisdom.
I abide in equability, which you do not know.
You are Aṅgulimāla, and I am a Samyak-Saṁbuddha.
I now give you the water of the unsurpassed good Dharma.
You should drink it quickly to end forever your thirst for birth and death.

Abide, abide, Aṅgulimāla, abide in the pure precepts.
I am a Samyak-Saṁbuddha, and give you the sword of wisdom.

I abide in the dharma realm, which you do not know.
You are Aṅgulimāla, and I am a Samyak-Saṁbuddha.
I now give you the water of the unsurpassed good Dharma.
You should drink it quickly to end forever your thirst for birth and death.

Abide, abide, Aṅgulimāla, abide in the pure precepts.
I am a Samyak-Saṁbuddha, and give you the sword of wisdom.
I abide in no entrance [into anything], which you do not know.
You are Aṅgulimāla, and I am a Samyak-Saṁbuddha.
I now give you the water of the unsurpassed good Dharma.
You should drink it quickly to end forever your thirst for birth and death.

Abide, abide, Aṅgulimāla, abide in the pure precepts.
I am a Samyak-Saṁbuddha, and give you the sword of wisdom.
I abide in pure goodness, which you do not know.
You are Aṅgulimāla, and I am a Samyak-Saṁbuddha.
I now give you the water of the unsurpassed good Dharma.
You should drink it quickly to end forever your thirst for birth and death.

Abide, abide, Aṅgulimāla, abide in the pure precepts.
I am a Samyak-Saṁbuddha, and give you the sword of wisdom.
I abide in transcending the world, which you do not know.
You are Aṅgulimāla, and I am a Samyak-Saṁbuddha.
I now give you the water of the unsurpassed good Dharma.
You should drink it quickly to end forever your thirst for birth and death.

Abide, abide, Aṅgulimāla, abide in the pure precepts.
I am a Samyak-Saṁbuddha, and give you the sword of wisdom.
I abide in no motion, which you do not know.
You are Aṅgulimāla, and I am a Samyak-Saṁbuddha.
I now give you the water of the unsurpassed good Dharma.
You should drink it quickly to end forever your thirst for birth and death.

Abide, abide, Aṅgulimāla, abide in the pure precepts.
I am a Samyak-Saṁbuddha, and give you the sword of wisdom.
I abide in the Dharma hall, which you do not know.
You are Aṅgulimāla, and I am a Samyak-Saṁbuddha.
I now give you the water of the unsurpassed good Dharma.
You should drink it quickly to end forever your thirst for birth and death.

Abide, abide, Aṅgulimāla, abide in the pure precepts.
I am a Samyak-Saṁbuddha, and give you the sword of wisdom.
I abide in no regrets, which you do not know.
You are Aṅgulimāla, and I am a Samyak-Saṁbuddha.
I now give you the water of the unsurpassed good Dharma.
You should drink it quickly to end forever your thirst for birth and death.

Abide, abide, Aṅgulimāla, abide in the pure precepts.
I am a Samyak-Saṁbuddha, and give you the sword of wisdom.

I abide in rest, which you do not know.
You are Aṅgulimāla, and I am a Samyak-Saṁbuddha.
I now give you the water of the unsurpassed good Dharma.
You should drink it quickly to end forever your thirst for birth and death.

Abide, abide, Aṅgulimāla, abide in the pure precepts.
I am a Samyak-Saṁbuddha, and give you the sword of wisdom.
I abide in the ultimate, which you do not know.
You are Aṅgulimāla, and I am a Samyak-Saṁbuddha.
I now give you the water of the unsurpassed good Dharma.
You should drink it quickly to end forever your thirst for birth and death.

Abide, abide, Aṅgulimāla, abide in the pure precepts.
I am a Samyak-Saṁbuddha, and give you the sword of wisdom.
I abide in the end of the three poisons [greed, anger, and delusion], which you do not know.
You are Aṅgulimāla, and I am a Samyak-Saṁbuddha.
I now give you the water of the unsurpassed good Dharma.
You should drink it quickly to end forever your thirst for birth and death.

Abide, abide, Aṅgulimāla, abide in the pure precepts.
I am a Samyak-Saṁbuddha, and give you the sword of wisdom.
I abide in the end of afflictions, which you do not know.
You are Aṅgulimāla, and I am a Samyak-Saṁbuddha.
I now give you the water of the unsurpassed good Dharma.
You should drink it quickly to end forever your thirst for birth and death.

Abide, abide, Aṅgulimāla, abide in the pure precepts.
I am a Samyak-Saṁbuddha, and give you the sword of wisdom.
I abide in the end of remnants, which you do not know.
You are Aṅgulimāla, and I am a Samyak-Saṁbuddha.
I now give you the water of the unsurpassed good Dharma.
You should drink it quickly to end forever your thirst for birth and death.

Abide, abide, Aṅgulimāla, abide in the pure precepts.
I am a Samyak-Saṁbuddha, and give you the sword of wisdom.
I abide in the depletion of the three poisons, which you do not know.
You are Aṅgulimāla, and I am a Samyak-Saṁbuddha.
I now give you the water of the unsurpassed good Dharma.
You should drink it quickly to end forever your thirst for birth and death.

Abide, abide, Aṅgulimāla, abide in the pure precepts.
I am a Samyak-Saṁbuddha, and give you the sword of wisdom.
I abide in the eradication [of afflictions], which you do not know.
You are Aṅgulimāla, and I am a Samyak-Saṁbuddha.
I now give you the water of the unsurpassed good Dharma.
You should drink it quickly to end forever your thirst for birth and death.

Abide, abide, Aṅgulimāla, abide in the pure precepts.
I am a Samyak-Saṁbuddha, and give you the sword of wisdom.
I abide in relinquishment, which you do not know.
You are Aṅgulimāla, and I am a Samyak-Saṁbuddha.
I now give you the water of the unsurpassed good Dharma.
You should drink it quickly to end forever your thirst for birth and death.

Abide, abide, Aṅgulimāla, abide in the pure precepts.
I am a Samyak-Saṁbuddha, and give you the sword of wisdom.
I abide in protecting [sentient beings], which you do not know.
You are Aṅgulimāla, and I am a Samyak-Saṁbuddha.
I now give you the water of the unsurpassed good Dharma.
You should drink it quickly to end forever your thirst for birth and death.

Abide, abide, Aṅgulimāla, abide in the pure precepts.
I am a Samyak-Saṁbuddha, and give you the sword of wisdom.
I abide as [sentient beings'] reliance, which you do not know.
You are Aṅgulimāla, and I am a Samyak-Saṁbuddha.
I now give you the water of the unsurpassed good Dharma.
You should drink it quickly to end forever your thirst for birth and death.

Abide, abide, Aṅgulimāla, abide in the pure precepts.
I am a Samyak-Saṁbuddha, and give you the sword of wisdom.
I abide on [sentient beings'] life-paths, which you do not know.
You are Aṅgulimāla, and I am a Samyak-Saṁbuddha.
I now give you the water of the unsurpassed good Dharma.
You should drink it quickly to end forever your thirst for birth and death.

Abide, abide, Aṅgulimāla, abide in the pure precepts.
I am a Samyak-Saṁbuddha, and give you the sword of wisdom.
I abide as a safe island [for sentient beings], which you do not know.
You are Aṅgulimāla, and I am a Samyak-Saṁbuddha.
I now give you the water of the unsurpassed good Dharma.
You should drink it quickly to end forever your thirst for birth and death.

Abide, abide, Aṅgulimāla, abide in the pure precepts.
I am a Samyak-Saṁbuddha, and give you the sword of wisdom.
I abide in accommodating all, which you do not know.
You are Aṅgulimāla, and I am a Samyak-Saṁbuddha.
I now give you the water of the unsurpassed good Dharma.
You should drink it quickly to end forever your thirst for birth and death.

Abide, abide, Aṅgulimāla, abide in the pure precepts.
I am a Samyak-Saṁbuddha, and give you the sword of wisdom.
I abide in no stinginess, which you do not know.
You are Aṅgulimāla, and I am a Samyak-Saṁbuddha.
I now give you the water of the unsurpassed good Dharma.
You should drink it quickly to end forever your thirst for birth and death.

Abide, abide, Aṅgulimāla, abide in the pure precepts.
I am a Samyak-Saṁbuddha, and give you the sword of wisdom.
I abide in no thirst [for rebirth], which you do not know.
You are Aṅgulimāla, and I am a Samyak-Saṁbuddha.
I now give you the water of the unsurpassed good Dharma.
You should drink it quickly to end forever your thirst for birth and death.

Abide, abide, Aṅgulimāla, abide in the pure precepts.
I am a Samyak-Saṁbuddha, and give you the sword of wisdom.
I abide in relinquishing everything, which you do not know.
You are Aṅgulimāla, and I am a Samyak-Saṁbuddha.
I now give you the water of the unsurpassed good Dharma.
You should drink it quickly to end forever your thirst for birth and death.

Abide, abide, Aṅgulimāla, abide in the pure precepts.
I am a Samyak-Saṁbuddha, and give you the sword of wisdom.
I abide in leaving everything behind, which you do not know.
You are Aṅgulimāla, and I am a Samyak-Saṁbuddha.
I now give you the water of the unsurpassed good Dharma.
You should drink it quickly to end forever your thirst for birth and death.

Abide, abide, Aṅgulimāla, abide in the pure precepts.
I am a Samyak-Saṁbuddha, and give you the sword of wisdom.
I abide in stopping everything, which you do not know.
You are Aṅgulimāla, and I am a Samyak-Saṁbuddha.
I now give you the water of the unsurpassed good Dharma.
You should drink it quickly to end forever your thirst for birth and death.

Abide, abide, Aṅgulimāla, abide in the pure precepts.
I am a Samyak-Saṁbuddha, and give you the sword of wisdom.
I abide in the end of suffering, which you do not know.
You are Aṅgulimāla, and I am a Samyak-Saṁbuddha.
I now give you the water of the unsurpassed good Dharma.
You should drink it quickly to end forever your thirst for birth and death.

Abide, abide, Aṅgulimāla, abide in the pure precepts.
I am a Samyak-Saṁbuddha, and give you the sword of wisdom.
I abide in the bliss of emptiness, which you do not know.
You are Aṅgulimāla, and I am a Samyak-Saṁbuddha.
I now give you the water of the unsurpassed good Dharma.
You should drink it quickly to end forever your thirst for birth and death.

Abide, abide, Aṅgulimāla, abide in the pure precepts.
I am a Samyak-Saṁbuddha, and give you the sword of wisdom.
I abide in removing fetters, which you do not know.
You are Aṅgulimāla, and I am a Samyak-Saṁbuddha.
I now give you the water of the unsurpassed good Dharma.
You should drink it quickly to end forever your thirst for birth and death.

Abide, abide, Aṅgulimāla, abide in the pure precepts.
I am a Samyak-Saṁbuddha, and give you the sword of wisdom.
I abide in the end of love [of being], which you do not know.
You are Aṅgulimāla, and I am a Samyak-Saṁbuddha.
I now give you the water of the unsurpassed good Dharma.
You should drink it quickly to end forever your thirst for birth and death.

Abide, abide, Aṅgulimāla, abide in the pure precepts.
I am a Samyak-Saṁbuddha, and give you the sword of wisdom.
I abide in no desire, which you do not know.
You are Aṅgulimāla, and I am a Samyak-Saṁbuddha.
I now give you the water of the unsurpassed good Dharma.
You should drink it quickly to end forever your thirst for birth and death.

Abide, abide, Aṅgulimāla, abide in the pure precepts.
I am a Samyak-Saṁbuddha, and give you the sword of wisdom.
I abide in nirvāṇa, which you do not know.
You are Aṅgulimāla, and I am a Samyak-Saṁbuddha.
I now give you the water of the unsurpassed good Dharma.
You should drink it quickly to end forever your thirst for birth and death.

Abide, abide, Aṅgulimāla, abide in the pure precepts.
I am a Samyak-Saṁbuddha, and give you the sword of wisdom.
Quickly cast away your sharp sword and return to radiant wisdom.
Do not follow the wisdom of an evil teacher, who claims that non-dharma is dharma.
Taste the supreme medicine and come to profound self-realization.

All [sentient beings] dread the pain of being clubbed, and love their lives.
Using yourself as an example, do not kill and do not tell others to kill.
As self and others are no different, so too are others and self.
Using yourself as an example, do not kill and do not tell others to kill.

Do not assume the form of a rākṣasa, who smears its body with human blood.
Do not wield a sharp sword stained with human blood.
Quickly cast away your finger garland and end the karma of a double life.[6]
Your double life does not accord with the Dharma, but is that of an evil rākṣasa.

Even a lamb knows devotion to its mother.
Sadly, you are pitiable because you were misguided by an evil teacher,
Wielded a sharp sword, and killed those born to live [their lives].
The karma you have done is more evil than that done by animal predators.
Your killings surpass a rākṣasa's.
You will enter the gang of evil māras, and be forever separate from humans.

Denounce the rebellious evil one, who does not requite his mother's kindness.
She carries, protects, and nourishes him in her womb for twelve months.
After he is born, she nurses him and endures his filth day and night.
Observe your mother, who is shedding bloody tears.
Out of love and concern for you, she has brought you food in person.
Her hair is disarrayed by wind, and her body is soiled by dust.
Her hands and feet are cracked, revealing the suffering of her deteriorating body.
Long distressed by hunger and thirst through winter and summer,
Her mind is perturbed as she laments her suffering.

When Aṅgulimāla's mother heard the dialogue between the Buddha-Bhagavān and her son, and saw that her son's mind was subjugated, because he lowered his menacing arm, concerned for her son, she spoke to the Buddha in verse:

Today a long-lost treasure store is recovered.
My eyes, impaired by dust and filth, have become bright and clear.
How sad that my son's mind was deranged
As he smeared his body with human blood.

Constantly holding a sharp sword in his hand,
He killed many people, who became a pile of corpses.
I would like my son to follow me
To reverently bow down to the Samyak-Saṁbuddha.
Many who see me scold me in foul language
Because I have such a son.

Then the World-Honored One told Aṅgulimāla, "Under this tree is your mother, who gave birth to you and reared you. Her great kindness is hard for you to requite. How can you kill her to have her be reborn in heaven? Aṅgulimāla, whoever claims that non-dharma is dharma is like a thirsty deer that seeks water in a mirage in springtime. Likewise are you. Because you follow an evil teacher's instruction, you are confused. Whoever does non-dharma and claims that it is dharma, after death, will fall into the indiscriminate hell.[7]

"Aṅgulimāla, come quickly to take refuge in the Tathāgata. Aṅgulimāla, have no fear. The Tathāgata's great lovingkindness is the place of no fear. He regards all sentient beings equally as Rāhula [His only son], and cures their diseases. For those without reliance, He serves as their reliance. The stability of the Tathāgata is their rest place. For those without kin, He serves as their kin. For those in poverty, He serves as their treasure store. To those who have lost the Buddha path, He indicates the unsurpassed path. For those in fear, he serves as their protector. For those adrift, He serves as their ship.

"You should quickly cast away your sharp sword, and renounce family life to train to attain bodhi. You should prostrate yourself at your mother's feet to repent and cleanse [off your sin]. Earnestly request her permission to renounce family life in order to deliver her from her suffering in the Three Realms of

Existence. I now approve your renouncement of family life and your acceptance of the complete monastic precepts. You now should drink the Dharma water like sweet dew. You are tired after long roaming in confusion on the evil path. You now should rest. You will become a giver like me, to give benefits to all those who abide by the law and enable them to cross the ocean of birth and death."

Forthwith Aṅgulimāla cast away his sharp sword. As a yearling infant recoils at once when he touches fire, and cries as his hands tremble, likewise Aṅgulimāla cast away his finger garland at once and cried aloud as his hands trembled. If a man in deep sleep is bitten on the foot by a snake, he immediately awakens and casts the snake far away. Likewise Aṅgulimāla cast away his finger garland. Then Aṅgulimāla, as if having exorcized possession by a nonhuman, regained his sense of shame and sense of dishonor. His entire body sweated blood, and his tears poured like rain. As a good doctor recites a mantra to a patient bitten by a snake to have him slither like a snake, so Aṅgulimāla slithered on his abdomen in a circle thirty-nine times. Then he moved forward, prostrated himself at the Buddha's feet, and spoke in verse:

> Amazing! The Saṁbuddha, the one who possesses the foremost lovingkindness,
> The tamer and teacher of men, comes to me,
> To enable me to cross the ocean of ignorance,
> Which abounds with dark waves of delusion and confusion.
>
> Amazing! The Saṁbuddha, the one who possesses the foremost compassion,
> The teacher and tamer of men, comes to me,
> To deliver me from the wilderness of birth and death,
> Which abounds with the thorn brushes of various afflictions.
>
> Amazing! The Saṁbuddha, the one who possesses the foremost sympathetic joy,
> The teacher and tamer of men, comes to me,
> To deliver me from my delusions,
> Caused by the wrong views, like the perils of tigers, wolves, and other predators.
>
> Amazing! The Saṁbuddha, the one who possesses the foremost equability,
> The teacher and tamer of men, comes to me,
> To deliver me from the indiscriminate hell
> And save me from immeasurable suffering.
>
> For those without reliance, He serves as their reliance.
> For those without kin, He serves as their kin.
> He now comes to me to be my refuge,
> Though I am laden with evil karmas and bound for tremendous suffering.

Then the World-Honored One told Aṅgulimāla, "Rise, quickly go to your mother, earnestly repent, and request her permission to renounce family life."

Aṅgulimāla rose from his place at the Buddha's feet and went to his mother. He circled her many times and prostrated himself. He earnestly repented and cried out in sorrow. Then he spoke to his mother in verse:

Alas, loving-kind mother, I have made grave mistakes,
Gathering evil karmas into a mass of sins.
I followed my evil teacher's instruction to commit murder
And killed nine hundred ninety-nine people, short of a thousand by only one.

I now take refuge in my mother
And take refuge in the Buddha-Bhagavān.
I bow down at my mother's feet
And request her permission to renounce family life.

His mother answered in verse:

I now give you permission
To renounce family life for the sake of your next life.
I also beseech the Tathāgata to permit me
To renounce family and accept the complete monastic precepts.

Amazing, inconceivable!
The Tathāgata is beyond analogy.
The Buddha, who now delivers my son,
Pities all in the world.

His sublime physical body
And virtues are unparalleled.
I now praise Him,
The supreme god of gods.

Then the World-Honored One answered in verse:

Very good, good woman!
You will enjoy uninterrupted joy
Because you permit your son
To renounce family life before me.

You now are old and feeble,
Already past the time to renounce family life.[8]
Nevertheless, you should have the joy of deep faith
And take the Dharma as your rest place.
You now should wait a little while,
For the arrival of King Prasenajit.

Then the god-king Śakra and his celestial multitude, including palace maids and retinues, emitted light from their bodies to illuminate the city of Śrāvastī. Having seen that Aṅgulimāla confronted the Buddha, lost his strength, changed his state of mind, and repented of his sins, they rejoiced, and the god-king Śakra spoke in verse:

Amazing! The hero who possesses the Ten Powers,
The tamer of men, the unequaled one,
Tamed Aṅgulimāla,
Who used to smear his body with blood.

When the generous god-king Indra, asuras, rākṣasas,
Violent yakṣas, dragons, kiṁnaras,
Strong garuḍas, and evil men
Heard of Aṅgulimāla, they closed their eyes out of fear.
How can a human king not be terrified upon seeing him?

When he was born, even dragons trembled with fear.
The armors of those in the kṣatriya caste fell apart, and their sabers and swords fell [to the ground].
How can a human king not be terrified upon seeing him?
However, the Tathāgata has tamed him, who has done such evil karma.
As the power of the Buddha is inconceivable, so too is His wisdom.
Amazing! Aṅgulimāla now well abides in the pure precepts,
And his Brahma way of life is pure like a mountain of gold.

Amazing! Today I rejoice that I have received the benefits of the good Dharma.
I now offer Aṅgulimāla a garment,
And pray that he will accept it because of the World-Honored One's compassion.
I now offer Aṅgulimāla the Dharma robe of a śramaṇa.
He will become a great mendicant king, as the World-Honored One can see.

Then the god-king Śakra said to Aṅgulimāla, "I pray that the great one will accept this celestial garment as his Dharma robe."

Aṅgulimāla said to the god-king Śakra, "What kind of mosquito or small insect are you? How can I accept alms from you? What kind of greedy donkey are you? You have not crossed the long flow of suffering from birth and death, and are in poor shape. How can you give away a robe as alms? You should know that you are in poor shape. How can you give anyone a priceless robe as alms?

"As an analogy, a king has a thousand strong men. However, before they see bandits, they already fall to the ground. How can they fight a thousand strong warriors of the enemy state? Hence, if I accepted this priceless robe, how could I subjugate a koṭi affliction māras and self-essence māras? I should eradicate countless afflictions, which is praised by the Buddha. I, a śramaṇa, should do the twelve dhūta practices.

"You are not a god-king because you are no different from those born blind. God-King Śakra, you do not know how to differentiate dharmas. What is called an atrocious evil karma? You are a mosquito. How can you know whether I am a violent evil man? Alas, God-King Śakra, if you regard Aṅgulimāla as a violent evil man, how can you understand the true meaning of the Buddha Dharma? What kind of śramaṇa would don a priceless robe when he has just renounced family life? You do not know the purity of renouncing family life.

"Alas, God-King Śakra, you are an outsider to the Tathāgata's true Dharma [saddharma]. His eldest son, Mahākāśyapa the Elder, had 80,000 treasure troves of jewels and countless other treasure stores, and various priceless precious garments. He discarded them all like spit. A śramaṇa has renounced family life to train to attain bodhi. He should do the twelve ascetic dhūta practices. Why does he not abandon self-restraint by donning a priceless robe?

"Mahākāśyapa the Elder forsook various kinds of delectable fine food and the flavor of flesh. He does spiritual training and refrains from eating flesh. When he begs for food from door to door, he never has any aversion. He remains the same, unchanged by pain or pleasure. When he begs for food, some say that they have no food for him, and some scold or insult him. He always responds, 'Have peace and joy,' then leaves, his mind never moving. If some say that they have food for him, he does not entertain greed or feel happy. He always responds, 'Have peace and joy,' accepts the food, and leaves, his mind never moving.

"If one gives great wealth as alms to monks, one's treasure stores will never be depleted. Why does one give alms not to monks, but to hungry ghosts, poor people, and forlorn beggars? God-King Śakra, a śramaṇa's way of life is not to accumulate things, not even salt or oil. Therefore, keeping slaves, servants, farmland, or houses, buying or selling impure things, or giving or accepting impure things is not a śramaṇa's way of life, but the way of one who lives a family life.

"Those who share your huge ignorance should be tamed, like treating weeds that harm seedlings. Those whom I killed and whose fingers I made into a garland were sentient beings that sabotaged the Dharma. None was a bhikṣu, bhikṣuṇī, upāsaka, or upāsikā."

Then the god-king Śakra asked Aṅgulimāla, "No harm is dharma. As the Tathāgata regards all sentient being equally as Rāhula, how can an evil man be tamed?"

Aṅgulimāla answered, "How do you know the difference between harm and no harm? Their appearances are like a magician's skillful means that others do not know. However, a Bodhisattva knows illusory states. You are an outsider to the Buddha Dharma. How can you know that there are two kinds of harm and no harm, such as no harm done by a Bodhisattva and no harm done by a voice-hearer? You are a puny mosquito. How can you know these two kinds of no harm? The difference between your state and a Bodhisattva's state is like a mosquito's wings that cover the open sky. Suppose that a śramaṇa is [in danger of] being abducted by a nonhuman. Should people safeguard him?"

The god-king Śakra answered, "They should."

Aṅgulimāla asked, "Indeed. If [that nonhuman] dies because of their safeguarding, who is guilty [of murder]?"

The god-king Śakra answered, "Those who have no intention to harm anyone are not guilty."

Aṅgulimāla said, "If the guardians kill evil ones in the process of taming them, they are not guilty of murder. Instead, they will acquire immeasurable excellent merit. This is called a Bodhisattva's doing no harm. Indeed, the difference between harm and no harm is hard to know.

"Suppose that a good doctor treats a patient. He uses a hook to hook out his tongue. If the patient dies, is the doctor guilty [of murder]?"

"No. That good doctor benefits patients, without any intention to harm any of them."

"When one tames evil ones, if one causes their death, is one guilty [of murder]?"

"No. One will acquire immeasurable merit, unless one intended to harm them."

"If a student studies under a teacher and dies because of his teachings, is his teacher guilty [of murder]?"

"No, unless he intended to harm his student."

"If evil ones die after seeing a dignified or prominent person, has he committed a sin subject to repentance?"

"No, unless he intended to harm them.

"Therefore, God-King Śakra, you do not know the difference between good karma and evil karma, nor that between a śramaṇa and a non-śramaṇa. The evil ones who sabotage the true Dharma should be tamed.

"For example, eighty great voice-hearers, such as Mahākāśyapa the Elder, relinquished their great treasure stores and renounced family life to train to attain bodhi. Abiding in the true Dharma, they have few desires and much contentment. Does a bhikṣu need to don a priceless robe? All bhikṣus shave off their hair and beard, travel alone with a begging bowl, and survive by begging for food. How can such a bhikṣu abandon self-restraint? He is oppressed by heat and cold, hunger and thirst. His feet tread dirt as do a wild deer's. He never violates even a minor precept, like a yak that loves its tail. He protects [the purity of] the precepts, like a bird sitting on its chicks. Like an elephant with a broken tusk, he has lost his good appearances. Why would he need a priceless robe? You are an outsider to the true Dharma and should take care not to speak [about the robe again]. As a non-Buddhist or caṇḍāla [outcaste] does not have two births[9] as does a śramaṇa, so too you do not because you are a caṇḍāla, outside the true Dharma. You, a puny mosquito, should keep quiet."

Notes

1. See "Brahmin caste" defined in the glossary's "four Indian castes."

2. Text 120 (T02n0120) states "age twelve." It is possible that the Chinese number twenty (二十) was erroneously written as twelve (十二).

3. See a sentient being's birth, aging, illness, and death in the glossary's "four appearances." In true reality, because a dharma has no birth, it has no death, no aging, no illness, no taints, etc.

4. See "no action" in the glossary's Three Liberation Doors.

5. That shore of bodhi (enlightenment) is opposite this shore of birth and death.

6. Aṅgulimāla is a human but leads the life of a rākṣasa.

7. The indiscriminate hell is Avīci Hell, the hell of interrupted suffering, which is indiscriminate of the gender and privileges of those who have committed the five rebellious sins, one of which is matricide. See the glossary's Avīci Hell and "five rebellious sins."

8. Considering that Aṅgulimāla is only twenty years of age, his mother is not old and not past the time to renounce family life.

9. According to text 1547, the Chinese version of the *Great Commentary* (Vibhāṣā), a bird is called two births because an egg is born from the mother bird, and a chick is born from the egg. Likewise a śramaṇa or Brahmin is called two births because he is born from his mother and is born again when he renounces family life to train to attain bodhi (T28n1547, 0522b26–28).

Fascicle 2 (of 4)

Then the Brahma-King Śikhin, the ruler of this Sahā World, emitted vast radiance to illuminate the city of Śrāvastī. Single-mindedly he joined his palms and bowed down at the Buddha's feet. After making offerings to the Tathāgata and Aṅgulimāla, he spoke in verse:

Amazing! Today I have seen a great battle, like a battle between two ferocious lions.
Amazing! The Tathāgata, the tamer of men, the teacher of gods and humans, has well tamed Aṅgulimāla.
As an analogy, when a venomous snake sees a mantra master, it spews venom.
But he has no fear and tames it to make it quiet.
Likewise the great master in the Three Realms of Existence
Has tamed the atrocious Aṅgulimāla.

I now bow down to the physician of the Three Realms of Existence, whose great spiritual power is inconceivable.
I now bow down to the sovereign king, whose establishings are extraordinary.
He has established Aṅgulimāla in the Dharma.
Because there is no analogy for His utmost excellent works, He is called the beyond-analogy honored one.

Now Aṅgulimāla does excellent karmas and tamely abides in the precepts and extreme quietness.
His body and mind are stable and fearless,
Just as one's true nature is golden,
Like the pure and wonderful Jambūnada gold.[1]

I pray that the Tathāgata, out of pity, will accept my offerings
And command Aṅgulimāla to don a celestial garment,
So that I will attain great bodhi.
When he dons this robe to protect his Brahma way of life,
His ultimate pure mind will remain motionless.

Aṅgulimāla said to the Brahma-king, "Who are you, speaking these superfluous divisive words? Your saying that Aṅgulimāla should don your robe to practice the Brahma way of life for a long time is an insult. You are an evil Brahma god, not an image of Brahmā. You, a mosquito, mention Brahma. What is meant by Brahma? What is meant by worldly Brahma karma? Why would I don a mosquito's garment to practice the Brahma way of life? Nor would I be a servant, take others' orders, or be a debtor. As a trapeze flyer quickly flies to and fro in the sky, likewise you, a puny mosquito, after enjoying the pleasures in your Brahma heaven, will fall to this human world. You do not know the true merit of a Bodhisattva's rebirth here, but take non-dharma as dharma. Gods like you are unaware of the deluded turning of the wheel of birth and death. Alas, Brahma-King, do you truly know good versus evil? You say that Aṅgulimāla has done huge evil karmas. How do you, a mosquito, an evil Brahma, know that? You should learn to take Bodhisattva actions."

The Brahma-king answered, "You killed nine hundred ninety-nine people, short of a thousand by only one. I see that you are still aggressive. Even an eagle or vulture dares not come near you. If you are not an aggressive one, where can a truly aggressive one be found? If you are not an evil māra, where can a truly evil māra be found? Aṅgulimāla, do not abandon self-restraint but use skillful means to obliterate your evil karmas. Very good! The Tathāgata has truly great compassion, which can deliver even atrocious sentient beings, such as Aṅgulimāla."

Aṅgulimāla said to the Brahma-king, "Evil Brahma mosquito, where will you go? Where will you go round and round in confusion? You do not know that evil sentient beings, after death, go down evil life-paths. As an analogy, someone goes to a forest at night. He sees fireflies on the trees and is terrified. He returns to the city and tells others, 'That forest is burning.' Then people go there and see fireflies, not a fire. It is the same with you, an evil Brahma god. You declare, 'I am deluded,' to deceive yourself and others. Later on, you and others will come to know that one's delusion is illusory. As an analogy, a deluded man goes to a forest. When he sees the [red] flowers of the aśoka trees,[2] he takes them as fire. He returns to the city and tells others, 'That forest is burning.' Then people go there and see that there is no fire. It is the same with you, a puny mosquito. Later on, you and others will come to know that good and evil are illusory. Do not speak such untrue words again. You should keep quiet and not tell lies."

Then the four world-protecting god-kings came to the Buddha. After making great offerings to the Buddha and Aṅgulimāla, they spoke to them in verse:

> Amazing! So extraordinary!
> Today the hero of this world fought a great battle.
> He answered questions about the highest truth [paramārtha]
> And used wisdom light to dispel the darkness of ignorance.
>
> Amazing! The tamer of men, the unsurpassed teacher of gods and humans,
> Because of His immeasurable power, is called the Tathāgata.
> He is the foremost padma [red lotus flower], completely pure and soft,
> Untainted by dust or water.
> Hence we bow down to the Buddha's feet and take refuge in Him.
> Single-mindedly we ask Him to grant our request for Aṅgulimāla to accept and use our bowl.
> Now Aṅgulimāla is excellent, like the moon in the sky.
> He is stately, and his observance of the precepts is perfect.

Aṅgulimāla said to the four world-protecting god-kings, "What kind of mosquitoes or small insects are you? Because you protect the world, you exalt yourselves. Your saying that you will give me a celestial bowl as alms is an insult. Although you now see my tribulations, you soon will see yourselves holding pottery vessels. Why do you use a luxurious bowl and call yourselves renowned world protectors? He who is called a world protector claims that he can tame evil ones. Actually, whoever is called a protector protects the true Dharma [saddharma], not the world. As an analogy, someone hears the sound of a kañjala [hill myna] and sees its shape. Then he sees a crow and gets confused. He keeps calling it 'kañjala, kañjala.' It is the same with you. You take non-dharma as dharma and safeguard it, just like that person who sees a crow and calls it kañjala. You should protect the Dharma, not the world. You four mosquito god-kings should keep quiet."

Then Pāpīyān, the evil māra-king, came to the Buddha. After making offerings to the Buddha, he stood aside and spoke to Aṅgulimāla in verse:

> You should quickly renounce family life as a hoax and enter my city.
> I do not care about you but will let you evade naraka [hell].

Aṅgulimāla answered in verse:

> Go far away, thieving dog māra, who speaks like a fearless mosquito.
> Before you are bound by five fetters, Pāpīyān, quickly go away.
> Do not force me to instantly kick a vile dog with my left foot.
> When I realize the emptiness of dharmas and that they have no self, I will freely visit [celestial] palaces.
>
> As a golden-winged garuḍa-king dwells atop Mount Sumeru
> And observes dragons frolicking in the vast ocean,
> Likewise a Bodhisattva dwells above hell,
> Joyfully drinks the water of liberation, and observes suffering sentient beings.
>
> You thieving dog māra should keep quiet and intently listen to the Dharma like drinking sweet dew,
> Then return to heaven and do whatever you want.

Then the Brahma-king Maheśvara made great offerings to the Tathāgata and Aṅgulimāla and stood aside. With joy and respect, he praised in verse:

> I now bow down at the feet of the World-Honored One, and speak stanzas with joy and respect.
> The Tathāgata's sublime physical body is like an utpala [blue lotus flower].
> His white teeth are like a kumuda [white lotus flower], and his pure eyes are like thousand-petaled flowers.
> His wisdom is taint free, purer than a puṇḍarīka [large white lotus flower].
>
> Amazing! Aṅgulimāla is excellent and so extraordinary.
> Although abiding on the ground of ordinary beings, he has tamed that māra.

He will quickly attain saṁbodhi [true enlightenment] and rescue all in the world.

Aṅgulimāla answered in verse:

On what lowly life-path are you, falsely calling yourself Maheśvara?
Īśvara [lord] is a false name because you are not truly a sovereign king.
How do you know whether I abide on the ground of ordinary beings?
Long-toothed piśāca, quickly answer my question.

Suppose that a mange victim with an unsightly body
Widely prescribes for the world the cure for mange.
Unable to cure his own disease, how can he cure others' diseases?
Likewise is a puny mosquito's delusion.

If you do not know your true nature, how can you know others' minds
And say that Aṅgulimāla abides on the ground of ordinary beings?
You should not be empowered to be a sovereign king.
To see [this problem], the ignorant should keep quiet.

Then the goddess of the tree under which the Tathāgata sat, saw Aṅgulimāla, and respect and faith rose in her heart. She praised in verse:

Come quickly, Aṅgulimāla, the brave, wise, and firm one.
I ask you to don the Dharma robe, and I will offer you your first meal.
Giving alms to you and the Tathāgata will bring me the highest fruit.

Aṅgulimāla answered in verse:

The Tathāgata has never eaten anything, nor have the voice-hearers.
To whom are you giving alms?
Speak quickly to resolve my doubts.

The tree goddess challenged him in verse:

As the Tathāgata regularly eats food, so too do voice-hearers.
If you firmly decide to renounce family life, you should not tell lies.
You should discard falsity and fawning, which are impure.
If one oversteps even one dharma, it becomes a lie.
Then one cannot transcend the world, but will do evil.

Aṅgulimāla answered in verse:

You are on a lowly life-path, and what do you want to do?
You should observe yourself because the Buddha speaks ill of women.
Who in the world tells lies, and who speaks the truth?
Who in the world is greedy for food, and who in the world falls ill and dies?
The Tathāgata possesses all the virtues of a vast self.[3]

If one says something that one cannot know, this is a lie.
If one does not eat food but claims that one does, this is a lie.
If one says that one does not understand veiled words, this is a lie.
If one has not even renounced family life, how can one accept the complete monastic precepts?
I do not overstep a single dharma, while you overstep countless dharmas.
Go quickly to the god of gods [the Buddha] to repent of your false speech.

The tree goddess challenged him in verse:

Why do you say that I am on a lowly life-path?
Not yet having discarded the way of a piśāca, how can you know that I am male or female?

Aṅgulimāla answered in verse:

As an analogy, a Wheel-Turning King possesses a jewel-adorned throne.
If a dog lies on it, even temporarily, it becomes impure.
You possess a lowly nature and live a life of convenience.
You assume a female body and indulge in the pleasures of the five desires.

You should use skillful means to quickly abandon your body, which is as lowly as a female dog's body.
You should discard [your attachment to] male or female appearances, and train to realize the emptiness of dharmas.
Once you realize their emptiness, you will quickly acquire a man's nature.

Then the venerable Śāriputra and Mahāmaudgalyāyana, like goose-kings, used their transcendental powers to soar across the sky. They came to the Buddha, bowed down at His feet, and stood aside. When they saw Aṅgulimāla, sympathetic joy rose in their hearts, and Mahāmaudgalyāyana praised in verse:

Outstanding! The brave and wise one excels in doing excellent karmas.
You should quickly follow the Buddha to renounce family life and observe the pure precepts.
Accompanied by those who practice the Brahma way of life, you can soar across the sky to the Jetavana garden.
I pray that the Buddha will compassionately give you permission to renounce family life and accept the complete monastic precepts,
So that all in the world will look up to you.
As you soar in the sky like a goose-king, you will be radiant and pure like the full moon.

Aṅgulimāla asked in verse:

What are transcendental powers in the world, and what are their roots?

The one honored as possessing the foremost transcendental powers,
Speak quickly to resolve my doubts.

Mahāmaudgalyāyana answered in verse:

If one practices pure relinquishment, one often gives away shoes and vehicles as alms.
If a bhikṣu observes the pure precepts, he stays far away from dissipation.
For these two reasons, one quickly acquires transcendental powers.

Aṅgulimāla again spoke in verse:

Alas, Mahāmaudgalyāyana practices the way of a mosquito
And cannot discern the truly foremost transcendental powers.
Even a mosquito can fly across the sky, and the ignorant should keep quiet.

One should constantly practice benefiting oneself and others, and wish to bring others peace.
If one trains in these skillful means, one will quickly acquire superior transcendental powers.
One should comfort Dharma expounders and those who endure tribulations.
If one sacrifices one's body to save and protect others, one will quickly acquire superior transcendental powers.

I now should take quick action to widely deliver sentient beings.
When I arrive at the Jetavana garden, I will acquire great transcendental powers.
Limitless is the Mahāyāna!
Immeasurable and boundless are Tathāgatas!

After speaking these stanzas, Aṅgulimāla asked Śāriputra in verse:

Why is Śāriputra honored in the world as one with great wisdom?
Whence does wisdom arise?
Speak quickly to resolve my doubts.

Śāriputra answered in verse:

Faithful observance of the five precepts bring great wisdom.
After one's death, wisdom always comes with one's rebirth.
As one's renown travels far, one's wisdom remains motionless.

Aṅgulimāla again spoke in verse:

Praising that Tathāgatas are eternal brings one great wisdom.
The Buddha says that great wisdom enables one to expound the Dharma.

Alas, Śāriputra practices the way of a mosquito
And does not know the true meaning of wisdom.
Crude is a mosquito's wisdom, and the ignorant should keep quiet.

Then the venerable Ānanda came to the Buddha. He bowed down at the Buddha's feet and stood aside. When he saw Aṅgulimāla, sympathetic joy rose in his heart, and he praised in verse:

Very good! Aṅgulimāla is training to do excellent karmas.
I now express sympathetic joy over his mastering sūtras in the nine categories.[4]

Aṅgulimāla asked in verse:

The Tathāgata praises you as foremost in hearing much [of the Dharma].
What is meant by hearing much [of the Dharma], and whence does it arise?

Ānanda answered in verse:

Recite and study sūtras in the nine categories and, without stinginess, expound them to others.
From these practices, one hears much [of the Dharma], and one's total retention of it is inconceivable.

Aṅgulimāla again spoke in verse:

Whoever praises that Tathāgatas are eternal
Is called foremost in hearing much [of the Dharma].
Alas, Ānanda practices the way of a mosquito
And does not know how to hear much [of the Dharma].
Crudity is what a mosquito upholds, and the ignorant should keep quiet.

Then the venerable Rāhula came to the Buddha. He bowed down at the Buddha's feet and stood aside. When he saw Aṅgulimāla, sympathetic joy rose in his heart, and he praised in verse:

Very good! Aṅgulimāla is training to acquire excellent merits.
I now express sympathetic joy over his respecting the precepts.

Aṅgulimāla asked in verse:

The Tathāgata praises you as foremost in respecting the precepts.
What is meant by respecting the pure precepts?
You are the Buddha's beloved son.
Speak quickly to resolve my doubts.

Rāhula answered in verse:

Intently and respectfully observe all precepts pronounced by the Buddha.
This is the foremost way to respect the precepts.

Aṅgulimāla again spoke in verse:

Saying that Tathāgatas are eternal
Is called the highest way to respect the precepts.
Alas, Rāhula practices the way of a mosquito
And does not know the truly foremost way to respect the precepts.
Crude is a mosquito's respect, and the ignorant should keep quiet.

Then Aniruddha came to the Buddha. He bowed down at the Buddha's feet and stood aside. When he saw Aṅgulimāla, sympathetic joy rose in his heart, and he praised in verse:

Amazing! Aṅgulimāla excels in doing excellent karmas.
I now express sympathetic joy over his soon acquiring the god eye.

Aṅgulimāla asked in verse:

The Tathāgata praises you as the one with the foremost god eye.
What is the god eye, and how is it acquired?
Speak quickly to resolve my doubts.

Aniruddha answered in verse:

Always give away bright lamps as alms and expound the Dharma to develop others.
From these practices, one acquires the god eye, to see faraway things hindrance free.

Aṅgulimāla again spoke in verse:

Diligently expounding the Tathāgata's profound Dharma store by skillful means,
With full disclosure and without concealment, brings one the most excellent eye.
Alas, Aniruddha practices the way of a mosquito
And does not know the skillful means to acquire the god eye.
Crude is a mosquito's eye, and the ignorant should keep quiet.

Then the venerable śramaṇa Dravya came to the Buddha. He bowed down at the Buddha's feet and stood aside. When he saw Aṅgulimāla, sympathetic joy rose in his heart, and he praised in verse:

Amazing! Aṅgulimāla excels in doing excellent karmas.

I now express sympathetic joy over his training in enduring adversity.

Aṅgulimāla asked in verse:

How does one acquire the foremost endurance?
How does one's endurance of adversity arise?
Speak quickly to resolve my doubts.

The śramaṇa Dravya answered in verse:

Whether one's right arm is smeared with sandalwood [perfume] or one's left hand is cut by a sharp knife,
If one's mind remains equable and motionless, one's foremost endurance arises.
Then one can endure superior self-restraint in the world.

Aṅgulimāla again spoke in verse:

If one reveals the Tathāgata store [tathāgata-garbha] to the world,
One can enable those who hold the wrong views to discard their self-view and train to realize that dharmas have no self.
One should declare that this is the Buddha's true Dharma, so that they will not dread to hear it.
One should discard arrogance and attachment to one's body and life, to widely expound the Tathāgata store.
This is called enduring superior self-restraint in the world.

Alas! The śramaṇa Dravya practices the way of a mosquito
And does not know the skillful means to acquire the highest endurance.
Even a mosquito can endure hunger, thirst, heat, cold, and pain.
Crude is a mosquito's endurance, and the ignorant should keep quiet.

Then the venerable Pūrṇa-Maitrāyaṇīputra came to the Buddha. He bowed down at the Buddha's feet and stood aside. When he saw Aṅgulimāla, sympathetic joy rose in his heart, and he praised in verse:

Very good! Aṅgulimāla is doing excellent karmas.
I express sympathetic joy over his comforting all sentient beings and expounding the Dharma.

Aṅgulimāla asked in verse:

The Tathāgata praises you as foremost in expounding the Dharma.
What is meant by expounding Dharma, and what is meant by knowing its meaning?
I pray that you will expound the Dharma to resolve my doubts.

Pūrṇa-Maitrāyaṇīputra answered in verse:

> There are things never found by Buddhas or holy voice-hearers.
> The truly enlightened one understands well what this means and widely expounds it to sentient beings.

[He said] "What does this stanza mean? It means that all past Buddhas delved into all dharmas by skillful means, and found neither the realm of sentient beings nor a self [ātman], a person, a sentient being, or an ever-lasting soul;[5] that all present and future Buddhas do delve and will delve into all dharmas by skill means, and do not and will not find these things; that all past, present, and future Pratyekabuddas and holy voice-hearers delved, do delve, and will delve into all dharmas by skillful means, and did not, do not, and will not find these things. Therefore, I tell sentient beings to discard [their perception of] the realm of sentient beings and [their imagination of] a self, a person, a sentient being, or an ever-lasting soul, because dharmas are empty and have no self. In this way I expound the Dharma."

Aṅgulimāla said to Pūrṇa-Maitrāyaṇīputra, "Alas, Pūrṇa-Maitrāyaṇīputra practices the way of a mosquito and does not know how to expound the Dharma. Alas, an ignorant mosquito does not know that the Tathāgata's teaching that dharmas have no self is a veiled teaching. It is like a moth throwing itself into the flame of the lamp of ignorance. Actually, what Buddha-Tathāgatas never find means that all past Buddha-Bhagavāns looked into all sentient beings by skillful means and did not find the absence of their Tathāgata store; that all present Buddha-Bhagavāns look into all sentient beings by skillful means and do not find the absence of their true self; that all future Buddhas will look into all sentient beings by skillful means and will not find the absence of their true nature; that all past, present, and future Pratyekabuddhas and holy voice-hearers looked, do look, and will look into all sentient beings by skillful means and did not, do not, and will not find the absence of their Tathāgata store. This is the true meaning of the Buddha's stanza.

"Moreover, what Buddha-Tathāgatas never find means that all past Buddha-Tathāgatas delved, do delve, and will delve into all dharmas by skillful means, and did not, do not, and will not find a self imagined by the world to have various features, such as its size being that of a thumb, a grain of rice, a sesame seed, a wheat berry, or a mustard seed; its color being blue, yellow, red, or white; its shape being square, round, long, or short. Some say that one's self is in one's heart, or above or below one's navel; some say that it is in one's head, eyes, or body parts; some say that it permeates one's body, like sweat; some say that it is constantly in peace and joy, and at rest. Such countless diverse, deluded thoughts are the worldly way to identify one's self. All Buddhas, Pratyekabuddhas, and holy voice-hearers never find such a self, and the truly enlightened one explains this to sentient beings. This is the true meaning of the Tathāgata's stanza, not what you just explained according to your deluded thinking.

"Moreover, what Buddha-Tathāgatas never find means that all past Buddha-Bhagavāns sought by skillful means and did not find the action of the Tathāgata store, because the Tathāgata in every sentient being by nature has no action, but has immeasurable purity and majesty and countless good characteristics; that all present Buddha-Bhagavāns seek by skillful means and do not find the action of one's Tathāgata store, because the Tathāgata in every sentient being by nature has no action, but has immeasurable purity and majesty and countless good characteristics; that all future Buddha-Bhagavāns will seek by skillful means and will not find the action of one's Tathāgata store, because the Tathāgata in every sentient being by nature has no action, but has immeasurable purity and majesty and countless good characteristics.

"All past, present, and future Pratyekabuddhas and holy voice-hearers did not, do not, and will not see with their eyes the Tathāgata store in their bodies. There is a reason. For example, because Rāhula respects the precepts, when he observes pure water, he does not understand that he sees an insect [in the water]. He wonders whether it is an insect, not an insect, or a dust particle. After intently observing for a long time, he gradually comes to see the tiny insect as it is. It is the same with a Bodhisattva on the tenth ground.[6] When he observes his true nature in his body, he entertains countless different views of this nature. Because it is hard to enter one's Tathāgata store, it is hard to comfort a Dharma expounder. In the blazingly evil world, not sparing his body or life, he expounds the Tathāgata store to sentient beings. Therefore, I say that Bodhisattva-Mahāsattvas, who are heroes among men, are [virtually] Tathāgatas.

"Aniruddha possesses the foremost god eye, and truly and clearly sees bird tracks in the sky, which cannot be seen by those who possess only the physical eye. However, they believe that Aniruddha sees bird tracks [in the sky]. Likewise Pratyekabuddhas, voice-hearers, and ordinary beings with the physical eye believe that they have the Tathāgata store because it is stated in the Buddha's sūtras. How can they see their Buddha nature [buddha-dhātu or buddha-gotra] as Buddhas do? Even Pratyekabuddhas and holy voice-hearers come to believe in it because of their trust in a source. How can ordinary beings, like the born blind, know [their Tathāgata store] on their own without learning about it from others?

"I heard from a past Buddha that in the initial kalpa of this world, the earth contained four flavors. Those who tasted these four flavors then still eat dirt now, because they do not abandon their longtime practice. It is the same with those who trained under past Tathāgatas to observe their Tathāgata store. Because of their longtime training, they now still believe in it with delight and train through the long night to requite the Tathāgatas' kindness. When they hear about one's Tathāgata store from a future Dharma expounder, they will also believe in it with delight. Those who believe [in one's Tathāgata store] with delight are the Tathāgata's sons and will requite His kindness.

"As an analogy, since the distant past, an owl has had no sense of shame and has never requited its mother's kindness. Even now, it never abandons its longtime habit. It is the same with sentient beings. Because in their past lives they had no sense of shame and no sense of dishonor, they continue in this way from the past to the present, and to the future. Likewise, because they did not believe in it with delight when they heard about one's Tathāgata store, they continue in this way from the past to the present, and to the future.

"As an analogy, an ugly monkey is constantly in fear, and its mind is restless, like raging waves. Because its past habit, it continues to be restless. It is the same with sentient beings, whose minds were, are, and will be restless in the past, present, and future. When they hear about one's Tathāgata store, they do not believe in it with delight.

"As a horned owl that sees better by night than by day prefers dark to light, likewise sentient beings prefer evil to good and, throughout past, present, and future, do not delight in seeing a Buddha or believing in one's Tathāgata store. Because a person has acquired the wrong views through the long night and is attached to the wrong doctrines of those on the wrong paths, he now does not abandon his past habit. It is the same with those who have long studied the veiled teaching that dharmas have no self. Like a fool attached to the wrong doctrines, throughout past, present, and future, they do not understand the secret teachings. When they hear about one's Tathāgata store, they do not believe in it with delight.

"Suppose that someone encountered Buddhas in the past, made offerings to Them, served Them, and heard about one's Tathāgata store even as briefly as a finger snap. Because of this good karma, his faculties became skilled, and he enjoyed unrestricted wealth and rank. In this life, sentient beings like him also have skilled faculties and enjoy unrestricted wealth and rank. Because in the past they briefly heard about one's Tathāgata store from Buddhas, when they hear about it in the future, they will believe in it with delight and train according to the teachings heard. Their faculties will be skilled, their wealth and rank will be unrestricted, their body will be strong, their wisdom will be radiant, and their Brahma tones will be pure and loved by all. They will become a Wheel-Turning King, a prince, or a great minister. They will possess worthy virtues and be free from arrogance and conceit. They will conquer the need for sleep, and study and train diligently, never abandoning self-restraint. They will acquire other merits and will even become the god-king Śakra or one of the four world-protecting god-kings. Because of the merit they acquired by hearing about the Tathāgata store, their body will always be stable, free from illness and trouble. Their lifespans will be prolonged, and they will be loved and respected by all. They will fully hear the sweet-dew teaching that a Tathāgata constantly abides in the great parinirvāṇa, and firmly and stably abides in the world in accord with the worldly ways. They will know that a Tathāgata is not born from desire, but born to widely expound the Dharma to the world. Through the benefits of their wisdom and merit, wherever they will be reborn, they will be reborn into an excellent clan and family and have many children and grandchildren, and their parents will live long. Throughout past, present, and future, they will always enjoy all pleasures in heaven or in the human world, because they have heard that the Tathāgata store forever abides in every sentient being.

"If sentient beings on the five life-paths have missing limbs and undergo all kinds of suffering as they transmigrate through birth and death throughout past, present, and future, it is because they have slighted one's Tathāgata store. If sentient beings serve Buddhas, and stay close and make offerings to Them, then they will come to hear about one's Tathāgata store. If they accept it, believe in it with delight, do not malign it, and truly comfort the [Dharma] expounder, know that they are [virtually] Tathāgatas. If sentient beings go against Buddhas, or malign one's Tathāgata store when they hear about it, they burn away their [bodhi] seeds. Alas, pain, pain! The nonbelievers in the three time frames are so pitiable.

"In this way a Dharma expounder should give teachings and praise the truth of a Tathāgata's eternity. If he does not do so, he abandons [the truth of] one's Tathāgata store. This person should not sit on a lion throne. Like a caṇḍāla [outcaste], he should not ride a great king's elephant.

"All Buddhas seek the birth of one's Tathāgata store by skillful means and never find it, because no birth is Buddha nature, which exists in every sentient being, has countless excellent characteristics, and is pure and majestic. All Buddhas seek the untruth of one's true nature by skillful means and never find it, because truth is one's Buddha nature, which exists in every sentient being, has countless excellent characteristics, and is pure and majestic. All Buddhas seek the impermanence of one's true nature by skillful means and never find it, because permanence is one's Buddha nature, which exists in every sentient being, has countless excellent characteristics, and is pure and majestic. All Buddhas seek the instability of one's Tathāgata store by skillful means and never find it, because stability is one's Buddha nature, which exists in every sentient being, has countless excellent characteristics, and is pure and majestic. All Buddhas seek the change in one's Tathāgata store by skillful means and never find it, because no change is one's Buddha nature, which exists in every sentient being, has countless excellent characteristics, and is pure and majestic. All Buddhas seek the inquietude of one's Tathāgata store by skillful means and never find it, because quietude is one's Buddha nature, which exists in every sentient being, has countless excellent characteristics, and is pure and majestic. All Buddhas seek the destruction of one's Tathāgata store by skillful means and never find it, because no destruction is one's Buddha nature, which exists in every sentient being, has countless excellent characteristics, and is pure and majestic. All Buddhas seek the damage to one's Tathāgata store by skillful means and never find it, because no damage is one's Buddha nature, which exists in every sentient being, has countless excellent characteristics, and is pure and majestic. All Buddhas seek the illness of one's Tathāgata store by skillful means and never find it, because no illness is one's Buddha nature, which exists in every sentient being, has countless excellent characteristics, and is pure and majestic. All Buddhas seek the aging and death of one's Tathāgata store by skillful means and never find them, because no aging and no death are one's Buddha nature, which exists in every sentient being, has countless excellent characteristics, and is pure and majestic. All Buddhas seek the impurity of one's Tathāgata store by skillful means and never find it, because purity is one's Buddha nature, which exists in every sentient being, has countless excellent characteristics, and is pure and majestic.

"As oil does not mix with water, likewise one's Buddha nature never mixes with one's afflictions, though one's countless afflictions shroud one's Tathāgata nature. Hence one's Buddha nature abides in one's afflictions, like a lamp contained in a bottle. When the bottle is broken, the lamp is revealed. The bottle means one's afflictions, and the lamp means one's Tathāgata store. An expounder of one's Tathāgata store, whether a Tathāgata, a Bodhisattva, or a voice-hearer, with or without afflictions, expounds it according to his ability. Pūrṇa-Maitrāyaṇīputra, I say that such an expounder is a truly enlightened one, who can shatter the hearer's bottle of a koṭi afflictions, enabling him to see his true nature, like seeing an āmra [mango] in his palm. As an analogy, when the sun or moon is covered by dense clouds, its light is obscured. When the clouds are removed, its radiance illuminates. It is the same with one's Tathāgata store. When it is shrouded by one's afflictions, it is unseen; when one's afflictions are removed, its radiance illuminates everywhere. One's Buddha nature is radiant and pure, like the sun or moon. Alas, Pūrṇa-Maitrāyaṇīputra practices the way of a mosquito and does not know how to expound the Dharma. He should quietly scurry away.

Then Sundara-Nanda[7] came to the Buddha. He bowed down at the Buddha's feet and stood aside. When he saw Aṅgulimāla, sympathetic joy rose in his heart, and he praised in verse:

> Very good! Aṅgulimāla is doing excellent karmas.
> He should use skillful means to acquire a Tathāgata's sublime physical body.

Aṅgulimāla asked in verse:

> The World-Honored One praises your respectable looks as foremost.
> What respectable looks are extraordinary?
> What is the cause of one's respectable looks?
> Explain now to resolve my doubts.

Sundara-Nanda answered in verse:

> Wash one's hands and join ten fingers;
> Bow down to a Buddha's śarīras [relics];
> Always make offerings to the ill.
> From these practices, one acquires respectable looks.

Aṅgulimāla again spoke in verse:

> As a Buddha's [dharma] body has no tendons or bones, how can it produce śarīras?
> Although a Tathagata is apart from śarīras, His dharma body [dharmakāya][8] possesses excellent skillful means.
> He is inconceivable, because He enables nonbelievers to believe [in His teachings] with delight,
> Using skillful means, He displays His śarīras.
> Leaving śarīras behind by skillful means is the way of Buddhas.
>
> The world has always made offerings to various images of
> The Brahma-king Maheśvara, god-sons, and goddess-daughters.
> Because they are not one's refuge, one erects a memorial pagoda [stūpa] to enshrine a Buddha's śarīras.
>
> If sentient beings understand this skillful means,
> Their applied wisdom-knowledge [jñāna] is the cause of their respectable looks.
> What you just said is a deluded guess of the cause of one's respectable looks.

Alas, Sundara-Nanda does not know the door to one's respectable looks.
Even a mosquito has its looks, and the ignorant should keep quiet.

Then the venerable Upāli came to the Buddha. He bowed down at the Buddha's feet and stood aside. When he saw Aṅgulimāla, sympathetic joy rose in his heart, and he praised in verse:

Amazing! Aṅgulimāla is doing excellent karmas.
I express sympathetic joy over his training to observe the pure Vinaya [rules of conduct].[9]

Aṅgulimāla asked in verse:

The Tathāgata praises you as foremost in upholding the Vinaya.
How does one uphold the Vinaya?
Speak quickly to resolve my doubts.

Upāli answered in verse:

Never do evil; always do good.
Train one's mind by skillful means.
This is the way to uphold the Vinaya.

Aṅgulimāla again spoke in verse:

If an evil bhikṣu, against the Vinaya, sabotages the Dharma or violates the precepts,
He should be stripped of a bhikṣu's six things[10] and all necessities of life.
He should be punished, dispelled, and tamed by skillful means.
The Brahma way of life precludes violation of the precepts.

As an analogy, a great king treasures his saber used to protect his body.
If it falls into a slaughter house, it should be forcefully retrieved.
The things treasured by a king should not belong to an evil man.
Likewise the things kept by those who practice the Brahma way of life
Should not belong to someone who sabotages the Dharma, and should be taken from him.
This is called the foremost way to uphold the Vinaya.
Do not commit any duṣkṛta [wrongdoing] or exhibit the wrong deportments.
Whoever upholds the Vinaya in this way fully upholds the Tathāgata's teachings.

The Tathāgata regards all as Rāhula [His only son].
Alas, Upāli practices the way of a mosquito
And does not know how to well uphold the Vinaya.
The ignorant should keep quiet.

Then Mañjuśrī the Dharma Prince came to the Buddha. He bowed down at the Buddha's feet and stood aside. When he saw Aṅgulimāla, sympathetic joy rose in his heart, and he praised in verse:

Very good! Aṅgulimāla is training to do excellent karmas.
He should train to realize the great emptiness, to see that dharmas are nonexistent.

Aṅgulimāla asked in verse:

Mañjuśrī the Dharma Prince, you are foremost in seeing the emptiness of dharmas.
What is meant by seeing that dharmas are empty?
What is meant by seeing that their emptiness is empty?
Speak now to resolve my doubts.

Mañjuśrī answered in verse:

Buddhas are like the open sky, which has no appearance of existence.
Buddhas are like the open sky, which has no appearance of birth.
Buddhas are like the open sky, which has no appearance of form.
Dharmas are like the open sky, and are a Tathāgata's wondrous dharma body.
Wisdom is like the open sky, and is a Tathāgata's great wisdom body.

A Tathāgata's hindrance-free wisdom cannot be grasped or touched.
Liberation is like the open sky, which has no appearance of existence.
A Tathāgata's liberation is empty and nonexistent.
How can you, Aṅgulimāla, understand this?

Aṅgulimāla again spoke in verse:

As an analogy, a fool sees hailstones and thinks deluded thoughts.
Mistaking them for aquamarine [vaiḍūrya] beads, he takes them home.
He places them in a bottle and guards them as if they are treasures.
Soon the hailstones melt and disappear, leaving him with their emptiness.
Then he thinks that true aquamarine is also empty.

Likewise Mañjuśrī trains to see the utter emptiness [of dharmas]
And constantly ponders their emptiness to destroy [his perception of] all dharmas.
Although liberation is actually not empty, he thinks that it is utterly empty.
As that person sees hailstones disappear, he indiscriminately decides that true treasures too will disappear.
Likewise you indiscriminately decide that all dharmas are utterly empty.
Having seen their emptiness, you declare that dharmas that are not empty are empty.

Some dharmas are empty; some dharmas are not empty.
All afflictions are like hailstones,
And destroying all evil is like hailstones melting.
True aquamarine is like a Tathāgata's forever abiding.
True aquamarine is like a Buddha's liberation.
While Buddhas take the open sky as Their form, riders of the Two Vehicles [see everything as] non-form.
While Buddhas take liberation as Their form, riders of the Two Vehicles [see everything as] non-form.
How can one say that perception of utter emptiness is true liberation?
Mañjuśrī should intently ponder and differentiate.

As an analogy, in an empty village the river is dry and vessels contain no water.
However, emptiness does not mean the empty space in a vessel.
A Tathāgata's true liberation is not empty.
Because liberation is free from all faults,
It is said to be empty.
Likewise a Tathāgata is actually not empty.
Because He has left behind all afflictions and the form of a god or human,
He is said to be empty.

Alas, [whoever practices] the way of a mosquito does not know the true meaning of emptiness.
Even non-Buddhists, such as Nirgranthas,[11] attempt to realize emptiness, and they should keep quiet.

Mañjuśrī asked in verse:

Aṅgulimāla, why do you intimidate voice-hearers and scorn Buddha-sons?
You wantonly display your atrocious behavior and roar like a ferocious tiger.
Who is practicing the mosquito's way and voicing such evil sounds?

Aṅgulimāla answered in verse:

As an analogy, a poor and timid person wanders a wilderness.
When he smells a ferocious tiger, he is terrified and scurries away.
Likewise a voice-hearer or Pratyekabuddha, who does not know the Mahāyāna,
Is terrified when he smells a Bodhisattva.

As an analogy, when a lion-king roams the mountain and roars,
All other animals are terrified.
Likewise, when a Bodhisattva, a hero among men, roars a lion's roar,
All voice-hearers and Pratyekabuddhas are terrified

Because through the long night they have trained to see that dharmas have no self,
Unaware that this is a veiled teaching.
Even if I howled a jackal's howl, no one could reply,
Not to mention replying to my unequaled lion's roar.

Mañjuśrī asked in verse:

You are a puny mosquito that did evil.
If you were a Bodhisattva, where could a māra be found?
Alas, people in the world have no self-awareness.
Unable to reflect upon their own faults, they see only others' evil.
Aṅgulimāla, how many sins have you committed?

Aṅgulimāla answered in verse:

Alas, there are two kinds of people who sabotage the true Dharma,
Those who declare that all dharmas are utterly empty and those who declare that dharmas have a self.
These two kinds of people sabotage the Buddha's true Dharma.
Alas, Mañjuśrī, you do not know that some evil is not evil.
Nor do you know Bodhisattva actions or that a mosquito and a lion are different.
Amazing! I can know the fearless Bodhisattvas.

Mañjuśrī, listen intently.
The Buddha praises Bodhisattva actions as a skillful magician's illusory displays,
Such as sawing or eating a person as a show to the public.
All things done by Buddhas and Bodhisattvas are illusory.

[A Bodhisattva] manifests being born or entering parinirvāṇa.
During times of famine, he gives away his body for others to eat.
[At the end of a] kalpa, he manifests fire that burns across the earth.
For those who perceive that dharmas are permanent, he enables them to know their impermanence.
During times of war, he manifests troops
To devastate and kill innumerable bandits.
In truth, he never harms anyone because his manifestations are illusory.

He puts all Three-Thousand Large Thousandfold Worlds into a mustard seed,
And not one sentient being is distressed or disturbed.
He puts the four oceans and Mount Sumeru into a pore, and they are not crammed or squeezed.
After the show he returns them to their own places.
He uses a toe to shake worlds in the ten directions, and no sentient being is distressed.
This is the way of Buddhas.

To comfort sentient beings, he manifests himself in countless forms, such as a Brahma-king,
The god-king Śakra, and any of the four world-protecting god-kings.
To comfort sentient beings, he manifests himself as a prince, a great minister,
A merchant leader, an elder, or a layman.
He may manifest as a god to change gods' wrong views.
Because He manifests the birth of all living things, he is called the birth itself.

As an analogy, when a magician sees the killing of a conjured sentient being,
He never laments that this is a tremendous evil,
Because he understands the nature of illusions.
Likewise I manifested killing sentient beings to tame those who sabotage the Dharma,
And did not actually harm anyone.
Just as a Buddha-Bhagavān manifests the times of war,
I now excel in taking Bodhisattva actions.

Alas, Mañjuśrī practices the way of a mosquito
And does not aspire to the great wisdom of the hero in the world, who is like a dragon elephant.[12]

Then the World-Honored One, who is all-knowing and all-seeing, spoke to Mañjuśrī in verse:

As Aṅgulimāla says, such are Bodhisattva actions.
You should know that, because he delivers sentient beings, he is not an ordinary being.
He is a great Bodhisattva, and his boldness equals yours.
Very good! Mañjuśrī, you should know his merits.

After saying these words, the Buddha praised in verse:

Very good! The exceptional hero among men, using skillful means
To comfort sentient beings, displays the great power of energetic progress.
I now will expound the merits, good karmas, and energetic progress required for whoever wants to quickly become an Arhat
To bring all sentient beings eternal peace and joy.

Śāriputra said to the Buddha, "World-Honored One, I pray that, out of pity for all sentient beings, You will tell me what merits, karmas, and energetic progress are required for whoever wants to quickly become an Arhat to benefit all sentient beings and bring them eternal peace and joy."

The World-Honored One answered in verse:

When parents are united, a child enters the mother's womb.
The parents are delighted and acquire consequent benefits,
Such as radiant looks and prosperity.
The father is extremely happy, and the mother dreams excellent dreams.
The birth of the child brings huge wealth to the family, and enemies become loving-kind.

At age seven the child enters school, where teachers and students are in harmony.
The household servants are happy and do their work diligently.
At age twenty he and his family members have no disputes.
They regard one another as parents, whose nurturance is like overflowing fragrant milk.

Great is this worthy and brilliant child, who has no greed, anger, arrogance,
Fawning, hypocrisy, excessive chatter, malice,
A child's misconduct, or evil karmas.
With lovingkindness and filial dutifulness, he makes offerings to dignitaries, and to his parents and teachers.
When he sees elders, he joins his palms to show respect.

He accommodates the middle-aged and frolics with the young.
Respectfully he gives relief to those in urgent need, and a child's love to those in pain.
He admonishes the evil to know shame and dishonor, and to aspire to training according to the true Dharma.
He never studies magic for fun but delights in seeing Buddhas.
He engages in reciting sūtras and rules of conduct, and in the five studies.

Staying far away from drinking and gambling, he pays reverence to the supreme.
He knows how much sleeping and eating is enough, and dislikes what is impure.
Gods love and remember him, and all people respect him.
His countless great merits are beyond analogy.
As he makes energetic progress in doing meritorious karmas, he will attain true enlightenment.

Śāriputra, know that Aṅgulimāla,
Like that youth, will quickly attain true enlightenment.
How can such a person be evil?
He has acquired countless extraordinary merits.
A majestic hero like Mañjuśrī, he surpasses even the uncommon kind [of people].
He regards all sentient beings as his only son.

Aṅgulimāla, know that a Bodhisattva-Mahāsattva
Vows to deliver all in the world who have not yet been delivered.

There is nothing right about making an excellent vow
To help all in the world, then doing evil.

The World-Honored One again spoke in verse:

Manifesting as a sun-moon god, or a Brahma-king who is the ruler of sentient beings,
Through earth, water, fire, wind, and space,
A Bodhisattva, a hero among men, uses countless merits to deliver sentient beings.

Mahāmaudgalyāyana praised in verse:

Amazing! Aṅgulimāla has such great merits that
Although he has seen the Buddha-Bhagavān only briefly, he will deliver all in existence.

Aṅgulimāla asked in verse:

Mahāmaudgalyāyana, why is it that some sentient beings
Have not seen a Buddha-Bhagavān, but can know the true Dharma?

Mahāmaudgalyāyana answered in verse:

As the Buddha-Bhagavān says, there are three groups:
The group that definitely is on the wrong path; the group that definitely progresses on the right path to bodhi; the group that is indecisive about its path.
A Buddha cannot transform those in the first group.
Mahākāśyapa and his peers are in the second group.
Before the Tathāgata appeared in the world, they entered the true Dharma.

Aṅgulimāla again spoke in verse:

Do not say that Mahākāśyapa the Elder
Entered the true Dharma before the Tathāgata appeared in the world.
Why not? Because a Tathāgata forever abides in the world.
If someone relies on the true Dharma, a Buddha constantly abides in his house.

As an analogy, a river flows when there is rain; it does not flow when there is no rain.
The wise should use skillful means to observe well.
There is nothing right about a river flowing when there is no rain.
Know that because of rainfall, a river flows endlessly.
Mahāmaudgalyāyana, all excellent worldly and supra-worldly dharmas
Flow out of a Buddha.
Therefore, Mahākāśyapa relied on the Buddha to renounce family life.

Mahāmaudgalyāyana asked in verse:

If Tathāgatas forever abide in the world,
Why do I and others not see Them?

Aṅgulimāla answered in verse:

Let Mahākāśyapa know that it is like [the river and] the rains.
Therefore, when no Buddha is in the world, sentient beings cannot deliver themselves.
Only when they see Tathāgatas can they achieve liberation.

As an analogy, someone enters a dark room
And cannot see sunlight or moonlight.
Therefore, Mahāmaudgalyāyana, do not say that no Buddha is in the world,
Because all Tathāgatas forever abide in the world
To deliver those who renounce family life and accept the complete monastic precepts.
Therefore, there are only two groups, one on the wrong path and the other on the right path.
There is no group that is indecisive about its path.

Mahāmaudgalyāyana asked in verse:

There are the five precepts in the world,
Whether or not a Buddha appears in the world.

Aṅgulimāla answered in verse:

Know that all precepts and right deportments,
Whether worldly or supra-worldly, are pronounced by a Buddha.

Mahāmaudgalyāyana asked in verse:

Why is disease classified into three kinds?
Some are cured by a treatment, some are cured without a treatment,
And some are not cured by any treatment.
Therefore, there are three kinds of disease.

Aṅgulimāla answered in verse:

Not so! Do not say that there are three kinds [of disease]
Because there are only two kinds, curable and incurable.
Some voice-hearers classify disease into three kinds,
And the Buddha says that the Voice-Hearer Vehicle is the Mosquito Vehicle.
Because of their ignorance, they classify disease into three kinds.

Those definitely on the wrong path are icchantikas.

Those definitely on the right path are Tathāgatas, holy Bodhisattvas, and riders of the Two Vehicles.
Mahāmaudgalyāyana, know that the two extraordinary kinds
Are Buddha-Bhagavāns and icchantikas.

While a Tathāgata is the highest, and no one is above Him,
An icchantika the vilest.
While a great Bodhisattva fully practices the ten pāramitās,
An icchantika fully does the ten evil karmas.
While a Bodhisattva gives away as alms his body, head, eyes, blood, brain, marrow,
And his countless bones piled higher than Mount Sumeru,
An icchantika gives away his evil karmas as alms
And is reborn as a hungry ghost with burning greed and desire.

Thought after thought, his greed and desire are responded to by many women.
He sires many children but derives no happiness [from them] in the long night.
Driven by hunger and thirst, he eats his own children.
A hungry ghost may manifest as a Brahmin.
Because of the evil karmas in his past lives, he asks people for their children to eat.
With unbridled desire, he even eats his own body.
Thus an icchantika finds gratification by doing evil karmas.

Therefore, while a Buddha-Bhagavān is the highest and extraordinary,
An icchantika is the lowest and extraordinary.
Those definitely on the wrong path are icchantikas;
Those definitely on the right path are Tathāgatas, Bodhisattvas abiding on Bodhisattva grounds, Pratyekabuddhas, and voice-hearers.

The World-Honored One said to Aṅgulimāla in verse:

Aṅgulimāla, renounce family life
And take the Three Refuges [the Buddha, the Dharma, and the Saṅgha].

Aṅgulimāla responded in verse:

The Mahāyāna is the vehicle that brings the hindrance-free wisdom-knowledge,
And this One Vehicle brings the one refuge.
The Buddha is the refuge in the highest truth.
The Dharma means a Tathāgata's wondrous dharma body.
The Saṅgha means a Tathāgata because He is the Saṅgha.

While the Dharma and the Saṅgha are the two refuges of convenience,

The Tathāgata is not a refuge of convenience, but the refuge in the highest truth.
Therefore, today I take refuge in the Tathāgata
Because He is the true refuge among refuges.

If someone wants to eat hiṅgu,[13] he should take the right plant.
If he discards the right one to eat the wrong one, he can benefit neither himself nor others.
A thousand physicians cannot save such a fool.
Therefore, if people abandon the one refuge to take refuges of convenience,
A thousand Buddhas cannot save such fools.

The World-Honored One told Aṅgulimāla, "You should accept and observe the pure precepts for an innocent youth.[14]"

Aṅgulimāla asked in verse:

What is meant by an innocent youth?
What is meant by the complete monastic precepts?
What is a true śramaṇa?
What are the fortune fields?[15]

As the World-Honored One abided in silence, Aṅgulimāla again spoke in verse:

If someone does not know that the one refuge is the refuge in the highest truth,
And does not know that the two refuges are established for convenience,
He is an innocent youth.

If someone has not received the complete monastic precepts, how can he be a śramaṇa?
If someone does not know the one refuge, how can he take it as the pure refuge?
If someone does not know that the Tathāgata is the refuge in the highest truth
And does not take [refuge in Him as] a pure refuge, how can he be a śramaṇa?
If someone does not know the true refuge, how can it be his fortune field?
Therefore, if someone does not know the difference between the true refuge and two refuges of convenience,
He is an innocent youth.

Then the World-Honored One told Aṅgulimāla, "You now should accept and observe the precept against killing."

Aṅgulimāla responded in verse:

I definitely can neither accept nor observe the precept against killing.
I will always accept and observe the precept for ending sentient beings' lives.
The so-called sentient beings mean countless afflictions.
Ending them is called observing the precept for killing.

The world-Honored One told him, "You now should accept and observe the precept against false speech."

Aṅgulimāla responded in verse:

I definitely can neither accept nor observe the precept against false speech.
I will always accept and uphold false words about dharmas.
Accepting and upholding false words are [accepting and upholding] the Buddha Dharma.
What is false is that all dharmas are empty.
What is false is that voice-hearers, Pratyekabuddhas,
And Bodhisattvas take action to follow worldly ways.

What is false is that I appear in the world,
Accept and observe the complete monastic precepts, and become an Arhat;
That I accept food and drink to establish someone's almsgiving;
That I walk to and fro in meditation as my afflictions flow through the nine life-paths;[16]
That I accept and use shoes, a willow tooth pick, and medicine;
That I get hungry or thirsty, sleep, cut my nails, and shave off my hair and beard;
That I take medicine to cure various diseases in my body;
That I will enter parinirvāṇa, like the extinction of a fire when its firewood is burnt away.
Words such as these are false words.
However, when I use skillful means to roam the world,
I never purify such false speech.

Now I reveal the real truth, and Mahāmaudgalyāyana, you should listen well.
The real truth is the Tathāgata store.
The eternal body in the highest truth is a Buddha's inconceivable body.
What never changes in the highest truth is His eternal body.
The quiet body in the highest truth is the truly wondrous dharma body.

How does such an inconceivable body appear?
Buddhas teach that false dharmas arise [as skillful means].
He who is free from all falsity is called a Buddha.

As an analogy, when a calf dies, to delight its mother, the cow herder
Takes its hide to cover other calves.
Likewise a Tathāgata follows worldly ways.
Like that cow herder, He manifests as a deaf man
In order to teach the deaf the Dharma.
Then sentient beings will think that a Tathāgata shares their world.

Like that cow herder, He manifests countless images
And uses various skillful means to guide sentient beings.
As that cow herder uses skillful means
To coax the cow to produce milk for other calves,
It is the same with a Tathāgata.
If He revealed His self-nature body, who in the world could see it?
Therefore, he uses skillful means to manifest Himself to suit worldly perceptions,
In order to enable all to achieve liberation.
This is the way of Buddhas.

Therefore, from now on, I will always do false things
And kill sentient beings as a false display.
I do not accept the precept against falsity, so that my observance of the precepts will be pure.

The World-Honored One told Aṅgulimāla, "You now should accept the precept against drinking alcohol."

Aṅgulimāla responded in verse:

I definitely can neither accept nor observe the precept against drinking alcohol.
I will always accept the precept for drinking alcohol and indulge [in drinking] in the long night.
I will shout throughout the five life-paths that
Extreme joy is called the alcohol produced by the Mahāyāna.
It is the alcohol of the unsurpassed Buddha store.
I now drink this alcohol to my fill and persuade sentient beings to do the same
And to joyfully praise, 'Very good! It forever abides and never changes.'
Eight times they should announce it aloud as their intoxication is endless.

The World-Honored told Aṅgulimāla, "You now should accept the pure precept against having sex."

Aṅgulimāla answered in verse:

I definitely can neither accept nor observe the precept against having sex.
I will always accept and follow my lust for what others love,
And constantly visit the house of prostitutes to frolic with them.
I will take samādhi as my wife, the truth as my son,

The loving-kind and compassionate mind as my daughter, the emptiness of dharmas as my house,
And countless pāramitās as my high and wide bed.
Guarding afflictions, I will take veiled teachings as my food,
Total retention [of teachings] as my garden, the Seven Bodhi Factors as flowers,
Dharma words as trees, and the wisdom-knowledge of liberation as fruits.
These are called the foremost entertainment in the world.
The true nature of the wise is not the state of the foolish.

The World-Honored One told Aṅgulimāla, "You now should accept the precept against taking things not given."

Aṅgulimāla responded in verse:

I definitely can neither accept nor observe the precept against taking things not given.
I will always take things not given and steal others' things.
What can never be given is bodhi because there exists no giver.
Therefore, I will take bodhi, which no one can give me.
When a Buddha sits under the bodhi tree, He neither gains nor loses [bodhi]
[Because] it is one's true nature, supreme and unsurpassed.

The Buddha told Aṅgulimāla, "You now should accept the precept against singing and dancing."

Aṅgulimāla responded in verse:

I will always enjoy the pleasure of dancing, and of singing a gandharva's songs
To proclaim the Tathāgata store and praise, 'Very good!'
I will hear from Buddhas that a Tathāgata forever abides.
I will constantly use wonderful tones to recite Mahāyāna sūtras,
Like the music played by kiṁnaras and gandharvas.
I will use countless wonderful tones as an offering to sūtras.
If sentient beings constantly make such offerings,
Buddhas will bestow upon them the prophecy that they will become Buddhas with the same name.

Notes

1. Jambūnada gold is gold from the river that flows through the jambū (rose apple) grove. It is renowned for its supreme quality and red-golden color with a purple tinge.

2. The Sanskrit word *aśoka* means carefree. The aśoka is an evergreen tree, important in the cultural traditions of the Indian subcontinent and adjacent areas. It is prized for its beautiful foliage and fragrant bright red flowers in heavy, lush bunches (Wikipedia.com).

3. A vast self means the true self, which never eats food, falls ill, or dies.

4. "Sūtras in the nine categories" are the glossary's "sūtras in the twelve categories," excluding categories (6) nidāna, causes of the discourses; (7) avadāna, parables; (12) upadeśa, pointing-out instructions.

5. See "a self, a person, a sentient being, and an ever-lasting soul" in the glossary's "four appearances."

6. See "ten Bodhisattva grounds" in the glossary's "stages of the Bodhisattva Way." Details of the ten Bodhisattva grounds are given in chapter 26 of text 279 (T10n0279), the 80-fascicle Chinese version of the *Mahāvaipulya Sūtra of Buddha Adornment* (Buddhāvataṁsaka-mahāvaipulya-sūtra). An English translation of this chapter appears in *The Bodhisattva Way* (Rulu 2013, 111–244).

7. See Sundara-Nanda's biography under the name Nanda in the glossary's "voice-hearer."

8. See "dharma body" defined in the glossary's "three bodies of a Buddha."

9. See Vinaya in the glossary's Tripiṭaka.

10. A monk's six things are (1) a ceremonial robe, (2) an upper robe, (3) a lower robe, (4) an iron Bowl, (5) a seating and sleeping mat, and (6) a pouch for filtering out insects in water.

11. Nirgrantha means free from worldly ties. See Nirgranthaputra in the glossary.

12. A huge elephant is called a dragon elephant, as a title of respect.

13. Hiṅgu (興渠) is a pungent vegetable, which may be a variety of foetida with edible stinking leaves.

14. Here, an innocent youth means a śrāmaṇera, a novice Buddhist monk, usually seven to twenty years old.

15. See "three fortune fields" in the glossary.

16. Sentient beings in the Three Realms of Existence delight in taking any of the nine life-paths: (1) the human world or any of the six desire heavens, (2) Brahma Multitude (Brahma-pāriṣadya) Heaven in the first dhyāna, (3) Pure Radiance (Ābhāsvara) Heaven in the second dhyāna, (4) Pervasive Splendor (Śubhakṛtsna) Heaven in the third dhyāna, (5) No Perception (Asaṁjña) Heaven in the fourth dhyāna, (6) Boundless Space Heaven, (7) Boundless Consciousness Heaven, (8) Nothingness Heaven, and (9) Neither With Nor Without Perception Heaven. The first life-path is in the desire realm, life-paths 2–5 are four of the eighteen heavens in the form realm, and life-paths 6–9 are the four heavens in the formless realm. Also see the glossary's "samādhi" and "eighteen heavens in the form realm."

Fascicle 3 (of 4)

Then the Buddha asked Aṅgulimāla, "What is meant by the one learning [śikṣā]?"

Aṅgulimāla answered in verse:

According to the Voice-Hearer Vehicle, not the Mahāyāna,
All sentient beings' lives are sustained by food and drink.
According to the Mahāyāna, their lives are apart from food and drink, and are always firm.

What is meant by one?
It means that the Tathāgata store [tathāgata-garbha] of all sentient beings constantly abides.

What is meant by two?
According to the Voice-Hearer Vehicle, not the Mahāyāna,
It means one's name and form [mind and body].[1]
Riders of the Voice-Hearer Vehicle and the Pratyekabuddha Vehicle
Claim that name and form are different.
They believe that only one's name achieves liberation, and do not say that it has a wonderful form.
All Tathāgatas' liberation has wondrous form,
Observable like an āmra [mango] in one's palm.

What is meant by three?
According to the Voice-Hearer Vehicle, not the Mahāyāna,
It means the three kinds of sensory reception [pleasure, pain, and neither].
According to the Mahāyāna, the three kinds of reception mean that
A Tathāgata is foremost in permanence, and is never born,
And that if the Dharma and the Saṅgha are destroyed, they will be born again.

What is meant by four?
According to the Voice-Hearer Vehicle, not the Mahāyāna,
It means the Four Noble Truths [suffering, accumulation of afflictions, cessation of suffering, and the path].
According to the Mahāyāna,
It means that all Tathāgatas are foremost in absolute permanence.
This, not suffering, is a truth in the Mahāyāna.
It means that all Tathāgatas are foremost in absolute perpetuity.
This, not accumulation of afflictions, is a truth in the Mahāyāna.
It means that all Tathāgatas are foremost in changelessness.
This, not cessation of suffering, is a truth in the Mahāyāna.
It means that all Tathāgatas are foremost in absolute quietness.
This, not the path, is a truth in the Mahāyāna.

These are the four truths in the Mahāyāna, which do not include suffering.
If suffering is a truth, then those on the four evil life-paths—hell-dwellers, hungry ghosts, animals, and asuras—should uphold this truth.

What is meant by five?
According to the Voice-Hearer Vehicle, not the Mahāyāna,
It means one's five faculties.
[According to the Mahāyāna] a Tathāgata's eyes are permanent,
As they definitely see with perfect discernment and are never impaired;
A Tathāgata's ears are permanent,
As they definitely hear with perfect discernment and are never impaired;
A Tathāgata's nose is permanent,
As it definitely smells with perfect discernment and is never impaired;
A Tathāgata's tongue is permanent,
As it definitely tastes with perfect discernment and is never impaired;
A Tathāgata's body is permanent,
As it definitely touches with perfect discernment and is never impaired.

What is meant by six?
According to the Voice-Hearer Vehicle, not the Mahāyāna,
It means one's six entrances.
[According to the Mahāyāna] a Tathāgata's eye entrance is permanent,
As His visual sense is perfect and never impaired;
A Tathāgata's ear entrance is permanent,
As His auditory sense is perfect and never impaired;
A Tathāgata's nose entrance is permanent,
As His olfactory sense is perfect and never impaired;
A Tathāgata's tongue entrance is permanent,
As His gustatory sense is perfect and never impaired;
A Tathāgata's body entrance is permanent,
As his tactile sense is perfect and never impaired;
A Tathāgata's mind entrance reveals one's Tathāgata store,
And those with pure faith and without rejecting it can enter it.

What is meant by seven?
According to the Voice-Hearer Vehicle, not the Mahāyāna,
It means the Seven Bodhi Factors.
These seven factors in the Mahāyāna are like udumbara flowers.[2]
As a Tathāgata forever abides, the seven bodhi flowers bloom.

What is meant by eight?
According to the Voice-Hearer Vehicle, not the Mahāyāna,
It means the Eightfold Right Path.
This path of the Mahāyāna leads to the teaching that a Tathāgata forever abides.
Through the power of hearing [this teaching], one will eventually arrive at the city of nirvāṇa.

A Tathāgata is forever, eternal, supreme, changeless, pure, and extremely quiet.
The dharma body [dharmakāya][3] revealed in one's true enlightenment
Is the profound Tathāgata store, which never grows old.
Thus the Mahāyāna fully encompasses the Eightfold Right Path.

What is meant by nine?
According to the Voice-Hearer Vehicle, not the Mahāyāna,
It means sūtras in the nine categories.[4]
The Mahāyāna is the One Vehicle that leads to a Tathāgata's hindrance-free wisdom-knowledge [jñāna].

What is meant by ten?
According to the Voice-Hearer Vehicle, not the Mahāyāna,
It means the Ten Powers.
The Mahāyāna brings countless powers because a Buddha is inconceivable.
He uses skillful means to give veiled teachings in countless sūtras.

What is meant by the one path,
One vehicle, one refuge, one truth,
One reliance, one realm, one birth, and one form?
[They all] mean a Tathāgata.
Therefore, the One Vehicle [Buddha Vehicle] is the only definitive vehicle.
All others are for convenience.

Then the World-Honored One praised, "Very good, very good, Aṅgulimāla! Come, bhikṣu. [5]" And Aṅgulimāla immediately became a śramaṇa, his deportment as perfect as that of a longtime bhikṣu.

Aṅgulimāla bowed down at the Buddha's feet and said, "World-Honored One, following Your voice, I have immediately become an Arhat."

The Buddha told him, "You should come to the Jetavana garden to widely deliver sentient beings."

Then, like a full moon surrounded by stars, the World-Honored One was attended by Aṅgulimāla, Śāriputra, Mañjuśrī, and all others in the multitude. Like a goose-king, He ascended from under the aśoka tree into the open sky, to a height of seven tāla [palm] trees, and went to the city of Śrāvastī, forty cows' bellows away. Aṅgulimāla, together with gods, dragons, yakṣas, gandharvas, asuras, kiṁnaras, and mahoragas, made huge offerings in the Jetavana garden. Like a goose-king, the World-Honored One entered the Jetavana garden, which had been donated by Anāthapiṇḍika the Elder, and ascended onto a lion throne. Then the ground of this Three-Thousand Large Thousandfold World became as level as a palm and carpeted with soft grass, as if it were [Amitābha Buddha's] Land of Peace and Bliss.

At that time all great Bodhisattvas [in worlds] in various directions wished to see Aṅgulimāla. Their Buddhas told them, "You all should go. Śākyamuni Buddha is fighting a Dharma battle, subjugating a great lion and delivering an innumerable multitude. He is staying in the Jetavana garden and will expound the unsurpassed Dharma to the multitude. You Buddha-sons should go to listen to and accept the Dharma, and to look upon Aṅgulimāla with respect."

These Bodhisattvas, who came from various directions, showered down lotus flowers as large as carriage wheels. When sentient beings smelled the fragrance of these lotus flowers, they all left their afflictions behind.

Then gods, dragon, yakṣas, gandharvas, asuras, kiṁnaras, mahoragas, and goddess-daughters made celestial offerings and showered down various treasures. With one mind and one voice, they spoke in verse:

> I now bow down to the one with the thirty-two physical marks of a great man.
> His countless merits are like a pure lotus flower in bloom.
> The white hair between His eyebrows is brighter and purer than moonlight.
>
> I now bow down to the muni [saint] with a sublime form.
> His great lovingkindness and comforting virtues are like a pure lotus flower in bloom.
> The white hair between His eyebrows is brighter and purer than moonlight.
>
> I now bow down to the one with the foremost ever-abiding body.
> The supreme muni is the unsurpassed one revered by gods and humans.
> His comforting of sentient beings is like the blooming of a pure lotus.
> The white hair between His eyebrows is brighter and purer than moonlight.
>
> I now bow down to the one with the foremost eternal merits.
> The supreme muni is the unsurpassed one revered by gods and humans.
> His comforting of sentient beings is like the blooming of a pure lotus.
> The white hair between His eyebrows is brighter and purer than moonlight.
>
> I now bow down to the one with changeless merits that never dwindle.
> The supreme muni is the unsurpassed one revered by gods and humans.
> His comforting of sentient beings is like the blooming of a pure lotus.
> The white hair between His eyebrows is brighter and purer than moonlight.
>
> I now bow down to the one with quiet and extraordinary merits.
> The supreme muni is the unsurpassed one revered by gods and humans.
> His comforting of sentient beings is like the blooming of a pure lotus.
> The white hair between His eyebrows is brighter and purer than moonlight.
>
> Namo [Homage to] Aṅgulimāla, who endures adversity and trains to observe the pure precepts and acquire countless merits.
> So I bow down to him.

Namo Aṅgulimāla, who upholds the path of the One Vehicle and the Mahāyāna's virtue of lovingkindness.
So I bow down to him.
Namo Aṅgulimāla, who uses [the power of] his body and voice, and their immeasurable secrets.
So I vow down to him.
Namo Aṅgulimāla, who uses the immeasurable wisdom light to give countless veiled teachings.
So I bow down to him.
Namo Aṅgulimāla, who uses countless illusions to subjugate countless māras.
So I bow down to him.
Namo Aṅgulimāla, who abides in the immeasurable nirvāṇa to follow innumerable sentient beings in the world.
So I bow down to him.

Then Aṅgulimāla asked the Buddha, "World-Honored One, You say, 'I abide in the state of no birth.' What is meant by that? Why does the World-Honored One, who abides in the state of no birth and on the ground of liberation, also abide here? Who can believe this? I pray that You will explain."

The Buddha answered Aṅgulimāla, "You and Mañjuśrī together should go north, passing worlds as numerous as the sands of one Ganges River, to the world called Immeasurable Bliss. Teaching there is a Buddha called Accumulation Ground of Immeasurable Wisdom and Merit Sovereign King, the Tathāgata, Arhat, Samyak-Saṁbuddha. You two should go there to ask that Buddha, 'Why does Śākyamuni Buddha, who abides in the state of no birth, also abide in this world called Sahā?'"

Mañjuśrī and Aṅgulimāla responded, "We gladly accept your instruction."

Using their transcendental powers, like goose-kings, they went north to the world called Immeasurable Bliss and arrived at the place of Accumulation Ground of Immeasurable Wisdom and Merit Sovereign King Tathāgata. They bowed down at His feet and said, "World-Honored One, we two came from the Sahā World because we are sent by Śākyamuni Buddha to ask you, 'Why does Śākyamuni Tathāgata, who abides in the state of no birth and on the ground of liberation, not enter parinirvāṇa but abides in the Sahā World?'

That Buddha told them, "Good men, I am one of the bodies of Śākyamuni Tathāgata. You should go back and tell your Buddha, 'Immeasurable Wisdom Buddha sent us back and said that You would explain to us.'"

Then, like goose-kings, they came back from that world and bowed down at the Buddha's feet. With joined palms they asked, "Amazing, World-Honored One! The Tathāgata is immeasurable, with an immeasurable body and immeasurable virtues. We two just saw Your amazing virtues because Immeasurable Wisdom Sovereign King Tathāgata said, 'I am that Buddha, who will explain to you.' We pray that the World-Honored One will compassionately explain why He, who abides in the state of no birth, also abides here."

The Buddha told Mañjuśrī and all others, "Why do I, who abide as Accumulation Ground of Immeasurable Wisdom and Merit Sovereign King Buddha in the world called Immeasurable Bliss, also abide here? Do not ask why I, who abide in the state of no birth, also abide here. A Tathāgata's body is boundless, and what He does is also boundless. A Tathāgata is indescribable, and what He does is also indescribable. A Tathāgata is immeasurable, and what He does is also immeasurable. Aṅgulimāla, you ask the Tathāgata why He displays the birth of a body that has no birth. The Tathāgata will now explain to you."

Aṅgulimāla said to the Buddha, "Very good! World-Honored One, I pray that you will explain, to pity all sentient beings and bring them peace and joy."

The Buddha told Aṅgulimāla, "For countless hundreds of thousands of koṭis of kalpas, I fully practiced the ten pāramitās to draw in innumerable sentient beings, and enabled those who had not activated the bodhi mind to activate it. Because I fully practiced countless pāramitās and planted roots of goodness for countless asaṁkhyeyas of kalpas, I display the birth of a body that has no birth."

Aṅgulimāla asked the Buddha, "World-Honored One, why does the Tathāgata display the birth of His body, as He abides in the true reality [of dharmas]?"

The Buddha told Aṅgulimāla, "You and Mañjuśrī together should go north, passing worlds as numerous as the sands of two Ganges Rivers, to the world called Unreal Lightning Garland. Teaching there is a Buddha called Vairocana, the Tathāgata, Arhat, Samyak-Saṁbuddha. You two should go there to ask Him, 'Why does Śākyamuni Tathāgata, who abides in the true reality [of dharmas], also abide in the Sahā World?'"

They acted upon His instruction and, like goose-kings, soared away to the world called Unreal Lightning Garland and arrived at the place of Vairocana Buddha. They bowed down at His feet and asked that question. However, that Buddha, as did Immeasurable Wisdom Buddha, sent them back to Śākyamuni Buddha.

Mañjuśrī and Aṅgulimāla said to the Buddha, "World-Honored One, we pray that you will tell us how the Tathāgata came to abide in the true reality [of dharmas]."

The Buddha told Mañjuśrī and all others, "For countless hundreds of thousands of koṭis of kalpas, I fully practiced the ten pāramitās to draw in innumerable sentient beings, and established them in the joy they never before had. Because I practiced asaṁkhyeyas of pāramitās for countless hundreds of thousands of koṭis of kalpas, I have realized this true-reality body."

Aṅgulimāla asked the Buddha, "World-Honored One, how did the Tathāgata come to abide in the asaṁskṛta [free from conditions] state?"

The Buddha answered, "You and Mañjuśrī together should go north, passing worlds as numerous as the sands of three Ganges Rivers, to the world called Taking by Intention. Teaching there is a Buddha called Immeasurable Intention, the Tathāgata, Arhat, Samyak-Saṁbuddha. You two should go there to ask Him, 'How did Śākyamuni Tathāgata come to abide in the asaṁskṛta state?' They went there and asked that Buddha, but He sent them back to Śākyamuni Buddha.

[Then the Buddha told them to] go north, passing worlds as numerous as the sands of four Ganges Rivers, to the world called Adorned with Colors, whose Buddha was called Supreme Subjugation; go north, passing worlds as numerous as the sands of five Ganges Rivers, to the world called Deep Dust, whose Buddha was called Deep Superior; go north, passing worlds as numerous as the sands of six Ganges Rivers, to the world called Wind, whose Buddha was called Like Wind; go north, passing worlds as numerous as the sands of seven Ganges

Rivers, to the world called Vajra Mind, whose Buddha was called Vajra Superior; go north, passing worlds as numerous as the sands of eight Ganges Rivers, to the world called Taint-Free Light, whose Buddha was called Taint-Free Superior; go north, passing worlds as numerous as the sands of nine Ganges Rivers, to the world called Moon Master, whose Buddha was called Moon Superior; go north, passing worlds as numerous as the sands of ten Ganges Rivers, to the world called Sunrise, whose Buddha was called Sunrise. However, each of those Buddhas sent them back to Śākyamuni Buddha.

[Then the Buddha told them to] go east, passing worlds as numerous as the sands of one Ganges River, to the world called Good Flavor, whose Buddha was called Good Flavor Superior; go east, passing worlds as numerous as the sands of two Ganges Rivers, to the world called Bandhujīva, whose Buddha was called Bandhujīva Light; go east, passing worlds as numerous as the sands of three Ganges Rivers, to the world called Fragrance-Suffused Garland, whose Buddha was called Fragrant Garland; go east, passing worlds as numerous as the sands of four Ganges Rivers, to the world called Tamālapatra [Cinnamon Tree], whose Buddha was called Tamālapatra Cool Fragrance; go east, passing worlds as numerous as the sands of five Ganges Rivers, to the world called Moon Master, whose Buddha was called Moon Store; go east, passing worlds as numerous as the sands of six Ganges Rivers, to the world called Agalloch Fragrance, where it Buddha was called Agalloch Fragrance Superior; go east, passing worlds as numerous as the sands of seven Ganges Rivers, to the world called Suffused with Powdered Incense, whose Buddha was called Powdered Incense; go east, passing worlds as numerous as the sands of eight Ganges Rivers, to the world called Radiance Illuminating, whose Buddha was called Radiance; go east, passing worlds as numerous as the sands of nine Ganges Rivers, to the world called Ocean Master, whose Buddha was called Ocean Virtues; go east, passing worlds as numerous as the sands of ten Ganges Rivers, to the world called Dragon Master, whose Buddha was called Dragon Store. However, each of those Buddhas sent them back to Śākyamuni Buddha.

[Then the Buddha told them to] go south, passing worlds as numerous as the sands of one Ganges River, to the world called Vermilion, whose Buddha was called Vermilion Light; go south, passing worlds as numerous as the sands of two Ganges Rivers, to the world called Great Cloud, whose Buddha was called Great Cloud Store; go south, passing worlds as numerous as the sands of three Ganges Rivers, to the world called Lightning Garland, whose Buddha was called Lightning Gained; go south, passing worlds as numerous as the sands of four Ganges Rivers, to the world called Vajra Wisdom, whose Buddha was called Vajra Store; go south, passing worlds as numerous as the sands of five Ganges Rivers, to the world called Turning Wheel, whose Buddha was called Holder of a Turning Wheel; go south, passing worlds as numerous as the sands of six Ganges Rivers, to the world called Treasure Ground, whose Buddha was called Holder of the Treasure Ground; go south, passing worlds as numerous as the sands of seven Ganges Rivers, to the world called Sky Wisdom, whose Buddha was called Equal to the Open Sky; go south, passing worlds as numerous as the sands of eight Ganges Rivers, to the world called Subjugation, whose Buddha was called Subjugation Superior; go south, passing worlds as numerous as the sands of nine Ganges Rivers, to the world called Superb Garland, whose Buddha was called Superb Store; go south, passing worlds as numerous as the sands of ten Ganges

Rivers, to the world called Lion Wisdom, whose Buddha was called Lion Store. However, each of those Buddhas sent them back to Śākyamuni Buddha.

[Then the Buddha told them to] go west, passing worlds as numerous as the sands of one Ganges River, to the world called Tranquility, whose Buddha was called Tranquility Flavor; go west, passing worlds as numerous as the sands of two Ganges Rivers, to the world called Eternal Garland, whose Buddha was called Eternal Virtue; go west, passing worlds as numerous as the sands of three Ganges Rivers, to the world called Universally Worthy, whose Buddha was called Universally Worthy Wisdom; go west, passing worlds as numerous as the sands of four Ganges Rivers, to the world called Splendid Garland, whose Buddha was called Splendid Garland Superior; go west, passing worlds as numerous as the sands of five Ganges Rivers, to the world called Boundless, whose Buddha was called Boundless Splendid Garland; go west, passing worlds as numerous as the sands of six Ganges Rivers, to the world called Worthy Master, whose Buddha was called Worthy Store; go west, passing worlds as numerous as the sands of seven Ganges Rivers, to the world called Eye, whose Buddha was called Eye King; go west, passing worlds as numerous as the sands of eight Ganges Rivers, to the world called Banner Master, whose Buddha was called Banner Store; go west, passing worlds as numerous as the sands of nine Ganges Rivers, to the world called Drumbeat, whose Buddha was called Drumbeat Mastery; go west, passing worlds as numerous as the sands of ten Ganges Rivers, to the world called Joyful Vision, whose Buddha was called Joyful Vision Superior. However, each of those Buddhas sent them back to Śākyamuni Buddha.

[Then the Buddha told them to] go northwest, passing worlds as numerous as the sands of one Ganges River, to the world called Delight, whose Buddha was called Delightful Progress; go northwest, passing worlds as numerous as the sands of two Ganges Rivers, to the world called Adornment, whose Buddha was called Adornment Store; go northwest, passing worlds as numerous as the sands of three Ganges Rivers, to the world called Cause of Wisdom, whose Buddha was called Cause of Wisdom Store; go northwest, passing worlds as numerous as the sands of four Ganges Rivers, to the world called Enjoying Aspiration Delight, whose Buddha was called Enjoying Aspiration Delight Superior; go northwest, passing worlds as numerous as the sands of five Ganges Rivers, to the world called Gathering of Sentient Beings, whose Buddha was called Above Sentient Beings; go northwest, passing worlds as numerous as the sands of six Ganges Rivers, to the world called Intelligence, whose Buddha was called Intelligence Superior; go northwest, passing worlds as numerous as the sands of seven Ganges Rivers, to the world called Aspiration Delight, whose Buddha was called Aspiration Delight Sound; go northwest, passing worlds as numerous as the sands of eight Ganges Rivers, to the world called Immeasurable, whose Buddha was called Immeasurable Life; go northwest, passing worlds as numerous as the sands of nine Ganges Rivers, to the world called Abiding, whose Buddha was called Abiding Superior; go northwest, passing worlds as numerous as the sands of ten Ganges Rivers, to the world called Water, whose Buddha was called Water Flavor Superior. However, each of those Buddhas sent them back to Śākyamuni Buddha.

[Then the Buddha told them to] go northeast, passing worlds as numerous as the sands of one Ganges River, to the world called Treasure Master, whose

Buddha was called Treasure Banner; go northeast, passing worlds as numerous as the sands of two Ganges Rivers, to the world called Maṇidhara, whose Buddha was called Maṇi [Jewel] Cool Store; go northeast, passing worlds as numerous as the sands of three Ganges Rivers, to the world called Precious Wisdom, whose Buddha was called Precious Wisdom Superior; go northeast, passing worlds as numerous as the sands of four Ganges Rivers, to the world called Golden Color, whose Buddha was called Sound of Golden Light; go northeast, passing worlds as numerous as the sands of five Ganges Rivers, to the world called Web, whose Buddha was called Web of Light; go northeast, passing worlds as numerous as the sands of six Ganges Rivers, to the world called Gold Master, whose Buddha was called Jambūnada Gold[6] Superior; go northeast, passing worlds as numerous as the sands of seven Ganges Rivers, to the world called Web, whose Buddha was called Web of Light;[7] go northeast, passing worlds as numerous as the sands of eight Ganges Rivers, to the world called Pure Water, whose Buddha was called Water King; go northeast, passing worlds as numerous as the sands of nine Ganges Rivers, to the world called Jade Continent, whose Buddha was called Jade Store; go northeast, passing worlds as numerous as the sands of ten Ganges Rivers, to the world called Treasure Continent, whose Buddha was called Treasure Ground. However, each of those Buddhas sent them back to Śākyamuni Buddha.

[Then the Buddha told them to] go southeast, passing worlds as numerous as the sands of one Ganges River, to the world called Vajra Accumulation, whose Buddha was called Vajra Wisdom; go southeast, passing worlds as numerous as the sands of two Ganges Rivers, to the world called Total Awareness, whose Buddha was called Total Awareness Banner; go southeast, passing worlds as numerous as the sands of three Ganges Rivers, to the world called Siddhānta [Doctrine] Master, whose Buddha was called Excellent Meaning of Siddhānta; go southeast, passing worlds as numerous as the sands of four Ganges Rivers, to the world called Taint-Free, whose Buddha was called Taint-Free Aquamarine [Vaiḍūrya]; go southeast, passing worlds as numerous as the sands of five Ganges Rivers, to the world called Pūrṇa [Abundant] Flavor, whose Buddha was called Pūrṇa Accumulation; go southeast, passing worlds as numerous as the sands of six Ganges Rivers, to the world called Fragrance, whose Buddha was called Adorned with Fragrance; go southeast, passing worlds as numerous as the sands of seven Ganges Rivers, to the world called Fragrance Master, whose Buddha was called Fragrance Store; go southeast, passing worlds as numerous as the sands of eight Ganges Rivers, to the world called Straight Action, whose Buddha was called Straight Victory; go southeast, passing worlds as numerous as the sands of nine Ganges Rivers, to the world called Priceless, whose Buddha was called Priceless Superior; go southeast, passing worlds as numerous as the sands of ten Ganges Rivers, to the world called Boundless Encompassment, whose Buddha was called Boundless King. However, each of those Buddhas sent them back to Śākyamuni Buddha.

[Then the Buddha told them to] go southwest, passing worlds as numerous as the sands of one Ganges River, to the world called Immeasurable Light, whose Buddha was called Immeasurable Life; go southwest, passing worlds as numerous as the sands of two Ganges Rivers, to the world called Immeasurable Eye, whose Buddha was called Immeasurable Sovereignty; go southwest, passing worlds as numerous as the sands of three Ganges Rivers, to the world called

Flaming, whose Buddha was called Flaming Light; go southwest, passing worlds as numerous as the sands of four Ganges Rivers, to the world called Dispelling Darkness, whose Buddha was called Dispelling Darkness King; go southwest, passing worlds as numerous as the sands of five Ganges Rivers, to the world called Taming Master, whose Buddha was called Taming Store; go southwest, passing worlds as numerous as the sands of six Ganges Rivers, to the world called No Birth, whose Buddha was called Mastery of No Birth; go southwest, passing worlds as numerous as the sands of seven Ganges Rivers, to the world called Fragrance Master, whose Buddha was called Fragrant Elephant's Frolic; go southwest, passing worlds as numerous as the sands of eight Ganges Rivers, to the world called Fragrance Chest, whose Buddha was called Fragrance Chest King; go southwest, passing worlds as numerous as the sands of nine Ganges Rivers, to the world called Delightful Praise, whose Buddha was called Dragon's Delight; go southwest, passing worlds as numerous as the sands of ten Ganges Rivers, to the world called Superb Garland, whose Buddha was called Victorious Subjugation Superior. However, each of those Buddhas sent them back to Śākyamuni Buddha.

[Then the Buddha told them to] go upward, passing worlds as numerous as the sands of one Ganges River, to the world called Enduring Vision, whose Buddha was called All in the World Delight in Seeing High King Display Spiritual Power to Adorn the Majestic Ground of Great Vows and the Door of Accumulation of All Radiance; go upward, passing worlds as numerous as the sands of two Ganges Rivers, to the world called Puṇḍarīka [Large White Lotus Flower], whose Buddha was called Puṇḍarīka of the Wondrous Dharma; go upward, passing worlds as numerous as the sands of three Ganges Rivers, to the world called Smiling Water Flower, whose Buddha was called Smiling Flower King; go upward, passing worlds as numerous as the sands of four Ganges Rivers, to the world called Carefree, whose Buddha was called Freedom from All Cares; go upward, passing worlds as numerous as the sands of five Ganges Rivers, to the world called Utpala [Blue Lotus Flower], whose Buddha was called Superb Treasure Flower; go upward, passing worlds as numerous as the sands of six Ganges Rivers, to the world called Padma [Red Lotus Flower] Master, whose Buddha was called Padma Store; go upward, passing worlds as numerous as the sands of seven Ganges Rivers, to the world called Kumuda [White Lotus Flower], whose Buddha was called Kumuda Store; go upward, passing worlds as numerous as the sands of eight Ganges Rivers, to the world called Bamboo, whose Buddha was called Bamboo Fragrance; go upward, passing worlds as numerous as the sands of nine Ganges Rivers, to the world called Kuṅganī [Plant], whose Buddha was called Victorious King; go upward, passing worlds as numerous as the sands of ten Ganges Rivers, to the world called Merit River, whose Buddha was called Sovereign King of All Rivers in the World. However, each of those Buddhas sent them back to Śākyamuni Buddha.

[Then the Buddha told them to] go downward, passing worlds as numerous as the sands of one Ganges River, to the world called Gathering of Lions, whose Buddha was called Lion's Frolic; go downward, passing worlds as numerous as the sands of two Ganges Rivers, to the world called Lion's Den, whose Buddha was called Lion's Roar; go downward, passing worlds as numerous as the sands of three Ganges Rivers, to the world called Enduring Action, whose Buddha was called Enduring Action Flower; go downward, passing worlds as numerous as the sands of four Ganges Rivers, to the world called Excellent, whose Buddha was called All Excellent Births; go downward, passing worlds as numerous as the sands of five Ganges Rivers, to the world called Hindrance-Free Accumulation, whose Buddha was called Mahāyāna Frolic King; go downward, passing worlds as numerous as the sands of six Ganges Rivers, to the world called Piṇḍa [Globe], whose Buddha was called Summit of Piṇḍa Mountain; go downward, passing worlds as numerous as the sands of seven Ganges Rivers, to the world called Hard-to-See Respect, whose Buddha was called Respected by All; go downward, passing worlds as numerous as the sands of eight Ganges Rivers, to the world called Possessing Wisdom, whose Buddha was called Possessing Wisdom King; go downward, passing worlds as numerous as the sands of nine Ganges Rivers, to the world called Ground Wisdom, whose Buddha was called Ground Wisdom King. After each of those nine Buddhas sent them back to Śākyamuni Buddha, the Buddha told them go downward, passing worlds as numerous as the sands of ten Ganges Rivers, to the world called Always Joyful King, whose Buddha was called Resolving All Doubts.

The Buddha told Aṅgulimāla, "You and Mañjuśrī together should go there to ask that Buddha, 'Why does Śākyamuni Buddha, who abides in the majestic state, also abide in the Sahā World, and not enter parinirvāṇa?' He will explain to you and resolve your doubts. Because He can resolve all doubts, He is called Resolving All Doubts Buddha."

Mañjuśrī and Aṅgulimāla bowed down to the Buddha and said, "World-Honored One, very good, very good! We gladly accept your instruction."

Like goose-kings, they soared away to the world called Always Joyful King, and bowed down at the feet of Resolving All Doubts Buddha. They sat aside and said to that Buddha, "We came from the place of Śākyamuni Buddha, in the Sahā World. We went to ten worlds in each of the ten directions and asked their Tathāgatas, 'Why does Śākyamuni Buddha abide in the Sahā World and not enter parinirvāṇa, the state of liberation?' They each answered, 'I am one of the bodies of Śākyamuni Buddha. He will resolve your doubts.' Then Śākyamuni Buddha told us, 'Resolving All Doubts Tathāgata will explain to you,' and sent us to You. Therefore, we now ask You, 'Why does Śākyamuni Buddha abide in the Sahā World and not enter parinirvāṇa?'"

That Buddha answered, "You should go back. Śākyamuni Buddha will resolve all your doubts. That is why innumerable Śākyamuni Tathāgatas sent you back."

Together they responded, "Very good, very good! We gladly accept Your instruction."

They bowed down at that Buddha's feet and returned to Śākyamuni Buddha's place. They bowed down to the Buddha and marveled, "Amazing, World-Honored One! Śākyamuni Buddha assumes countless asaṁkhyeyas of bodies. They each tell us, 'You should go back, and Śākyamuni Buddha will resolve your doubts. I am that Buddha-Bhagavān's body.'"

Then the World-Honored One asked Mañjuśrī, "Did those Tathāgatas each tell you, 'I am that Tathāgata's body'?"

Mañjuśrī answered, "Indeed, World-Honored One. All those Tathāgatas said so."

Then the World-Honored One asked Mañjuśrī, "How are those Tathāgatas' worlds?"

Mañjuśrī answered, "Those worlds have no grit, and their ground is level, like [the surface of] clear water. The ground is soft to the touch, like cotton. Like the Land of Peace and Bliss, those worlds do not have the five turbidities, nor are there women, voice-hearers, or Pratyekabuddhas. They have the One Vehicle only, no other vehicles."

The Buddha told Mañjuśrī and all others, "If a good man or woman, whether following others or taking the initiative, says all those Buddhas' names, whether he or she is reading, writing, listening [to something], or even frolicking or speaking, all things that terrify him or her will be eliminated. No god, dragon, yakṣa, gandharva, asura, garuḍa, kiṁnara, or mahoraga can disturb him or her. Whoever hears those names will shut the door to the four evil life-paths. Whoever has not activated the bodhi mind will acquire the cause of attaining bodhi, not to mention those who with a pure mind [think of those names], whether they are reading, reciting, writing, or listen [to something].

"Aṅgulimāla, a Tathāgata has extraordinary awesome powers to totally retain the teachings in all sūtras. Eighty koṭi Buddhas are but one Buddha, myself. As Buddha Lands are countless, so too are Tathāgatas. A Tathāgata's body is immeasurable and boundless because He has acquired immeasurable merit. How is it possible that His body can be impermanent or have illnesses? A Tathāgata forever abides in His boundless body. I now broadly say that it has roots, and causes and conditions. All Buddhas have reasons to dislike being born in this world, because sentient beings here are incurable. However, to cure incurable sentient beings in this world, time and again I abandoned my bodies, so I have realized this body that has no birth and no action.[8]

"For countless asaṁkhyeyas of kalpas, to protect the Dharma I abandoned my bodies, as numerous as the sands of the Ganges. Because each and every body was injured, battered, or broken, I have realized this indestructible asaṁskṛta body. For countless asaṁkhyeyas of kalpas, in many dwelling places, I purposely abandoned my bodies, as numerous as the sands of the Ganges. Because each and every body energetically practiced asceticism for countless kalpas, I have realized this never-aging body. For countless asaṁkhyeyas of kalpas, I was [repeatedly] born in times of epidemics to provide good medicine. Because each and every body abided for kalpas as numerous as the sands of the Ganges, I have realized this no-illness body. For countless asaṁkhyeyas of kalpas, I displayed my births, as numerous as the sands of the Ganges. Because, to end the hunger of innumerable sentient beings, I gave them as alms the flavor of the Mahāyāna, I have realized this no-death body. For countless asaṁkhyeyas of kalpas, I displayed my births, as numerous as the sands of the Ganges. Because, to remove the filth of innumerable sentient beings' afflictions, I did difficult things for them and indicated to them their Tathāgata store, I have realized this filth-free body. For countless asaṁkhyeyas of kalpas, I displayed my births, as numerous as the sands of the Ganges. Because, to end the hunger and thirst of innumerable hungry ghosts, I gave them the flavor of the One Vehicle to satiate them, I have realized this body that has no afflictions to discharge. For countless asaṁkhyeyas of kalpas, I displayed my births, as numerous as the sands of the Ganges. Because, to love and think of all sentient beings equally, I regarded them as a father, mother, child, or sibling, I have realized this no-sin body. For countless asaṁkhyeyas of kalpas, I displayed my births, as numerous as the sands of the Ganges. Because I established in the

Mahāyāna innumerable sentient beings, such as gods and humans, who told lies, I have realized this permanent body. For countless asaṁkhyeyas of kalpas, I displayed my births, as numerous as the sands of the Ganges. Because I established in the supra-worldly dharmas innumerable sentient beings, such as gods and humans, who did non-dharmas, I have realized this dharma body. For countless asaṁkhyeyas of kalpas, I displayed my births, as numerous as the sands of the Ganges. Because I established in the right views innumerable sentient beings, such as gods and humans, who followed the wrong views, I have realized this quietest body.

"For countless asaṁkhyeyas of kalpas, I displayed my births, as numerous as the sands of the Ganges. Because I established in fearlessness innumerable sentient beings, such as gods and humans, who were in fear, I have realized this stable body. For countless asaṁkhyeyas of kalpas, I displayed my births, as numerous as the sands of the Ganges. Because I established in freedom from anxiety innumerable sentient beings, such as gods and humans, who were in anxiety, I have realized this anxiety-free body. For countless asaṁkhyeyas of kalpas, I displayed my births, as numerous as the sands of the Ganges. Because I established in great moral conduct all gods and humans who indulged in sex, I have realized this taint-free body. For countless asaṁkhyeyas of kalpas, I displayed my births, as numerous as the sands of the Ganges. Because I drew in innumerable evil sentient beings, purified them, and established them in the true Dharma [saddharma], I have realized this weakness-free dharma body. For countless asaṁkhyeyas of kalpas, I displayed my births, as numerous as the sands of the Ganges. Because I gave material things and the Dharma as two stores to innumerable sentient beings, such as gods and humans, who were in poverty, and set them on the bodhi [path], I have realized this disaster-free dharma body. For countless asaṁkhyeyas of kalpas, I displayed my births, as numerous as the sands of the Ganges. Because I established in freedom from desire innumerable sentient beings, such as gods and humans, who followed their love and desire, I have realized this immeasurable vexation-free dharma body. For countless asaṁkhyeyas of kalpas, I displayed my births, as numerous as the sands of the Ganges. Because I removed all afflictions, like removing venomous snakes, of innumerable sentient beings such as gods and humans, I have realized this trouble-free dharma body. For countless asaṁkhyeyas of kalpas, I displayed my births, as numerous as the sands of the Ganges. Because I formed a Dharma family, stronger than all worldly families, with innumerable sentient beings such as gods and humans, I have realized this no-action wondrous body revealed in dharma illumination. For countless asaṁkhyeyas of kalpas, I displayed my births, as numerous as the sands of the Ganges. Because I gave apt teachings on the pure Tathāgata store to innumerable sentient beings such as gods and humans, I have realized this beyond-existence body. For countless asaṁkhyeyas of kalpas, I displayed my births, as numerous as the sands of the Ganges. Because I established innumerable sentient beings such as gods and humans, and enabled them to abide in a Tathāgata's extraordinary secret, I have realized this extraordinary body.

"For countless asaṁkhyeyas of kalpas, I displayed my births, as numerous as the sands of the Ganges. Because a Buddha brings to accomplishment innumerable sentient beings such as gods and humans, I have realized this immeasurable, boundless, supreme body. For countless asaṁkhyeyas of kalpas, I displayed my births, as numerous as the sands of the Ganges. Because, to deliver innumerable sentient beings, I displayed everywhere my births with various names, I have realized this exalted body. For countless asaṁkhyeyas of kalpas, I displayed my births, as numerous as the sands of the Ganges. Because I enabled innumerable sentient beings to transcend all existence and be set on the bodhi [path], I have realized this unsurpassed body. For countless asaṁkhyeyas of kalpas, I displayed my births, as numerous as the sands of the Ganges. Because I followed the world and manifested [bodies with] missing limbs to set innumerable sentient beings on the bodhi [path], I have realized this unexcelled dharma body. For countless asaṁkhyeyas of kalpas, I displayed my births, as numerous as the sands of the Ganges. Because I never withheld [teachings on] the eternal Tathāgata store but explained it with comforting words to all sentient beings, I have realized this eternal body. For countless asaṁkhyeyas of kalpas, I displayed my births, as numerous as the sands of the Ganges. Because I observed the pure precepts and never entertained lust when I saw celestial, māra, or human women, I have realized this non-fragile body. For countless asaṁkhyeyas of kalpas, I displayed my births, as numerous as the sands of the Ganges. Because I never entertained lust when I saw honored women in the world, I have realized this never-collapsing body. For countless asaṁkhyeyas of kalpas, I displayed my births, as numerous as the sands of the Ganges. Because I cured the diseases of innumerable sentient beings such as gods and humans, I have realized this unparalleled body. For countless asaṁkhyeyas of kalpas, I displayed my births, as numerous as the sands of the Ganges. Because I established in the profound Dharma innumerable sentient beings, including animals, I have realized this profound body. For countless asaṁkhyeyas of kalpas, I displayed my births, as numerous as the sands of the Ganges. Because, to reveal their Buddha nature [buddha-dhātu or buddha-gotra], I explained to all gods and humans that one's Tathāgata store is like a bird track in the sky, I have realized this invisible body.

"For countless asaṁkhyeyas of kalpas, I displayed my births, as numerous as the sands of the Ganges. Because I converted innumerable sentient beings, such as gods and humans, who held the view of no self, and revealed to them their hard-to-see Tathāgata store, I have realized this body that all sentient beings find hard to see. For countless asaṁkhyeyas of kalpas, I displayed my births, as numerous as the sands of the Ganges. Because, to establish the true Dharma, I enabled all gods and humans not to harm others, I have realized this unobservable body. For countless asaṁkhyeyas of kalpas, I displayed my births, as numerous as the sands of the Ganges. Because I enabled all gods and humans to experience Dharma delight, I have realized this perfect body. For countless asaṁkhyeyas of kalpas, I displayed my births, as numerous as the sands of the Ganges. Because I indicated to all gods and humans their Tathāgata store as clearly as they could see Mañjuśrī, I have realized this easy-to-see body. For countless asaṁkhyeyas of kalpas, I displayed my births, as numerous as the sands of the Ganges. Because I untied all sentient beings' fetters and established them in liberation, I have realized this extremely hard-to-see body. For countless asaṁkhyeyas of kalpas, I displayed my births, as numerous as the sands of the Ganges. Because I abided among all gods, humans, and those on evil life-paths, in the Three Realms of Existence, and established them in true liberation, I have realized this non-discriminating body. For countless asaṁkhyeyas of kalpas, I displayed my births, as numerous as the sands of the Ganges. Because I enabled all gods and humans to observe with purity the five precepts, I have realized this body with neither muscles nor bones. For countless asaṁkhyeyas of kalpas, I displayed my births, as numerous as the sands of the Ganges. Because I made a great vow to deliver all sentient beings, I have realized this ubiquitous liberation body. For countless asaṁkhyeyas of kalpas, I displayed my births, as numerous as the sands of the Ganges. Because I pulled out the arrows of all sentient beings' wrong views and established them in the true Dharma, I have realized this quiet, changeless body. For countless asaṁkhyeyas of kalpas, I displayed my births, as numerous as the sands of the Ganges. Because I regarded all sentient beings equally as Rāhula [my only son] and enabled them to see the equality of all, I have realized this still body.

"For countless asaṁkhyeyas of kalpas, I displayed my births, as numerous as the sands of the Ganges. Because I trained myself to be content and enabled others to do the same, I have realized this superior still body. For countless asaṁkhyeyas of kalpas, I displayed my births, as numerous as the sands of the Ganges. Because I taught voice-hearers to be content without [attachment to] food, I have realized this pāramitā body that has ended all seeking. For countless asaṁkhyeyas of kalpas, I displayed my births, as numerous as the sands of the Ganges. Because I relinquished fine food such as fish and meat, and taught sentient beings to do the same, I have realized this splendid body. For countless asaṁkhyeyas of kalpas, I displayed my births, as numerous as the sands of the Ganges. Because I enabled innumerable sentient beings, such as gods and humans, to purge all their afflictions, I have realized this falsity-free body. For countless asaṁkhyeyas of kalpas, I displayed my births, as numerous as the sands of the Ganges. Because I destroyed the dwellings of innumerable evil sentient beings and drove them away like huge hailstones, I have realized this body that destroys [evil] dwellings. For countless asaṁkhyeyas of kalpas, I displayed my births, as numerous as the sands of the Ganges. Because I gave the drink of Dharma flavor to innumerable sentient beings confused by the four inverted views,[9] I have realized this arrogance-free Brahma body. For countless asaṁkhyeyas of kalpas, I displayed my births, as numerous as the sands of the Ganges. Because I enabled innumerable sentient beings to take the quiet, perpetual path of their Tathāgata store, and to leave behind their disturbing faults to become upright and truthful, I have realized this quiet, equable body. For countless asaṁkhyeyas of kalpas, I displayed my births, as numerous as the sands of the Ganges. Because, for innumerable sentient beings that only received a Tathāgata's teaching that dharmas have no self, like pointing at the moon, I established [that one has a true] self, I have realized this body that has abandoned [provisional teachings]. For countless asaṁkhyeyas of kalpas, I displayed my births, as numerous as the sands of the Ganges. Because I never entered parinirvāṇa though there were countless opportunities to do so, I have realized this dharma body in accord with the Dharma. For countless asaṁkhyeyas of kalpas, I displayed my births, as numerous as the sands of the Ganges. Because I used skillful means to look for the taints of innumerable sentient beings' Tathāgata store and never found any, I have realized this [dharma-]realm body, and all sentient beings have this realm.

"For countless asaṁkhyeyas of kalpas, I displayed my births, as numerous as the sands of the Ganges. Because I imparted the Mahāyāna hindrance-free wisdom-knowledge and the true door to see that dharmas have no self and its belongings, I have realized this no-entrance body. For countless asaṁkhyeyas of kalpas, I displayed my births, as numerous as the sands of the Ganges. Because I brought innumerable sentient beings to achievement and enabled them to fear their afflictions, I have realized this supra-worldly, supreme body. For countless asaṁkhyeyas of kalpas, I displayed my births, as numerous as the sands of the Ganges. Because I served as the refuge for all sentient beings, the reliance for those without reliance, and the kin for those without kin, I have realized this body that is like a vast ocean, into which myriad streams flow. For countless asaṁkhyeyas of kalpas, I displayed my births, as numerous as the sands of the Ganges. Because with a fearless mind I expounded sūtras on the Tathāgata store, I have realized this securely abiding body. For countless asaṁkhyeyas of kalpas, I displayed my births, as numerous as the sands of the Ganges. Because I abandoned superb palaces, [the reign of] a Wheel-Turning King, and countless pleasures to enter a mountain and train to attain bodhi, I have realized this palace-like, blissful, motionless body. For countless asaṁkhyeyas of kalpas, I displayed my births, as numerous as the sands of the Ganges. Because I shunned arrogant sentient beings as if they were caṇḍālas [outcaste] and regarded those who observe the precepts as various Dharma vessels, I have realized this no-regret body. For countless asaṁkhyeyas of kalpas, I displayed my births, as numerous as the sands of the Ganges. Because I lightened innumerable sentient beings' burden of afflictions, I have realized this luminously apparent, restful body. For countless asaṁkhyeyas of kalpas, I displayed my births, as numerous as the sands of the Ganges. Because I denounced family life as a prison, I have realized this body that all sentient beings seek. For countless asaṁkhyeyas of kalpas, I displayed my births, as numerous as the sands of the Ganges. Because I enabled innumerable sentient beings to end their greed, anger, and delusion, I have realized this body that has no illness, no fear, and no belongings. For countless asaṁkhyeyas of kalpas, I displayed my births, as numerous as the sands of the Ganges. Because I enabled innumerable sentient beings, such as gods and humans, to guard against women, amusements, and afflictions, as if they were a venomous snake, I have realized this [hindrance-]eliminating body.

"For countless asaṁkhyeyas of kalpas, I displayed my births, as numerous as the sands of the Ganges. Because I trained in Bodhisattva actions under Lamp Lighter [Dīpaṁkara] Tathāgata, received His prophecy [of my attaining Buddhahood], and never maligned the Dharma, I have realized this house[-like] body.[10] For countless asaṁkhyeyas of kalpas, I displayed my births, as numerous as the sands of the Ganges. Because, having heard the teaching that all sentient beings possess the Tathāgata store and will attain Buddhahood when they end their afflictions, I protected those who believed and delighted [in this teaching], I have realized this protective body. For countless asaṁkhyeyas of kalpas, I displayed my births, as numerous as the sands of the Ganges. Because when I was a ṛṣi called Endurance Advocate [Kṣāntivādin],[11] I cultivated the Four Immeasurable Minds [lovingkindness, compassion, sympathetic joy, and equability], I have realized this body on which all sentient beings rely. For countless asaṁkhyeyas of kalpas, I displayed my births, as numerous as the sands of the Ganges. Because I often expounded the hindrance-free wisdom-knowledge from the Mahāyāna, the One Vehicle, the unexcelled vehicle, to greatly illuminate the vehicle that all sentient beings are destined to ride, so that they could use the Mahāyāna to eliminate asaṁkhyeya evils, I have realized this destined body. For countless asaṁkhyeyas of kalpas, I displayed my births, as numerous as the sands of the Ganges. Because I praised the taint-free Tathāgata store as the secure realm, the foremost realm of all sentient beings, which has no aggregation, I have realized this non-aggregate body.[12] For countless asaṁkhyeyas of kalpas, I displayed my births, as numerous as the sands of the Ganges. Because I enabled innumerable sentient beings, such as gods and humans, to enter the celestial abode of pure liberation, I have realized this vast, unlimited, encompassing body. For countless asaṁkhyeyas of kalpas, I displayed my births, as numerous as the sands of the Ganges. Because I regarded innumerable sentient beings, whether male or female, as my parents, brothers, or sisters, I have realized this fatherly body that is supreme everywhere. For countless asaṁkhyeyas of kalpas, I displayed my births, as numerous as the sands of the Ganges. Because I gave away countless bodies as food in times of famine, I have realized this body that is free from hunger and thirst. For countless asaṁkhyeyas of kalpas, I displayed my births, as numerous as the sands of the Ganges. Because I denounced the evil of an icchantika to innumerable sentient beings to make them fearful [of becoming one], I have realized this body that has discarded all existence. For countless asaṁkhyeyas of kalpas, I displayed my births, as numerous as the sands of the Ganges. Because I displayed countless skillful-means bodies and medicinal-trees bodies, and never increased the cause of evil, I have realized this no-action, still body.

"For countless asaṁkhyeyas of kalpas, I displayed my births, as numerous as the sands of the Ganges. Because I delivered innumerable sentient beings, enabled them to end their afflictions, and indicated to them their true nature [for them to see it like] an āmra [mango] in the palm, I have realized this prahāṇa-mārga[13] body. For countless asaṁkhyeyas of kalpas, I displayed my births, as numerous as the sands of the Ganges. Because I denounced to sentient beings all existence, which is like an empty bottle and like the four venomous snakes [earth, water, fire, and wind], I have realized this body that is free from fluid, muscles, and veins. For countless asaṁkhyeyas of kalpas, I displayed my births, as numerous as the sands of the Ganges. Because I enabled innumerable sentient beings to end countless afflictions in all their existences, discard their desires, and enter parinirvāṇa, I have realized this motionless, joyful body in nirvāṇa.

"Aṅgulimāla, for countless asaṁkhyeyas of kalpas, I, who abide in all boundless places, also abide here. Aṅgulimāla, nirvāṇa is liberation, and liberation is [an attainment of] a Tathāgata.[14]"

Notes

1. See "name and form" defined in the glossary's "five aggregates."

2. Udumbara, the ficus glomerata, a tree that produces fruit with hidden flowers. Hence the appearance of its bloom is likened to the rare appearance of a Buddha.

3. See "dharma body" defined in the glossary's "three bodies of a Buddha."

4. "Sūtras in the nine categories" are the glossary's "sūtras in the twelve categories," excluding categories (6) nidāna, causes of the discourses; (7) avadāna, parables; (12) upadeśa, pointing-out instructions.

5. When the Buddha says to someone, "Come, bhikṣu," he immediately becomes a fully ordained monk. No ceremony is needed.

6. Jambūnada gold is gold from the river that flows through the jambū (rose apple) grove. It is renowned for its supreme quality and red-golden color with a purple tinge.

7. The name of this world and the name of its Buddha are identical to an earlier pair.

8. In the following paragraphs, the Buddha gives seventy-three reasons for, and descriptions of, the dharma body that He has realized.

9. See "inversion" in the glossary.

10. Later in this paragraph, the dharma body is described as vast, unlimited, and encompassing. Therefore, it is not a house or like a house.

11. According to fascicle 1 of text 673 (T16n0673), the Chinese version of the *Sūtra of Achieving a Clear Understanding of the Mahāyāna* (Mahāyānābhisamaya-sūtra), in a past life, the Buddha was a ṛṣi called Endurance Advocate [Kṣāntivādin], who sought bodhi. When His body was mutilated by the king of Kaliṅga, He endured pain without harboring malice toward that king. Then He expounded the Dharma to that king and his queen to delight them. The English translation of this sūtra appears in *Transcending the World* (Rulu 2015, 192–230).

12. A sentient being's body is composed of the five aggregates.

13. Prahāṇa-marga (斷道) means the path that has the power to eliminate all one's affliction hindrances and attain bodhi. It is also called the uninterrupted path (ānantarya-mārga, 無間道). On this path, one enters the Vajra-Like Samādhi (vajropamā-samādhi, 金剛喻定) and, without interruption, enters the liberation path and eliminates all remaining traces of afflictions, thus attaining bodhi. A Bodhisattva also eliminates all hindrances to wisdom-knowledge (jñeyāvaraṇa, 智障), thus attaining Buddhahood. Also see "two kinds of hindrances" in the glossary.

14. For the differences in attainments between a Buddha and an Arhat or Pratyekabuddha, see "deliverance" and "bodhi" in the glossary.

Fascicle 4 (of 4)

Then Aṅgulimāla said to the Buddha, "Amazing! World-Honored One, pitying all sentient beings is the foremost difficult thing."

The Buddha told Aṅgulimāla, "For a Tathāgata, that is not the foremost difficult thing. There are other foremost difficult things. During the remaining eighty years when the true Dharma [saddharma] abides in the world, to say comforting words about this Mahāyāna sūtra on the eternal and changeless Tathāgata store [tathāgata-garbha] will be very difficult. For sentient beings to uphold this sūtra will also be very difficult. For those who have heard a Tathāgata's teaching on the eternal and changeless Tathāgata store, truly to follow it will also be very difficult."

Aṅgulimāla asked the Buddha, "World-Honored One, how difficult are these things?"

The Buddha answered, "As an analogy, the great earth bears four heavy burdens. What are these four? They are (1) immense waters, (2) huge mountains, (3) grass and trees, and (4) sentient beings. These are the four burdens that the great earth bears."

Aṅgulimāla agreed, "Indeed, World-Honored One."

The Buddha told Aṅgulimāla, "It is not just the great earth that bears four heavy burdens. Why? Because there are people who bear heavy burdens."

Aṅgulimāla asked the Buddha, "Who, World-Honored One?"

The Buddha told Aṅgulimāla, "During the remaining eighty years when the true Dharma abides in the world, every Bodhisattva-Mahāsattva who expounds to all sentient beings a Tathāgata's teaching on the eternal and changeless Tathāgata store should bear four burdens. What are these four? When the evil kind wants to harm him, he should disregard his survival and even abandon his body and life, to expound a Tathāgata's teaching on the eternal and changeless Tathāgata store. This is the first burden, which is heavier than the totality of all mountains. When the evil kind slanders him as an icchantika and scolds him, he should endure it. This is the second burden, which is heavier than the totality of all immense waters. If he cannot stay in prosperous and pleasurable cities or places, he should stay on their edges or in trouble-ridden places, where necessities, such as food, clothing, and medicine, are coarse, men are slanderous, women have little faith, and all his experiences are painful. This is the third burden, which is heavier than the totality of all grass and trees. If conditions do not permit him to expound the Tathāgata store to kings, ministers, strong warriors, and their retinues, he should endure in expounding it to the lowly, the handicapped, the poor, or the vagrant. This is the fourth burden, which is heavier than the totality of all sentient beings. Whoever can bear these four heavy burdens is called a Bodhisattva-Mahāsattva capable of bearing huge burdens.

"During the remaining eighty years as the true Dharma perishes, for a Bodhisattva-Mahāsattva who can abandon his body and life, to expound a Tathāgata's teaching on the eternal and changeless Tathāgata store will be very difficult. For him to sustain [the belief of] sentient beings will also very difficult.

For those who have heard a Tathāgata's teaching on the eternal and changeless Tathāgata store, to elicit belief and delight will also very difficult.

"However, Aṅgulimāla, for a Tathāgata, those things are not the foremost difficult things. I now will tell you other difficult things. Suppose that a man has an immeasurable lifespan. For countless hundreds of thousands of koṭis of years, he uses the tip of a hair to take a drop of water from the immense ocean until it is depleted, like a puddle in a cow's track. Is that difficult?"

Aṅgulimāla answered, "Very difficult, World-Honored One. That is indescribably difficult."

The Buddha told Aṅgulimāla, "That is not difficult. There are truly difficult things."

Aṅgulimāla asked, "Who [does them], World-Honored One?"

The Buddha told Aṅgulimāla, "During the remaining eighty years when the true Dharma abides in the world, for a Bodhisattva-Mahāsattva who can abandon his body and life, to expound a Tathāgata's teaching on the eternal and changeless Tathāgata store will be very difficult."

"However, Aṅgulimāla, for a Tathāgata, that is not the foremost difficult thing. There are other difficult things. Suppose that a man bears Mount Sumeru, the great earth, and the immense ocean for a hundred koṭi years. Is that the foremost difficult thing for a strong man?"

Aṅgulimāla said to the Buddha, "That is a Tathāgata's state, and no voice-hearer or Pratyekabuddha can match it."

The Buddha told Aṅgulimāla, "That would not be difficult for a strong man. Suppose that he divides each dust particle in the immense ocean into a hundred thousand koṭi pieces and takes away one dust particle every hundred thousand koṭi kalpas until [all dust particles] are depleted [and the ocean] resembles a cow's track. And suppose that he can bear Mount Sumeru, the great earth, and the immense ocean for a hundred thousand koṭi kalpas. However, during the remaining eighty years when the true Dharma abides in the world, he cannot expound a Tathāgata's teaching on the eternal and changeless Tathāgata store. Only a Bodhisattva who is a hero among men can expound it to protect and uphold the true Dharma. I say that he does the foremost difficult thing."

"Moreover, Aṅgulimāla, suppose that a man can use water to extinguish the blazing fire of a Three-Thousand Large Thousandfold World. Is that man doing a very difficult thing?"

Aṅgulimāla answered, "World-Honored One, to extinguish the fire of even one [small] world is very difficult, much more a Three-Thousand Large Thousandfold World. It is very difficult."

The Buddha said, "Indeed, Aṅgulimāla. In the future, those who observe the precepts will decrease, and those who violate the precepts will increase. During the remaining eighty years when the true Dharma abides in the world, if a Bodhisattva-Mahāsattva abandons his body and life, slaves and servants, cows and sheep, and material things, propagates with purity the true Dharma, and expounds a Tathāgata's teaching on the eternal and changeless Tathāgata store, what kind of man is he?"

Aṅgulimāla answered, "Only a Buddha, not a voice-hearer or Pratyekabuddha, can know. At that time, supporting even worldly pure dharmas will be difficult, not to mention a Tathāgata's supreme supra-worldly teaching on the eternal and changeless Tathāgata store. If that man can use water to extinguish the blazing fire of a Three-Thousand Large Thousandfold World, it is very difficult. In the future, during the remaining eighty years when the true Dharma abides in the world, if a Bodhisattva-Mahāsattva abandons his body and life to expound a Tathāgata's teaching on the eternal and changeless Tathāgata store, he is [virtually] a Tathāgata."

The Buddha told Aṅgulimāla, "Very good, very good! Good man, I say the same. All Tathāgatas say that all the difficult things done by that man cannot reach even the edge [of what this Bodhisattva does]."

"Moreover, good man, as an analogy, hundreds of rivers enter the immense ocean and no longer appear. Likewise, all men enter the wisdom acquired by one man and no longer appear.

"Moreover, good man, as an analogy, the immense ocean does not accept corpses. Likewise a man who never does non-dharmas should not associate with those who malign the Tathāgata store. To be such a man is very difficult. To sustain his group and those who hear the Dharma is also very difficult."

Aṅgulimāla asked the Buddha, "World-Honored One, what things should a Bodhisattva-Mahāsattva achieve to indicate that he is not a novice?"

The Buddha answered, "Good man, if a Bodhisattva-Mahāsattva achieves the following eight things, he is not a novice. What are these eight? They are (1) know the Dharma, (2) ponder and uphold the Dharma, (3) support his parents, (4) acknowledge the kindness of his teachers, (5) reject the wrong views, (6) stay away from attitudes of disdain, and from unruly, evil, or impure things, (7) do not entertain thoughts of desire [objects], even in dreams, and (8) respect the precepts. If a Bodhisattva-Mahāsattva achieves these eight things, he is not a novice.

"Moreover, if a Bodhisattva-Mahāsattva achieves the following eight things, he is not a novice. What are these eight? They are (1) explain the Mahāyāna; (2) clearly expound the Tathāgata store, never tiring; (3) do not covet material things; (4) have lovingkindness, compassion, sympathetic joy, equability, and endurance; (5) regard all sentient beings as his only son; (6) stay close to beneficent learned friends; (7) stay far away from evil learned ones; (8) be content with worldly benefits. If a Bodhisattva achieves these eight things, he is not a novice.

"Moreover, if a Bodhisattva achieves the following eight things, he is not a novice. What are these eight? They are (1) speak comforting words well, (2) do not be mischievous, (3) endure slight afflictions, (4) endure in hearing all sūtras, (5) conquer the need for sleep, (6) do not be indolent, (7) be diligent and exercise self-restraint, and (8) delight in seeking [to accept] the precepts. If a Bodhisattva achieves these eight things, he is not a novice.

"Moreover, if a Bodhisattva achieves the following eight things, he is not a novice. What are these eight? They are (1) be truthful, (2) delight in doing pure things, (3) be radiant, (4) be civil, (5) stay far away from women, (6) stay far away from [attachment to] kin, (7) feel terrified, with body hair standing on end, when hearing evil, and (8) think compassionately of sentient beings. If a Bodhisattva achieves these eight things, he is not a novice.

"Moreover, if a Bodhisattva achieves the following eight things, he is not a novice. What are these eight? They are (1) know well what the Buddha says about māras and their differences, (2) have respect for those who know the sūtras, (3) know the differences between [the right] code of conduct and the wrong code, without concealment, (4) know well a Tathāgata's veiled teachings, (5) know a Tathāgata's secret, (6) know well how to follow worldly matters, (7) know well that a Tathāgata is eternal and changeless, and (8) know well that, according to time and place, a Bodhisattva's [seeming] evil is not truly evil. If a Bodhisattva achieves these eight things, he is not a novice.

"If a Bodhisattva achieves these forty things, he is not a novice. If a good man or woman can acquire only half of these forty merits, it means that he or she neither abides in the Mahāyāna nor enters the status of a Bodhisattva. Therefore, Bodhisattva actions are very difficult. What are a Bodhisattva's excellent virtues? If he has no thoughts of desire [objects], even in dreams, know that he has the virtues of all bodhi elements.[1]"

Then Mañjuśrī said to Aṅgulimāla, "What is meant by the Tathāgata store? If all sentient beings possess the Tathāgata store, they all will become Buddhas even if they have track records of evil karmas, such as killing, stealing, sexual misconduct, lying, and drinking alcohol. Why? Because all sentient beings have Buddha nature [buddha-dhātu or buddha-gotra] and will someday achieve deliverance. Because one has [and cannot lose] Buddha nature, should one commit the rebellious sins[2] or become an icchantika? If one had a self [ātman], its self-realm [ātman-dhātu] could deliver all in existence. However, one has neither a self nor its realm. Buddhas teach that all dharmas have no self."

The Buddha told Mañjuśrī, "All sentient beings possess the Tathāgata store. However, like a lamp in a bottle, it is shrouded by countless afflictions. For example, Kāśyapa Tathāgata bestowed a prophecy upon a young [spiritual] trainee. He prophesied, 'After seven years, you will become a Wheel-Turning King and use the true Dharma to rule and transform the world, while after seven days, I will enter parinirvāṇa.' After hearing His prophecy, the young trainee exuberantly rejoiced and thought, 'The one with all wisdom-knowledge prophesied that I will become a Wheel-Turning King. I have no doubt [that it will come true].' He told his mother, 'Get me various kinds of fine food, such as fish, meat, milk, cheese, sesame, and beans, to build up my strength.' Then he ate all these things in a mixture and died an untimely death. Mañjuśrī, did that Buddha lie? Did He not have all wisdom-knowledge? Did that young trainee not have the roots of goodness to deserve the good requital of becoming a Wheel-Turning King?"

Mañjuśrī answered, "World-Honored One, his past evil karmas must have caused his death."

The Buddha told Mañjuśrī, "Do not say so. His untimely death was not a requital for his past evil karmas. Mañjuśrī, how could that Buddha not know the requital for his past evil karmas and bestow upon him a prophecy [by mistake]? He had no past evil karmas, but lost his life because of his own doing. Mañjuśrī, a man or woman might think, 'My body possesses the Tathāgata store. Because I will achieve deliverance, I now might as well do evil.' If someone does evil, will he achieve deliverance because of his Buddha nature? In that story, the young trainee had the nature of a king, but failed to use it. Why? Because he abandoned self-restraint. Likewise sentient beings fail to reveal their Buddha nature because they abandon self-restraint. Do sentient beings not have Buddha nature? They truly do have it. Was that Buddha's prophecy of the young trainee's becoming a Wheel-Turning King a lie? Sentient beings tell lies and abandon self-restraint. Although they hear the Dharma, they abandon self-restraint. It is their own fault that they do not become Buddhas."

Mañjuśrī asked the Buddha, "Do not all sentient beings have past karmas?"

The Buddha answered, "They have past karmas. However, if they have heard even a little of this sūtra, their countless asaṁkhyeyas of sins will be expunged. Why? Because throughout countless asaṁkhyeyas of kalpas the Tathāgata [Śākyamuni Buddha] made a great vow: 'I will deliver all sentient beings that have not been delivered, and liberate all those who have not been liberated.' Because of this vow and His roots of goodness, the radiance of the Tathāgata's wisdom sunlight can expunge countless asaṁkhyeyas of sins. Moreover, Mañjuśrī, as an analogy, before sunrise, clouds and fogs cover the world. When the sun rises, all darkness in the world is dispelled. Likewise, before this sūtra-sun rises, all sentient beings transmigrate through [their cycles of] birth and death. When this sūtra-sun rises, the darkness of asaṁkhyeyas of one's accumulated huge evil is dispelled in a finger snap. Even for someone who jokes about a Tathāgata's teaching on the eternal and changeless Tathāgata store, or follows those on the wrong paths, his asaṁkhyeya sins, such as parājikas, and sins that would result in uninterrupted suffering in hell,[3] will be expunged in an instant. Why? Because whoever hears the name Śākyamuni Tathāgata, even if he has not yet activated the bodhi mind, is already a Bodhisattva. Why? Because the Tathāgata made a great vow to deliver all in the world who have not yet been delivered, to transform them by using the true Dharma, and to enable them to come to realization [of the truth]. Therefore, Mañjuśrī, whoever hears the name of the Tathāgata is a Bodhisattva. He not only can quickly remove his afflictions but also will realize the [dharma] body,[4] just as I have realized it. Mañjuśrī, I now speak in verse:

> I have described the path
> That can pull out the poisonous thorns of care and sorrow.
> You all should act
> [In accordance with] the Tathāgata's words.

"What is the path? There are two paths, the voice-hearer path and the Bodhisattva path. The voice-hearer path is the Eightfold Right Path. The Bodhisattva path is [the understanding] that all sentient beings possess the Tathāgata-store self and should, step by step, eradicate their afflictions and reveal their Buddha nature, which is motionless, delightful, and lovable. Those who do not eradicate [their afflictions] transmigrate forever through [their cycles of] birth and death. [In these lines] 'I have described the path / That can pull out the poisonous thorns of care and sorrow,' care and sorrow mean afflictions, and one who has pulled out poisonous thorns is a Tathāgata. I have eradicated countless afflictions and become a great medicine king. You should follow me and accept [my teachings], and I will indicate to you your Tathāgata store. 'You all should act' means that you should act in accordance with the veiled teachings in 'the Tathāgata's words,' which never deceive you. The appearing of a Buddha in the world is like the appearing of an udumbara flower.[5] One's belief in Him is like a speck of gold in the sands of the Ganges, also like a blind turtle chancing [to find] a hole in a piece of driftwood. If you encounter a Tathāgata, Arhat, Samyak-Saṁbuddha, who expounds a sūtra on the Tathāgata store and never deceives you about the consequences of one's birth and death, then you can deliver yourselves from all your existences and affliction diseases. This is what is meant by 'the Tathāgata's words.'"

Diligently do good dharmas
And subjugate evil minds.
Whoever is tardy in acquiring merit
Has intentions [āśaya] attached to evil dharmas.

"I spoke this stanza for voice-hearers' sake. [Teachings on] the Tathāgata store are hard to obtain. Nothing in the world is so hard to obtain as such teachings. Quickly observe how one's intentions are attached to evils. A bhikṣu who emulates the faults of evil learned ones is surrounded by many afflictions, headed by the five filths that cover his inherent pure mind. What five filths are the root of afflictions that surround him? They are (1) greed, (2) anger, (3) stupor, (4) restlessness, and (5) doubt.[6] These five filths taint his mind. To remove these five filths and other afflictions, he should diligently use the power of his inherent pure mind as skillful means, in order not to malign sūtras, nor to become an icchantika, but to train to deliver himself [from his cycle of birth and death]. Because of this meaning, I say that he should quickly pull out the root of countless visitor-like afflictions [āgantuka kleśa][7] in his mind."

One's mind initiates [everything],
And one's excellent mind produces dharmas.
If one's mind has pure belief
While speaking or doing things,
Joy follows one,
Like the shadow of a form.

"This stanza explains to voice-hearers that the Tathāgata store means one's inherent pure mind. As one's Tathāgata store transcends all dharmas, all dharmas are one's Tathāgata store. If one does things with pure belief and intention, it is because one has ended all one's afflictions and seen one's self-realm. As one has pure belief in one's Tathāgata store whenever one speaks or does things, likewise after one attains Buddhahood, one will speak or do things to deliver all in the world. As one sees the shadow of a form, likewise one sees one's Tathāgata store. That is why I say, 'Like the shadow of a form.'"

One's mind initiates [everything],
And one's excellent mind produces intentions.
If one's mind does evil
Through speaking or doing things,
Pains follow one,
Like wheels [of a cart] that follow a track.

"This stanza explains what is meant by *afflictions*. 'One's mind does evil' means that one's mind, shrouded by countless afflictions, initiates evildoing. So it is called evil. If one does not know that one's inherent pure mind is the Tathāgata store, one succumbs to countless afflictions. Because one is restless and confused, whether one speaks or does things, pains endlessly follow. 'Like wheels that follow a track' means that evils accumulate as one transmigrates through [one's cycle of] birth and death, and that evils drive sentient beings to take the three evil life-paths, like wheels that follow a track. That is why I say that whoever is tardy in acquiring merit delights in evil dharmas.

"Moreover, Mañjuśrī, because one knows that milk contains butter, one churns milk to get butter; because water contains no butter, one does not churn it. Likewise, Mañjuśrī, because one knows that one possesses the Tathāgata store, one diligently observes the pure precepts and practices the Brahma way of life. Moreover, because one knows that a mountain contains gold, one excavates the mountain to get gold; because a tree contains no gold, one does not excavate it. Likewise, Mañjuśrī, because one knows that one possesses the Tathāgata store, one diligently observes the pure precepts and practices the Brahma way of life, and declares, 'I will definitely attain Buddha bodhi.' Moreover, Mañjuśrī, if one had no Tathāgata store, practicing the Brahma way of life would be futile, like churning water for a kalpa but never getting butter."

Mañjuśrī asked the Buddha, "World-Honored One, what is meant by the Brahma way of life? Why has the Tathāgata discarded the pleasures of the five desires?"

Aṅgulimāla said to Mañjuśrī, "Innumerable gods know that [desire] will cause them to fall, so they stay away from thoughts of desire."

The Buddha told Aṅgulimāla, "Do not say so. All sentient beings possess the Tathāgata store. Therefore, all men are brothers, and all women are sisters."

Aṅgulimāla asked the Buddha, "World-Honored One, if King Śuddhodana and Queen Māyā were brother and sister, how could they become the Buddha's parents?"

The Buddha answered, "[Their being my parents] was a skillful display to deliver sentient beings. Otherwise sentient beings could not be delivered. As an analogy, a great king has two thousand strong men. Then two men display skills and subjugate them all, to delight the king and entertain the multitude. Only they know [that it is a staged show], and others are unaware. Likewise a Buddha displays that He has parents as do humans, in order to deliver innumerable sentient beings and enable them to leave the boundless immense ocean of birth and death. However, sentient beings do not know this. As an analogy, an actor plays various roles to entertain the multitude. Likewise Buddha-Bhagavāns produce various manifestations to deliver sentient beings, but sentient beings do not know this. As an analogy, a magician manifests severing his body parts to entertain the multitude, but actually his body is unharmed. Likewise Buddha-Bhagavāns, like a magician, produce various manifestations to deliver sentient beings. Mañjuśrī, a Tathāgata possesses all wisdom-knowledge and knows everything. He observes all sentient beings in the world, and sees that without a beginning each appears as someone's parent, brother, or sister, and repeatedly rises high or falls low [in station], just like an actor playing various roles. Therefore, a Tathāgata lives the Brahma way of pure life.

"Moreover, Mañjuśrī, for pleasure, a man and a woman enter each other's realm. How can they experience pleasure? Know that such pleasure is an aggregate of tremendous suffering. As a woman possesses the Tathāgata store, so too does a man. As they have the same [Buddha] nature, why should they be attached to each other? Having the same nature, a Tathāgata lives the Brahma way of life and abides on His own ground, the no-regress ground, the Tathāgata ground."

Mañjuśrī asked the Buddha, "World-Honored One, why does the Tathāgata not establish an upāsaka and an upāsikā in the Brahma way of life? Why, World-Honored One, do You say that a bhikṣu, a bhikṣuṇī, an upāsaka, and an upāsikā are like four pillars of a hall? An upāsaka or upāsikā lives an impure life [does not practice celibacy]. How can they be established in the way of the true Dharma?"

The Buddha answered, "This odd thought is called a worldly thought. The Tathāgata regards all sentient beings as Rāhula [His only son] and always wants to establish them on the Buddha ground without ranking or graduation. A Buddha's thoughts are different from worldly thoughts. Your question is called a non-question."

Mañjuśrī asked the Buddha, "World-Honored One, is it because the realms of all sentient beings are one realm that Buddhas refrain from killing?"

The Buddha answered, "Indeed, killing another in the world is like killing oneself because all are in the same realm."

Mañjuśrī asked the Buddha, "World-Honored One, why do You regard all sentient beings as Rāhula, then teach people to tame and subjugate the evil kind in the same realm?"

The Buddha told Mañjuśrī, "Good man, do not say so. The Tathāgata regards all sentient beings as Rāhula. For example, a man usually eats more than one meal a day. However, because he loves the Dharma, he eats only one meal a day, which means starving 80,000 worms [bacteria in his body]. His act should be called killing, but it is not impure killing. Moreover, Mañjuśrī, a sage turns away from the pleasures of countless desire [objects]. To end his desire, he could kill himself, but he would be guilty of suicide. When his sexual desire blazes, he should go to someone and say, 'Because my desire has arisen, I pray to be admonished to have a sense of shame, lest I should disregard my survival and commit suicide.' Does it mean that he has destroyed his realm?"

Mañjuśrī answered, "No, World-Honored One, he has accumulated merits."

The Buddha told Mañjuśrī, "Indeed. Mañjuśrī, why do [some] sages kill themselves? It is because of their venomous affliction snakes, not to mention other causes. Buddhas teach that if one's afflictions are strong, one should teach the evil kind and those who sabotage the true Dharma, to do difficult things. This would be an offering to one's realm. When one discards the pleasures of desire [objects], clothing, food, or even life, in order to seek the ultimate bliss, or lets oneself be harmed in order to tame another, it means that one knows well one's Tathāgata store."

Mañjuśrī asked the Buddha, "World-Honored One, is it because [all sentient beings possess] the Tathāgata store that Buddhas do not eat flesh?"

The Buddha said, "Indeed. Without a beginning, all sentient beings transmigrate through [their cycles of] birth and death. They have been parents, brothers, or sisters, just like an actor's various roles. One's flesh and others' flesh are one flesh. Therefore, Buddhas do not eat flesh. Moreover, Mañjuśrī, one's realm and the realms of all sentient beings are one realm, and all flesh is one flesh. Therefore, Buddhas do not eat flesh."

Mañjuśrī asked the Buddha, "World-Honored One, are conch shells, bee wax, honey, leather, and soft silk not the flesh from some sentient beings' realm?"

The Buddha told Mañjuśrī, "Do not say so. The Tathāgata stays away from worldly ways and does not eat flesh. It is not right to say that He stays close to worldly things. Using worldly things is a convenience. One can use anything that arrives through a chain of stations, but should not use it at its origin. One can touch anything that arrives through a chain of stations that do not involve killing."

Mañjuśrī said to the Buddha, "In this city there is cobbler who makes leather shoes. If someone buys [shoes from him] and gives them to You as an offering, will the Buddha accept them because they arrive through a chain of stations? Moreover, if a cow dies from natural causes, and if its owner has a caṇḍāla [an outcaste] remove its hide and give it to a cobbler to make shoes, can someone who observes the precepts accept the shoes given to him as alms because they arrive through a chain of stations?"

The Buddha told Mañjuśrī, "You ask whether someone who observes the precepts should accept leather shoes made by a cobbler from the hide of a cow that died from natural causes, and offered by that cow's owner. If he does not accept them, he complies with a bhikṣu's way of life. If he accepts them, he has no compassion but does not violate the precepts."

Mañjuśrī said to the Buddha, "World-Honored One, a bhikṣu should not accept food cooked with impure water."

The Buddha told Mañjuśrī, "This is called a worldly thought. If a layperson is available, he should use pure [insect-free] water to cook food. If no layperson is available, what can a Buddha do? There are insects in the earth, the water, and the air. If purity is evil, how can the world cultivate purity? Your question is called a non-question."

Mañjuśrī asked the Buddha, "World-Honored One, there are those in the world who decided long ago not to eat flesh."

The Buddha told Mañjuśrī, "Those in the world who follow my words know that they are a Buddha's words."

Mañjuśrī said to the Buddha, "World-Honored One, some in the world talk about liberation, but their liberation is not [true] liberation. Only the Buddha Dharma leads to liberation. Some in the world talk about renouncing family life, but their renunciation is not [true] renunciation. Only the Buddha Dharma leads to renunciation of family life. World-Honored One, some in the world talk about not eating flesh, because they believe that they have no self that eats flesh. Only the Dharma of the World-Honored One reveals one's [true] self, which definitely does not eat flesh."

The Buddha asked Mañjuśrī, "Do you want to know the origins of the paths established outside the right path? I will tell you."

Mañjuśrī answered, "Yes, World-Honored One, I would be delighted to hear."

The Buddha told Mañjuśrī, "Countless asaṁkhyeya kalpas ago, a Buddha called Kucchandabhadra appeared in the world, in this city. At that time the world had no grit and no paths other than the Mahāyāna, and all sentient beings were happy. After that Tathāgata stayed in the world for a long time, he entered parinirvāṇa. After his parinirvāṇa, the true Dharma abided in the world for a long time. When it began to perish, those who observed the precepts decreased, and those who did non-dharmas increased.

"At that time in an araṇya [a temple in a remote place] lived a bhikṣu named Buddha Wisdom. A benevolent man gave him as alms a priceless robe. Out of pity for the almsgiver, that bhikṣu accepted it and showed it to hunters. When the hunters saw his fine garment, they decided to steal it. At night they took that bhikṣu deep into a mountain, beat him, bound his hands, and hung him naked from a tree. That night, a Brahmin went to that araṇya to pick flowers. When he saw a tiger, he was terrified and ran into the mountain. Then he saw that bhikṣu, with a beaten body and bound hands, hanging naked from a tree. Astonished, he said, 'Alas! Earlier this śramaṇa wore a kaṣāya [yellowish red robe], and now he is naked. He must know that wearing a kaṣāya is not the cause of liberation. The ascetic practice of hanging himself from a tree is the right training to attain bodhi. How could he have abandoned good dharmas? This clearly is the liberation path.' Mistaking it for the true Dharma, that Brahmin shed his clothes, pulled out his hair, and became a naked śramaṇa. This is the origin of naked śramaṇas.[8]

"After that bhikṣu was released from his fetters, to cover his body, he took tree barks, dyed them with [the pigment of] red stone, and made a grass duster to dispel mosquitoes. Then another flower-picking Brahmin saw him and thought, 'This bhikṣu wore a fine robe, and now he wears this. How could he have abandoned good dharmas? This clearly is the liberation path.' That Brahmin then followed suit. This is the origin of Brahmins' renunciation of family life.

"At dusk that bhikṣu entered a river to bathe. To wash the lesions on his head, he used a wash cloth to cover them. And he took the ragged clothes discarded by a cow herder to cover his body. Then another Brahmin saw him and thought, 'This bhikṣu wore a kaṣāya, and now he has discarded it. He must know that wearing a kaṣāya is not the cause of liberation. Therefore, he wears ragged clothes, bathes three times a day and night, and practices asceticism. How could he have abandoned good dharmas? This clearly is the liberation path.' That Brahmin then followed suit. This is the origin of Brahmins' practice of asceticism.

"After that bhikṣu bathed, he was plagued by flies biting the lesions on his body. So he smeared white ash on the lesions and used a wash cloth to cover his body. Another Brahmin who saw him thought that this was the way to attain bodhi, and followed suit. This is the origin of Brahmins' smearing themselves with ash.

"Then that bhikṣu used fire to cauterize his lesions. When the pain became unbearable, he committed suicide by jumping off a cliff. The one who saw him thought, "This bhikṣu wore a fine robe, and now he has ended up like this. How could he have discarded good dharmas? Jumping off a cliff must be the liberation path.' This is the origin of worshipping fire and jumping off a cliff.

"Thus ninety-six paths arose because people saw that bhikṣu in various appearances, entertained various thoughts, and formed their own views. As an analogy, people in a country look at one another and entertain violent thoughts. Then they kill one another. Likewise ninety-six paths were established on people's different thoughts. As an analogy, a thirsty deer chases a mirage that looks like water, until the deer dies from exhaustion. Likewise, when the true Dharma is perishing, some people took that bhikṣu's non-dharma behavior as the Dharma. When the true Dharma is perishing, such things happen. Then the true Dharma ends.

"Mañjuśrī, all things in the world, such as the precepts and the right deportments, are a Tathāgata's manifestations. However, Mañjuśrī, people in the world hold wrong views and entertain strange thoughts about one's true self, as they describe liberation and self. Those who seek the supra-worldly truth do not know a Tathāgata's veiled teachings but claim that a Buddha has taught "no self" [only]. They ponder their words as did those who established the wrong paths. The world follows ignorance, and those who seek the supra-worldly truth have lost the wisdom-knowledge of making veiled statements. Therefore, a Tathāgata expounds the Middle Way[9] of the One Vehicle [Buddha Vehicle], which is apart from the two opposites, and reveals that one's true self, the Buddha, the Dharma, and the Saṅgha are true. Therefore, the Middle Way is called the Mahāyāna."

Then Aṅgulimāla said to the Buddha, "World-Honored One, sentient beings do not know the Middle Way but fancy that they can expound it."

The Buddha told Aṅgulimāla, "Few people who have heard this sūtra believe it. Most people in the future will malign this sūtra."

Aṅgulimāla said to the Buddha, "World-Honored One, I pray that You will tell us how many sentient beings from which directions will malign this sūtra and how many sentient beings will become icchantikas. Where can one find those who can say comforting words to sentient beings? I pray that the Tathāgata, out of compassion, will tell us."

The Buddha answered, "In the future, in the central region, 98 hundred thousand koṭi sentient beings will malign this sūtra, and 70 koṭi sentient beings will become icchantikas; in the east, 98 thousand koṭi sentient beings will malign this sūtra, and 60 koṭi sentient beings will become icchantikas. In the west, 98 hundred koṭi sentient beings will malign this sūtra, and 50 koṭi sentient beings will become icchantikas; in the south, 98 koṭi sentient beings will malign this sūtra, and 40 koṭi sentient beings will become icchantikas. The Kophen Kingdom [in present-day Kashmir] will preserve my remaining Dharma, and My Dharma will not perish in the Bharukaccha Kingdom [present-day Bharuch, in northwestern India], nor the kingdom of the Vindhya mountain range [in central India]. Half of the bhikṣus in Kophen will practice the Mahāyāna, and half of them will delight in the Mahāyāna and expound it. In the south, there will be those who, free from the eight evil ways, walk the firm path, train in a Tathāgata's actions, and expound that a Tathāgata is eternal and changeless, in accordance with a Tathāgata's store of teachings. Bodhisattva-Mahāsattvas, bhikṣus, bhikṣuṇīs, upāsakas, and upāsikās will walk the firm path, and bear and uphold my Dharma."

Then Mañjuśrī said to the Buddha, "Amazing! World-Honored One, the Buddha Dharma will abide in the south.[10]"

The Buddha told Mañjuśrī, "Indeed, indeed. When my Dharma abides in the south for a while, you Bodhisattvas who practice asceticism should not spare your bodies and lives and, to comfort all sentient beings, should expound a Tathāgata's teaching on the eternal and changeless Tathāgata store. As other Buddhas do not delight in being born here to bear innumerable sentient beings in this Three-Thousand Large Thousandfold World, I alone have come here to deliver them. Likewise, during the remaining eighty years as the true Dharma perishes, [most] Bodhisattva-Mahāsattvas will not delight in bearing and upholding the true Dharma. However, you and other Bodhisattvas will bear and uphold the true Dharma in Jambudvīpa [the southern continent] and other continents. Not sparing your bodies and lives, you all will expound a Tathāgata's teaching on the eternal and changeless Tathāgata store. At that time, whether or not sentient beings believe it, you Bodhisattvas should think, 'Even if my [physical] body is chopped into pieces, I will realize the ever-abiding body.'

"Therefore, for you and innumerable other Bodhisattva-Mahāsattvas to bear and uphold the true Dharma in the south is the foremost difficult thing. Therefore, I often praise the south as the final place to expound the Dharma. Because of the power of Mañjuśrī Bodhisattva's awesome virtue and renown, or because of fear or a sense of shame, sentient beings in Jambudvīpa and other continents will turn to [the Dharma]. As an analogy, a king hears other kings' ways in order to rule his country. Likewise [some people in] Khopen and Bharukaccha, out of fear or a sense of shame, will expound the secret store in the Mahāyāna. However, they will not expound a Tathāgata's teaching on the eternal and changeless Tathāgata store.

"Mañjuśrī, as an analogy, when grassland is set on fire, it burns in the middle, not the edges. Likewise the firm path in my birthplace is gone, but my remaining Dharma will abide on the edges of the south because Bodhisattvas there will bear and uphold the true Dharma. Know that a Tathāgata will [virtually] be in their midst."

Then the god-king Śakro-Devānām-Indra and his retinue from the Thirty-three Heavens [Trayastriṁśa Heaven] bowed down at the Buddha's feet. After making great offerings, he said to the Buddha, "World-Honored One, together we will protect and uphold this sūtra. We request Your permission, and pray that, out of compassion for all sentient beings, You will tell us the name of this sūtra."

The Buddha told the god-king Śakra, "Kauśika, this sūtra is called Aṅgulimālika. Uphold it as such. Kauśika, this sūtra is as hard to acquire as is an udumbara flower."

Then Abhimaṁru,[11] the god-king Śakra's eldest son, bowed down at the Buddha's feet and said, "World-Honored One, when my father-king battles asuras, he tells his chariot driver, 'You should gloriously subjugate the asura army.' The driver says to him, 'Have no worry. I will never let the king die before I die. I am resolved to fight to my death. Others will also do their best, not sparing their bodies.' Likewise, World-Honored One, during the remaining eighty years as the true Dharma perishes, Bodhisattva-Mahāsattvas who will expound a Tathāgata's teaching on the eternal and changeless Tathāgata store might think, 'When I expound the Dharma, many sentient beings cannot endure hearing it. So I will not expound it.' At that time, do not allow good men who hear about difficulties to quit. [They should] know how to drive well the majestic Dharma vehicle [to deliver teachings on] the Tathāgata store, and know that a Tathāgata, who is eternal, quiet, and changeless, widely expounds [the Dharma] in the world. At that time, if a good man will expound a Tathāgata's teaching on the eternal and changeless Tathāgata store, I will become a bhikṣu to protect him, not sparing my body and life."

Then the god-king Śakra's many children, male and female, and other gods bowed down at the Buddha's feet and vowed, 'I will become a bhikṣu, a bhikṣuṇī, an upāsaka, or an upāsikā to protect him, not sparing my body and life.'

Then the Buddha praised, "Very good, very good! Good men, you all are seekers of the true Dharma. I too will protect those who delight in the Dharma. Like a skillful [chariot] driver, I will go before them. You all should stand firm, acknowledge a Tathāgata's kindness, and widely expound a Tathāgata's permanence, eternity, quietness, and changelessness."

Then King Prasenajit, commander of the four types of troops, told his ministers, "Now someone like a rākṣasa has killed nine hundred ninety-nine people, short of a thousand by only one, made a garland with their fingers, and smeared his body with their blood. Bold and agile, he has devastated this area. He is now forty cows' bellows from this city. Maybe he will kill me and my ministers to make his quota. Together we should eliminate this killer. In this city, men and women dare not leave their homes, and even birds and animals are too scared of him to come forth. You now should announce inside and outside [the city]: 'King Prasenjit is leading the four types of troops to crush that rākṣasa Aṅgulimāla. All of you should take up arms and fight him with all your strength. Whether or not you can kill him, you will receive a reward according to your merit. You will be rewarded with elephants, horses, treasures, cities, or land. You will be given whatever you want.'

However, people were terrified of Aṅgulimāla's evil name, and no one responded to the announcement, except the king's attendants, who had no choice but to obey, because of their respect for the king. Then his queen and concubines wept and pleaded, "We would rather that you lose the position of a king than go to battle in person."

Then King Prasenajit summoned divinators and inquired about the favorable or unfavorable outcome. He asked, "Will I be able to subjugate Aṅgulimāla?" And all divinations stated: "He will perish."

Although the king received these words, he still disbelieved them. He took his four types of troops to visit the Buddha. Upon arrival, he bowed down at the Buddha's feet. Looking fearful and with sweat flowing down his forehead, he sat aside.

Although the World-Honored One, who possessed all wisdom-knowledge, knew everything, He purposely asked, "Great King, why do you perspire?"

The King answered, "Now there is a rākṣasa called Aṅgulimāla. He has killed a thousand people, short only by one, made a garland with their fingers, and smeared his body with their blood. I fear that he will attack me. The people in my entire kingdom are terrified. Afraid to go outside their doors, they have neglected their work. Even birds and animals dare not go near him. I will lead these four types of troops to battle him."

The Buddha asked the king, "Does the great king want to battle him today?"

The king answered, "I now single-mindedly place my faith at the Buddha's feet."

While the four types of troops were in huge fear, the king withheld his fear because he relied on the Buddha's awesome virtue. The king said to the Buddha, "If he comes, he will be by himself."

Then the World-Honored One pointed at Aṅgulimāla and said, "This is the ever-victorious Aṅgulimāla."

The king stared at Aṅgulimāla without a blink. Observing his body, bloodshot eyes, and commanding bearing, the king was astounded, and his hair stood on end, as if he were seized by a non-human. His courage dissipated, and his saber fell to the ground. He drew near the Tathāgata's lion throne, earnestly taking refuge in the Tathāgata, who regarded all as Rāhula. Meanwhile the four types of troops were even more terrified. In confusion and disorder, they scurried away. Then, to comfort sentient beings, the Tathāgata emitted the radiance of fearlessness, illuminating sentient beings and bringing them peace and joy. King Prasenajit, his retinues inside and outside [the city], and his people in the city thought, "Aṅgulimāla must have been subjugated by the World-Honored One."

King Prasenajit praised, "Amazing! World-Honored One, You are truly the foremost yoke [of a cart]. You are truly the unsurpassed teacher of gods and humans, who has skillfully established in the true Dharma such a violent man who did huge, evil karmas."

Then the World-Honored One praised in verse:

> If someone who abandoned self-restraint
> Has quit his violation [of the precepts],
> He illuminates the world,
> Like the moon after the clouds are gone.

"If a Bodhisattva-Mahāsattva first displays abandonment of self-restraint, then displays his merit, he illuminates the world, like the moon after the clouds are gone. He delivers innumerable sentient beings to display a Tathāgata's merit. Great King, know that he is not an evil man, but a Bodhisattva versed in using skillful means."

The king asked the Buddha, "Why do You say that he is not an evil man? He ravaged his teacher's wife, then followed his evil teacher's command to act like a piśāca."

The Buddha told the king, "He did not ravage his teacher's wife. That teacher and wife were a manifestation to convert his mind because he delighted in learning from his teacher and in speaking pure words. Great King, know that this event is extraordinary. As an analogy, the thrust of a dragon elephant[12] is beyond that of a donkey. Indeed, Great King, a Tathāgata is a great elephant-king. He gives veiled teachings in secret words, which are beyond voice-hearers and Pratyekabuddhas. Only Buddhas can do so.

"Great King, south of here, past worlds as numerous as the sands of sixty-two Ganges Rivers, there is a world called Adorned with All Treasures, whose Buddha is called Superior Great Energetic Progress That the World Is Delighted to See, the Tathāgata, Arhat, Samyak-Saṁbuddha. He teaches in that world, where there is neither the Voice-Hearer Vehicle nor the Pratyekabuddha Vehicle. The Mahāyāna is the only vehicle, and even the names of other vehicles do not exist. The sentient beings there have no aging, illness, or suffering. Enjoying only happiness, they have an immeasurable lifespan and immeasurable radiance. The wonderful things there are beyond analogies in all worlds. That is why that world is called Adorned with All Treasures and why its Buddha is called Superior Great Energetic Progress That the World Is Delighted to See. Great King, you should express sympathetic joy and join your palms in reverence. Is that Tathāgata a different person? Aṅgulimāla is none other than [the self-manifestation of] that Buddha. Know that Buddhas' states are inconceivable."

Then King Prasenajit said to the divinators, "All you said is a lie. You should quickly go far way. Do not lie again."

Then gods, humans, dragons, voice-hearers, Bodhisattvas, King Prasenajit, and people from all cities and villages, through the Buddha's awesome spiritual power, gathered there. They bowed down at Aṅgulimāla's feet and, with one voice, praised in verse:

Namo the Tathāgata with a boundless body.
Namo Aṅgulimāla, who uses skillful means.
I now bow down at the holy one's feet
And repent at the honored one's soft feet.
I now repent to the honored Tathāgata,
Aṅgulimāla, whose body lives a double life.

For our sake, he has come here
And manifested a Buddha's image in superb flaming radiance,
To illuminate sentient beings and give teachings.
I repeatedly repent to the immeasurable body of a Samyak-Saṁbuddha,
Who serves as the reliance for those without reliance
And as the kin for those without kin.

Amazing! Two Buddhas have appeared in the world.
What never before happened in the world has now happened.
It is extraordinary to see two Buddhas in the world,
Like a lotus flower born from fire.

Then the World-Honored One told King Prasenajit, "North of here, past worlds as numerous as the sands of forty-two Ganges Rivers, there is a world called Constant Joy, whose Buddha is called Joy Store Jewel Accumulation, the Tathāgata, Arhat, Samyak-Saṁbuddha. He teaches in that world, where there is neither the Voice-Hearer Vehicle nor the Pratyekabuddha Vehicle. The Mahāyāna is the only vehicle, and even the names of other vehicles do not exist. The sentient beings there have no aging, illness, or suffering. Enjoying only happiness, they have an immeasurable lifespan and immeasurable radiance. The wonderful things there are beyond analogies in all worlds. That is why that world is called Constant Joy and why its Buddha is called Joy Store Jewel Accumulation. Great King, you should express sympathetic joy and join your palms in reverence. Is that Tathāgata a different person? Mañjuśrī is none other than that Buddha [His self-manifestation].

"If one reverently pays respects to Aṅgulimāla and Mañjuśrī and has heard their names, one will see the world Constant Joy as if seeing one's own home. Because one has heard their names, one can close the door to the four evil life-paths. Even if one jokes, follows others for fame and profit, follows those on the wrong paths, violates the grave prohibitions,[13] or commits sins that will result in suffering in the hell of the five no interruptions, one also can close the door to the four evil life-paths. If good men or women use these two names for protection, in their present and future lives, they will be protected in wilderness and perilous or terrifying places, and will have no fear anywhere. Even gods, dragons, yakṣas, gandharvas, asuras, garuḍas, kiṁnaras, mahoragas, and piśācas will not disturb them."

Then the World-Honored One told King Prasenajit, "A Tathāgata's words have such great, awesome virtues. A Bodhisattva's actions also have such great, awesome virtues. Mañjuśrī and Aṅgulimāla also have such great, awesome virtues. If one expresses sympathetic joy over their virtues, one can take a Bodhisattva's immeasurable actions. Great King, you should make an offering to Aṅgulimāla's mother. Do not forget that his mother is protected by my skillful means."

Then Aṅgulimāla's mother ascended into the sky, to a height of seven tāla [palm] trees, and spoke in verse:

A Tathāgata's manifestations
Are unknown to sentient beings.
The illusions manifested by a Tathāgata
Are the king of illusions.
A Tathāgata can manifest
A huge or skillful-means body.

After speaking this stanza, she vanished. Then King Prasenajit asked the Buddha, "World-Honored One, was that an illusion?"

The Buddha told the great king, "It was a manifested mother. As this manifested mother said, likewise are Bodhisattva actions."

Then Aṅgulimāla's teacher, Maṇibhadra, ascended into the sky, to the height of seven tāla trees, and spoke in verse:

Suppose that a jackal
Often roams with a lion.
Although it stays near the lion,
Its voice can never compare with the lion's.
As it is scared to death by the lion's sound,
How can it mimic a lion's roar?

I am like that small animal.
Although I have long been Aṅgulimāla's teacher,
I can never emit
The fearless sounds of a hero among men.
If he did not use skillful means,
I would be dead.

I am like a jackal.
How can I accept his offerings?
My actions are foolish,
And Bodhisattvas stay far away from me.

Regarding all sentient beings
Equally as His only son,

The Buddha manifests countless illusions,
But sentient beings cannot know this.

Even if He manifests a hundred thousand koṭi
Brahmin teachers,
Sentient beings cannot know this.
Only a Buddha knows another Buddha's illusions.
Know that a Buddha-Bhagavān
Is the king of illusions.

Then Maṇibhadra's wife spoke in verse:

Alas! Sentient beings do not know a Buddha's virtues.
They say that the Ciñcā-mānavika was real,[14]
Because they do not know that she was manifested by the Tathāgata.

He manifested my body,
Which is an illusion.
Great King should know that
A Buddha's body is inconceivable.

Caṇḍālas [outcaste] cannot get near the king
Because they constantly fear death,
Not to mention speaking to the king.
Although they are humans,
They dare not get near another human,
Not to mention gods or a Buddha.

Innumerable gods, dragons, and other protectors of the Dharma[15]
Constantly make offerings to the Tathāgata.
They end the lives of
Those who have evil intentions toward the Buddha.

The Buddha uses skillful means
To display various illusions
In order to restrain future sentient beings
From doing countless non-dharmas.
As a Buddha's manifestations are a great illusion,
So too is His skillful-means body.

After speaking these words, she vanished. King Prasenajit, after hearing and seeing these extraordinary things, exuberantly rejoiced. He asked the Buddha, "Was that an illusion?"

The Buddha said, "Great King, know that Aṅgulimāla's mother, teacher, and teacher's wife [who each just spoke and vanished] were manifested by me. The way I display manifestations is inconceivable as I teach and transform Aṅgulimāla, in order to deliver innumerable sentient beings."

Then King Prasenajit said to the Buddha, "World-Honored One, I will give great alms for seven days because Aṅgulimāla Tathāgata is a fortune field.[16]"

The Buddha approved, "Indeed, indeed."

Then gods, dragons, and other protectors of the Dharma spoke together in verse:

Namo the king of illusions,
Who displays great energetic progress.
A Tathāgata's skillful-means body
Is an appearance of skillful means.
He enters parinirvāṇa by skillful means
And displays distribution of His relics [śarīra].

A Tathāgata has a boundless body,
Boundless wisdom,
Countless good names,
And countless strong guards.

As a Tathāgata's body is boundless,
So too are His secret marks.
As His words are boundless,
So too are His veiled statements.

As He boundlessly illuminates the world,
His radiance is boundless.
His merits are beyond number,
Description, and measure.

With hindrance-free wisdom like the open sky,
And a body like the open sky,
The Tathāgata comforts Mañjuśrī
And all of us.

Because of Aṅgulimāla,
The Buddha-Bhagavān has come.
Whether or not He comes
Is not something we can know.
The Tathāgata regards all
Equally as Rāhula.

After the World-Honored One pronounced this sūtra, all in the assembly, such as gods, dragons, other protectors of the Dharma, voice-hearers, Bodhisattvas, and King Prasenajit, admired the actions of Aṅgulimāla and Mañjuśrī Bodhisattva. Wishing to be born in their Buddha Lands, the multitude activated the anuttara-samyak-saṁbodhi mind and exuberantly rejoiced.

Notes

1. See Thirty-seven Elements of Bodhi in the glossary.
2. See "five rebellious sins" and "ten evil karmas" in the glossary.
3. See "hell of the five no interruptions" in the glossary.
4. See "dharma body" in the glossary's "three bodies of a Buddha."
5. Udumbara, the ficus glomerata, a tree that produces fruit with hidden flowers. Hence the appearance of its bloom is likened to the rare appearance of a Buddha.
6. In other texts, these five filths are called "five coverings." See "five coverings" in the glossary.
7. See note 39 in Sūtra 3 in the presentbook.
8. Some followers of Jainism are also naked śramaṇas. The Jain community is divided into two denominations: the Digambara, clad in no clothes, and the Śvetāmbara, clad in white clothes. See Nirgranthaputra in the glossary, who is the 24th and last patriarch of the Jain School, and revered as the Mahāvīra (great hero).
9. The word *middle* does not mean a midpoint or a compromise between opposites, nor is it their union. The Middle Way (Mādhyamaka) means that emptiness is non-dual, above the plane of polar opposites, which are illusory appearances of dharmas through illusory causes and conditions, all with false names. Emptiness is also a false name. Although the Buddha often likens emptiness to the open sky, one should not take emptiness as nothingness or as a metaphysical base for saṁskṛta dharmas (Rulu 2012a, 25).
10. In fascicle 2 of text 270 (T09n0270), the Chinese version of the *Sūtra of the Great Dharma Drum* (Mahā-bherīhāraka-parivarta-sūtra), the Buddha says that during the last eighty years as the Dharma perishes, a youth of the Licchavi clan, called Entire World Is Delighted to See, will be reborn in the south as a bhikṣu to uphold the Dharma and pronounce the *Sūtra of the Great Dharma Drum*. An English translation of text 270 appears in *Teachings of the Buddha* (Rulu 2012a, 151–83).
11. The name Abhimaṁru is phonetically translated from Chinese. Maybe it should be Abhimanyu, which is a well-known Sanskrit name.
12. A large elephant is called a dragon elephant, as a title of respect.
13. See "four grave prohibitions" in the glossary.
14. The Sanskrit word *mānavikrayin* means selling one's honor. Ciñcā-mānavika refers to the Brahmin woman who attempted to hinder the Buddha's delivering the multitude. Hiding a wooden bowl inside her clothes, she entered the ashram in the Jetavana garden, where the Buddha was giving teachings, and declared that she was pregnant with the Buddha's child. Then the god-king Śakra manifested himself as a white mouse, entered her clothes, chewed off the string that tied the bowl to her clothes, and exposed the bowl. As the multitude was relieved of its doubts, the earth cracked open, and that woman fell into Avīci Hell (Buddha's Light Dictionary 1988, 4119a).
15. See "eight classes of Dharma protectors" in the glossary.
16. See "three fortune fields" in the glossary.

About Sūtra 5

Text 669 (T16n0669) in 2 fascicles is the Chinese version of the *Sūtra of the Unsurpassed Reliance* (Anuttarāśraya-sūtra). It was translated from Sanskrit in 557 during the Southern Liang Dynasty (502–57) by Paramārtha (真諦, 499–569) from northwestern India. In addition, comparable to chapter one of text 669 are texts 688, 689, 690, and 691 (T16n0688–91), each a Chinese version of the *Sūtra of the Unprecedented* (Adbhuta-sūtra). Text 688 was translated from Sanskrit in the Eastern Han Dynasty (25–220) by an unknown person; text 690 was translated in the Sui Dynasty (581–619) by Jñānagupta (闍那崛多, 523–600) form northern India; texts 689 and 691 were translated in the Tang Dynasty (618–907) by Xuanzang (玄奘, 600– or 602–64) from China.

The term "a Tathāgata's realm" (Tathāgata-dhātu) introduced in this sūtra is synonymous with "the Tathāgata store" (tathāgata-garbha) used in other sūtras, such as the *Mahāvaipulya Sūtra of the Tathāgata Store* (T16n0666), the *Mahāparinirvāṇa Sūtra* (T12n0374), and the *Vaipulya Sūtra of Śrīmālā's Lion's Roar* (T12n0353). Therefore, this sūtra belongs in the category of teachings on the Tathāgata store. Although its words are cited in many commentaries written by Chinese masters, they are cited in only two treatises, texts 1595 and 1610, both translated from Sanskrit by Paramārtha. Text 1595 (T31n1595) in 15 fascicles is the Chinese version of Vasubandhu's *Mahāyāna-saṁgraha-bhāṣya,* his commentary on Asaṅga's *A Treatise on Adopting the Mahāyāna* (Mahāyāna-saṁparigraha-śāstra); text 1610 (T31n1610) in 4 fascicles is the Chinese version of Vasubandhu's *A Treatise on Buddha Nature* (Buddhagotra-śāstra).

Text 669 comprises seven chapters. In chapter 1, the Buddha praises the merit of erecting memorial pagodas (stūpa) after a Buddha's parinirvāṇa. In chapter 2, He says that a Tathāgata is extraordinary and inconceivable for four reasons: (1) His realm and nature are inconceivable; (2) His bodhi and attainment are inconceivable; (3) His merit and Dharma are inconceivable; (4) His benefits and works are inconceivable. These four reasons are explained in chapters 2 through 5, respectively. In chapter 6, Ānanda praises the Buddha in verse. In chapter 7, the Buddha entrusts this sūtra to Ānanda.

Jikido Takasaki (高崎直道, 1926–2013) notes that this sūtra uses, as its own, words from other sūtras, which are cited in *Ratnagotravibhāga Mahāyānottaratantraśāstra* [Discerning the jewel nature: A Mahāyāna treatise on higher tantra], whose Chinese version is text 1611 (T31n1611) in 4 fascicles. He finds that the ten elements of bodhi in chapter 3 are also covered in that treatise, which does not cite this sūtra. Therefore, he concludes that this sūtra is an imitation of that treatise (Takasaki 2014a, 50; Takasaki 2014b, 157–58).

Sūtra 5 in the present book is an English translation of text 669, which has never before been translated into English. For the convenience of the reader, headings are added to some of its seven chapters, which are summarized below.

Fascicle 1 (of 2)

Chapter 1 - A Comparison of Merits.

The Buddha compares merits acquired by honoring innumerable Pratyekabuddhas or holy voice-hearers on the four continents. Suppose that a good man or woman of pure faith builds 100,000 koṭi towers just like the god-king Śakra's soaring tower, and gives them away as alms to monks and nuns in places in the four directions. Then suppose that after a Tathāgata's parinirvāṇa, someone takes one of His relics the size of a mustard seed and enshrines it in a memorial pagoda. His merit surpasses that of the former donor.

Chapter 2 - A Tathāgata's Realm.

A Tathāgata is extraordinary and inconceivable because (1) His realm and nature are inconceivable; (2) His bodhi and attainment are inconceivable; (3) His merit and Dharma are inconceivable; (4) His benefits and works are inconceivable.

A Tathāgata's realm has neither birth nor death, and neither diminishes nor ends. It is eternal, constant, quiet, and ever abiding. It is by nature pure and free from taints. Apart from taints, it is free from afflictions and beyond liberation. It fully accords with and is never apart from a Tathāgata's Dharma. It never abandons wisdom and is inconceivable. A Tathāgata's realm within one is immeasurable and boundless, but shrouded by one's afflictions. A Tathāgata as a realm is inconceivable because, when a Tathāgata's realm is on the tainted ground, pure and impure dharmas coexist. Their coexistence is inconceivable. Suppose that someone follows the profound doctrine and achieves liberation, becoming an Arhat or a Pratyekabuddha. It is not his place to know a Tathāgata's realm. There are two things that he cannot understand: (1) the dharma realm, which is by nature pure, and (2) one's affliction hindrances. Only Bodhisattvas at the spiritual level of avinivartanīya (no regress) can hear, accept, and uphold this great dharma, a Tathāgata's realm. Voice-hearers, Pratyekabuddha, and other Bodhisattvas come to know it because they believe in a Buddha's words. A Tathāgata's realm is inconceivable.

Chapter 3 - The Unsurpassed Bodhi

A Tathāgata's unsurpassed bodhi comprises ten elements: (1) nature [svabhāva], (2) causes and conditions, (3) freedom from affliction hindrances, (4) perfect fruits, (5) works, (6) inclusiveness, (7) action range [vṛtti], (8) being ever abiding [nitya], (9) exclusivity [āveṇika], and (10) inconceivability [acintya].

A Tathāgata's unsurpassed bodhi comes with four fruits: (1) eternity, (2) bliss, (3) a true self, and (4) purity. Stated in another way, a Tathāgata's dharma body has four pāramitās (virtues): (1) the eternity pāramitā, (2) the bliss pāramitā, (3) the true-self pāramitā, and (4) the purity pāramitā.

The benefits of bodhi are acquiring two kinds of wisdom-knowledge: (1) differentiation-free wisdom-knowledge (root wisdom-knowledge) and (2) consequent wisdom-knowledge. The first benefits oneself, and the second benefits others. Benefiting oneself and benefiting others are the two works of bodhi. The action range of bodhi is revealed in a Tathāgata's three bodies: (1)

dharma body [dharmakāya], (2) reward body [saṁbhogakāya], and (3) response body [nirmāṇakāya].

The unsurpassed bodhi is inconceivable for six reasons: (1) it is beyond the description of words, (2) it is encompassed in the highest truth, (3) it is beyond perception, differentiation, and thinking, (4) it is beyond analogy, (5) it is the highest among all dharmas, and (6) it is where neither saṁsāra nor nirvāṇa can dominate. That is why the unsurpassed bodhi is inconceivable.

Moreover, bodhi is inconceivable for two reasons: (1) its ineffability, because it is beyond the description of words; (2) its transcendence, because it is beyond analogy in the world.

Fascicle 2 (of 2)

Chapter 4 - A Tathāgata's Merits

A Tathāgata's merits are revealed by one hundred eighty dharmas: (1) thirty-two physical marks, (2) eighty excellent physical characteristics, and (3) sixty-eight attainments. In brief, a Tathāgata's merits have six characteristics: (1) complete, (2) taint-free, (3) immovable, (4) hindrance-free, (5) altruistic, and (6) skillful. Throughout kalpas as numerous as the sands of the Ganges, all of a Tathāgata's boundless merits, whether acquired on the tainted ground or the pure ground, encompass and accord with one another, and are never apart from one another. Beyond purity and impurity, they are inconceivable.

Chapter 5 - A Tathāgata's Works

To deliver sentient beings, a Tathāgata does eighteen things, and His actions pervade everywhere, without omission, throughout the three time frames (past, present, and future), revealing the nature of the Three Jewels. Why are the things done by a Tathāgata inconceivable? A Tathāgata does countless things, but sentient beings in the world neither are aware of nor understand them because they cannot be displayed or described by words. As a Tathāgata abides in such things, His body is in the nature of the open sky as He appears in all Buddha Lands. As He speaks sentient beings' languages to expound the true Dharma, His speech is not in the nature of sounds. Although a Tathāgata does not take anyone's mind as an object, He fully knows all sentient beings' minds, capacities, natures, desires, and preferences. That is why the things done by a Tathāgata to deliver sentient beings are inconceivable.

Chapter 6 - Ānanda's Praise

Ānanda speaks in verse in praise of the Buddha, who is unequaled in the human realm and the dharma realm.

Chapter 7 - Entrusting This Sūtra

There are ten ways to uphold this sūtra. They are to (1) copy it, (2) make offerings to it, (3) propagate it, (4) listen to it, (5) study it, (6) memorize it, (7) widely expound it, (8) recite it, (9) ponder it, and (10) train accordingly. If someone upholds this sūtra in these ten ways, his accumulating merits will be immeasurable and endless.

5 佛說無上依經
Buddha Pronounces the Sūtra of the Unsurpassed Reliance

Translated from Sanskrit into Chinese in the Southern Liang Dynasty
By
The Tripiṭaka Master Paramārtha from India

Fascicle 1 (of 2)

Chapter 1 – A Comparison of Merits

Thus I have heard:

At one time the Buddha-Bhagavān was staying in the Kalandaka bamboo grove,[1] north of the city of Rājagṛha, together with 1,250 great bhikṣus. All of them were Arhats, who had ended their afflictions, accomplished their undertakings, shed the heavy burden, ended the bondage of existence, and acquired benefits for themselves. Their minds had achieved liberation and ease, and they were accomplished in practicing śamatha and vipaśyanā. These great bhikṣus included Ājñātakauṇḍinya, Aśvajit, Bhadrajaya, Vāṣpa, Mahānāma, Uruvilvākāśyapa, Gayākāśyapa, Nadīkāśyapa, Yaśoda, Mahākāśyapa, Śāriputra, Mahāmaudgalyāyana, Subhūti, Suvahula, Mahākauṣṭhila, Upāli, Pūrṇa-Maitrāyaṇīputra, Mahācunda, Mahākapphiṇa, Revata, Pilindavatsa, Aniruddha, Sundara-Nanda, Rāhula, and Ānanda.[2] Among these 1,250 great bhikṣus, only Ānanda was still on the learning ground.[3] Present as well were five hundred great bhikṣuṇīs, including Mahāprajāpatī,[4] Yaśodharā,[5] Utpalavarṇā,[6] Cimā, Bhadrā, and Nandā, together with their retinues.

Also gathered there were innumerable hundreds of thousands of Bodhisattva-Mahāsattvas from worlds in other directions. Headed by Maitreya Bodhisattva, who would become the next Buddha [in this world], these Bodhisattvas in this Worthy Kalpa had a full understanding of the profound dharma nature [dharmatā]. With an impartial mind, they tamed and transformed sentient beings, and performed good works as they walked the Bodhisattva Way. They truly were sentient beings' beneficent learned friends. They acquired hindrance-free dhāraṇīs, made offerings to innumerable Buddhas, and continued to turn the no-regress Dharma wheel.

Present as well were billions of upāsakas headed by Bimbisāra, king of Magadha, and innumerable hundreds of thousands of upāsikās headed by Queen Vaidehī.[7]

While the World-Honored One was being revered, esteemed, and attended by gods and humans making offerings to Him, through the Buddha's spiritual power Ānanda rose from his seat, bared his right shoulder, and bowed down at the Buddha's feet. Kneeling on his right knee, with joined palms, he said to the Buddha, "Today, I dressed appropriately, took my begging bowl, and went into the city of Rājagṛha. As I begged for food from one house to the next, I saw a newly built tower, tall and majestic. It was decorated with carvings and paintings inside and outside. After seeing it, I had a thought: 'Suppose that a good man or woman of pure faith builds a grand tower like that one, gives it away as alms to monks in places in the four directions, and provides them with the four necessities. Then suppose that after a Tathāgata's parinirvāṇa, someone takes one of His relics [śarīra] the size of a mustard seed and enshrines it in a memorial pagoda [stūpa]. And suppose that the pagoda he builds is the size of an āmra's [mango] seed, its spire the size of a needle, its dew-catching plates the size of a jujube leaf, and its Buddha statue the size of a wheat berry. Which one of these two acquires more merit?' Now I ask the World-Honored One and pray that He will explain."

The Buddha said, "Very good, very good! Ānanda, you can ask the Tathāgata about this important matter because you can do training, acquire multiple benefits, pity the world, serve as a refuge, indicate the right path to gods and humans, bring them peace and happiness, and rescue sentient beings from their suffering. Therefore, Ānanda, now hearken, intently ponder my words, and believe in and accept them with a reverent mind."

"Very good, World-Honored One. I would be delighted to hear them."

The Buddha said, "Ānanda, this southern continent, Jambudvīpa, is 7,000 yojanas long and wide. It is wide in its north and narrow in its south, as is a human face here. Suppose that it is filled with holy voice-hearers[8]—Srotāpannas, Sakṛdāgāmins, Anāgāmins, and Arhats—and Pratyekbuddhas, like densely growing sugar canes, bamboos, reeds, hemp plants, and rice plants, without any gaps. Then, Ānanda, suppose that someone in Jambudvīpa, throughout his life, offers these holy beings clothing, food and drink, medicine, and bedding. After any of them dies, he erects a huge memorial pagoda and offers lit lamps, burning incense, powdered incense, solid perfumes, garlands, clothing, umbrellas, and banners. Ānanda, what is your opinion? Does he acquire much merit through these causes and conditions?"

Ānanda answered, "A great deal, World-Honored One. A great deal, Sugata.[9]"

The Buddha said, "Ānanda, the western continent, Aparagodānīya, is 8,000 yojanas long and wide. It is half-moon shaped, as is a human face there. Suppose that it is filled with holy beings, from Srotāpannas to Pratyekabuddhas, like densely growing sugar canes, bamboos, reeds, hemp plants, and rice plants, without any gaps. Then, Ānanda, suppose that someone in Aparagodānīya, throughout his life, offers these holy beings clothing, food and drink, medicine, and bedding. After any of them dies, he erects a huge memorial pagoda and offers lit lamps, burning incense, powdered incense, solid perfumes, garlands, clothing, umbrellas, and banners. Ānanda, what is your opinion? Does he acquire much merit through these causes and conditions?"

Ānanda answered, "A great deal, World-Honored One. A great deal, Sugata."

The Buddha said, "Ānanda, the eastern continent, Pūrvavideha, is 9,000 yojanas long and wide. It is full-moon shaped, as is a human face there. Suppose that it is filled with holy beings, from Srotāpannas to Pratyekabuddhas, like densely growing sugar canes, bamboos, reeds, hemp plants, and rice plants, without any gaps. Then, Ānanda, suppose that someone in Pūrvavideha, throughout his life, offers these holy beings clothing, food and drink, medicine, and bedding. After any of them dies, he erects a huge memorial pagoda and offers lit lamps, burning incense, powdered incense, solid perfumes, garlands, clothing, umbrellas, and banners. Ānanda, what is your opinion? Does he acquire much merit through these causes and conditions?"

Ānanda answered, "A great deal, World-Honored One. A great deal, Sugata."

The Buddha said, "Ānanda, the northern continent, Uttarakuru, is 10,000 yojanas long and wide. It is square shaped, as is a human face there. Suppose that it is filled with holy beings, from Srotāpannas to Pratyekabuddhas, like densely growing sugar canes, bamboos, reeds, hemp plants, and rice plants, without any gaps. Then, Ānanda, suppose that someone in Uttarakuru, throughout his life, offers these holy beings clothing, food and drink, medicine, and bedding. After any of them dies, he erects a huge memorial pagoda and offers lit lamps, burning incense, powdered incense, solid perfumes, garlands, clothing, umbrellas, and banners. Ānanda, what is your opinion? Does he acquire much merit through these causes and conditions?"

Ānanda answered, "A great deal, World-Honored One. A great deal, Sugata."

The Buddha said, "Ānanda, in the place where the god-king Śakra's celestial palace is situated is a great soaring tower called Forever Victory Hall. It is surrounded by 84,000 tall towers with 84,000 aquamarine [vaiḍūrya] pillars. It is covered with a jeweled net of pure gold, and its four sides are draped with nets, with bells hanging off gold cords. Its ground is scattered with various celestial flowers and gold, silver, and gem dust, and sprinkled with sandalwood-perfumed water. It has 84,000 windows with beautiful decorations. It is adorned with interlaced aquamarine, crystal, jewels in the colors of lotus flowers, and the god-king Indra's jewels. It has 84,000 stairs and railings made of pure blue aquamarine. Ānanda, suppose that a good man or woman of pure faith builds 100,000 koṭi towers just like the god-king Śakra's soaring tower called Forever Victory Hall, and gives them away as alms to monks [and nuns] in places in the four directions. Then suppose that after a Tathāgata's parinirvāṇa, someone takes one of His relics the size of a mustard seed and enshrines it in a memorial pagoda. And suppose that the pagoda he builds is the size of an āmra's seed, its spire the size of a needle, its dew-catching plates the size of a jujube leaf, and its Buddha statue the size of a wheat berry. His merit surpasses that of the former donor more than a hundred times, ten million koṭi times, or an asaṁkhyeya times, and even beyond analogy. Why? Because a Tathāgata is immeasurable.

"Ānanda, suppose that this Sahā World with its four continents—Jambudvīpa, Aparagodānīya, Pūrvavideha, and Uttarakuru—vast seas, Mount Sumeru, and the Iron Mountain Range [Cakravāḍa-parvata], is pulverized into dust particles. Then suppose that there are holy beings, such as Srotāpannas, Sakṛdāgāmins, Anāgāmin, Arhats, and Pratyekabuddhas, as numerous as those dust particles. And suppose that a good man or woman of pure faith, throughout his or her life, makes offerings to them. After any of them dies, he or she erects a memorial pagoda and makes offerings. What is your opinion? Does this man or woman acquire much merit?"

"A great deal, World-Honored One. A great deal, Sugata."

The Buddha told Ānanda, "Suppose that someone, whether a good man or woman, after a Buddha's parinirvāṇa, takes one of His relics the size of a mustard seed and enshrines it in a memorial pagoda. And suppose that the pagoda he builds is the size of an āmra's seed, its spire the size of a needle, its dew-catching plates the size of a jujube leaf, and its Buddha statue the size of a wheat berry. His merit surpasses that of the former donor more than a hundred times or ten million koṭi times, and even beyond measure or analogy. Ānanda, even if he does not transfer this merit to his attaining anuttara-samyak-saṁbodhi, it will bring him fortunate requitals as numerous as the dust particles in this Sahā World, and will enable him to be reborn as the god-king of any of the top five desire heavens[10]—Paranirmita-vaśa-vartin Heaven, Nirmāṇa-rati Heaven, Tuṣita Heaven, Yāma Heaven, or Trayastriṁśa Heaven—or reborn as a Wheel-Turning King."

Chapter 2 – A Tathāgata's Realm

The Buddha told Ānanda, "The merit of and the fortunate requitals to someone who erects temples, memorial pagodas, and Buddha images after a Buddha-Bhagavān's parinirvāṇa are immeasurable, beyond measure. Why? Because, Ānanda, a Tathāgata is extraordinary and inconceivable. Why? Because a Tathāgata's realm and nature are inconceivable; His bodhi and attainment are inconceivable; His merit and Dharma are inconceivable; His benefits and works are inconceivable.

"Ānanda, what is a Tathāgata's realm [Tathāgata-dhātu]?[11] Why is a Tathāgata as a realm inconceivable? Ānanda, every sentient being is composed of the five aggregates, the six faculties, and the eighteen spheres. His various appearances are displays of his internal and external elements, in a continuous flow without a beginning. However, his nature is utmost radiance and wondrous goodness.

"If one's mind [citta], mental faculty [manas], and consciousness [vijñāna] do not arise through conditions, one's perception and differentiation cannot arise through conditions. Then one's wrong thinking cannot arise through conditions. Free from wrong thinking, a Tathāgata's realm within one never activates one's ignorance. Never activating one's ignorance, it is not the condition for the action of one's Twelve Links of Dependent Arising. Not being the condition for the action of one's Twelve Links of Dependent Arising, a Tathāgata's realm has no appearance. Without appearances, it is not formed, has neither birth nor death, and neither diminishes nor ends. It is eternal, constant, quiet, and ever abiding. It is by nature pure and free from taints. Apart from taints, it is free from afflictions and beyond liberation. It fully accords with and is never apart from a Tathāgata's Dharma [with teachings] more numerous than the sands of the Ganges. It never abandons wisdom and is inconceivable.

"Ānanda, as an analogy, a priceless wish-fulfilling jewel is superb, lustrous, lovely, and pure. Its body is perfectly clean, without spots. However, it is left in filthy mud for 100,000 kalpas. Then someone picks it up, washes it, and protects it from falling [into mud]. After it is cleaned, this wish-fulfilling jewel recovers the purity of a treasure.

"Indeed, Ānanda, when all Tathāgatas were on the Cause Ground, as Bodhisattvas They knew that a sentient being's nature is pure, but tainted by his visitor-like afflictions [āgantuka kleśa].[12] They thought: 'Visitor-like afflictions do not enter a sentient being's pure realm because his filthy afflictions are external hindrances formed by his false thinking. We can expound the profound wondrous Dharma to sentient beings to have them eliminate their affliction hindrances.[13] We should not regard them as lowly. Because of our magnanimity, we will (1) respect sentient beings, (2) revere great teachers, (3) develop wisdom [prajñā], (4) acquire wisdom-knowledge [jñāna], and (5) elicit great compassion [for sentient beings]. Following these five ways, a Bodhisattva will reach avinivartanīya [the spiritual level of no regress].'

"These Bodhisattvas then thought: 'One's dirt-like afflictions have neither power nor ability, incoherent [asambaddha] with one's root [true mind]. While one's true mind is the pure root, they have no root of reality and no root of reliance. With no root, they arise from one's false thinking and perverted habits. While the four domains—earth, water, fire, and wind—abide in one's root, which relies on nothing, one's afflictions have no root of reality. If one truly knows this, and observes one's afflictions with right thinking, they cannot go against one's true mind. I now should observe my afflictions so that they cannot taint me. If my afflictions cannot taint me, this is very good. If we are tainted by our afflictions, how can we expound the Dharma to sentient beings to free them from the fetters of their afflictions? Therefore, I should discard my afflictions and expound the true Dharma [saddharma] to sentient beings, enabling them to cut off their fetters. However, if afflictions that drive one's repeated birth and death respond to one's roots of goodness, I should accept such afflictions[14] in order to bring sentient beings to [spiritual] maturity through mastering the Buddha Dharma.'

"Thus, Ānanda, when a Tathāgata on the Cause Ground relied on the true reality [bhūta-koṭi][15] of dharmas to acquire knowledge and to train [as a Bodhisattva], He understood that a Tathāgata's realm [within Him], which is free from taints and attachments, could undergo repeated birth and death, unfettered by His afflictions, and enable Him to acquire great skillful means, abide in quiet nirvāṇa that abides nowhere,[16] and quickly attain anuttara-samyak-saṁbodhi.

"Ānanda, a Tathāgata's realm [within one] is immeasurable and boundless, but shrouded by one's afflictions. When it follows one's births and deaths to transmigrate through the six life-paths, I say that it is called a sentient being. Ānanda, when a sentient being tires of his suffering through repeated birth and death, discards his desires for the six sense objects, enters 84,000 Dharma Doors [dharma-paryāya] encompassed in the ten pāramitās, and trains to attain bodhi, I say that he is called a Bodhisattva. Ānanda, when a sentient being has ended his afflictions, cleansed off their filth, passed all his suffering, and revealed his innate purity, become someone whom sentient beings wish to see, ascended to the wondrous highest ground of all wisdom-knowledge free from all hindrances, abided there until he has acquired the unparalleled ability and a Dharma King's great commanding power, I say that he is called a Tathāgata, Arhat, Samyak-Saṁbuddha.

"Ānanda, a Tathāgata's realm within sentient beings in these three positions is the same in every way and is hindrance free, because it has always been quiet. As an analogy, the open sky cannot be covered, filled, or stuffed by any objects. The space in an earthen vessel, a silver vessel, and a gold vessel is the same. Likewise a Tathāgata's realm within sentient beings in these three positions is the same in every way and is hindrance free.

"Ānanda, when all Tathāgatas were on the Cause Ground, as Bodhisattvas They relied on the true reality of dharmas to acquire knowledge and to train. They observed the five virtues of a Tathāgata's realm: (1) ineffability, (2) sameness, (3) beyond sameness and difference, (4) beyond the states of perception, and (5) having the one flavor [the flavor of emptiness] wherever it is.

"When a Bodhisattva sees these five virtues, he removes his perceptions of a sentient being's appearances, the different appearances of dharmas, and the appearances of his huge afflictions. Using his unimpeded wisdom-knowledge[17] to observe a Tathāgata's realm within sentient beings undergoing successive lives, he has an extraordinary thought: 'Sentient beings are amazing! Although a Tathāgata is in their bodies, they cannot see Him in accord with true reality. Therefore, I will reveal to them the complete holy path[18] and explain to them the hindrance caused by their attachment to appearances, which has no beginning, enabling them to use the power of the holy path to remove their attachment to appearances and to see in accord with true reality that the Tathāgata [within them] remains the same wherever they are.'[19] Why does he do so? Because all sentient beings, fettered by their attachment to appearances, do not recognize the Tathāgata within them, do not see Him, and cannot realize Him.

"Ānanda, when a Tathāgata was on the Cause Ground, He observed a Tathāgata's realm [within Him] and fully understood it. He rightly realized that all dharmas are equal in their suchness, rightly turned the unsurpassed, wondrous Dharma wheel, and rightly brought to spiritual maturity innumerable holy disciples, who reverently surrounded Him. He abided in the tranquil nirvāṇa without remnants,[20] benefited sentient beings, and never abandoned them, even at the end of the world.

"Ānanda, a Tathāgata's realm is by nature pure and is the same within sentient beings, without any difference. It accords with equality, purity, brightness, and smoothness, and responds [to sentient beings] with the most wondrous tenderness and goodness. Ānanda, as an analogy, water is by nature pure and wet and can wet and grow all medicinal herbs and trees. Likewise, Ānanda, when all Tathāgatas were on the Cause ground, as Bodhisattvas They relied on a Tathāgata's realm [within them] to develop roots of goodness and benefit sentient beings. For this reason, They entered the Three Realms of Existence and appeared to undergo birth, old age, illness, and death, which were unreal. Why? Because they had truly seen a Tathāgata's realm.

"Ānanda, as an analogy, a rich and powerful elder has an only son, who is handsome and intelligent. He protects, cherishes, watches, and cares for him without interruption. This boy is young and loves to frolic. He missteps and falls into a deep pit of feces and putrid corpses. When his mother and relatives see him fall into the pit, they cry, 'Alas, pain, trouble, distress!' Although they wail in sorrow, they are too weak and timid to enter the pit to rescue him. Then the elder quickly arrives. Concerned about his son, undaunted by the filth and stench, he enters the pit and carries his son out of it. Thus, Ānanda, I use this analogy to reveal the true meaning. The pit of feces and corpses is like the Three Realms of Existence. The only son is like sentient beings, who are ordinary beings. The mother and relatives are like voice-hearers and Pratyekabuddhas. When these riders of the Two Vehicles see sentient beings drifting and sinking in the flow of existence, although out of compassion they worry about and pity them, they have no ability to relieve them and pull them out. The rich and powerful elder is like Bodhisattvas, who are pure, taint free, and free from an impure mind. They have already seen [a Tathāgata's realm within them] without any study or training, and they accept their requital bodies in order to enter the filthy and stinking place of births and deaths, and relieve and rescue sentient beings.

"Ānanda, know that a Bodhisattva's great compassion is rare and ineffable. Although he has shed his fetters and transcended the Three Realms of Existence, he enters them and accepts his rebirths there. By upāya-kauśalya [skillful means], he practices prajñā-pāramitā [the wisdom pāramitā],[21] and his afflictions cannot taint him. In this way he expounds the true Dharma to end sentient beings' suffering.

"Ānanda, know that a Tathāgata's realm has vast, awesome powers, and is changeless and gentle. Therefore, Ānanda, sentient beings have holy nature [Buddha nature], which is unaffected by cultivation or no cultivation, action or no action. It has neither mind nor mental functions, neither karma nor karmic requital, neither pain nor pleasure. When one enters it, one sees that this nature is the same [within all], has no different appearances, and stays far away from afflictions. It follows [sentient beings' needs], and is vast and free from a self and its belongings, high or low. It is real, endless, ever abiding, radiant, and pure. Ānanda, why is this nature called the holy nature? Because all holy teachings are founded on it, and all holy beings rely on it to attain Buddhahood. Hence I say that it is the holy nature.

"Ānanda, Tathāgata nature is the exclusive truth of all Tathāgatas, who are more numerous than the sands of the Ganges. They arise from this nature, which is also called a Tathāgata's realm. All should believe and delight in this true teaching, and appreciate and value [a Tathāgata's realm within them], through which the precept, meditation, and wisdom bodies[22] of all sages and holies are formed. Therefore, this dharma [a Tathāgata's realm] is called the dharma body [dharmakāya].[23] It is all-encompassing, inseparable from wisdom, and free from understandings [based on one's consciousness]. It is the reliance, support, and base of all dharmas. Even if a sentient being departs from its purity and wisdom, and relies on understandings based on his consciousness, it is still the reliance, support, and base of all dharmas. Therefore, I say that because it is the changeless store of all dharmas, it is called true suchness [bhūta-tathātā]; because it is never perverted, it is called the true reality [bhūta-koṭi]; because it has no appearances, it is called quietness; because it is the place walked by a holy being with differentiation-free wisdom-knowledge, it is called the highest truth. Ānanda, a Tathāgata's realm is neither existent nor nonexistent, neither pure nor impure. It is by nature taint free and accords with purity. You should know this.

"Ānanda, why is a Tathāgata as a realm inconceivable? Because, Ānanda, when a Tathāgata's realm is on the tainted ground, pure and impure dharmas coexist. Their coexistence is inconceivable. Suppose that someone follows the profound doctrine and achieves liberation, becoming an Arhat or a Pratyekabuddha. It is not his place to know a Tathāgata's realm. Ānanda, there are two things that he cannot understand: (1) the dharma realm, which is by nature pure, and (2) one's affliction hindrances.[24] Only Bodhisattvas at the spiritual level of avinivartanīya can hear, accept, and uphold this great dharma [a Tathāgata's realm]. Voice-hearers, Pratyekabuddha, and other Bodhisattvas come to know it because they believe in a Buddha's words. Ānanda, a Tathāgata's realm is inconceivable."

Chapter 3 – The Unsurpassed Bodhi

The Buddha told Ānanda, "What is a Tathāgata's anuttara-samyak-saṁbodhi? When a Buddha-Bhagavān abides in the affliction-free realm [nirvāṇa], He has forever eliminated all kinds of hindrances and realized His quiet, radiant, and pure [mind]. His unsurpassed bodhi comprises ten elements, and you should know them. What are these ten? They are (1) nature [svabhāva], (2) causes and conditions, (3) freedom from affliction hindrances, (4) perfect fruits, (5) works, (6) inclusiveness, (7) action range [vṛtti], (8) being ever abiding [nitya], (9) incomparability, and (10) inconceivability [acintya].

The Nature of Bodhi

"Ānanda, what is the nature of bodhi? It is the quietness, radiance, and purity acquired through one's proper training to transcend the world by practicing the ten pāramitās on the ten Bodhisattva grounds.[25] It is beyond the state of a voice-hearer or Pratyekabuddha. This is called the nature of bodhi.

"However, one has not removed one's afflictions. So I reveal that one's Tathāgata store [tathāgata-garbha] is the extremely pure dharma for one to turn to and rely on. One's reliance on it is the condition for (1) the arising of the bodhi path, (2) ending one's afflictions, (3) acquiring the Dharma fruit through intense pondering, and (4) realizing the body of the purest dharma realm. Why does the bodhi path arise? It arises so that Tathāgatas in all worlds will continue to appear. How does one end one's afflictions? By following the bodhi path, one will end forever one's three grades of afflictions—low, middling, and high—that arise from one's ignorance [of the truth], the root affliction. How does one acquire the Dharma fruit? One acquires it when one has fully realized the true suchness of dharmas and attained bodhi. What is the body of the dharma realm? It is the purest dharma realm revealed by ending one's afflictions and attachment to appearances. Ānanda, what one turns to and relies on is a Buddha-Bhagavān's unsurpassed bodhi, also called the nature of bodhi.

The Causes of Bodhi

"Ānanda, there are four working causes [kāraṇa-hetu][26] of attaining the unsurpassed bodhi. What are these four? They are (1) delighting in learning Mahāyāna teachings, (2) practicing prajñā-pāramitā, (3) entering the samādhi door that ends the view of void,[27] and (4) learning a Tathāgata's great compassion.

The Four Affliction Hindrances to Attaining Bodhi

"Ānanda, there are four afflictions that hinder one from acquiring the bodhi fruit. What are these four? They are (1) rejecting Mahāyāna teachings, (2) holding wrong views such as the wrong view that one has a self [ātman], (3) dreading suffering through repeated birth and death, and (4) refusing to do things to benefit others.

The Four Fruits of Bodhi

"Ānanda, the unsurpassed bodhi comes with four fruits. What are these four? They are (1) eternity, (2) bliss, (3) a true self, and (4) purity."[28]

Ānanda's Request for Teachings

After hearing the Buddha's worlds, Ānanda, in the midst of the multitude, rose from his seat. He bared his right shoulder, bent over, and bowed down at the Buddha's feet. Then, kneeling on his right knee, with joined palms, he asked the Buddha in verse:

> You have revealed the profound principle for our training
> To cross the flow of existence, never regressing,
> And to end all our afflictions and fears.
> So I bow down to ask Gotama.[29]
>
> What are the causes of bodhi?
> What are its hindrances and what are its fruits?
> I pray that the great loving-kind and compassionate honored one
> Will pity us and explain in detail.

Three Kinds of Sentient Beings

Then the World-Honored One praised, "Very good, very good! You can ask the Tathāgata about this great profound meaning because you have benefited many sentient beings, indicated the right path to gods and humans, and brought them peace and joy. Now hearken to, believe in, and accept my words with earnest longing and reverence."

"Very good, World-Honored One. I would be delighted to hear them."

The Buddha told Ānanda, "There are three kinds of sentient beings in the world: (1) those attached to existence, (2) those attached to nonexistence, and (3) those attached to neither.

"Those attached to existence are divided into two groups. The first group comprises those who turn away from the path to nirvāṇa because they have no proclivity for nirvāṇa. They do not seek nirvāṇa because they delight in their repeated birth and death. The second group comprises those who do not aspire to my Dharma but malign the Mahāyāna. Ānanda, these two groups are not a Buddha's disciples because they think that a Buddha is not a great teacher and not a place of refuge. Foolish and blind, they fall into steep, terrifying, vast darkness. Wandering in a wilderness, they enter a filthy, dark, dense forest of thorns. Continuing to be fettered by birth and death in their future, they fall into the net of icchantikas [those who cut off their roots of goodness] and cannot break away on their own.

"Those attached to nonexistence are divided into two groups. The first group trains without skillful means, and the second group trains with skillful means. The first group training without skillful means is further divided into two bands: (1) those who follow any of the ninety-six non-Buddhist doctrines, such as [the doctrine advocated by] Ajita Kesakambala,[30] and (2) those who believe in the Buddha Dharma. However, in the second band are those who obstinately hold the view that one has a self and do not appreciate the true principle. I say that they are the same as those non-Buddhists [in the first band]. Then there are those with exceeding arrogance.[31] Although they observe the emptiness of dharmas in accordance with the true Dharma, they hold either the view of existence or the view of nonexistence. A true understanding of the emptiness of dharmas as revealed by a Tathāgata leads one to the one path to the unsurpassed bodhi through the pure liberation door. However, if someone holds the view of void, I say that he is beyond cure. Ānanda, if someone holds the view that one has a self, and his wrong view is as huge as Mount Sumeru, I will not be alarmed, nor will I rebuke him. However, if someone with exceeding arrogance holds the view of void, and his wrong view is as small as one sixteenth of a hair, I will not permit him. The second group training with skillful means is also divided into two bands: (1) riders of the Voice-Hearer Vehicle, who train with a view to benefiting themselves but do nothing to benefit others, and (2) riders of the Pratyekabuddha Vehicle, who rarely benefit others and are satisfied with their few deeds.

"Those attached to neither existence nor nonexistence have the highest and keenest capacity to do spiritual training by riding the Mahāyāna, and they are attached to neither birth nor death.

"An icchantika neither does spiritual training nor has any skillful means; a non-Buddhist trains without skillful means. How should a rider of either of the Two Vehicles do spiritual training [like a Bodhisattva]? He should observe that saṁsāra and nirvāṇa are the same in the one appearance [the appearance of emptiness] in order to attain bodhi with his mind steadily abiding in pure nirvāṇa that abides nowhere, to roam through births and deaths without being tainted, to cultivate great compassion as his root, and to firmly abide in his high aspirations."

The Buddha said, "Ānanda, whoever maligns the Mahāyāna and is attached to existence and greedy for lingering in the Three Realms of Existence is called an icchantika. He falls into the group that definitely is on the wrong path. Whoever is attached to nonexistence and trains without skillful means falls into the group that is indecisive about its path.[32] Whoever is attached to nonexistence and trains with skillful means, and whoever is attached to neither existence nor nonexistence and trains on the path of equality, fall into the group that definitely progresses on the right path to bodhi.[33]

Four Kinds of People Cannot Realize a Tathāgata's Dharma Body

"Ānanda, excepting those who are attached to neither existence nor nonexistence and train on the path of equality, there are four kinds of people who cannot attain the unsurpassed bodhi to realize a Tathāgata's dharma body. Who are these four? They are (1) icchantikas, (2) non-Buddhists, (3) voice-hearers, and (4) Pratyekabuddhas. Each kind has its own affliction hindrance. What are their hindrances? First, rejecting the Mahāyāna is an icchantika's hindrance. To eliminate this hindrance, I expound that a Bodhisattva believes and delights in Mahāyāna teachings and trains accordingly. Second, holding the wrong view that wherever one is one has a self is a non-Buddhist's hindrance. To eliminate this hindrance, I expound that a Bodhisattva practices prajñā-pāramitā. Third, dreading his repeated birth and death is a voice-hearer's hindrance. To eliminate this hindrance, I expound that a Bodhisattva enters the samādhi door that ends the view of void. Fourth, benefiting others rarely and feeling satisfied with his small deeds are a Pratyekabuddha's hindrance. To eliminate this hindrance, I expound that a Bodhisattva cultivates great compassion [for all sentient beings].

"These four kinds of people have these four afflictions. To remove them, I expound the Four Noble Truths because the truth can correct their four inverted views, enabling them to realize a Tathāgata's supreme and wondrous dharma body with the four virtues, which is the fruit of practicing the wisdom pāramitā.

The Four Inversions

"Ānanda, dharmas such as form are impermanent, yet one perceives them as permanent. Dharmas boil down to suffering, yet one perceives them as happiness. Dharmas have no self, yet one perceives [that they have] a self. Dharmas are impure, yet one perceives them as pure. This is the meaning of inversion. Then perceiving dharmas as impermanent, suffering, having no self, and impure is not called an inversion. However, if one applies this [non-inversion] to a Tathāgata's wondrous dharma body, it becomes an inversion. To correct this inversion, I expound that a Tathāgata's dharma body has four virtues. What are these four? They are (1) the eternity pāramitā, (2) the bliss pāramitā, (3) the true-self pāramitā, and (4) the purity pāramitā.[34]

"Ānanda, an ordinary being entertains the four inverted perceptions of the five aggregates, which constitute a sentient being. He takes impermanence as permanence, suffering as happiness, a nonexistent self as a self, and impurity as purity.

"Ānanda, a Tathāgata's dharma body is the object of His knowledge of all wisdom-knowledge [sarvajña-jñāna].[35] A voice-hearer or Pratyekabuddha cannot realize a Tathāgata's dharma body because his inverted training cannot be rectified. Why not? Because he thinks that (1) he should train to realize a Tathāgata's supreme eternal dharma body by taking it as impermanence, not permanence; (2) he should train to realize a Tathāgata's supreme blissful dharma body by taking it as suffering, not bliss; (3) he should train to realize a

Tathāgata's supreme dharma body symbolized as a true self by taking it as no self, not a true self; (4) he should train to realize a Tathāgata's supreme pure dharma body by taking it as impurity, not purity. Therefore, a voice-hearer or a Pratyekabuddha, who does inverted training on his path, cannot realize a Tathāgata's dharma body with the four virtues. Therefore, its four virtues—eternity, bliss, a true self, and purity—are beyond his state.

Correction of Inversions

"Ānanda, if someone believes in a Tathāgata's words and can see that His dharma body is eternity, bliss, a true self, and purity, his mind is not inverted and truly holds the right views. Why? Because, Ānanda, a Tathāgata's dharma body has four virtues—the eternity, bliss, true-self, and purity pāramitās. If someone follows the excellent wondrous path to observe a Tathāgata's body, he goes from illumination to higher illumination, and from a secure place to the utmost joyful place. He is a Buddha's true son and is loved and remembered by Him. He is born from a Buddha's mouth [i.e., from hearing the Dharma] and will attain what a Buddha has attained. He is born from being transformed by the Dharma and will acquire the Dharma wealth.

"Ānanda, an icchantika rejects the true Dharma because he is greedy for and delights in his stinking and filthy births and deaths. To remove this affliction, I expound that one should delight in the Mahāyāna and train accordingly in order to acquire the purity pāramitā as the fruit. Ānanda, a non-Buddhist holds the wrong view that one has a self, which leads to grasping and attachment. However, dharmas such as form have no self because they never contend. While other Buddhas everywhere in the three time frames [past, present, and future] and I expound that a Tathāgata is a true self, a non-Buddhist takes the five aggregates, which constitute a sentient being, as a self and feels secure and happy. To remove this affliction, I expound that one should practice prajñā-pāramitā in order to acquire the true-self pāramitā as the fruit. Ānanda, a voice-hearer dreads his repeated birth and death, and delights in cessation of his suffering. To remove this affliction, I expound that one should enter the samādhi door that ends the view of void in order to acquire the bliss pāramitā as the fruit. Ānanda, a Pratyekabuddha overlooks things that can benefit others, does not live with others, but enjoys pondering the truth in solitude. To remove this fixation, I expound that one should cultivate a Bodhisattva's great compassion in order to go everywhere in the ten directions to do things that benefit sentient beings. Forever abiding in altruistic deeds, one acquires the eternity pāramitā as the fruit. Ānanda, because of these four virtues, a Tathāgata is actually called the dharma realm, which, like the vast open sky, the ultimate domain of space, is attached to neither existence nor nonexistence and is ever abiding, beyond past, present, and future.

A Holy Being's Hindrances to Attaining Bodhi

"Ānanda, a holy being, such as an Arhat, a Pratyekabuddha, or a Bodhisattva on any Bodhisattva ground, cannot realize a Tathāgata's dharma body with the four virtues because of four kinds of hindrances. What are these four? They are (1) the condition for the arising of his [subtle] afflictions, (2) the cause of the arising of his [subtle] afflictions, (3) his existence, and (4) his unreal existence.

"What is the condition for the arising of a holy being's [subtle] afflictions? It is his ground-abiding ignorance, which produces his actions, just like an ordinary being's ignorance, which produces his karmas. What is the cause of the arising of a holy being's [subtle] afflictions? It is his actions produced by his ground-abiding ignorance, just like an ordinary being's karmas produced by his ignorance. What is a holy being's existence? Through his ground-abiding ignorance as the condition and his affliction-free karmas as the cause, his three kinds of mind-created bodies[36] arise, just like an ordinary being's karmic bodies, which arise in the Three Realms of Existence through his four kinds of grasping[37] as the condition and his affliction-driven karmas as the cause. What is a holy being's unreal existence? Through his three kinds of mind-created bodies as the condition, he experiences imperceptible, subtle death, just as an ordinary being in the Three Realms of Existence undergoes old age and death, thought after thought.

"Because his ground-abiding ignorance upon which his [subtle] afflictions depend is not ended, an Arhat, a Pratyekabuddha, or a holy Bodhisattva cannot reach the great purity pāramitā, which is free from all his filthy afflictions and habits. Because his ground-abiding ignorance triggers his subtle afflictions, he has not completely ended his false thinking; hence he cannot reach the great true-self pāramitā, which is quiet, takes no action, and does nothing. Because of his ground-abiding ignorance as the condition and his affliction-free karmas arising from his subtle thinking as the cause, he has not completely eliminated his mind-created bodies, each composed of the five aggregates; hence he cannot reach the great bliss pāramitā, which is free from all suffering.[38] Because he has not realized a Tathāgata's realm of sweet dew by ending all his afflictions, karmas, and rebirths, the flow of his changeable death continues; hence he cannot reach the great eternity pāramitā, which is changeless.

"Ānanda, in the Three Realms of Existence, an ordinary being, who undergoes karmic birth and death, has four troubles: (1) afflictions, (2) karmas, (3) requitals, and (4) faults. [Outside the Three Realms of Existence, a holy being, such as an Arhat, a Pratyekabuddha, or a Bodhisattva on any Bodhisattva ground, has similar troubles.] Arising from his ground-abiding ignorance are his four kinds of changeable birth and death:[39] (1) his birth and death as skillful means are like the afflictions in the Three Realms of Existence; (2) his birth and death through causes and conditions are like the karmas in the Three Realms of Existence; (3) his birth and death as existence are like the existence in the Three Realms of Existence; (4) his birth and death as unreal existence are like the faults in the Three Realms of Existence.[40] You should know this. Ānanda, because he has not ended these four kinds of changeable birth and death, he continues to use his three kinds of mind-created bodies, which do not have the eternity, bliss, true-self, and purity pāramitās as the fruits. Only a Buddha's dharma body has the eternity, bliss, true-self, and purity pāramitās [as the fruits of bodhi]. You should know this.

The Four Fruits of Bodhi, the Four Pāramitās

"Ānanda, a Tathāgata's dharma body has the great purity pāramitā with two appearances: (1) purity by nature as its general appearance [in all sentient beings], and (2) purity free from taints as its particular appearance [in Buddhas]. His dharma body has the great true-self pāramitā for two reasons: (1) He stays far away from the fixation of those on non-Buddhist paths [tīrthika] because He has transcended their fantasy that one has a self, and (2) He stays far away from the fixation of riders of the Two Vehicles because He has transcended their limited understanding that one has no self. His dharma body has the great bliss pāramitā because He has achieved cessation of all His suffering in two ways: (1) ending His accumulation of afflictions and continuation of habits, and (2) eliminating His mind-created bodies. His dharma body has the great eternity pāramitā for two reasons: (1) He does not denounce impermanent processes [in saṁsāra] because He has transcended the view of cessation [uccheda-dṛṣṭi], and (2) He does not grasp the ever-abiding nirvāṇa because He has transcended the view of perpetuity [śāśvata-dṛṣṭi].[41] Seeing impermanent processes cease is called the view of cessation, while seeing nirvāṇa ever abide is called the view of perpetuity. Because He has eliminated the four affliction hindrances and corrected the four inversions, He harvests the perfect fruits of bodhi—eternity, bliss, a true self, and purity.

The Works of Bodhi

"Ānanda, what are the benefits of bodhi? One acquires two kinds of wisdom-knowledge: (1) differentiation-free wisdom-knowledge [root wisdom-knowledge] and (2) consequent wisdom-knowledge.[42] The first benefits oneself, the second benefits others. What are the benefits to oneself? Acquiring the liberation body, realizing the dharma body, eliminating affliction hindrances, and eliminating all hindrances to wisdom-knowledge are the benefits to oneself, brought by differentiation-free wisdom-knowledge. What are the benefits to others? After acquiring the differentiation-free wisdom-knowledge, manifesting, without thinking, the two kinds of bodies[43] throughout the endless future, and expounding the Dharma with no limit, interruption, or end, in order to rescue sentient beings on the three evil life-paths from their suffering, establish them [in the Dharma], and set them on the good paths of the Three Vehicles are the benefits to others.

"Moreover, the benefits to oneself are not apart from three virtues: (1) freedom from afflictions, (2) pervasiveness, and (3) freedom from causes and conditions. And the benefits to others are not apart from four virtues because one's consequent wisdom-knowledge protects sentient beings from falling into four things: (1) wrong views, delusions, and doubts, (2) evil and painful life-paths, (3) maligning the true Dharma out of jealousy and hatred, and (4) delighting in the Small Vehicle because of a lowly mind. Ānanda, benefiting oneself and benefiting others are the two works of bodhi.

The Concomitant Virtues of Bodhi

"Ānanda, what virtues accord with bodhi? The unsurpassed bodhi is the ultimate truth, with nineteen virtues: (1) inconceivability, (2) subtlety, (3) truthfulness, (4) profundity, (5) invisibility, (6) unfathomability, (7) eternity, (8) constant presence, (9) quietness, (10) constancy, (11) tranquility, (12) pervasiveness, (13) freedom from differentiation, (14) freedom from attachment, (10) freedom from hindrance, (16) compliance, (17) ungraspability, (18) purity, and (19) clarity. These nineteen virtues are never apart from the unsurpassed bodhi. That is why they are called the concomitant virtues of bodhi.

The Action Range of Bodhi

"Ānanda, what is the action range of bodhi? It is revealed in [a Tathāgata's] three bodies based on three principles respectively: (1) the profound principle, (2) the vast principle, and (3) the principle with myriad virtues.

"Ānanda, His first body [the dharma body] has five virtues and five attributes. Its five virtues are (1) freedom from causes and conditions, (2) constant presence, (3) freedom from polar opposites, (4) freedom from all hindrances, and (5) pure nature. Its five attributes are (1) immeasurability, (2) uncountability, (3) inconceivability, (4) incomparability, and (5) absolute purity.

"His second body [the reward body] is manifested from His dharma body and formed with a Tathāgata's immeasurable merit, great wisdom, and great compassion. It has five virtues: (1) freedom from differentiation, (2) freedom from an effortful mind, (3) benefiting sentient beings according to their preferences, (4) never being apart from the dharma body, and (5) never abandoning sentient beings.

"His third body [the response body] is manifested from His great wisdom and great compassion. It takes a physical form and has four virtues: (1) thirty-two physical marks [of a great man], (3) eighty excellent physical characteristics, (3) awe-inspiring dignity, and (4) strength. It responds to sentient beings' capacities, natures, desires, and actions. In an impure Buddha Land, it displays various events in a Buddha's life—ascending to Tuṣita Heaven, descending from Tuṣita Heaven into the human world, entering His mother's womb, being born, living as a youth, engaging in eighteen studies, frolicking in a palace garden, renouncing family life, practicing asceticism, entering His bodhi place [bodhimaṇḍa], attaining Buddhahood, turning the wondrous Dharma wheel, and entering parinirvāṇa in a forest. It displays such events throughout the endless future. Ānanda, the unsurpassed bodhi encompasses these three bodies. Therefore, they are called the action range of bodhi.

The Ever-Abiding Bodhi

"Ānanda, why is the unsurpassed bodhi ever abiding? It is ever abiding because it has (1) neither birth nor death and (2) no end. That is why bodhi is ever abiding.

The Exclusivity of Bodhi

"Ānanda, what are the exclusive appearances of the unsurpassed bodhi? It is exclusive for two reasons: (1) it is unknowable because no ordinary being, voice-hearer, or Pratyekabuddha can understand it, for it is not their state, and (2) it is unattainable except by a Buddha. It has five exclusive appearances: (1) it is profound as is the true suchness of dharmas, (2) it is immovable and hindrance free, (3) it is encompassed in the affliction-free pure realm, (4) it knows all there is to know hindrance free, and (5) it completes works that benefit sentient beings. These are called the exclusive appearances of bodhi.

The Inconceivability of Bodhi

"Ānanda, why is the unsurpassed bodhi inconceivable? It is inconceivable for six reasons: (1) it is beyond the description of words, (2) it is encompassed in the highest truth, (3) it is beyond perception, differentiation, and thinking, (4) it is beyond analogy, (5) it is the highest among all dharmas, and (6) it is where neither saṁsāra nor nirvāṇa can dominate. That is why the unsurpassed bodhi is inconceivable.

"Ānanda, why is a Tathāgata abiding in the unsurpassed bodhi inconceivable? Ānanda, all Tathāgatas abiding in the unsurpassed bodhi are inconceivable for five inconceivable reasons: (1) a Tathāgata as the nature of bodhi, (2) a Tathāgata as the bodhi place, (3) His abiding, (4) His being the same as or different [from other Tathāgatas], and (5) His performing beneficial works.

"Ānanda, why is a Tathāgata as the nature of bodhi inconceivable? Because a Tathāgata can be captured neither in nor not in one's form; neither in nor not in one's sensory reception, perception, mental processing, or consciousness;[44] neither in nor not in the domain of earth; neither in nor not in the domain of water, fire, or wind; neither in nor not in one's eye; neither in nor not in one's ear, nose, tongue, or body; neither in nor not in the Dharma. That is why a Tathāgata as the nature of bodhi is inconceivable.

"Ānanda, why is a Tathāgata as the bodhi place inconceivable? Because a Tathāgata in or not in the desire realm is inconceivable; in or not in the form realm or the formless realm is inconceivable; in or not in the human world is inconceivable; on or not on the six life-paths is inconceivable; in or not in places in the ten directions is inconceivable.

"Ānanda, why is a Tathāgata's abiding inconceivable? Because a Tathāgata's abiding in peace and joy is inconceivable, abiding in quietness [nirvāṇa] is inconceivable, abiding in a mind is inconceivable, and abiding in no mind is inconceivable. Indeed, a Tathāgata's abiding in purity and holiness is inconceivable. That is why His abiding is inconceivable.

"Ānanda, why is a Tathāgata being the same as or different [from other Tathāgatas] inconceivable? Because Tathāgatas in the three time frames abide in one place. What is the one place? It is the affliction-free pure dharma realm. It is inconceivable whether They are the same or different. That is why a Tathāgata's being the same or different is inconceivable.

"Ānanda, why is a Tathāgata's performing beneficial works inconceivable? Because Tathāgatas are the same as the one dharma realm. Their wisdom, spiritual power, right endeavors, and awesome virtues are the same. Abiding in the affliction-free pure dharma realm, They give sentient beings immeasurable benefits. That is why a Tathāgata's performing beneficial works is inconceivable.

"Moreover, bodhi is inconceivable for two reasons: (1) its ineffability, because it is beyond the description of words; (2) its transcendence, because it is beyond analogy in the world. That is why bodhi is inconceivable. Moreover, the true suchness of dharmas has never been tainted, which is inconceivable. Ānanda, that is why bodhi is inconceivable."

Notes

1. For the Buddha and His disciples, an elder named Kalandaka had a monastery built in the bamboo grove given to the Buddha by Bimbisāra (558–491 BCE), king of Magadha. In another account, Kalandaka offered his bamboo grove, and Bimbisāra had a monastery built there. This Veṇuvana (Bamboo Grove) Monastery north of Rājagṛha and Jetavana Monastery outside Śrāvastī were the two major centers of the Buddha's teaching activities.

2. Their short biographies are in the glossary, except Mahācunda, Bhadrajaya and Suvahula, whose names, here translated from Chinese, are uncertain.

3. Voice-hearers on the learning ground are "those who are still learning" as defined in the glossary's "voice-hearer fruits."

4. Mahāprajāpatī (摩訶波闍波提) was Śākyamuni Buddha's aunt, the sister of His mother, Mahāmāyā, who died seven days after His birth. Mahāprajāpatī raised the Buddha. Five years after the Buddha attained Buddhahood, His father, King Śuddhodana, died. Then Mahāprajāpatī, leading five hundred women in the Śākya clan, requested the Buddha's permission to renounce family life, and they became the first Buddhist nuns. Three months before the Buddha's parinirvāṇa, to avoid her grief over His parinirvāṇa, she entered meditation, which deepened from the first dhyāna to the fourth dhyāna, and died.

5. Yaśodharā (耶輸陀羅) was the Buddha's wife when He was Prince Siddhārtha, and the mother of Rāhula. Five years after the Buddha attained Buddhahood, she and Mahāprajāpatī, the Buddha's aunt, became nuns, along with five hundred Śākya women.

6. Utpalavarṇā means the color of a blue lotus. She was from Ujayana, the capital of Avanti, in northwestern India, where she married and gave birth to a daughter. She left her husband after she found out that he was sleeping with her mother. Then she went to Vārāṇasī and married an elder there. He went to Ujayana to do business and married a young girl. When he brought her home, Utpalavarṇā discovered that the young girl was her daughter. Utterly disgusted

with her unfortunate life, she went to Vaiśālī and lived as a prostitute. One day she heard Mahāmaudgalyāyana expound the Dharma, and she became a nun under Mahāprajāpatī. Utpalavarṇā acquired the six transcendental powers and became an Arhat. When Devadatta attempted to murder the Buddha, she rebuked him. He beat her to death.

7. As described in text 365 (T12n0365), the Chinese version of the *Sūtra of Visualization of Amitāyus Buddha,* an English translation of which appears in *Thinking of Amitābha Buddha* (Rulu 2012b, 89–105), King Bimbisāra was imprisoned by his son, the crown prince Ajātaśatru. His queen Vaidehī, on her visit to him in prison, prayed to the Buddha. Then the Buddha appeared to them and gave them teachings on visualizing Amitāyus Buddha in order to be reborn in His land. King Bimbisāra later died in prison.

8. For "holy voice-hearers," see "voice-hearer fruits" in the glossary.

9. Sugata, Well-Gone One, is the fifth of a Buddha's ten epithets.

10. See "six desire heavens" in the glossary.

11. In fascicle 1 of text 481 (in 4 fascicles), the Chinese version of the *Sūtra of People-Supporting Bodhisattva*, a passage states that no realm is a Tathāgata's realm, and all realms are a Tathāgata's realm (T14n0481, 0629a7–8). As stated in a following paragraph in chapter 2 of the present sūtra, "a Tathāgata's realm [within one] is immeasurable and boundless, but shrouded by one's afflictions." This meaning is the same as that of one's Tathāgata store (tathāgata-garbha). Later in chapter 2, it is revealed that it is also called true suchness, true reality, the dharma body (dharmakāya), and the holy nature (Tathāgata nature).

12. See note 39 in Sūtra 3 in the present book.

13. See "affliction hindrances" defined in the glossary's "three kinds of hindrances."

14. A Bodhisattva retains his love of being, which is an affliction, in order to be reborn in the Three Realms of Existence to deliver sentient beings.

15. See "true reality" defined in the glossary's "true suchness."

16. See "nirvāṇa that abides nowhere" defined in the glossary's "nirvāṇa."

17. For "unimpeded wisdom-knowledge," see the glossary's "four kinds of unimpeded wisdom-knowledge."

18. For "complete holy path," see the glossary's Eightfold Right Path.

19. A similar passage appears in fascicle 51 of text 279, the 80-fascicle Chinese version of the *Mahāvaipulya Sūtra of Buddha Adornment* (Buddhāvataṁsaka-mahāvaipulya-sūtra), in which a Buddha says, "Amazing! Amazing! Why do these sentient beings, deluded and confused, not know and not see that they have a Tathāgata's wisdom? I will teach them the holy path, enabling them to discard forever their attachments and deluded perceptions. Then they will be able to see within them vast Tathāgata wisdom, no different from a Buddha's" (T10n0279, 0272c25–0273a1).

20. See "nirvāṇa without remnants" defined in the glossary's "nirvāṇa."

21. See "prajñā-pāramitā" defined in the glossary's "six pāramitās."

22. By merging the first four into the second one, the six pāramitās are summarized into the Three Learnings (三學): śīla (precept), dhyāna (meditation), and prajñā (wisdom). By observing the precepts (śīla), one purifies one's body, voice, and mind karmas. With purity one practices meditation (dhyāna), training in śamatha (mental stillness) and vipaśyanā (correct observation). The former leads to the right samādhi (meditative absorption),

which subjugates one's afflictions, and the latter develops one's wisdom (prajñā), which ends one's afflictions. With wisdom, and compassion for sentient beings, one attains Buddhahood, realizing a Buddha's dharma body.

23. See "dharma body" defined in the glossary's "three bodies of a Buddha." According to text 353, the earlier of the two Chinese versions of the *Sūtra of Śrīmālā's Lion's Roar,* "when a Tathāgata's dharma body is not free from one's store of afflictions, it is called the Tathāgata store" (T12n0353, 0221c10–11).

24. These two things are stated in another way in the *Śrīmālā Sūtra,* in which the Buddha says, "There are two things that are hard to know: (1) one's inherent pure mind and (2) its being tainted by afflictions" (Ibid., 0222c4–5).

25. See "ten Bodhisattva grounds" in the glossary's "stages of the Bodhisattva Way." Details of the ten Bodhisattva grounds are given in chapter 26 of the *Mahāvaipulya Sūtra of Buddha Adornment* (Buddhāvataṁsaka-mahāvaipulya-sūtra). An English translation of this chapter appears in *The Bodhisattva Way* (Rulu 2013, 111–244).

26. See "working cause" defined in the glossary's "six causes."

27. The samādhi door leads to all samādhis; the view of void is the wrong view that the emptiness of dharmas means nothingness, like the open sky, and that therefore causality can be ignored.

28. In this passage, the four fruits of bodhi are eternity, bliss, a true self, and purity. In a later section of this chapter 3, the four virtues of a Tathāgata's dharma body, the four pāramitās, are also called the four fruits of bodhi. In different fascicles of text 374 (T12n0374), the 40-fascicle Chinese version of the *Mahāparinirvāṇa Sūtra,* these four virtues variously belong to nirvāṇa, Buddha nature, a Tathāgata, or His dharma body.

29. Gotama, or Gaugama, is Śākyamuni Buddha's family name.

30. Ajita Kesakambala was one of the six principal philosophers in ancient India, who were the Buddha's contemporaries. Their and their students' non-Buddhist doctrines number ninety-six.

31. See "exceeding arrogance" defined in the glossary's "arrogance."

32. It seems that whoever follows any non-Buddhist doctrine to train without skillful means falls into the group that definitely is on the wrong path, and that whoever neither follows nor rejects any path falls into the group that is indecisive about its path.

33. See "three groups" in the glossary.

34. See note 34 in Sūtra 3 in the present book.

35. See "knowledge of all wisdom-knowledge" defined in the glossary's "three kinds of wisdom-knowledge."

36. According to fascicle 3 of text 670, the 4-fascicle Chinese version of the *Laṅkāvatāra Sūtra,* the three kinds of mind-created body (manomaya-kāya, 意生身) are (1) a body that arises from the joy of samādhi and samāpatti, (2) a body that arises from the realization of the illusory nature of dharmas and enters all Buddha Lands at will, and (3) a body that arises from the realization that all doctrines are the Buddha Dharma and instantly manifests, without action, countless bodies of various kinds (T16n0670, 0497c20–22). A Bodhisattva on any of first five Bodhisattva grounds can produce the first kind of body; a Bodhisattva on any of the next three grounds can produce the second kind of body; a Bodhisattva on the ninth ground or above can produce the third kind of body.

37. All afflictions can be classified into four kinds of grasping (catur-upādāna, 四取): (1) grasping desire objects, (2) grasping wrong views, (3) grasping useless precepts as the cause of liberation, and (4) grasping claims that one has a self.

38. A holy being who undergoes changeable birth and death is still subject to causes and conditions, and experiences subtle suffering because of continuous change in every process. See "three kinds of suffering" defined in the glossary's "suffering."

39. See "changeable birth and death" defined in the glossary's "two kinds of birth and death."

40. These four troubles of a holy being are also described in text 1610 (in 4 fascicles), the Chinese version of *A Treatise on Buddha Nature* (Buddhagotra-śāstra). In fascicle 2, a passage states: "His ground-abiding ignorance is like an ordinary being's ignorance, his affliction-free karmas are like an ordinary being's [affliction-driven] karmas, his three kinds of mind-created bodies are like an ordinary being's requital bodies, and his inconceivable regress is like an ordinary being's faults" (T31n1610, 0799b12–14).

41. In the *Śrīmālā Sūtra,* Śrīmālā says, "An ordinary being holds the wrong view that there is a self [ātman] in the five aggregates that constitute a sentient being and, from that view, derives two opposite views, perpetuity and cessation. When he sees that all processes are impermanent, he holds the view of cessation, which is not the right view. When he seeks nirvāṇa, he holds the view of perpetuity, which is not the right view. These two opposite views arise from deluded thinking" (T12n0353, 0222a10–14).

42. See "root wisdom-knowledge" and "consequent wisdom-knowledge" defined in the glossary's "two kinds of wisdom-knowledge."

43. The "two kinds of bodies" refer to the reward body and the response body of a Buddha. See "three bodies of a Buddha" in the glossary.

44. See "form, sensory reception, sensory perception, mental processing, and consciousness" in the glossary's "five aggregates."

Fascicle 2 (of 2)

Chapter 4 – A Tathāgata's Merits

The Buddha told Ānanda, "A Tathāgata's wondrous merits are revealed by one hundred eighty dharmas: (1) thirty-two physical marks, (2) eighty excellent physical characteristics,[1] and (3) sixty-eight attainments.

His Thirty-two Physical Marks

"What are His thirty-two physical marks? While a Bodhisattva, He developed four causes and conditions: (1) observing the precepts, (2) practicing meditation, (3) enduring adversities, and (4) relinquishing His wealth and ending His afflictions. Because He persistently developed these four causes, He has acquired these two marks: (1) flat soles, which make the ground He treads smooth without potholes, and (2) a steady gait, never wobbly. Because He diligently and repeatedly made various offerings to his parents and teachers and gave various alms to the needy, He has acquired the mark of a thousand-spoke wheel on each sole. Because He never distressed others, never stole, robbed, or coveted things attractive to Him, was never conceited or arrogant, always rose to greet His elders or teachers, and respectfully attended them with His palms joined, He has acquired these two marks: (1) slender and not nubby fingers and (2) a well-formed, majestic body. Because of His preceding three karmas, He has acquired the mark of long heels. Because, in addition to doing the preceding three karmas, He practiced the Four Drawing-in Dharmas to benefit others, He has acquired the mark of finely webbed fingers and toes like a goose-king's toes. Because He attended His parents and teachers, rubbed oil and medicinal ointment on them, massaged and bathed them, provided them with soft candies, and visited them, He has acquired the mark of soft smooth hands and feet, and red palms like red lotus flowers. Because He tirelessly practiced good dharmas, He has acquired the mark of plump ankles. Because He studied the true Dharma [saddharma] and tirelessly went everywhere to expound it to others, He has acquired the mark of [sinewy] calves like a deer-king's. Because He diligently sought teachings that He had not received, benefited and transformed others with teachings that he had received, ended His evil body, voice, and mind karmas, kept His body and mind untainted by the six sense objects and evil dharmas, gave medicinal potions to the physically ill, and served as a good physician to the mentally ill, He has acquired the mark of a straight body. Because He rescued and protected those in fear, gave food and clothing to the poor and naked, and prevented His evildoing by having a sense of shame and a sense of dishonor,[2] He has acquired the mark of a hidden male organ. Because he protected His body, voice, and mind to keep them constantly pure, knew how much was enough of the things received, knew the right quantity of things to consume, gave medicine to the ill, gave money to the deprived, and taught sentient beings to stop doing inequitable karmas, which would bring them corresponding requitals, and to do things based on the principle of equality, He has acquired the mark of a well-proportioned body whose height and arm-span are equal, like a ficus tree. Because He used skillful means to do good dharmas to develop others, whether they were of low, middling, or high capacities, He has acquired the mark of body hair that swirls upward and clockwise. Because He used His keen capacity to ponder the meaning [of the Dharma], stayed close to the wise, encountered beneficent learned friends, cleaned His elders' houses, bathed and massaged them, removed feces and filth from the surroundings of caityas [temples or funeral monuments], and prevented visitor-like afflictions from tainting His mind, He has acquired the mark of one body hair in each and every pore of His fine and smooth skin, free from dust and water. Because He delighted in giving away, without regrets, things such as clothing, food and drink, bedding, vehicles, and adornments, He has acquired the mark of a golden body with a halo ten feet across. Because he gave away fine food and drink without limit to sentient beings, to satiate them, He has acquired the mark of fullness in seven places [hands, feet, shoulders, and neck]. Because He gave good teachings to good sentient beings, taught them to make a right livelihood, served as their guide, established them in goodness, and ended their evildoing, He has acquired the mark of a chest like a lion's. Because He trained in the Four Right Endeavors[3] with a lion-king's fearless mind in order to benefit sentient beings, He has acquired these two marks: (1) level shoulders with fullness in the armpits and (2) rounded long arms that, like an elephant-king's trunk, reach below the knees. Because He never used divisive speech, but spoke uniting words to those in conflict, carried out the Four Drawing-in Dharmas to draw sentient beings in, pondered the profound meaning [of the Dharma], and cultivated impartial lovingkindness, He has acquired these two marks: (1) forty well-aligned teeth without gaps and white like snow, and (2) four incisors like a new moon. Because He gave sentient beings to their satisfaction what they needed or desired, whether wealth or teachings, He has acquired these two marks: (1) cheeks like a lion's and (2) a rounded clean neck. Because He protected and cared for sentient beings like an only son, trusted them, thought of them with immeasurable lovingkindness, and widely gave them medicine without ulterior motives, He has acquired these two marks: (1) a throat with a thousand veins that savor fine flavors moistened with saliva, and (2) collar bones like the god-king Nārāyaṇa's. Because He did the ten good karmas and taught others to do the same, appreciated and praised spiritual trainees, pitied sentient beings with great compassion, and made vast vows to accept the true Dharma, He has acquired these two marks: (1) a bony bulge like a topknot on the crown of His head and (2) a broad, thin, and long tongue like a lotus flower petal. Because He always spoke truthful words, loving words, and beautiful words, and expounded the true Dharma without distortion, He has acquired the mark of a beautiful voice, like a kalaviṅka bird's, that emits Dharma tones far and wide, like a sounding celestial drum. Because he respected all in the world and regarded them as His parents, and never exuded the three poisons [greed, anger, and delusion] or glared at sentient beings, He has acquired these two marks: (1) eyelids like a blue lotus flower and (2) purple eyelashes like an ox-king's. Because He praised good sentient beings for their training in the Three Learnings [precepts, meditation, and wisdom],[4] never criticized them, and safeguarded them from slanderers, He has acquired the mark of a white hair between His eyebrows that swirls upward and clockwise.

"Moreover, Ānanda, a Tathāgata has acquired these thirty-two marks because of His four right karmas: (1) unwavering resolve, (2) scrupulous observation, (3) uninterrupted training, and (4) right action. Because of His first karma, He has acquired the mark of flat soles. Because of His second karma, He has acquired these nine marks: (1) the image of a thousand-spoke wheel on each sole, (2) plump ankles, (3) webbed fingers and toes, (4) fine and soft skin, (5) fullness in seven places, (6) level shoulders with fullness in the armpits, (7) rounded arms, (8) a broad and long tongue, and (9) a chest like a lion's. Because of His third karma, He has acquired these five marks: (1) slender long fingers, (2) long heels, (3) a straight body, not bent, (4) a well-proportioned body whose height and arm-span are equal, and (5) a rounded clean neck. Because of His fourth karma, He has acquired the other marks.

"Moreover, Ānanda, suppose that all sentient beings [in worlds] in the ten directions do the ten good karmas, and that their acquired merits increase a hundredfold. Because of these good karmas, they can acquire the mark of only one of a Tathāgata's hairs. When they acquire the mark of all His hairs, their merits will increase another hundredfold. Then they can acquire one of a Tathāgata's eighty excellent physical characteristics. When they acquire all His physical characteristics, their merits will increase another hundredfold. Then they can acquire one of a Tathāgata's thirty-two physical marks. When they acquire all His physical marks, excepting the mark of a white hair between His eyebrows and the mark of a bony bulge on His crown, their merits will increase another hundredfold. Then they can acquire a Tathāgata's mark of a white hair between His eyebrows, and their merits will increase another hundredfold. Then they can acquire a Tathāgata's mark of a bony bulge on His crown, and their merits will increase a thousandfold. Because they have acquired a Tathāgata's exclusive physical marks and characteristics, they can acquire a Tathāgata's one sound that pervades countless worlds in the ten directions.

"Ānanda, a Tathāgata's thirty-two physical marks are inconceivable for three reasons: (1) the required time is inconceivable, because He trained for three asaṁkhyeya kalpas; (2) His joy is inconceivable, because He trained to benefit all sentient beings and bring them peace and joy; (3) the kinds of His training are inconceivable, because He trained to do all good karmas and stayed away from all evil karmas, both of countless kinds. Therefore, the excellent marks of a Tathāgata's body are inconceivable.

His Eighty Excellent Physical Characteristics

"Ānanda, what are a Tathāgata's eighty excellent physical characteristics? They are (1) an invisible crown of His head, (2) a strong bone that forms His crown, (3) a wide smooth forehead, (4) high-set long eyebrows like a purple new moon, (5) broad and long eyes, (6) a high and straight nose with unexposed nostrils, (7) broad, thick, long ears with perfect earlobes, (8) a strong body like the god-king Nārāyaṇa's, (9) strong limbs, (10) well-connected strong joints, (11) a body that can turn quickly, like an elephant-king's, (12) a limber body, (13) a straight body, (14) an unblemished body, (15) a sleek body, (16) an upright body, not crooked, (17) perfect limbs, (18) perfect consciousness, (19) perfect looks and bearings, (20) an awesome spirit that reaches far, (21) [an appearance that] no one turns his back on, (22) [the ability] to abide and remain immovable, (23) a well-proportioned face, neither too wide nor too long, (24) a broad and beautiful face, (25) a clear face like a full moon, (26) perfect facial features, (27) good facial colors, (28) a majestic bearing like a lion's, (29) a serene gait like an elephant-king's, (30) an elegant gait like a goose-king's, (31) a head like the fruit of a madana tree, (32) feet with plump tops, each leaving a footprint after it is four fingers' width above the ground, (33) thin and lustrous fingernails [and toenails] the color of copper, (34) strong and rounded kneecaps, (35) splendid lines on each palm, (36) deep lines on each palm, (37) clear and straight lines on each palm, (38) long lines on each palm, (39) unbroken lines on each palm, (40) deft hands and feet, (41) pink hands and feet the color of a lotus flower, (42) perfect orifices, (43) evenly spaced steps, neither too long nor too short, (44) a rounded waist, (45) an unobtrusive abdomen, (46) a round and deep navel, (47) red-tinged blue hair the color of a peacock's neck, (48) clean hair, (49) hair that swirls clockwise, (50) a mouth that emits [breath with] unsurpassed fragrance, and body hair that emits fragrance, (51) red lips like the fruit of the bimba tree, (52) a red tongue, (53) a thin tongue, (54) being a delightful sight to all beholders, (55) speaking kindly to sentient beings according to their minds, (56) speaking benevolent words in all situations, (57) speaking first [before a question is asked], (58) speaking neither too loudly nor too softly, according to sentient beings' preferences, (59) expounding the Dharma in the languages of multitudes, (60) expounding the Dharma without attachment, (61) regarding sentient beings equally, (62) doing things after looking into them, (63) emitting one tone in response to multiple sounds, (64) expounding the Dharma systematically through causes and conditions, (65) [an appearance that] cannot be fully taken in by any sentient being's eyes, (66) [an appearance that] beholders never tire of beholding, (67) emitting perfect sounds, (68) displaying good works, (69) [such an awe-inspiring presence that] when sentient beings see Him, the strong-willed are tamed and the timid acquire peace and joy, (70) a clear and pure voice, (71) a body that does not sway, (72) a large body, (73) a tall body, (74) an untainted body, (75) a body surrounded by light ten feet across, (76) a body illuminated by light when walking, (77) a clean body, (78) untangled shiny long hair the color of a blue jewel, (79) plump hands and feet, and (80) virtuous marks on His hands and feet. Ānanda, these eighty excellent characteristics adorn a Buddha's body.

His Sixty-eight Attainments

"Ānanda, a Tathāgata has Ten Powers. What are these ten? He has the power of perfect wisdom-knowledge [jñāna] of (1) everyone's right or wrong action in every situation, and its corresponding karmic consequences; (2) the karmic requitals of every sentient being; (3) all stages of dhyāna, liberation, and samādhi; (4) the capacity of every sentient being; (5) the desires and preferences of every sentient being; (6) the nature and kind of every sentient being; (7) the consequences of all actions, with or without afflictions; (8) all past lives of every sentient being; (9) all future rebirths of every sentient being; (10) the permanent ending of all His afflictions and habits [upon attainment of Buddhahood]. Because of the power of His wisdom-knowledge, a Tathāgata reveals the greatest state [Buddhahood], turns the unsurpassed pure Dharma wheel, and roars the lion's roar in the midst of multitudes.

"Ānanda, a Tathāgata has Four Fearlessnesses. He has (1) fearlessness because He has acquired the knowledge of all wisdom-knowledge [sarvajña-jñāna];[5] (2) fearlessness because He has eradicated all His afflictions; (3) fearlessness in explaining hindrances to one's attaining bodhi; (4) fearlessness in explaining the right path to end one's suffering.

"Ānanda, a Tathāgata has three kinds of mindfulness: (1) right mindfulness of right actions, (2) right mindfulness of wrong actions, and (3) right mindfulness of mixed actions. Also, Ānanda, a Tathāgata has great compassion.

"Ānanda, a Tathāgata has Eighteen Exclusive Dharmas [which Arhats, Pratyekabuddhas, and Bodhisattvas do not have]. They are (1–3) faultless body, voice, and mind karmas, (4) impartiality to all; (5) abiding in constant meditation; (6) equability toward pleasure or pain; (7) never-diminishing desire to deliver sentient beings; (8) never-diminishing energy for delivering sentient beings; (9) never-diminishing memory of the Buddha Dharma; (10) never-diminishing wisdom; (11) never-diminishing liberation from afflictions and habits; (12) never-diminishing knowledge and views of liberation; (13–15) all body karmas, voice karmas, and mind karmas, led by wisdom; (16–18) perfect wisdom-knowledge of the past, present, and future.[6]

"Ānanda, only a Tathāgata has these [thirty-three] attainments: (1) hindrance-free transcendental power of instant arrival anywhere, (2) boundless transcendental power of manifestations, (3) countless transcendental powers, (4) a hindrance-free mind, (5) the ability of telepathy, (6) the ability of the god ear, (7) the ability to know the differences among sentient beings in the formless realm, (8) the ability to know holy beings' states after they have entered parinirvāṇa, (9) the wisdom to give various answers, (10) [mastery of] the great [wisdom] pāramitā[7] to answer questions, (11) the ability to expound the Dharma in detail without faults, (12) the ability to develop sentient beings without fail, (13) being the foremost guiding teacher, (14) the ability not to be harmed or killed, (15) abiding in the Vajra Samādhi, (16) knowing all things, even if they are not material, not mental, or not coherent [sambaddha] with the mind, (17) hindrance-free liberation, (18) the three protection-free dharmas [faultless body, voice, and mind karmas], (19) complete end of His habits, (20) the knowledge of all wisdom-knowledge, (21) a vajra [adamantine] body, (22) the ability to accomplish all things without a thought, (23) complete purity in all His appearances and places, (24) certainty of His prophecies coming true, (25) the ability to forbid those anxious about victory or defeat to see a Buddha, (26) the ability to turn all wondrous Dharma wheels, (27) the ability to support all sentient beings and enable them to shed their heavy burdens, (28) the ability to enter parinirvāṇa and reactivate His mind, (29) completion of the causes of bodhi without remnants, (30) completion of the fruits of bodhi without remnants, (31) completion of works that benefit others without remnants, (32) endless unimpeded eloquence, and (33) expounding the Dharma in accord with the principle.

"Ānanda, in brief, a Tathāgata's merits have six characteristics: (1) complete, (2) taint-free, (3) immovable, (4) hindrance-free, (5) altruistic, and (6) skillful. Ānanda, why are a Tathāgata's merits inconceivable? Because, throughout kalpas as numerous as the sands of the Ganges, all of a Tathāgata's boundless merits, whether acquired on the tainted ground or the pure ground, encompass and accord with one another, and are never apart from one another. Beyond purity and impurity, they are inconceivable.

Chapter 5 – A Tathāgata's Works

"Ānanda, [to deliver sentient beings] a Tathāgata does eighteen things. (1) A Tathāgata is unparalleled, most wondrous, and supreme, with whom no one can compare. He inspires sentient beings to reverently make offerings to Him with an awestruck mind. This first thing is accomplished because of His body, with the thirty-two physical marks of a great man and the eighty excellent physical characteristics. (2) A Tathāgata fully understands causality according to the principle. If a śramaṇa or Brahmin claims that there is no causality or that a cause does not lead to a corresponding effect, He will refute him and make him realize that he is wrong. This second thing is accomplished because of the power of His wisdom-knowledge of everyone's right or wrong action in every situation, and its corresponding karmic consequences. (3) A Tathāgata knows and sees that one, never another, receives the requital of one's karma. If a śramaṇa or Brahmin expounds the [evil] doctrine that one can avoid one's karmic requital, He will refute him and make him realize that he is wrong. This third thing is accomplished because of the power of His wisdom-knowledge of various kinds of karmas. (4) A Tathāgata uses three wheels—transcendental powers, mental powers, and teachings—to teach and guide His disciples to become a holy multitude. If a śramaṇa or Brahmin anxious about victory or defeat expounds wrong theories against the true Dharma, He will refute him and make him realize that he is wrong. This fourth thing is accomplished because of the power of His wisdom-knowledge that arises from meditation. (5) A Tathāgata knows and sees sentient beings of high, middling, and low capacities, and teaches them accordingly, enabling them to plant bodhi seeds to come to [spiritual] maturity and achieve liberation. This fifth thing is accomplished because of the power of His wisdom-knowledge of various capacities. (6) A Tathāgata knows and sees the good and evil desires and preferences of three grades of sentient beings, and He ends their evil desires and increases their good desires. This sixth thing is accomplished because of the power of His wisdom knowledge of various desires and preferences. (7) A Tathāgata knows and sees three kinds of sentient beings—coarse, average, and fine—and enables them to enter various Dharma Doors [dharma-paryāya]. This seventh thing is accomplished because of the power of His wisdom-knowledge of various natures. (8) A Tathāgata clearly sees that the path of transcendence leads to liberation and that the path of hindrance leads to repeated birth and death. He enables sentient beings to leave the path of hindrance and take the path of transcendence. This eighth thing is accomplished because of the power of His wisdom-knowledge of the consequences of all actions. (9) A Tathāgata clearly sees everyone's past lives and narrates past events to enable sentient beings to tire [of their repeated birth and death]. If a śramaṇa or Brahmin holds the view of perpetuity [of dharmas], He will refute him and make him realize that he is wrong. This ninth thing is accomplished because of the power of His wisdom-knowledge of past lives. (10) A Tathāgata clearly sees all sentient beings' deaths here and rebirths there as properly recorded [in their consciousnesses]. If a śramaṇa or Brahmin holds the [wrong] view of cessation, He will refute him and make him realize that he is wrong. This tenth thing is accomplished because of the power of His wisdom-knowledge of birth and death. (11) A Tathāgata knows that He has achieved complete liberation. If a śramaṇa or Brahmin with exceeding arrogance[8] claims that he has become an Arhat though he has not, He will refute him and make him realize that he is wrong. This eleventh thing is accomplished because of the power of His wisdom-knowledge that He has ended all His afflictions. (12) A Tathāgata uses the best skillful means to benefit sentient beings. If someone asks about a Tathāgata's Ten Powers, He will give him truthful answers to resolve his doubts, because His right words can defeat others' wrong words. This twelfth thing is accomplished because of His Four Fearlessnesses. (13) A Tathāgata is free from joy and woe in regard to the group that trains according to His teachings, the group that does not, and the group that comprises those who train accordingly and those who do not. This thirteenth thing is accomplished because of His three abidings of mindfulness. (14) A Tathāgata uses His Buddha eye day and night to constantly observe sentient beings in distress and rescues them. This fourteenth thing is accomplished because of His great compassion. (15) A Tathāgata can act and speak, and acts according to His words. This fifteenth thing is accomplished because of His three protection-free dharmas [faultless body, voice, and mind karmas]. (16) A Tathāgata does things to completion and without omission to benefit sentient beings. This sixteenth thing is accomplished because His right mindfulness never forgets anything. (17) A Tathāgata appropriately carries out His four deportments [walking, standing still, sitting, and lying down] without faults. This seventeenth thing is accomplished because He has ended all His habits. (18) A Tathāgata observes three kinds of actions—beneficial, harmful, and both—and teaches only beneficial actions. This eighteenth thing is accomplished because of His knowledge of all wisdom-knowledge and His exclusive dharmas. Ānanda, you should know that a Tathāgata does these things.

"Ānanda, why are the things done by a Tathāgata [to deliver sentient beings] inconceivable? Ānanda, a Tathāgata does countless things, but sentient beings in the world neither are aware of nor understand them because they cannot be displayed or described by words. All Buddha Lands are hindrance free, and all Tathāgatas abide in the equality of dharmas, which is beyond one's state of mind. Like the open sky, all Tathāgatas make no differentiation because They accord with the dharma realm.

"Therefore, good men, I say that the things done by a Tathāgata are inconceivable and that His actions pervade everywhere, without omission, throughout the three time frames [past, present, and future], revealing the nature of the Three Jewels. As a Tathāgata abides in such things, His body is in the nature of the open sky as He appears in all Buddha Lands. As He speaks sentient beings' languages to expound the true Dharma, His speech is not in the nature of sounds.[9] Although a Tathāgata does not take anyone's mind as an object, He fully knows all sentient beings' minds, capacities, natures, desires, and preferences. Ānanda, that is why the things done by a Tathāgata [to deliver sentient beings] are inconceivable."

After the Buddha pronounced this sūtra, in this huge assembly, 75,000 Bodhisattva-Mahāsattvas realized the perfect dharma body,[10] 75,000 Bodhisattva-Mahāsattvas acquired the Mahāyāna Samādhi of Wondrous Light, and 75,000 Bodhisattva-Mahāsattvas acquired endurance in their realization that dharmas have no birth. Also, innumerable asaṁkhyeyas of sentient beings activated the unsurpassed bodhi mind without regress, and innumerable asaṁkhyeyas of sentient beings shunned dust and filth [their afflictions] and acquired the pure dharma eye. Also, innumerable sentient beings acquired higher fruits [of their training].

Chapter 6 – Ānanda's Praise

Then, after hearing the Buddha's words, Ānanda rejoiced exuberantly because he acquired an understanding he never before had. He rose from his seat, bared his right shoulder, and bowed down at the Buddha's feet. Kneeling on his right knee, with joint palms, he reverently gazed at the Buddha's face and, with a pure mind, praised Him in verse:

In the midst of sentient beings in the three time frames,
The Tathāgata is beyond analogy.
Unequaled in the human realm and the dharma realm,
He regards all equally.

He has forever ended what should be ended,
And fully knows all dharmas that should be known.
None but a Buddha-Bhagavān
Has such foremost splendid wisdom.

Truly He has power and fearlessness,
Because the Tathāgata has the Ten Powers and the Four Fearlessnesses.
That nothing can impair the World-Honored One's great abilities
Is inconceivable and extraordinary.

Using skillful means to transform sentient beings
Cannot be accomplished by an evil or deluded mind.
Although sentient beings are arrogant and self-exalting,
The World-Honored One tames them and enables them to discard their ways.

If someone claims that he can surpass the Tathāgata,
His words are false and faulty.
If someone points out the Tathāgata as the Supreme Honored One,
His words are true and faultless.

If someone asks a Tathāgata challenging questions according to the principle,
There is no way he can defeat Him [in debate].

The invincible Tathāgata has no shortcomings,
And He guides sentient beings to the joyful place [enlightenment].

His four body karmas[11] are pure and faultless,
So He does not need to protect them.
Using the four kinds of unimpeded wisdom-knowledge,
He endlessly expounds the Dharma to fill sentient beings with Dharma flavors.

His wisdom-knowledge of dharmas has no lack,
And His abidings of mindfulness[12] are never lessened or lost.
He has equal compassion for all sentient beings,
And His mind is never tainted by worldly things.

He fully understands sentient beings' capacities and natures,
And gives them teachings to deliver them.
For different kinds of afflictions,
He reveals different kinds of remedial measures.

The World-Honored One is foremost in expounding the Dharma,
But ordinary beings who encounter Him do not understand [His teachings].
Shrouded by the darkness of ignorance,
They are extremely hard to deliver.

The renown of the World-Honored One inspires one's longing [to see Him],
And seeing Him brings one endless joy.
The Buddha's words can purify one's mind,
And His true teachings enable one to end one's repeated birth and death.

Praising the Buddha can rid one of inauspicious things,
And thinking of Him can bring one constant joy.
Seeking the Buddha can bring one great wisdom,
And understanding His teachings can bring one wisdom-knowledge.

The Tathāgata is pure because He has observed the precepts,
And His mind is clear because He has practiced meditation,
The Tathāgata is immovable because of His wisdom,
And His Dharma is an ocean of sweet dew.

While sentient beings are asleep [unenlightened], only the Buddha is awake,
And He pervasively observes their capacities, natures, and desires.
While sentient beings abandon self-restraint, the Buddha does not,
And He regards all sentient beings equally.

The Buddha has revealed the methods to annihilate one's affliction bandits,

And has removed the illusions produced by the māra-king.
He has indicated the faults of one's repeated birth and death,
And revealed the direction of the place of fearlessness.

To give teachings that can deliver sentient beings,
The World-Honored One uses great compassion.
Devadatta is the best example of[13]
The World-Honored One giving bodhi to all sentient beings.

Although I cannot yet attain Buddhahood through the right training,
I will train in accordance with this sūtra to requite the kindness of the World-Honored One.
Even if someone has attained nirvāṇa without remnants,
He has not yet requited the Buddha's kindness.

Even if someone can do the right training taught by the Buddha,
Maybe he trains only to benefit himself.
The World-Honored One tirelessly teaches sentient beings.
How can we requite His profound kindness?

The Tathāgata expounds His true Dharma,
Enabling one to train accordingly and teach it to others.
If He did not appear in the world,
Everyone would be oppressed by suffering,
Evil life-paths would prevail in the world,
And sentient beings' loud wailing would be heard.

Sentient beings on the six life-paths undergo suffering just the same
Because they are fettered by their afflictions.
To untie the knots of their fetters,
The World-Honored One forever ties Himself to great compassion.

The World-Honored One is the unsurpassed fortune field[14]
For those who rely on Him in order to do the right training.
If I fail to see this great treasure, I will fall into poverty.
If I do evil karmas, I will fall as well.

If someone disregards the Buddha,
He will fall to the ground of poverty.
If someone hates and criticizes the Buddha,
He will without doubt forever remain in darkness.

As a great master recognizes his [dharma] body,
So too can other great masters recognize [their dharma bodies].
However, ordinary beings cannot.
I now make obeisance to all Buddhas in worlds in the ten directions,
Whose merits, wisdom, and powers are equal.
The World-Honored One has appeared in the world and revealed His dharma body.

Out of great compassion, He wants sentient beings to recognize [their dharma bodies].
Hence I now prostrate myself at His feet.

His wonderful fragrant body is a sight that beholders never tire of beholding.
His perfect physical marks are sublime.
A lovely flower is in bloom day and night,
And I make obeisance to such a Buddha flower.

The World-Honored One knows well the unsurpassed place [Buddhahood],
Which is free from all perils and tribulations,
And has no trace, no assemblage, and no falsity.
Hence I now make obeisance to the Two-Footed Honored One.

The World-Honored One has washed off all taints
And abides in the true Dharma and the water of His merits.
He has always been pure inside and outside,
And I now make obeisance to the truly pure body.

The World-Honored One has completed all good works
And always gives sentient beings bountiful benefits.
He widely showers down sweet dew for sentient beings to drink their fill,
And I now make obeisance because He benefits others.

Although He is the Supreme One most revered in the world,
He still reveres other Buddhas.
He has ended all His evildoing and attained perfect enlightenment.
Hence I now make obeisance to the Supreme Honored One.

To rescue sentient beings,
He never omitted learning even one skillful means
To enable all to avoid the perilous pit of birth and death.
I now make obeisance to the refuge of the world.

I make obeisance to the sublime physical body beyond analogy
And make obeisance to the one who can give teachings like sweet dew.
I make obeisance to His pure wisdom
And make obeisance to His forest of merits.

Chapter 7 – Entrusting This Sūtra

The Buddha told Ānanda, "You should uphold this true Dharma Door."

Ānanda fell on his knees and said to the Buddha, "Just now I received from the Buddha this profound teaching, and acquired what I never before had. I will uphold it with the utmost respect. World-Honored One, what is the name of this sūtra and how should we uphold it?"

The Buddha said, "Ānanda, this sūtra is called *Unsurpassed Reliance,* also called *Unprecedented,* also called *Accepting Good Dharmas,* also called *Pure Action,* also called *Definitive Action.* Ānanda, there are ten ways to uphold this sūtra. What are these ten? They are to (1) copy it, (2) make offerings to it, (3) propagate it, (4) listen to it, (5) study it, (6) memorize it, (7) widely expound it, (8) recite it, (9) ponder it, and (10) train accordingly.

"Ānanda, if someone upholds this sūtra in these ten ways, his accumulating merits will be immeasurable and endless. Ānanda, as an analogy, wherever a wish-fulfilling jewel is, all treasures appear. Likewise whoever upholds this sūtra can accomplish all good dharmas. Ānanda, as another analogy, all trees and medicinal herbs depend on the earth to grow. Likewise good dharmas grow because of this sūtra. Ānanda, as another analogy, all good dharmas in the past, present, and future are accomplished through exercising self-restraint, because it is the foremost dharma. Likewise, among sūtras, whether they give voice-hearer teachings, Pratyekabuddha teachings, or Bodhisattva teachings, this sūtra is the foremost sūtra. Ānanda, as another analogy, if a Wheel-Turning King abides in the world, his seven precious things[15] always follow him. Likewise, if this sūtra abides in the world, the Three Jewels will continue without end.

"Ānanda, you should successively expound this sūtra to bhikṣus, bhikṣuṇīs, upāsakas, upāsikās, gods, dragons, gandharvas, asuras, garuḍas, kiṁnaras, mahoragas, humans, and nonhumans. Why? Because this is the way to enable all sentient beings to plant roots of goodness where a Tathāgata is."

After the Buddha pronounced this sūtra, in this huge assembly, Ānanda, Bodhisattva-Mahāsattvas, the god-king Śakra, the four world-protecting god-kings, and all others, having heard this extraordinary Dharma Door revealed by the Buddha, rejoiced exuberantly. They believed in, accepted, and carried out His teachings.

Notes

1. A Buddha's thirty-two physical marks are easily discernible, but His eighty excellent physical characteristics, or secondary marks, are subtle and hard to discern. The two sets combined are called excellent marks. Although a Wheel-Turning King has the thirty-two physical marks as well, a Buddha's are superior. Also, only a Buddha has the eighty excellent physical characteristics.

2. "Having a sense of shame" and "having a sense of dishonor" are two of the glossary's "seven noble treasures."

3. See "Four Right Endeavors" defined in the glossary's "Thirty-seven Elements of Bodhi."

4. For Three Learnings, see note 22 in fascicle 1 of this sūtra.

5. See "knowledge of all wisdom-knowledge" defined in the glossary's "three kinds of wisdom-knowledge."

6. Another set of eighteen comprises the Ten Powers, the Four Fearlessnesses, the three abidings of mindfulness, and great compassion. The three abidings of mindfulness means that a Buddha's mind abides in right mindfulness and wisdom, free from joy and woe in regard to (1) the group that believes in the Dharma and trains accordingly, (2) the group that neither believes in the Dharma nor trains accordingly, and (3) the group that comprises believers and nonbelievers.

7. See "wisdom pāramitā" defined in the glossary's "six pāramitās."

8. See "exceeding arrogance" defined in the glossary's "arrogance."

9. As stated in text 358, the Chinese version of the *Sūtra of Entering the States of All Buddhas Adorned with Wisdom,* like echoes, the sounds voiced by a Tathāgata are neither inside nor outside nor in the middle, and have neither birth nor death, neither names nor appearances. He voices various sounds according to sentient beings' preferences to make them understand (T12n0358, 0251c5–8). An English translation of this text appears in *Transcending the World* (2015, 165–78).

10. See "dharma body" defined in the glossary's "three bodies of a Buddha."

11. The "four body karmas" are the first four of the glossary's "ten good karmas."

12. See "Four Abidings of Mindfulness" in the glossary.

13. See Devadatta's life story in the glossary's "voice-hearer."

14. For a Buddha as a fortune field, see the glossary's "three fortune fields."

15. According to text 456, the Chinese version of the *Sūtra of Maitreya Bodhisattva's Attainment of Buddhahood,* a Wheel-Turning King with a gold wheel possesses seven precious things: (1) the gold wheel, (2) the white elephant, (3) the blue horse, (4) the divine jewel, (5) exquisite maidens, (6) the treasure minister, and (7) the military minister (T14n0456, 0429c27–0430a6; Rulu 2012a, 82).

About Sūtra 6

Text 273 (T09n0273) in one fascicle is the Chinese version of the *Sūtra of the Vajra Samādhi,* translated from Sanskrit in the Northern Liang Dynasty (397–439), in the northwestern region of China, by an unknown person. It is classified under the Dharma Flower section of the Chinese Canon, because it is conjectured that the Buddha pronounced this sūtra shortly after He pronounced the *Lotus Sūtra,* whose three Chinese versions are texts 262–64 (T09n0262–64).

The Tibetan version of the *Vajra Samādhi Sūtra* was translated from Chinese. In 1989, Robert E. Buswell Jr. was the first to translate text 273 into English. Sūtra 6 in the present book is also an English translation of text 273.

Commentaries on This Sūtra

There are three ancient Chinese commentaries on this sūtra: text 1730 in the Chinese Canon (Taishō Tripiṭaka), and texts 651 and 652 in the Extension of the Chinese Canon (Shinsan Zokuzōkyō).

Text 1730 (T34n1730) in 3 fascicles was written in the Tang Dynasty (618–907) by the Korean scholar Yuanxiao (元曉, 617–86), or Wŏnhyo. His interpretations of the *Vajra Samādhi Sūtra* are influenced by the doctrine of the Consciousness-Only School. In his commentary, he repeatedly brings up the terms "inherent awareness" (benjue 本覺) and "developed awareness" (shijue 始覺) used in text 1666 (T32n1666), the earlier of the two Chinese versions of *A Treatise on Eliciting Faith in the Mahāyāna* (Mahāyāna-śraddhotpāda-śāstra), attributed to Aśvaghoṣa (馬鳴, circa 100–60) from central India, translated in the Southern Liang Dynasty (502–57) by Paramārtha (真諦, 499–569) from northwestern India. A prolific writer, Yuanxiao wrote other commentaries. For example, text 1844 (T44n1844) in 2 fascicles and text 757 (X45n0757) in 5 fascicles are his two commentaries on that treatise; text 1759 (T36n1759) in one fascicle is his commentary on the *Sūtra of Amitāyus Buddha* (T12n0360).

Text 651 (X35n0651) in 4 fascicles was written in the Ming Dynasty (1368–1644) by the Chinese Chán (dhyāna) master Yuancheng (圓澄, 1561–1626) of the Caodong School (曹洞宗), a branch of the Chán School of China. Text 652 (X35n0652) in 12 fascicles was written in the Qing Dynasty (1644–1912) by the Chinese master Jizhen (寂震, dates unknown) of the Huading Temple (華頂寺) atop the Tiantai Mountain (天台山). Because the wording of text 273 is terse and obscure, these three commentaries differ in their interpretations of some of its passages.

In the 20th century, the Chinese master Zhiyü (智諭, 1924–2000) published his commentary in a book (Shi Zhiyü 2002), in which he often cites Yuanxiao's words. Each of these four commentators presents the words in the copy of this sūtra he used and his explanations of them.

In 2007, Buswell published his English translation of text 1730, Yuanxiao's commentary. However, Yuanxiao's explanations are based on a particular copy of this sūtra, in which some words differ from those in text 273. In deference to

Yuanxiao, Buswell made a minor revision to his 1989 translation of this sūtra in order to conform to Yuanxiao's interpretation.

Catalog Listings of This Sūtra

The earliest listing of this sūtra is found in fascicle 3 of text 2145 (T55n2145), a 15-fascicle catalog of Buddhist texts compiled in the Southern Liang Dynasty by Sengyou (僧祐, 445–518). This sūtra in one fascicle is listed in the section "Odd Sūtras (yijing 異經) Collected by Dao-an in the Liang territory (涼土)." Although the catalog compiled by Dao-an (道安, 314–85) in 374 during the Eastern Jin Dynasty (317–420), which is China's first catalog of Buddhist texts, was lost, its content is included in fascicles 2–5 of text 2145, and its title, *Zongli Zhongjing Mulu* 綜理眾經目錄 [Catalog of collected sūtras], is listed in four later catalogs: texts 2034, 2149, 2154, and 2157. Dao-an's catalog is evidence that this sūtra existed in the latter part of the 4th century.

Texts 2034, 2146, and 2147 are three catalogs compiled during the Sui Dynasty (589–618). Text 2034 (T49n2034), compiled in 597 by Fei Changfang (費長房), lists this sūtra among 234 Mahāyāna sūtras entered into the Chinese Canon. It is also listed in texts 2146 and 2147 (T55n2146–47). Text 2146 was compiled in 594 by Fajing (法經) et al. Text 2147 was compiled in 602 by Yancong (彥琮, 557–610), a renowned scholar monk. However, text 2147 lists this sūtra among 378 missing texts (queben 闕本).

Then it is listed in seven catalogs compiled between 644 and 799 during the Tang Dynasty, which are texts 2148, 2149, 2151, 2153, 2154, 2155, and 2157 (T55n2148, 49, 51, 53, 54, 55, 57).

Texts 2146, 2149, 2151, 2153, 2154, 2155, and 2157, in recognition of Dao-an's catalog included in text 2145, also state that this sūtra's translator is unknown. Based on text 2147 (compiled in 602), both text 2148 (compiled in 644) and text 2153 (compiled in 695) also list this sūtra as a missing text.

Then in the 8th century, this sūtra is listed as extant, in two catalogs: text 2154, the Kaiyuan (開元) catalog compiled in 730 by Zhisheng (智昇), and text 2157, the Zhenyuan (貞元) catalog compiled in 799 by Yuanzhao (圓照). Both catalogs list it as a text translated in the Northern Liang Dynasty by an unknown translator, in two fascicles (or one fascicle) with twenty-seven pages (T55n2154, 0688c20–21; T55n2157, 1036b10), compiled into the catalog by shiyi (shiyi bianru 拾遺編入) (T55n2154, 0605b15–16; T55n2157, 0938c10–12).[1]

Commentaries on this sūtra are listed in two catalogs compiled during the Northern Song Dynasty (960–1126). Text 2183 (T55n2183) in one fascicle, a catalog of Buddhist texts that circulated in Japan, was compiled in 1094 by the Japanese scholar Yongchao (永超). It lists two commentaries on this sūtra, one in 3 fascicles and the other in 5 fascicles, each without the commentator's name. Text 2184 (T55n2184) in 3 fascicles, a catalog of commentaries that circulated in Korea, was compiled in 1091 by the Korean monk Yitian (義天, 1055–1101). It lists two commentaries on this sūtra, one in 6 fascicles (or 3 fascicles) dictated by Yuanxiao and the other in four fascicles dictated by Sengdun (僧遁).

Because this sūtra was listed as a missing text in three catalogs compiled between 602 and 695, then listed in text 2154, the Kaiyuan catalog compiled in 730, as an extant text, Buswell agrees with Japanese scholars' deduction that this sūtra now available as text 273 in the Chinese Canon is the sūtra listed in text 2154, but different from that listed in Dao-an's catalog (Buswell 1989, 37). They contend that because Yuanxiao died in 686, during the years when this sūtra was listed as a missing text, the copy he used to write his commentary must have been a text written by someone. They disregard the possibility that although a cataloger may fail to acquire a copy of a sūtra at the time and list it as missing, some of its copies may be available elsewhere and be acquired later. Also, according to text 2034 (T49n2034), the catalog compiled in 594 by Fei Changfang, this sūtra had already been entered into the Chinese Canon before it was listed as missing. Scholars make no comment on whether or not this sūtra already entered into the Chinese Canon in 594 was the original one listed in Dao-an's catalog and no comment on how it could be replaced by text 273, which is claimed to be a different text.

This Sutra's Authenticity

In the 20th century, some scholars showed a great deal of interest in identifying apocryphal texts in the Chinese Canon. Bibliographies of such studies published in English, Japanese, and Korean can be found in Buswell's books (1989, 1990). Scholars, based on their studies and certain criteria, came up with a list of apocryphal texts, one of which is the *Vajra Samādhi Sūtra*.

The most influential argument against its authenticity comes from the Japanese scholar Kōgen Mizuno (水野弘元, 1901–2006). In his 1955 journal article, he argues that the three Chinese words *huai* 淮, *he* 河, and *jiang* 江 in text 273, chapter 7, which suggest the sizes of three rivers, indicate three actual rivers in China, i.e., the Huai River, the Yellow River, and the Yangtze River, and that these words serve as evidence that this sūtra was an apocryphal text written in China. Also, he claims that the source of the two entrances into the true reality of dharmas, presented in text 273, chapter 5, is Bodhidharma's (菩提達摩, ?–535) teaching on attaining bodhi through two entrances and four actions, in text 1217 (X63n1217) in the Extension of the Chinese Canon, as presented by his student Tanlin (曇林, ?–585). Moreover, he notes that the four mantra names in text 273, chapter 6, also appear in text 251, a Chinese version of the *Heart Sūtra* translated from Sanskrit by Xuanzang (玄奘, 600– or 602–64), after his return from India to China in 645. Mizuno concludes that text 273 was written in China in the seventh century, after Xuanzang translated the *Heart Sūtra* and before Yuanxiao wrote his commentary.

In text 2061 (T50n2061), a collection of biographies of exalted monks, compiled by Zanning (贊寧, 919–1002) in 982 during the Northern Song Dynasty (960–1127), appears a short tale of Yuanxiao, who lived in the Korean kingdom of Silla (新羅, 57 BCE–935 CE). In this tale, the king of Silla sends an agent to sail to China to find a cure for his queen's brain tumor. An old man rises from the sea and takes the agent to the dragon-king's palace. The dragon-king gives him a text of the *Vajra Samādhi Sūtra* with thirty-some disarrayed pages and tells him that in order to cure the queen's illness, Da-an (大安), or Taean, has to organize these pages into a text, and Yuanxiao has to write a commentary on it. Upon the agent's return to Silla, at the king's command to organize the pages, Da-an divides the text into eight chapters and gives it to Yuanxiao for him to expound it. Then Yuanxiao writes his commentary in two versions. The extensive version in 5 fascicles is stolen, and the brief version in 3 fascicles comes to China.

This tale implies that the sūtra given by the dragon-king was a Chinese text with thirty-some pages, but the sūtra listed in text 2154 has twenty-seven pages. Nevertheless, this tale serves to elevate the status of this sūtra to that of the *Sūtra of Mahāvaipulya Sūtra of Buddha Adornment* (Buddhāvataṁsaka-mahāvaipulya-sūtra) because legend has it that Ācārya Nāgārjuna (龍樹菩薩, circa 150–250) went to a dragon palace and brought a Sanskrit text of the *Buddha Adornment Sūtra* back to the human world.

Based on this tale, some scholars suggest that this sūtra was written in Korea. Buswell estimates that it was written in Korea between 668 and 685 (Buswell 1989, 71). Among the four Korean candidates for authorship—Taean (Da-an), Wŏnhyo (Yuanxiao), Chidŏk, and Pŏmnang (Falang 法朗)—Buswell claims that Pŏmnang would be the most likely author (Ibid., 174–77). Pŏmnang reputedly went to China sometime between 632 and 646 and received a mind transmission from Daoxin (道信, 580–651), the fourth patriarch of the Chán School of China. Buswell believes that Pŏmnang was well qualified to write this sūtra with a view to propagating in Korea the principle and practice of Chán.

The Chinese scholar Xü Wen-ming 徐文明, in his 1997 journal article, notes that the copy of this sūtra used by Yuanxiao to write his commentary contains some words different from those in text 273. He cites these differences passage by passage and compares Yuanxiao's interpretations of these words with the meanings of the corresponding words in text 273. He concludes that it is impossible that Yuanxiao wrote this sūtra. Xü claims that text 273 is an apocryphal text written in China around the time of Huike (慧可, 487–593), the second patriarch of the Chán School of China.

The Chinese scholar Yü De-long 于德隆, in his 2002 journal article, refutes Mizuno's contentions. Yü notes that the three Chinese words in text 273 that suggest the sizes of three rivers also appear in other texts, which are not classified as apocrypha.[2] He agrees with the statement, in fascicle 7 of Jizhen's commentary (X35n0652, 0296b15–c21), that text 273's two entrances into the true reality of dharmas are the source of Bodhidharma's teaching on the two entrances and four actions, not vice versa as claimed by Mizuno. Yü notes that the four mantra names in text 273 also appear in earlier texts, which were translated from Sanskrit into Chinese way before Xuanzang's time.[3] He claims that the *Vajra Samādhi Sūtra* listed in text 2145 as an odd sūtra was a fragmented text, and that text 273 is a translation done later by Paramārtha (真諦, 499–569), because one's inherent awareness and amala consciousness addressed in text 273 also appear in texts 1593, 1595, and 1666, which are treatises translated from Sanskrit into Chinese by Paramārtha (see Paramārtha's biography in the Ancient Translators section of the present book).

Although arguments over the authenticity of some texts in the Chinese Canon continue, many of these texts, including text 273, are highly valued in China. Buddhist masters generally advise their students against engaging in textual research and criticism, even for texts translated by unknown translators in unknown years. In case of doubt, one should measure the correctness of a text's teachings against the Four Dharma Seals (see Dharma Seal in the glossary).

This Sūtra's Teachings

The title of this sūtra is *Vajra Samādhi.* As vajra is an adamantine substance that can destroy all things, the Vajra Samādhi can penetrate the truth of all things. As stated in chapter 1, whoever enters the Vajra Samādhi, the samādhi that verifies the truth, definitely will eliminate all doubts and regrets in accordance with one dharma, the true reality of dharmas. In fascicle 24 of text 374, the 40-fascicle Chinese version of the *Mahāparinirvāṇa Sūtra,* the Buddha uses fourteen analogies to describe the supremacy of this samādhi (T12n0374, 0509b11–c29). According to fascicle 27, Vajra Samādhi is one of the five names of the Śūraṅgama Samādhi, which are (1) Śūraṅgama Samādhi, (2) Prajnā-Pāramitā, (3) Vajra Samādhi, (4) Lion's Roar Samādhi, and (5) Buddha Nature (Ibid., 0524c18–25).

This sūtra is not to be confused with the *Sūtra of the Pure and Indestructible Nature of the Vajra Samādhi* (T15n0644). In that short sūtra, also translated from Sanskrit into Chinese by an unknown person, the Buddha names a hundred samādhis in which a Bodhisattva on the tenth ground,[4] who abides in the Śūraṅgama Samādhi, should train, in order to enter the Vajra Samādhi. In this context the Śūraṅgama Samādhi is a prerequisite of the Vajra Samādhi.

On the uninterrupted path (ānantarya-mārga, 無間道), one enters the Vajra-Like Samādhi (vajropamā-samādhi, 金剛喻定) and eliminates all one's afflictions. Then, without interruption one enters the liberation path and eliminates all remaining traces of afflictions, thus attaining bodhi. A voice-hearer becomes an Arhat; a Bodhisattva becomes a Buddha (Buddha's Light Dictionary 1988, 5123a). In text 1730, Yuanxiao differentiates between the Vajra-like Samādhi and the Vajra Samādhi. According to him, the former eliminates all afflictions while the latter penetrates all dharmas; the former is for those who are still learning (śaikṣa) while the latter is for those who have nothing more to learn (aśaikṣa) (T34n1730, 0962a9–12). Indeed, in this sūtra, the Buddha enters the Vajra Samādhi. Moreover, in fascicle 2 of text 669 (in 2 fascicles), the Chinese version of the *Sūtra of the Unsurpassed Reliance,* whose English translation is Sūtra 5 in the present book, the Buddha says that only a Buddha can abide in the Vajra Samādhi (T16n0669, 0475c10).

This sūtra has two more titles, *Adopting the Mahāyāna* and *Tenet of Immeasurable Meaning,* because it gives definitive Mahāyāna teachings. As a sūtra, it belongs in the Sūtra-piṭaka. Because it mentions the precepts, it also belongs in the Vinaya-piṭaka. Because it gives explanations of the profound principle, it also belongs in the Abhidharm-piṭaka. Thus this sūtra serves as a compendium of the Tripiṭaka.

In this sūtra, the Tathāgata gives teachings to reveal the truth, teachings that follow the One Vehicle, the Buddha Vehicle, and have no mixed flavors. This sūtra reveals the One Vehicle as does the *Lotus Sūtra,* whose popular Chinese version is text 262 (T09n0262) in 7 fascicles; it reveals the Dharma in one flavor as does the *Sūtra of Buddha Adornment* (Buddhāvataṁsaka-mahāvaipulya-sūtra), whose three Chinese versions are text 278 (T09n0278) in 60 fascicles, text 279 (T10n0279) in 80 fascicles, and text 293 (T10n0293) in 40 fascicles; it reveals one's true nature, or Buddha nature, as does the

Mahāparinirvāṇa Sūtra, whose three Chinese versions are text 374 (T12n0374) in 40 fascicles, text 375 (T12n0375) in 36 fascicles, and text 376 (T12n0376) in 6 fascicles. For a Bodhisattva's training, it touches upon the six pāramitās, the six stages of training, the three clusters of Bodhisattva precepts, and the Thirty-seven Elements of Bodhi, all of which are benefits of one's inherent awareness.

This sūtra reveals the Middle Way because, in chapter 8, it states that all dharma appearances abide on neither of the two opposite shores, such as subject and object, existence and nonexistence, saṁsāra and nirvāṇa, nor in the stream between them. It repeatedly states that dharmas have no birth because their true reality is emptiness, which is true suchness. When one realizes one's boundless mind, one enters the true reality of dharmas. This sūtra uses such terms as one's inherent awareness, true nature, true mind, Tathāgata store (tathāgata-garbha), ālaya consciousness (ālaya-vijñāna), and amala consciousness (amala-vijñāna). In chapter 2, it explains that one's mind, which has no birth, is one's Tathāgata store, which has always been quiet and motionless. While the Tathāgata store is one's true mind shrouded by the perceptions of one's false mind, one's inherent awareness, the pure awareness of one's true mind, is free from subject and object, and knowing and not knowing, and has a mass of benefits. Buddhas use the one realization of one's inherent awareness to awaken all sentient beings, enabling them to realize their inherent awareness. Attaining nirvāṇa is realizing one's inherent awareness. Because nirvāṇa and one's inherent awareness are no different, attaining nirvāṇa is no attainment. When one eventually attains bodhi, one's enlightenment is but realizing one's inherent awareness.

It is well known that the Chán School of China upholds the *Diamond Sūtra* (T08n0235), whose full title is *Vajra Prajñā-Pāramitā Sūtra.* While the *Diamond Sūtra* reveals vajra wisdom, the *Vajra Samādhi Sūtra* reveals vajra samādhi. As wisdom and samādhi are of equal importance, the *Vajra Samādhi Sūtra* is highly valued, though not explicitly so, by the Chán School of China. In chapter 4 of text 2008, the *Sixth Patriarch's Platform Sūtra,* the sixth patriarch, Huineng (慧能, 638–713), says, "Samādhi and wisdom are one thing, not two things. Samādhi is the body of wisdom, and wisdom is the use of samādhi. As one's wisdom is revealed, samādhi underlies one's wisdom; as one abides in samādhi, wisdom is revealed from one's samādhi" (T48n2008, 0352c14–16). Many believe that his words echo the teachings in the *Vajra Samādhi Sūtra.* For example, in chapter 8 of this sūtra, the Buddha says, ". . . wisdom and samādhi accord with true suchness. . . . When one's wisdom and samādhi are perfected, one transcends the Three Realms of Existence."

Also, in chapter 4 of text 2008, the sixth patriarch says, "This Dharma Door of mine has always used no thought as its principle, no appearance as its essence, and no abiding as its root" (Ibid., 0353a11–12). These words accord with the teachings in the *Vajra Samādhi Sūtra* on no thought, no birth, no appearance, and no abiding.

Chapter Summaries

Sūtra 6 in the present book is an English translation of text 273, which comprises eight chapters. Although text 273 is a text in one fascicle, at the end of chapter 5, it states that fascicle 1 ends here and fascicle 2 begins with chapter 6. Sūtra 6 is accordingly divided into 2 fascicles. Chapter 8 covers two events: (1) the interlocution between Earth Store Bodhisattva and the Buddha and (2) the Buddha's entrusting of this sūtra to Ānanda. For clarity, the second event is put into chapter 9. Below are summaries of the nine chapters.

Fascicle 1 (of 2)

Chapter 1 - Preface

The Buddha is staying on the Gṛdhrakūṭa Mountain, near the city of Rājagṛha, accompanied by 10,000 Arhats, 2,000 Bodhisattva-Mahāsattvas, 80,000 koṭi Dharma protectors, such as gods and dragons. He pronounces a Mahāyāna sūtra called *The Truth in One Flavor, [Dharmas Have] No Appearance, [Actions Have] No Birth, the Absolute True Reality [of Dharmas], and the Benefits of One's Inherent Awareness.* After He enters the Vajra Samādhi, a bhikṣu named Agada (Panacea) praises the Buddha for revealing the highest truth, which follows the One Vehicle, the Buddha Vehicle. He praises the Vajra Samādhi because it verifies the truth and resolves all one's doubts.

Chapter 2 - Dharmas Have No Appearance

The Buddha rises from samādhi and tells Liberation Bodhisattva that the One Vehicle and the Dharma in one flavor enable all sentient beings to realize their inherent awareness. When one discards the view of opposite appearances of dharmas, such as existence and nonexistence, one realizes quiet nirvāṇa but does not abide in it, because one enters the true reality of dharmas, which is free from appearances and actions. One's mind, which has no birth, neither enters something to learn it nor exits anything after learning it, because it is one's Tathāgata store (tathāgata-garbha), which has always been quiet and motionless. Empty and motionless, one's mind encompasses the six pāramitās, which are benefits of one's inherent awareness and accord with one's true nature, or Buddha nature. They enable one to transcend the world and achieve hindrance-free liberation.

Chapter 3 - Actions Have No Birth

The Buddha tells Mind King Bodhisattva that endurance in one's realization that dharmas have no birth means an enduring understanding that dharmas have never had any birth; for example, all actions have no birth.

One's mind has no birth because it is not born from itself, from something else, from both itself and something else, or from no cause. As it abides in its true nature, or true suchness, it cannot be described as born or not born, or as having or not having endurance. Whatever has no birth takes no action. Although actions appear, they have no birth. As all one's mental actions are quiet and have no appearance and no birth, so too all one's consciousnesses are quiet and have no appearance and no birth.

Chapter 4 - The Benefits of One's Inherent Awareness

The Buddha praises Not Abiding Bodhisattva because he has acquired the benefits of his inherent awareness and abides in it, as he, neither coming nor going, benefits sentient beings.

Buddhas use the one realization of one's inherent awareness to awaken all sentient beings, enabling them to realize their inherent awareness and see that their emotion-driven consciousnesses are empty and quiet, and have no birth, because a sentient being's true nature, or Buddha nature, has always been motionless.

The holy power of realizing one's inherent awareness and the ground of the four kinds of wisdom-knowledge revealed by the Tathāgata are benefits of every sentient being's inherent awareness. Its benefits are motionless and constantly present, free from existence and nonexistence, awareness and no awareness.

Attaining nirvāṇa is realizing one's inherent awareness. As one's inherent awareness by nature is changeless, so too nirvāṇa is changeless. Because nirvāṇa and one's inherent awareness are no different, attaining nirvāṇa is no attainment.

Chapter 5 - Entering the True Reality of Dharmas

The Buddha tells Great Power Bodhisattva that if a Bodhisattva knows that realizing the emptiness of dharmas is a benefit of one's inherent awareness, he will attain bodhi. When one enters the no-grasping ground, one enters the three emptinesses: (1) the appearance of emptiness, (2) the wisdom that sees the emptiness of dharmas, and (3) whatever is seen as empty.

Although all dharmas appear to arise through conditions, they have no birth because the nature of their arising is true suchness, which never moves. Moreover, the appearances of conditions are by nature empty. As each condition also arises through conditions, in true reality there is no dependent arising of dharmas.

Whoever perceives the existence or nonexistence of a dharma sees only his mind and consciousnesses. One's mind does not arise even when one makes the two entrances into the true reality of dharmas. The two entrances are (1) the entrance through the principle and (2) the entrance through action. When one realizes one's boundless mind, one enters the true reality of dharmas.

One should retain three things, abide in one thing, and enter a Tathāgata's dhyāna. Retaining three things means retaining the three liberations. Abiding in one thing means abiding in the true suchness of one's mind. Entering a Tathāgata's dhyāna means using the principle to observe that one's mind is true suchness. When one enters one's mind ground in this way, one enters the true reality of dharmas.

Fascicle 2 (of 2)

Chapter 6 - Dharma Nature Is Emptiness

The Buddha tells Śāriputra that good and evil dharmas are manifested by one's mind. All one's perceptions of objects are differentiations made by one's consciousnesses and words. If one sets one's mind in one place, then one's perceptions of various objects will not arise.

Ending one's perception of a dharma's birth and death means realizing that its true reality is emptiness. One's realization of this emptiness is the wisdom fire that burns away one's afflictions. Then one realizes that all dharmas are equal in their emptiness as one enters one's ninth consciousness, or amala consciousness, which is bright and pure, free from one's mental projections.

The nature of dhyāna is no motion. It neither taints nor is tainted, is neither a mental object nor a mental projection, and is apart from making differentiations, because it is a benefit of one's inherent awareness. Doing meditation according to this observation is called dhyāna.

Chapter 7 - The Tathāgata Store

The Buddha tells the elder Brahma Way that all dharma appearances have only one true meaning. If one abides in one Dharma flavor, one tastes all flavors. Entering one's Tathāgata store is like a seedling coming to bear fruit without entering any place. When one uses the power of the benefits of one's inherent awareness to realize one's inherent awareness, one acquires limitless wisdom. To put one's wisdom to great use, one must do three great things to benefit oneself and others, enter the Bodhisattva Way, transcend the Three Realms of Existence, and not abide in nirvāṇa.

One's mind that knows that dharmas are in nirvāṇa is not the mind in nirvāṇa, because the mind constantly in nirvāṇa is one's true awareness, which is free from knowing and not knowing an object. Turning away from perceiving a grasper and an object grasped, one enters one's Tathāgata store.

Chapter 8 - Total Retention of Teachings

The Buddha tells Earth Store Bodhisattva that a dharma is neither existent nor nonexistent, nor does it have a self versus others. Although all dharmas are empty and quiet, they are quiet but not empty because they vividly appear in one's perception. As dharmas have always been in nirvāṇa, so too one's mind has always been in nirvāṇa. As nirvāṇa and emptiness cannot be grasped, they are true suchness.

The true reality of dharmas is encompassed in one's inherent awareness, which has a mass of profound virtues. When one ends one's perception of a dharma's birth and death, one realizes the eternality of nirvāṇa, which never ends and is apart from motion and no motion in the Three Realms of Existence. When one eventually attains bodhi, one's enlightenment is but realizing one's inherent awareness.

Chapter 9 - Entrusting This Sūtra

The Buddha tells Ānanda that this inconceivable sūtra is called *Adopting the Mahāyāna,* also called *Vajra Samādhi,* also called *Tenet of Immeasurable Meaning.* It is the hub of the teachings in all sūtras. Accepting and upholding this sūtra is accepting and upholding the teachings of 100,000 Buddhas. The merit acquired in this way is inconceivable and boundless, like the open sky. Then the Buddha entrusts this sūtra to him.

Notes

1. In everyday usage, the term *shiyi* 拾遺 means picking up something lost or left behind. Here, shiyi is a state advisory post established in the Tang Dynasty. Conceivably, one of its functions was to recover lost texts. "Shiyi bianru" 拾遺編入 (transliterated by Buswell as "shih-i p'ien-ju") means that an official in this post, by his authority compiled this text into the catalog. These words do not mean "having been reconstructed from scattered folios," as interpreted by Buswell, based on Mizuno's, Hayashiya's, and Kimura's works (Buswell 1989, 37).

2. These three Chinese words also appear in texts 985 (T19n0985, 0473b2–3), 1045b (T20n1045b, 0042a7–8), and 1332 (T21n01332, 0548a24–25), which are not classified as apocrypha.

3. For example, the last three of the four mantra names appear in fascicle 2 of text 227 (T08n0227, 0543b28–29), the Chinese version of the *Small Prajñā-Pāramitā Sūtra,* translated from Sanskrit in the Later Qin Dynasty (384–417) by Kumārajīva (鳩摩羅什, 344–413) from Kucha. They also appear in fascicle 1 of text 643 (T15n0643, 0647b4–5), the Chinese version of the *Sūtra of the Ocean Samādhi of Visualizing a Buddha,* translated from Sanskrit in the Eastern Jin Dynasty (317–420) by Buddhabhadra (佛馱跋陀羅, 359–429) from India. Moreover, the first of the four mantra names appears in many texts translated from Sanskrit into Chinese before Xuanzang's time.

4. See "ten Bodhisattva grounds" in the glossary's "stages of the Bodhisattva Way." Details of the ten Bodhisattva grounds are given in chapter 26 of the *Mahāvaipulya Sūtra of Buddha Adornment* (Buddhāvataṁsaka-mahāvaipulya-sūtra). An English translation of this chapter appears in *The Bodhisattva Way* (Rulu 2013, 111–244).

6 金剛三昧經
Sūtra of the Vajra Samādhi

Translated from Sanskrit into Chinese in the Northern Liang Dynasty
by
An Unknown Person

Fascicle 1 (of 2)

Chapter 1 – Preface

Thus I have heard:

At one time the Buddha was staying on the Gṛdhrakūṭa Mountain, near the city of Rājagṛha. He was accompanied by 10,000 great bhikṣus who all had completed the Arhat path, including Śāriputra, Mahāmaudgalyāyana, and Subhūti. Also present were 2,000 Bodhisattva-Mahāsattvas, including Liberation Bodhisattva, Mind King Bodhisattva, and Not Abiding Bodhisattva. In attendance as well were 80,000 elders, including Brahma Way, Great Brahma Way, and Jyotiṣka. Also gathered there were 600,000 koṭi gods, dragons, yakṣas, gandharvas, asuras, garuḍas, kiṁnaras, mahoragas, humans, and nonhumans.

At that time the World-Honored One, surrounded by the multitude, pronounced to all a Mahāyāna sūtra called *The Truth in One Flavor, [Dharmas Have] No Appearance, [Actions Have] No Birth, the Absolute True Reality [of Dharmas], and the Benefits of One's Inherent Awareness.*[1] Whoever heard this sūtra, and accepted and upheld even one four-line stanza, would enter a Buddha's wisdom ground and be able to use skillful means to teach and transform sentient beings, and to serve as their great beneficent learned friend. After the Buddha pronounced this sūtra, He sat cross-legged and entered the Vajra Samādhi,[2] His body and mind motionless.

Then, in the midst of this multitude, a bhikṣu named Agada [Panacea] rose from his seat, knelt on his right knee, and joined his palms. [Wishing the Buddha] to restate the meaning of this sūtra, he spoke in verse:

The World-Honored One, who has great lovingkindness,
Wisdom, and hindrance-free transcendental powers
To widely deliver sentient beings,
Has revealed the meaning of the one truth.

Using the one flavor,
Never the path of the Small Vehicle [Hīnayāna],[3]
The meaning He has revealed
Is apart from falsity.

It enters Buddhas' wisdom ground
To reveal the absolute true reality[4] [of dharmas].
Whoever hears it will transcend the world
And achieve liberation.

To deliver sentient beings,
Innumerable Bodhisattvas, for the sake of this multitude,
Ask profound questions,
In order to know that dharmas are in quiet nirvāṇa
And to enter their absolute place [true reality].

Using wisdom and skillful means,
The Tathāgata has given teachings to reveal the truth,
Teachings that follow the One Vehicle [Buddha Vehicle]
And have no mixed flavors.

As a rain brings wetness,
All grasses thrive according to their different natures.
As the Dharma in one flavor
Pervades everywhere,
Bodhi sprouts grow,
Like grasses wetted by a rain.

[Whoever] enters the Vajra Samādhi,
The samādhi that verifies the truth,
Definitely will eliminate all doubts and regrets
In accordance with one dharma [the true reality of dharmas].

Chapter 2 – Dharmas Have No Appearance

Then the World-Honored One rose from samādhi and said, "Buddhas' wisdom ground reveals the true reality of dharmas. Their skillful means and spiritual powers have no appearance because dharmas are by nature absolutely empty [śūnya].[5] However, the definitive meaning of the one realization [of one's inherent awareness[6]] is hard to understand and fathom, and beyond the knowledge and views of riders of the Two Vehicles. Only Buddhas and Bodhisattvas can know it. To sentient beings ready to be delivered, I expound the Dharma in one flavor."

Then Liberation Bodhisattva rose from his seat. Kneeling on his right knee, with joined palms, he asked the Buddha, "World-Honored One, after the Buddha enters parinirvāṇa, the true Dharma [saddharma] will be gone, and a likeness of the Dharma will abide in the world. In its final kalpa with the five turbidities,[7] sentient beings will do evil karmas as they endlessly transmigrate in the Three Realms of Existence. I pray that the Buddha, out of lovingkindness and compassion, will expound the Dharma in one flavor and reveal the absolute true reality of dharmas, to enable future sentient beings to achieve equal liberation."

The Buddha answered, "Good man, you ask why I have appeared in the world. It is because I want to transform sentient beings and enable them to acquire the spiritual fruit, i.e., to transcend the world. This great matter [of a Buddha's appearance in the world] is inconceivable because it arises from great compassion. If I would not give you teachings out of great compassion, stinginess would be a fault of mine. All of you should intently hearken as I explain to you.

"Good man, when transforming sentient beings, if one neither regards oneself as a transformer who transforms them nor regards them as objects to be transformed, and if one does not regard their transformation as no transformation, then this is a great transformation. One should enable every sentient being to discard the wrong view that one has a mind and an embodied self,[8] because they have always been empty and quiet. If he realizes that his mind is empty, it will not produce illusions [perceived or conceived dharmas]. Free from illusions, he will realize that dharmas have no birth. His realization that one's mind has no birth lies in its freedom from producing illusions."

Liberation Bodhisattva asked the Buddha, "World-Honored One, a sentient being's mind by nature has always been empty and quiet. An empty and quiet mind has no form. Then how should one train in order to realize that it has always been empty? I pray that the Buddha, out of lovingkindness and compassion, will explain to me."

The Buddha answered, "Bodhisattva, all one's mental appearances have no root, no place, and no birth, and are empty and quiet. If one's mind has no birth, it must be empty and quiet. By clearing one's mind ground, one realizes that one's mind has always been empty and had no appearance. Good man, as one's mind with no appearance has no mind and no self, so all dharma appearances [have no mind and no self]."

Liberation Bodhisattva asked the Buddha, "World-Honored One, if sentient beings imagine that they have a self and a mind,[9] what teachings should be used to enable them to free themselves from their fixations?"

The Buddha answered, "Good man, if someone holds the view that one has a self, you should have him observe the Twelve Links of Dependent Arising, which are based on cause and effect and arise from one's mental actions. Even one's mind does not exist, much less one's body. If someone holds the view that one has a self, you should have him discard the view of its existence. If someone holds the view that one has no self, you should have him discard the view of its nonexistence.[10] If someone thinks that one's mind has a birth, you should have him discard his misconception that it will die. If someone thinks that one's mind has a death, you should have him discard his misconception that it was born.[11] Once he discards these views [existence versus nonexistence, birth versus death], he will enter the true reality of dharmas. Why? Because whatever has no birth has no death and whatever has no death has no birth. Hence all dharmas have neither birth nor death, neither death nor birth."

Liberation Bodhisattva asked the Buddha, "World-Honored One, when a sentient being perceives the birth of a dharma, what view should he discard? When he perceives the death of a dharma, what view should he discard?"

The Buddha answered, "Bodhisattva, when a sentient being perceives the birth of a dharma, you should have him discard the view of its nonexistence. When he perceives the death of a dharma, you should have him discard the view of its existence. If he discards these views, he will realize that dharmas are by nature absolutely empty and definitely have no birth."

Liberation Bodhisattva asked the Buddha, "World-Honored One, if a sentient being abides in the view that dharmas have no birth, has he realized the truth that dharmas have no birth?"

The Buddha answered, "Abiding in the view of no birth means birth [of a thought]. Why? Because not abiding in the view of no birth means no birth [of a thought]. Bodhisattva, if one has the thought that dharmas have no birth, one is using the birth of a thought to end the view of birth. Only when one ends [one's perception of] birth and death of dharmas will one realize that dharmas have never had any birth, and that one's mind is constantly empty and quiet, and abides in nothing. When one's mind abides in nothing, it has no birth."

Liberation Bodhisattva asked the Buddha, "World-Honored One, if one's mind abides in nothing, how does one train and learn? Does one still have something to learn or have nothing to learn?[12]"

The Buddha answered, "Bodhisattva, one's mind, which has no birth, neither enters something [to learn it] nor exits anything [after learning it], because it is one's Tathāgata store [tathāgata-garbha], which has always been quiet and motionless. It has neither something to learn nor nothing to learn. Freedom from learning and not learning means having nothing to learn. What one has learned is that one's mind has nothing to learn."

Liberation Bodhisattva asked the Buddha, "World-Honored One, why is one's Tathāgata store by nature quiet and motionless?"

The Buddha answered, "Although one's Tathāgata store is hidden by the appearances of birth and death of one's thoughts and concerns, it is by nature quiet and motionless."

Liberation Bodhisattva asked the Buddha, "World-Honored One, what are the appearances of the birth and death of one's thoughts and concerns?"

The Buddha answered, "Bodhisattva, the principle [of one's true mind] is free from duality. If one differentiates between approval and disapproval [acceptance and rejection], thousands of thoughts will arise and expire. These are the appearances of birth and death. Bodhisattva, observe that one's true nature [Buddha nature] fully accords with the principle, while thousands of thoughts and concerns disaccord with the principle. They are a turmoil that shrouds one's mind.

"If one has no thoughts or concerns, then their births and deaths will not appear, and one's [eight] consciousnesses[13] will remain quiet and motionless. Then one's five dharmas [five aggregates] will become pure.[14] This is a Mahāyāna teaching.

"Bodhisattva, when one enters the purity of one's five dharmas, one's mind will be free from delusion. Without delusion, one enters a Tathāgata's holy wisdom ground of self-realization. Having entered the wisdom ground, one will know well that no dharma has ever been born. Knowing that dharmas have never been born, one will not have deluded thinking."

Liberation Bodhisattva said to the Buddha, "World-Honored One, if one has no deluded thinking, then one does not need to stop it."

The Buddha said, "Bodhisattva, because one's delusion has never been born, there is no delusion to end. If one knows that one's mind is no mind, there is no mind to stop. Free from differentiation, one's manifesting consciousness [ālaya consciousness] does not arise. Then it has no birth to stop. However, no stopping is not no stopping. Why? Because there is nothing to stop."

Liberation Bodhisattva asked the Buddha, "Although stopping does not have anything to stop, to stop something means the birth [of a thought]. Then what is no birth?"

The Buddha answered, "Bodhisattva, one should stop the birth of a thought. After stopping it, one has nothing else to stop. As one does not abide in one's no stopping or no abiding, how can there be the birth [of a thought]?"

Liberation Bodhisattva asked the Buddha, "If one's mind [in true reality] has no birth, how does one accept or reject anything? In what dharma appearances does one abide?"

The Buddha answered, "One's mind, which has no birth, neither accepts nor rejects anything. It abides in no mind and no dharma.[15]"

Liberation Bodhisattva asked the Buddha, "World-Honored One, how does one abide in no mind and no dharma?"

The Buddha answered, "If one's mind does not arise, one abides in no mind. If a dharma does not arise [from one's mind], one abides in no dharma. Good man, as dharmas and one's mind do not arise, one relies on nothing. As one does not abide in actions [body, voice, and mind karmas], one's mind is constantly empty and quiet, free from various appearances. As an analogy, the open sky neither moves nor abides, neither arises nor does anything, and never differentiates between this and that. When one acquires the eye that sees that one's mind is empty, and acquires the mind that knows that dharmas are empty, one realizes that one's five aggregates and six faculties are empty and quiet.

"Good man, to train to realize this emptiness, one does not rely on the Three Realms of Existence or various precepts, because one's mind has no thoughts, and is pure and free from restraint and unrestraint. Although it is by nature as adamantine as vajra, it never damages [one's inherent] Three Jewels. Empty and motionless, one's mind encompasses the six pāramitās."

Liberation Bodhisattva asked the Buddha, "World-Honored One, the six pāramitās have their appearances. How can one use dharmas with appearances to transcend the world?"

The Buddha answered, "Good man, the six pāramitās that I expound have no appearances and are asaṁskṛta [free from conditions]. Why? Because if one discards desires,[16] one's mind will always be pure. If one uses truthful words and skillful means to reveal the benefits of one's inherent awareness, to benefit others, this is dāna-pāramitā [the almsgiving pāramitā]. If one's resolve is firm, and if one's mind is pure, abides in nothing, and has no attachment to the Three Realms of Existence, this is śīla-pāramitā [the precept pāramitā]. If one delves into the emptiness of dharmas, cuts off one's fetters, quiets one's three karmas [body, voice, and mind karmas], and does not abide in one's body or mind, this is kṣānti-pāramitā [the endurance pāramitā]. If one stays far way from names and numbers, discards the opposite view, whether that a dharma is empty or that it is existent, and delves into the emptiness of one's five aggregates, this is vīrya-pāramitā [the progress pāramitā]. If one's meditation stays away from blankness and does not abide in various emptinesses,[17] and if one's mind abides in nothing, not even great emptiness, this is dhyāna-pāramitā [the meditation pāramitā]. If one knows that one's mind has no appearance but is not a blank like the open sky, does not give birth to actions or enter nirvāṇa, does not rely on the Bodhisattva grounds[18] or abide in one's wisdom, neither enters nor exits anything, but constantly abides in equality [of dharmas] and definitely accords with the true reality of dharmas, this is prajñā-pāramitā [the wisdom pāramitā].

"Good man, these six pāramitās are the benefits of one's inherent awareness and accord with one's true nature. They enable one to transcend the world and achieve hindrance-free liberation. Good man, this liberation has neither appearance nor action. Freedom from liberation and no liberation is called liberation. Why? Because it has no appearance, no action, no motion, and no disorder. It is quiet nirvāṇa without the appearance of nirvāṇa."

After Liberation Bodhisattva heard these words, he found great joy in his heart because he acquired an understanding he never before had. To affirm the meaning of the Buddha's words, he spoke in verse:

The World-Honored One, who is fully enlightened,
Has Expounded the Dharma to this multitude.
His teachings reveal the One Vehicle,
Not the paths of the Two Vehicles.

[The Dharma] in one flavor and with no appearance
Is like the vast open sky, which encompasses all things.
It enables all those with different natures
To realize their own place [inherent awareness].

If one discards the view that one has a mind and a self,
One will realize that all things are manifested by one dharma [one's true mind].
Whether sentient beings in the Three Realms of Existence take the same or different actions,
They all receive the benefits of their inherent awareness.

When one discards the view of opposite appearances [of dharmas], such as existence and nonexistence,
One realizes quiet nirvāṇa
But does not abide in it,
Because one enters the absolute place [true reality of dharmas],
Which is free from appearances and actions.

One's empty mind on the nirvāṇa ground
Is the nirvāṇa mind, which has no birth.
It is by nature as adamantine as vajra,
And never damages [one's inherent] Three Jewels
It has the six pāramitās
To deliver all sentient beings.

One never rides the Small Vehicle
To transcend the Three Realms of Existence,
Because the seal of the Dharma in one flavor
Is formed by the One Vehicle.

After the multitude heard this meaning, all found great joy in their hearts, discarded the wrong view that one has a mind and a self, entered the vastness of emptiness and no appearance, and definitely cut off their fetters and ended their afflictions.

Chapter 3 – Actions Have No Birth

At that time, Mind King Bodhisattva heard the Buddha's inconceivable teaching on transcending the Three Realms of Existence. He rose from his seat, joined his palms, and asked in verse:

> According to the Tathāgata's teaching,
> One's transcendence of the world has no appearance.
> If all sentient beings
> End their afflictions, cut off their fetters,
> And know that one's mind and self are empty,
> They will realize that dharmas have no birth.
> As dharmas have no birth,
> How can one acquire endurance in one's realization that dharmas have no birth?

Then the Buddha told Mind King Bodhisattva, "Good man, endurance in one's realization that dharmas have no birth means an enduring understanding that dharmas have never had any birth; for example, all actions have no birth. It is false that one can take action that has birth to acquire endurance in one's realization that dharmas have no birth."

Mind Kind Bodhisattva said, "World-Honored One, if perceiving as an attainment one's endurance in one's realization that dharmas have no birth is false, then perceiving no attainment and no endurance must not be false."

The Buddha said, "Not so. Why not? Because perceiving no attainment and no endurance implies attainment [of his negations]. Any attainment and one's endurance in it mean birth, the birth of an attainment. Whether one perceives attainment or no attainment, one's perception is false."

Mind Bodhisattva asked, "World-Honored One, why is one's mind, which has no birth and no abiding in anything, not false?"

The Buddha answered, "What is meant by one's mind, which has no birth and no abiding in anything? One's mind has no shape or sections, just as the nature of fire is hidden in wood but has no place. Fire has a name, which is a word, but its true nature cannot be captured. To describe its principle, one gives it a false name, which also cannot be captured. Likewise one's mind does not have a place. Such is one's mind that it has no birth.

"Good man, one's mind is like an āmra [mango], which is not born from itself, from something else, from both itself and something else, or from no cause.[19] It has no birth. Why? Because conditions arise and expire. When a condition arises, it is no birth; when a condition expires, it is no death. Whether conditions are hidden or visible, they have no appearance because their basic principle is nirvāṇa. The presence of one's mind cannot be identified with a place because it abides in its true nature.

"This true nature is neither the same nor different, neither perpetual nor ceasing, neither entering nor exiting, and has neither birth nor death.[20] It is free from the four falsities[21] and beyond the way of words. Likewise one's mind by nature has no birth. How can it be described as born or not born, or as having or not having endurance? If someone claims that his mind attains, abides in, or sees something, he has not attained anuttara-samyak-saṁbodhi. [Without] prajñā [wisdom],[22] he remains in the long night [of births and deaths]. To understand one's mind and its nature, one should know that one's mind is true suchness [bhūta-tathātā][23] and that its nature is true suchness as well. They have no birth and no action."

Mind King Bodhisattva said, "World-Honored One, if one's mind is true suchness, it will not give birth to actions, and actions will not be born from one's mind. Although actions appear, they have no birth. Whatever has no birth takes no action. Hence actions have no birth."

The Buddha asked, "Good man, do you use [the principle of] no birth to prove that actions have no birth?"

Mind King Bodhisattva answered, "Not so. Why not? Because as the appearances of one's actions, which have no birth, are by nature empty and quiet, there is no seeing or hearing, no gain or loss, no words or speech, no knowing or appearing, and no accepting or rejecting. Then how does one verify anything? Any claim of verifying [the truth] would be disputable. Actions, which have no birth, are free from dispute and discussion."

The Buddha asked, "Have you attained anuttara-samyak-saṁbodhi?"

Mind King Bodhisattva answered, "World-Honored One, I do not attain anuttara-samyak-saṁbodhi. Why not? Because bodhi by nature has neither gain nor loss, neither perception nor knowledge, and makes no differentiation. Its freedom from differentiation is purity, and its nature is unadulterated, indescribable by words, and free from existence and nonexistence, and knowing and not knowing. Likewise are Dharma actions. Why? Because all Dharma actions have no place, because of their true nature. They are free from attainment and no attainment. Therefore, how can one attain anuttara-samyak-saṁbodhi?"

The Buddha said, "Indeed, indeed. As all one's mental actions are quiet and have no appearance and no birth, so too all one's consciousnesses are quiet and have no appearance and no birth. Why? Because as eye and what it touches are empty and quiet, eye consciousness is empty and quiet, free from motion and no motion, and from the three kinds of internal sensations [pleasant, unpleasant, and neither], which are in nirvāṇa. So too are ear consciousness, nose consciousness, tongue consciousness, body consciousness, mental consciousness [the sixth consciousness], manas consciousness [the seventh consciousness], and ālaya consciousness [the eighth consciousness]. All one's consciousnesses are free from the notion that they are in nirvāṇa and the notion that they have no birth. If one entertains these two notions, then one's actions have birth, not no birth, and one is not free from the three kinds of sensations, the three kinds of actions [good, evil, and neural], and the three kinds of precepts.[24]

"If one has attained nirvāṇa, one's mind does not arise but is quiet and free from effort and usage. It abides in neither attainment nor no attainment of nirvāṇa. As one's mind remains in no abiding and no appearance, one is free from the three kinds of sensations, the three kinds of actions, and the three kinds of precepts. One's mind is quiet and pure, has neither birth nor action, and abides in nothing, whether dhyāna or samādhi.

Mind King Bodhisattva asked, "Dhyāna can control one's moving mind and still one's chaotic illusions. Why should one not abide in dhyāna?"

The Buddha answered, "Bodhisattva, dhyāna is motion.[25] No motion and no dhyāna are dhyāna, which has no birth. Dhyāna by nature has no birth and is apart from its appearances. It by nature does not abide in anything and is apart from the motion of abiding in dhyāna. If one knows that dhyāna by nature has neither motion nor quietness, one will understand that it has no birth. Likewise prajñā, which has no birth, does not abide in anything, and one's mind does not move. Because of this wisdom-knowledge [jñāna], one achieves prajñā-pāramitā, which has no birth."

Mind King Bodhisattva said, "World-Honored One, prajñā, which has no birth, neither abides nor departs anywhere. One's mind abides nowhere, and there is nowhere one's mind can abide. Having nowhere to abide, one's mind has no birth and no abiding. Abiding in this way, one's mind abides in no birth and no abiding. World-Honored One, one's mind, which has no birth and no abiding, is inconceivable. What is inconceivable is describable and indescribable.[26]"

The Buddha said, "Indeed, indeed."

After Mind King Bodhisattva heard these words, he marveled at them as unprecedented teachings and praised the Buddha in verse:

> The World-Honored One, who is adorned with great wisdom,
> Has broadly expounded that dharmas have no birth.
> These teachings never before heard
> Are now given.
>
> They are like pure sweet dew,
> Which appears once in a long while.
> They are inconceivable, hard to encounter,
> And hard to hear.
>
> Like an unsurpassed fortune field[27]
> And a supreme remedy,
> To deliver sentient beings,
> These teachings are now given.

After the multitude heard these words, all acquired endurance in their realization that dharmas have no birth and acquired prajñā, which has no birth.

Chapter 4 – The Benefits of One's Inherent Awareness

At that time, Not Abiding Bodhisattva heard the Buddha expound the inconceivable truth in one flavor. Having come from a distant place, he stayed close to the Tathāgata's seat to listen with intent mindfulness. He entered a pure state, his body and mind motionless.

Then the Buddha asked Not Abiding Bodhisattva, "Whence have you come and where have you come to?"

Not Abiding Bodhisattva answered, "I came from nowhere and came to nowhere."

The Buddha praised, "Inconceivable! Because you came from nowhere and came to nowhere, you have acquired the benefits of your inherent awareness. You are a Bodhisattva-Mahāsattva."

Then He emitted vast radiance that illuminated everywhere in the Three-Thousand Large Thousandfold World, and spoke in verse:

Great is a Bodhisattva
Whose wisdom is fully developed!
He always uses the benefits of his inherent awareness
To benefit sentient beings.

Neither coming nor going,
As he carries out his four majestic deportments,
He constantly abides in the benefits of his inherent awareness
To guide sentient beings.

Then Not Abiding Bodhisattva asked the Buddha, "World-Honored One, what benefits should be used to enable a sentient being's emotion-driven consciousnesses to become amala [stainless]?[28]"

The Buddha said, "Buddha-Tathāgatas always use the one realization [of one's inherent awareness] to turn a sentient being's consciousnesses into amala. Why? Because all sentient beings have their inherent awareness. So Buddhas use the one realization to awaken all sentient beings, enabling them to realize their inherent awareness and see that their emotion-driven consciousnesses are empty and quiet, and have no birth. Why? Because a sentient being's true nature has always been motionless."

Not Abiding Bodhisattva asked, "One's eight consciousnesses depend on objects to arise. How can they not move?"

The Buddha said, "All [perceived or conceived] objects and one's consciousnesses have always been empty. Emptiness is free from dependency. Then how can one's consciousnesses depend on objects to arise?"

Not Abiding Bodhisattva asked, "If all objects are empty, how does one perceive them?"

The Buddha said, "One's perception is false. Why? Because all dharmas in existence have no birth, no appearance, and no names. As all dharma appearances are empty and quiet, so too are all sentient beings' bodies. Even one's body does not exist, much less its perception."

Not Abiding Bodhisattva said, "If one's body, [perceived or conceived] objects, and consciousnesses are empty, one's inherent awareness must also be empty."

The Buddha said, "One's inherent awareness is indestructible because of its true nature. It is neither empty nor not empty, and free from emptiness and non-emptiness."

Not Abiding Bodhisattva said, "Likewise the appearances of all objects are neither empty nor not empty."

The Buddha said, "Indeed. The true nature of an object is emptiness. Moreover, the root of this nature has no place."

Not Abiding Bodhisattva said, "Likewise one's inherent awareness has no place."

The Buddha said, "Indeed. Because one's inherent awareness has no place, it is pure. In its purity, it has no perception. Because a [perceived] thing has no place, it is pure. In its purity, it has no form."

Not Abiding Bodhisattva said, "Likewise one's mind, eye, and consciousness are inconceivable."

The Buddha said, "Likewise one's mind, eye, and consciousness are inconceivable. Why? Because an object has no place, and is pure and without a name, it does not come inside [to enter one's mind]. Because one's eye has no place, and is pure and without perception, it does not go outside [to touch anything]. Because one's mind has no place and is pure, it neither arises from nor stops anywhere. Because one's consciousness has no place, and is pure and motionless, it makes no differentiation. The nature [of one's mind, eye, and consciousness] is emptiness, which has no perception. Realization of its emptiness is enlightenment.

"Good man, when one realizes that one's inherent awareness is free from perception, one's consciousnesses enter [one's true mind]. Why? Because when one arrives on the ground of vajra wisdom, one has completed the liberation path and entered the no-abiding ground [the Buddha Ground], free from entering and exiting, and one's mind abides nowhere on the ground of its true nature. This ground is pure like lucid aquamarine [vaiḍūrya]; its nature is equality, like the nature of the great earth; its discerning observations are like the wisdom sunlight; its benefits that enable sentient beings to realize their inherent awareness are like a great Dharma rain. Acquiring these four kinds of wisdom-knowledge[29] is entering the ground of a Buddha's wisdom-knowledge, where one's consciousnesses do not arise."

Not Abiding Bodhisattva said, "The holy power of realizing one's inherent awareness and the ground of the four kinds of vast wisdom-knowledge revealed by the Tathāgata are the benefits of every sentient being's inherent awareness. Why? Because every sentient being has always had them in his body."

The Buddha said, "Indeed. Why? Because all sentient beings have always been free from afflictions and had the benefits of their inherent awareness. However, they have not yet conquered their desires,[30] which are like thorns."

Not Abiding Bodhisattva asked, "If sentient beings have not yet acquired the benefits of their inherent awareness and are still collecting [appearances of objects], how can they conquer what is hard to conquer?"

The Buddha answered, "Whether one is collecting [appearances] or letting one's perception be alone, whether one is making differentiations or forming attachments [to appearances], whether one draws one's mind back to stay in an empty cavern [the emptiness of dharmas], one will be able to conquer what is hard to conquer, and to liberate oneself from the fetters of māras, because when one sits loftily [in meditation] on the open ground, one's consciousness enters nirvāṇa."

Not Abiding Bodhisattva said, "When one's mind abides in nirvāṇa alone, unaccompanied [by one's consciousnesses], one should achieve liberation."

The Buddha said, "Constantly abiding in nirvāṇa is being fettered by nirvāṇa. Why? Because nirvāṇa is a benefit of one's inherent awareness, and because the benefits of one's inherent awareness are in nirvāṇa. Attaining nirvāṇa is realizing one's inherent awareness. As one's inherent awareness is by nature changeless, so too nirvāṇa is changeless. As one's inherent awareness has neither birth nor death, so too nirvāṇa has neither birth nor death. Because nirvāṇa and one's inherent awareness are no different, attaining nirvāṇa is no attainment. As attaining nirvāṇa is no attainment, how can one abide in it?

"Good man, an enlightened person does not abide in nirvāṇa. Why not? Because one's inherent awareness has no birth and is apart from one's filthy afflictions. One's inherent awareness has no death and is apart from the motion of entering nirvāṇa. Abiding on this wisdom ground, one's mind abides in nothing. Free from entering and exiting, it enters amala consciousness."

Not Abiding Bodhisattva said, "Entering amala consciousness means that there is a place to enter. Entrance into this place means attainment."

The Buddha said, "Not so. Why not? As an analogy, a confused son possesses gold coins but does not know that he has them. He roams in the ten directions for fifty years, undergoing poverty and hardship. He has to beg for things to live a life of privation. When the father sees his son in such a plight, he says to him, 'You have gold coins. Why do you not use them? Then you can get whatever you need in full.' The son is awakened and sees his gold coins. With great joy in his heart, he declares that he has gotten gold coins. His father says, 'Confused child, do not rejoice. The gold coins have always been yours. You did not get them. There is no reason to rejoice.'[31]

"Good man, likewise is one's amala consciousness. Because it has never left one, it does not enter one. When one is confused, it is not absent. One's awakening [to its presence] does not mean that it enters one."

Not Abiding Bodhisattva asked, "The father knows that his son is confused. Why does he let him wander in the ten directions for fifty years, undergoing poverty and hardship, then tell him [that he has gold coins]?"

The Buddha answered, "Passing fifty years describes how one's mind moves in one thought. Roaming in the ten directions in pursuit of the appearances of objects describes how one travels far away [from one's true mind]."

Not Abiding Bodhisattva asked, "What is meant by 'one's mind moves in one thought'?"

The Buddha answered, "When one's mind moves in one thought, one's five aggregates arise, which bring fifty evils.[32]"

Not Abiding Bodhisattva asked, "Roaming in the ten directions in pursuit of the appearances of objects, far away from one's true mind, describes how a thought in one's mind brings fifty evils. How can a sentient being be enabled not to have any thoughts?"

The Buddha answered, "Have a sentient being quiet his mind and abide on the vajra ground, where no thought arises. If his mind remains peaceful and calm, not a single thought will arise."

Not Abiding Bodhisattva said, "Inconceivable! When one has no thought, one's mind remains peaceful and calm. This is a benefit of one's inherent awareness. Its benefits are motionless, constantly present, and free from existence and nonexistence, and awareness and unawareness. Free from perception, one's inherent awareness is pure, changeless, taint free, and attachment free, because its pure nature is inconceivable."

The Buddha said, "Indeed."

After hearing these words, Not Abiding Bodhisattva acquired an understanding he never before had, and spoke in verse:

The World-Honored One, the one with great enlightenment,
Has given teachings on how to have no thoughts.
One's true mind with neither birth nor thoughts,
Is constantly present, never ceasing.

Once realizing one's inherent awareness,
One uses its benefits to guide sentient beings to realize their inherent awareness,
Like that son who comes to see his gold coins
And whose gain is no gain.

When the multitude heard these words, all achieved prajñā-pāramitā, a benefit of their inherent awareness.

Chapter 5 – Entering the True Reality of Dharmas

Then the Tathāgata said, "Bodhisattvas who have entered deep into their inherent awareness and acquired its benefits can deliver sentient beings. After the true Dharma age, even when the times are not right, they should explain to them a sentient being's inherent awareness. They should give them pertinent teachings, whether the same or different, whether in accord with or against their views, to guide their emotion-driven consciousness into the sea of sarvajña [overall wisdom-knowledge],[33] and to enable those ready to be delivered not to puff their false wind of ignorance but to drink the wondrous Dharma milk in one flavor.

"Whether one engages in worldly or supra-worldly matters, one should abide nowhere to observe the five emptinesses, and should neither grasp nor discard them when one enters or exits one's observation. Why? Because dharmas have empty appearances. Their true nature is neither existence nor nonexistence, though they may appear to be existent or nonexistent. Without a fixed appearance, they abide in neither existence nor nonexistence. Their true nature cannot be fathomed by an ordinary being or a holy voice-hearer,[34] based on his understanding of existence and nonexistence. If a Bodhisattva knows that realizing the emptiness of dharmas is a benefit of one's inherent awareness, he will attain bodhi."

Then, in the midst of this multitude, a Bodhisattva called Great Strength rose from his seat and came forward. He asked the Buddha, "World-Honored One, as the Buddha says, one should neither grasp nor discard the five emptinesses when one enters or exits [one's observation of them]. What are these five emptinesses?"

The Buddha answered, "Bodhisattva, the five emptinesses are the emptiness of (1) the Three Realms of Existence, (2) the six life-paths,[35] which are projections of one's mind, (3) the appearances of dharmas, (4) the names of dharmas, and (5) the meanings of one's mind and consciousnesses [based on their names]. Bodhisattva, emptinesses such as these do not abide in emptiness and have no appearance of emptiness. How can one grasp or discard a dharma, which has no appearance? When one enters the no-grasping ground, one enters the three emptinesses."

Great Strength Bodhisattva asked, "What are the three emptinesses?"

The Buddha answered, "The three emptinesses are the emptiness of (1) the appearance of emptiness, (2) the wisdom that sees the emptiness of dharmas, and (3) whatever is seen as empty. Not abiding in their appearances, these three emptinesses are true, beyond the way of words, and inconceivable."

Great Strength Bodhisattva said, "Whatever is true implies its existence."

The Buddha said, "Existence does not abide in existence; nonexistence does not abide in nonexistence. An existent dharma does not mean that it abides in its existence; a nonexistent dharma does not mean that it abides in its nonexistence. One cannot use the existence or nonexistence of a dharma to explain its principle [i.e., emptiness]. Bodhisattva, it is inconceivable that a dharma with no name and no meaning appears to have a name and a meaning. Why? Because a dharma has no name but is given a name, and because a name has no meaning but is given a meaning."

Great Strength Bodhisattva said, "Then the name and meaning of a dharma are actually an appearance of true suchness, just as a Tathāgata is an appearance of true suchness. True suchness does not abide in true suchness and has no appearance of true suchness. Although the appearance of a dharma is not true suchness, it is no different from the appearance of a Tathāgata. Likewise a sentient being's mental appearances are a Tathāgata's appearance. Then his mind must not have differentiated objects."

The Buddha said, "Indeed. A sentient being's mind has no differentiated objects. Why? Because one's mind has always been pure and should have no taints. However, it is tainted by one's afflictions[36] and perceives the Three Realms of Existence. The Three Realms of Existence perceived by one's mind are called its differentiated objects. These objects are false because they are manifested by one's mind. If one's mind is not deluded, it will not manifest differentiated objects."

Great Strength Bodhisattva said, "If one's mind is pure, it does not give birth to objects. If one's mind is pure, one does not perceive the Three Realms of Existence."

The Buddha said, "Indeed. Bodhisattva, one's mind does not give birth to objects, and objects do not give birth to one's mind. Why? Because when one sees objects, one sees only one's mind. If one's mind does not give birth to illusions, then one does not see them. If one sees no sentient being within oneself and sees the emptiness of the three natures [good, evil, and neither] of one's karma, then one sees neither oneself nor others. Even when one makes the two entrances [into the true reality of dharmas], one's mind does not arise. After one acquires this benefit [of one's inherent awareness], the Three Realms of Existence will not arise in one's mind."

Great Strength Bodhisattva asked, "What is meant by making the two entrances while one's mind does not arise? If one's mind has never had any birth, how does it make an entrance?"

The Buddha answered, "The two entrances are (1) the entrance through the principle and (2) the entrance through action.[37]

"The entrance through the principle means having a deep belief that sentient beings are no different from their true nature. They and their true nature are neither the same nor different. Although their true nature is shrouded by their visitor-like afflictions [āgantuka kleśa], it neither comes nor goes. One should focus one's awareness and intently observe that one's Buddha nature is neither existent nor nonexistent, does not differentiate between itself and other things, and is the same in an ordinary being and a holy being. When one firmly abides on the ground of one's vajra mind, remains in quietness, and makes no differentiation, this is called the entrance through the principle.

"The entrance through action means keeping one's mind quiet, free from forming attachments, producing illusions, and seeking something, and, like the great earth, remaining immovable by winds.[38] One should discard the view that one has a mind and a self, and should rescue and deliver sentient beings. Using one's mind, which has neither birth nor appearance, one neither grasps nor discards anything.

"Bodhisattva, one's mind neither enters nor exits. Realizing that it neither enters nor exits is called entering [one's true mind], though entering is no entering. Bodhisattva, entering [the true reality of dharmas] in this way, one does not regard dharma appearances as empty or false. Why not? Because a dharma that is not nonexistent has merits. As [dharma nature is] neither one's mind nor its projections, it is naturally pure."

Great Strength Bodhisattva asked, "What is neither one's mind nor its projections, and is naturally pure?"

The Buddha answered, "[Dharma nature is] emptiness, or true suchness, which cannot be identified by one's mind, consciousnesses, or mental functions. It is free from the appearance of emptiness and the appearance of form, and is neither coherent [sambaddha] nor incoherent [asambaddha] with one's mind through or not through conditions. It is not one's mental projections or indications. It has no self-essence, makes no differentiation, and has no appearance, no name, and no meaning. Why? Because the meaning of a name is words, not true suchness. There is no dharma whose nature is not true suchness, because true suchness pervades all dharmas. Why? Because true suchness is the root principle of all dharmas, but is neither a root nor a principle, is apart from dispute, and has no appearance. Bodhisattva, this pure dharma is beyond birth and death."

Great Strength Bodhisattva said, "Inconceivable! A dharma appearance is not formed compositely or singly, and is not constrained by existence or nonexistence, neither gathers nor disperses, has neither birth nor death, and neither comes nor goes, nor abides. It is inconceivable."

The Buddha said, "Indeed. As a dharma appearance is inconceivable, so too is one's mind. Why? Because one's mind is no different from true suchness, and because it has always been true suchness. A sentient being and his Buddha nature are neither the same nor different. His nature has neither birth nor death because the nature of birth and death is nirvāṇa.

"Dharma nature and appearance are true suchness, which never moves. Although all dharmas appear to arise through conditions, they have no birth because the nature of their arising is true suchness, which never moves. Moreover, the appearances of conditions are by nature empty. As each condition also arises through conditions, in true reality there is no dependent arising of dharmas. However, one's deluded mind sees dharmas arise through conditions, not knowing that their appearances have no birth because the conditions they depend upon are nonexistent. One's mind accords with the principle of dharmas because its essence is emptiness. Like the open sky, it abides nowhere. However, an ordinary being's mind takes dharma appearances as real and differentiates them. Because the appearance of true suchness is beyond existence and nonexistence, whoever perceives the existence or nonexistence of a dharma sees only his mind and consciousnesses.

"Bodhisattva, one's mind has no self-essence, and is neither existent nor nonexistent. It has neither appearance nor no appearance, and is beyond the description of words. Why? Because true suchness, like the open sky, has no appearance, and is beyond riders of the Two Vehicles. Like the open sky, it has no inside or outside that one can measure. Only those who train through the six stages can know it."

Great Strength Bodhisattva asked, "What are the six stages of training? I pray that you will reveal them."

The Buddha answered, "They are (1) the ten levels of faith, (2) the ten levels of abiding, (3) the ten levels of action, (4) the ten levels of transference of merit, (5) the Ten Grounds, and (6) the ground of virtually perfect enlightenment.[39] Those who train in this way can know true suchness."

Great Strength Bodhisattva asked, "The benefits of one's inherent awareness neither enter nor exit. What dharma can enable one's mind to enter the true reality of dharmas?"

The Buddha answered, "The true reality of dharmas is boundless. When one realizes one's boundless mind, one enters the true reality of dharmas."

Great Strength Bodhisattva asked, "One's boundless mind has limitless wisdom. It is hindrance free, and with hindrance-free wisdom enters the true reality of dharmas. However, an ordinary being has a weak mind that jitters. What dharma should be used to enable him to develop a firm mind in order to enter the true reality of dharmas?"

The Buddha answered, "Bodhisattva, his mind jitters because it is driven by internal faculties and external objects to accumulate his afflictions, which form a sea with waves agitated by strong winds. Like a terrified great dragon, his terrified mind jitters. Bodhisattva, have him retain three things, abide in one thing, and enter a Tathāgata's dhyāna. Through dhyāna, his mind will not jitter."

Great Strength Bodhisattva asked, "What is meant by retaining three things, abiding in one thing, and entering a Tathāgata's dhyāna?"

The Buddha answered, "Retaining three things means retaining the three liberations. Abiding in one thing means abiding in the true suchness of one's mind. Entering a Tathāgata's dhyāna means using the principle to observe that one's mind is true suchness. When one enters one's mind ground in this way, one enters the true reality of dharmas."

Great Strength Bodhisattva asked, "What are the three liberations? How does one use the principle to observe [one's mind]?"

The Buddha answered, "The three liberations are (1) sky liberation, (2) vajra liberation, and (3) prajñā liberation.[40] When one uses the principle to observe, one sees that one's mind is as pure as the principle and never differentiates between approval and disapproval [acceptance and rejection]."

Great Strength Bodhisattva asked, "What is meant by making use [of the three liberations]? How does one observe [one's mind]?"

The Buddha answered, "Making use [of the three liberations] means seeing that one's mind is no different whether one is in meditation or is doing things. One's mind is no different whether one is observing one's internal actions or is taking external actions, whether one is entering or exiting meditation. Not abiding in any appearance, free from any sense of gain or loss, one's pure mind flows with the same or different appearances. This is called using the principle to observe."

"Bodhisattva, whoever observes his mind in this way does not abide in opposite appearances. Although he does not renounce family life, he does not abide in family life. Although he does not don a Dharma robe, does not observe the prātimokṣa precepts, and does not participate in the poṣadha practice, he does self-purification by letting his mind be, and acquires the holy fruit. He does not ride either of the Two Vehicles, but enters the Bodhisattva Way. Then he completes his training on all Bodhisattva grounds and attains Buddha bodhi."

Great Strength Bodhisattva said, "Inconceivable! Such a person neither renounces nor does not renounce family life. Why? Because he enters the house of nirvāṇa, dons a Tathāgata's robe, and sits on a bodhi seat. Even śramaṇas should respect him and make offerings to him."

The Buddha said, "Indeed. Why? Because entering the house of nirvāṇa means that his mind transcends the Three Realms of Existence; donning a Tathāgata's robe means that he realizes the emptiness of dharmas; sitting on a bodhi seat means that he ascends to the ground of true enlightenment. The mind of such a person is beyond riders of the Two Vehicles, not to mention śramaṇas. How can they not make offerings to him?"

Great Strength Bodhisattva said, "His wisdom ground and his [realization of the] ocean of emptiness cannot be seen by riders of the Two Vehicles."

The Buddha said, "Indeed. Riders of the Two Vehicles are attached to the flavor [their experience] of samādhi and acquire a samādhi body. As if in a coma caused by drinking alcohol, even after several kalpas, they still cannot awaken to their inherent awareness. Only after the alcohol has worn off can they begin to train and then to acquire a Buddha's body.

"By contrast, as soon as a person sheds the status of an icchantika [a nonbeliever or one who has cut off his roots of goodness], he trains through the six stages. On his training ground, in one thought from his pure mind, he absolutely understands the truth, acquires the power of vajra wisdom, reaches the spiritual level of avinivartanīya [no regress], and, with endless lovingkindness and compassion, begins to deliver sentient beings."

Great Strength Bodhisattva said, "Such a person has no need to observe the precepts or show respect for śramaṇas."

The Buddha said, "Buddhas pronounce the precepts to transform those whose evil ways and arrogance are like ocean waves. However, on that person's mind ground, the ocean of his eighth consciousness is clear, and the flow of his ninth consciousness [amala consciousness] is pure, immovable by winds that agitate ocean waves. The precepts are by nature empty, but those who observe them are attached to their appearances. However, that person's seventh and sixth consciousnesses[41] do not arise, and his accumulation of afflictions has ended in his samādhi. He is never apart from the three Buddhas, under whom he activates the bodhi mind. He penetrates a dharma's three appearances [arising, continuing, and ending] to see that they have no appearance, and reveres the Three Jewels. Displaying his majestic deportments, he never fails to show respect for śramaṇas. Bodhisattva, that kindly one abides in neither action nor no action in the world. He enters the three emptinesses and ends his attachment to the Three Realms of Existence."

Great Strength Bodhisattva said, "That kindly one activates the bodhi mind under the three Buddhas: the Tathāgata-store Buddha[42] [the dharma body of a Buddha], the Buddha fulfilled in all required merits [the reward body of a Buddha], and the Buddha in physical form [the response body of a Buddha]. He enters the three clusters of Bodhisattva precepts[43] but does not abide in their appearances. He ends his attachment to the Three Realms of Existence but does not abide on the nirvāṇa ground. He enters the place where the untamed reside and never abandons those ready to be delivered. He is inconceivable."

Then Śāriputra rose from his seat, came forward, and spoke in verse:

Sailing in the ocean of prajñā,
A Buddha does not abide in the city of nirvāṇa.
He is like a wonderful lotus flower,
Which does not grow on a plateau.

For countless kalpas,
Bodhisattvas never discard their afflictions
As they deliver the world and attain Buddhahood,
Like a lotus flower that rises from mud.

The six stages of training
Are a Bodhisattva's training ground.
The three emptinesses
Are the right path to bodhi.

I now abide in not abiding in [nirvāṇa]
In accordance with the Buddha's teachings,
And I will come to this world again and again [to deliver sentient beings].
After completing all Bodhisattva actions, I will transcend the world.

I will enable sentient beings
To do the same, no different from me,
And enable those who are ready now and those who will be ready later
To attain true enlightenment.

Then the Buddha told Śāriputra, "[Your resolve is] inconceivable! You will attain bodhi and enable innumerable sentient beings to cross the ocean of suffering from birth and death."

At that time all riders of the Mahāyāna attained bodhi, and riders of the Small Vehicle entered the ocean of the five emptinesses.

Notes

1. The name of that sūtra comprises several topics, which are addressed in the following chapters.

2. As vajra is an adamantine substance that can destroy all things, the Vajra Samādhi can penetrate the truth of all things. In fascicle 24 of text 374, the 40-fascicle Chinese version of the *Mahāparinirvāṇa Sūtra,* the Buddha uses fourteen analogies to describe the supremacy of this samādhi (T12n0374, 0509b11–c29). According to fascicle 27, Vajra Samādhi is one of the five names of the Śūraṅgama Samādhi, which are (1) Śūraṅgama Samādhi, (2) Prajñā-Pāramitā, (3) Vajra Samādhi, (4) Lion's Roar Samādhi, and (5) Buddha Nature (Ibid., 0524c18–25).

3. See Small Vehicle defined in the glossary's Two Vehicles.

4. See "true reality (bhūta-koṭi)" defined in the glossary's "true suchness."

5. See "emptiness" in the glossary.

6. One's inherent awareness is the pure awareness of one's true mind. The word *awareness* means the radiance of great wisdom that illuminates the entire dharma realm. In text 1666 (T32n1666), the earlier of the two Chinese versions of *A Treatise on Eliciting Faith in the Mahāyāna* (Mahāyāna-śraddhotpāda-śāstra), attributed to Aśvaghoṣa (馬鳴, circa 100–60) from central India, translated from Sanskrit in the Southern Liang Dynasty (502–57) by Paramārtha (真諦, 499–569) from northwestern India, Aśvaghoṣa explains one's inherent awareness (benjue 本覺), unawareness (bujue 不覺), and developed awareness (shijue 始覺). As one follows one's consciousnesses, and differentiates and pursues the appearances of dharmas, one's ignorance of one's true mind is called one's unawareness. Using the internal power of one's inherent awareness and the external power of hearing the Dharma, one's awareness developed through

training taps into the purity and radiant wisdom of one's true mind. When one eventually realizes that one's fully developed awareness is the same as one's inherent awareness, one acquires great awareness (dajue 大覺), or great enlightenment. Without using the term "developed awareness," this sūtra states that one's enlightenment is but realizing one's inherent awareness.

7. The true Dharma will not be gone right after the Buddha's passing. It will gradually perish through the true Dharma age, the Dharma-likeness age, and the Dharma-ending age. See "three ages of the Dharma" and "five turbidities" in the glossary.

8. According to text 842, the Chinese version of the *Mahāvaipulya Sūtra of Perfect Enlightenment,* "without a beginning, all sentient beings . . . mistake the four domains [earth, water, fire, and wind] for appearances of their bodies, and mistake the images of the six sense objects for appearances of their minds" (T17n0842, b24–25). An English translation of this sūtra appears in *Transcending the World* (Rulu 2015, 233–66).

9. According to text 1730, a commentary on this sūtra, written by the Korean scholar Yuanxiao (元曉, 617–86), or Wŏnhyo, the wrong view that one has a self is a fixation on the existence of an imaginary self, and the wrong view that one has a mind is a fixation on the existence of a dharma [e.g., one's mind] (T34n1730, 0966b14–15).

10. According to text 669, the Chinese version of the *Sūtra of the Unsurpassed Reliance,* fascicle 1, chapter 3, "a Tathāgata's dharma body . . . has the great true-self pāramitā for two reasons: (1) He stays far away from the fixation of those on non-Buddhist paths [tīrthika] because He has transcended their fantasy that one has a self, and (2) He stays far away from the fixation of riders of the Two Vehicles because He has transcended their limited understanding that one has no self" (T16n0669, 0472b25–28).

11. The birth or death of one's mind can be understood as the perceptible arising and expiring of thoughts. Although a thought appears to arise and expire through causes and conditions, it has neither birth nor death. So too does one's mind.

12. See "those who are still learning (śaikṣa)" and "those who have nothing more to learn (aśaikṣa)" defined in the glossary's "voice-hearer fruits." Here, the answer given by the Buddha is a Mahāyāna teaching on one's mind, unrelated to the ranks of voice-hearers.

13. See "eight consciousnesses" defined in the glossary's "eighteen spheres."

14. According to text 251, one of the seven Chinese versions of the *Heart Sūtra,* "as Avalokiteśvara Bodhisattva went deep into prajñā-pāramitā, he saw in his illumination the emptiness of the five aggregates, the realization of which delivers one from all suffering and tribulations" (T08n0251, 0848c7–8). Therefore, the purity of one's five aggregates means their emptiness. An English translation of text 251 appears in *Teachings of the Buddha* (Rulu 2012a, 121).

15. Here, "dharma" means anything perceived or conceived by one's thinking mind.

16. See "five desires" in the glossary.

17. See "eighteen emptinesses" in the glossary.

18. See "ten Bodhisattva grounds" in the glossary's "stages of the Bodhisattva Way." Details of the ten Bodhisattva grounds are given in chapter

26 of the *Mahāvaipulya Sūtra of Buddha Adornment* (Buddhāvataṁsaka-mahāvaipulya-sūtra). An English translation of this chapter appears in *The Bodhisattva Way* (Rulu 2013, 111–244).

19. That dharmas have no birth is explained in text 1564 (in 4 fascicles), the Chinese version of Ācārya Nāgārjuna's *Fundamental Verses on the Middle Way* (Mūla-madhyamaka-kārikā), annotated by Piṅgalanetra (青目, 4th century) and translated from Sanskrit by Kumārajīva (鳩摩羅什, 344–413). In fascicle 1, the four negations of the birth of dharmas are stated in this way: "Dharmas are not born from themselves, from other things, from themselves and other things, or from no cause. So we know that they have no birth" (T30n1564, 0002b6–7).

20. In text 1564, fascicle 1, Nāgārjuna establishes the emptiness of dharmas on the Middle Way, which negates four pairs of opposite perceptions of dharmas. The eight negations are "neither birth nor death, neither perpetual nor ceasing, neither the same nor different, and neither coming nor going" (Ibid., 0001b14–16). The emptiness of dharmas lies in the first pair of negations, neither birth nor death, with the other three pairs of negations as its corollaries. Further simplified, the principal thesis of the Middle Way is that dharmas have no birth because without birth there cannot be death. In fascicle 4, Nāgārjuna concludes, "I say that dharmas born through causes and conditions are emptiness, which is a false name and is the meaning of the Middle Way" (Ibid., 0033b11–13).

21. The four falsities refer to the four wrong views of true suchness: (1) existent, (2) nonexistent, (3) both existent and nonexistent, and (4) neither existent nor nonexistent. The first is a falsity that the dharma realm can increase; the second is a falsity that the dharma realm can decrease; the third is a contradictory falsity; the fourth is a ludicrous falsity.

22. The word *prajñā* is omitted in the corresponding passages in this sūtra in the Yuan and Ming editions of the Chinese Buddhist Canon.

23. According to *A Treatise on Eliciting Faith in the Mahāyāna,* true suchness has two meanings, empty and not empty. It is empty because it never responds to the thoughts and differentiations of one's false mind, and has neither appearance nor no appearance, neither one appearance nor various appearances. It is not empty because one's true mind is eternal and changeless, and encompasses pure dharmas (T32n1666, 0576a24–b7). The pure dharmas encompassed in one's true mind correspond to the benefits of one's inherent awareness addressed in this sūtra, because in chapter 8 the Buddha says that one's inherent awareness has a mass of profound virtues.

24. The three kinds of precepts are (1) precepts for laity, such as the eight precepts; (2) precepts for monastics, such as the ten precepts and the complete monastic precepts; (3) precepts common to both laity and monastics, such as the five precepts. See "eight precepts," "ten precepts," and "five precepts" in the glossary.

25. As one's meditation deepens, one's mind moves from the first dhyāna, to the second, third, and fourth. When one exits meditation, one's mind moves in reverse order.

26. To describe the inconceivable, all descriptions are no description, and no description is a description.

27. See "three fortune fields" in the glossary.

28. Ālaya consciousness (ālaya-vijñāna), one's eighth consciousness, stores the pure, impure, and neutral seeds of one's experience without a beginning. When one attains Buddhahood, only pure seeds remain, which will neither change nor manifest karmic rebirth. Hence the name ālaya (storehouse) is changed to amala (stainless). In chapter 4, the Buddha says that amala consciousness (amala-vijñāna) has never left one. Because it is revealed when one attains perfect enlightenment, in this sūtra amala consciousness is called the ninth consciousness.

29. The mirror-like wisdom-knowledge is likened to the lucid aquamarine ground. The equality wisdom-knowledge is likened to the great earth. The discernment wisdom-knowledge is likened to the wisdom sunlight. The accomplishment wisdom-knowledge is likened to a great Dharma rain. See "four kinds of wisdom-knowledge" defined in the glossary's "five kinds of wisdom-knowledge." For details, see text 680 (T16n0680), the Chinese version of the *Sūtra of the Buddha Ground,* whose English translation appears in *Transcending the World* (Rulu 2015, 153–64).

30. See "five desires" in the glossary.

31. A similar story of a wandering confused son is told in fascicle 4 of text 262 (T09n0262), a Chinese version of the *Lotus Sūtra,* and in fascicle 2 of text 270 (T09n0270), the Chinese version of the *Sūtra of the Great Dharma Drum* (Mahābheri-haraka-parivarta). An English translation of text 270 in 2 fascicles appears in *Teachings of the Buddha* (Rulu 2012a, 154–83).

32. According to text 945 (T19n0945), the Chinese version of the *Śūraṅgama Sūtra,* fascicles 9 and 10, each of the five aggregates is subjected to ten māra works, totaling fifty.

33. See "sarvajña" defined in the glossary's "three kinds of wisdom-knowledge."

34. A holy voice-hearer is a voice-hearer who has become a holy being. For the ranks of holy voice-hearers, see the glossary's "voice-hearer fruits."

35. See good and evil life-paths defined in the glossary's "life-journey."

36. In text 353, the earlier of the two Chinese versions of the *Vaipulya Sūtra of Śrīmālā's Lion's Roar,* the Buddha says, "There are two things that are hard to know: (1) one's inherent pure mind and (2) its being tainted by afflictions" (T12n0353, 0222c4–5).

37. Bodhidharma (菩提達摩, ?–535) is the first patriarch of the Chán School of China. Text 1217 (X63n1217) in the Extension of the Chinese Canon (Shinsan Zokuzōkyō) is his teaching on attaining bodhi through two entrances and four actions, as presented by his student Tanlin (曇林, ?–585). The description of the first entrance, the entrance through the principle, is similar to that in this sūtra, but the description of the second entrance, the entrance through action, specifies four actions, which are not in this sūtra. Most followers of the Chán School of China believe that the two entrances presented in this sūtra are the source of Bodhidharma's "two entrances and four actions."

38. See "eight winds" in the glossary. One's perception of these eight winds arises from one's ignorance.

39. See these trainings defined in the glossary's "stages of the Bodhisattva Way." For details, see text 1485 (T24n1485), the Chinese version of the *Sūtra of the Garland of a Bodhisattva's Primary Karmas,* whose English translation appears in *The Bodhisattva Way* (Rulu 2013, 33–88).

40. Sky liberation means one's realization of the dharma body, which is like the open sky. Vajra liberation means one's realization that the dharma body is adamantine like vajra and penetrates dharma appearances. Prajñā liberation means one's realization of the wisdom that all dharmas are empty and have no appearance and no action. These three liberations are one liberation. For comparison, see Three Liberation Doors in the glossary.

41. According to the Consciousness-Only School, one's seventh consciousness (manas-vijñāna) has an inborn sense of self, characterized by four defilements: (1) self-delusion, (2) self-love, (3) self-view, and (4) self-arrogance. See "seventh consciousness" defined in the glossary's "eighteen spheres."

42. Tathāgata store (tathāgata-garbha) means a Tathāgata in storage, or the dharma body fettered by one's afflictions. Therefore, everyone has the Tathāgata-store Buddha within.

43. The "three clusters of Bodhisattva precepts" are (1) restraining precepts, (2) precepts for doing good dharmas, and (3) precepts for benefiting sentient beings. See "Bodhisattva precepts" in the glossary.

Fascicle 2 (of 2)

Chapter 6 – Dharma Nature Is Emptiness

Then Śāriputra said to the Buddha, "World-Honored One, trainings on the Bodhisattva Way have neither names nor appearances. Then the three clusters of Bodhisattva precepts have no descriptions. How can one accept them and explain them to sentient beings? I pray that the Buddha, out of lovingkindness and compassion, will explain to me."

The Buddha said, "Good man, hearken. I will explain to you. Good man, good and evil dharmas are manifested by one's mind. All one's perceptions of objects are differentiations made by one's consciousnesses and words. If one sets one's mind in one place, then one's perceptions of various objects will not arise. Why? Because, good man, as one's inherent awareness never arises, the three clusters of Bodhisattva precepts have no use. [As one's mind] abides in true suchness [bhūta-tathātā], the doors of the six life-paths shut, and the four conditions accord with true suchness and encompass the three clusters of Bodhisattva precepts."

Śāriputra asked, "What is meant by 'the four conditions accord with true suchness and encompass the three clusters of Bodhisattva precepts'?"

The Buddha answered, "The four conditions are as follows: (1) the power of choosing to end one's evil actions is the condition for observing the restraining precepts; (2) the power of the benefits of one's inherent awareness gathered by one's pure faculties is the condition for observing the precepts for doing good dharmas; (3) the power of one's innate wisdom and great compassion is the condition for observing the precepts for benefiting sentient beings; (4) the power of wisdom arising from one's inherent awareness is the condition that accords with true suchness. These are the four conditions.[1]

"Bodhisattva, the power of these four conditions does not abide in anything's appearances but has its usefulness. However, one cannot acquire it if one fails to set one's mind in one place. Good man, one's inherent awareness is the one thing that encompasses the six stages of training and is Buddha bodhi, which is an ocean of wisdom."

Śāriputra said, "[This power] does not abide in anything's appearances but has its usefulness [because one's inherent awareness is] absolute emptiness and has the four virtues: eternity, bliss, a true self, and purity.[2] It is free from the two wrong views (1) that a person has a self and (2) that a dharma has a self. It is the great nirvāṇa but has no attachment to it. According to one's direct observation, one's inherent awareness must encompass the Thirty-seven Elements of Bodhi."

The Buddha said, "Indeed. It encompasses the Thirty-seven Elements of Bodhi: (a) Four Abidings of Mindfulness, (b) Four Right Endeavors, (c) Four Ways to Attain Samādhi, (d) Five Roots, (e) Five Powers, (f) Seven Bodhi Factors, and (g) Eightfold Right Path.[3] As these thirty-seven elements with different names have only one meaning, they are neither the same nor different. Their names and numbers are mere words, which cannot capture their true meaning. This one meaning that cannot be captured has no words and no appearances because it is emptiness, which means true suchness. The principle of true suchness encompasses all dharmas. Good man, whoever abides in this principle will cross the ocean of the three kinds of suffering.[4]"

Śāriputra asked, "All dharmas are described by words, whose appearances are not the true meaning. If the true meaning of a dharma is indescribable by words, how does the Tathāgata expound the Dharma?"

The Buddha answered, "I expound the Dharma because you sentient beings use speech in your lives. I expound the Dharma to express what is ineffable. What I say is the true meaning, not mere words. What sentient beings say is mere words, not the true meaning. Speech that does not reveal the true meaning is void, and void words have no meaning. Speech devoid of meaning is false speech. Speech in accord with the meaning of true suchness is apart from opposite appearances, such as empty and not empty, or real and unreal, and does not abide in the middle. Not abiding in a dharma's three appearances[5] [arising, continuing, and ending], it abides nowhere. Speech in accord with the meaning of true suchness reveals that true suchness abides in neither existence nor nonexistence. Such is a description of true suchness."

Śāriputra asked, "To reach a Tathāgata's state and attain a Tathāgata's reality, starting with an icchantika's mind, through what steps should all sentient beings develop?"

The Buddha answered, "For an icchantika's mind to reach a Tathāgata's state and attain a Tathāgata's reality, he should develop through five steps. The first step is belief. Belief means that one should believe that the seed of true suchness in one's body is shrouded by one's false mind. By discarding one's false mind, one's pure mind reveals its purity, and one knows that one's perceptions of objects are differentiations made by one's consciousnesses and words. The second step is pondering. Pondering means that one should observe that one's perceptions of objects are displays of differentiations made by one's consciousnesses and words, and that one's perceptions are not one's root consciousness [ālaya consciousness], which is neither a mental object nor its meaning, neither a grasper nor an object grasped. The third step is training. Training means that one can activate the bodhi mind and let it constantly arise. As the arising of the bodhi mind and one's training are concurrent, one should be guided by wisdom to eliminate hindrances and difficulties and free oneself from the fetters of one's mental coverings.[6] The fourth step is completion of training. Completion of training means that one leaves all training grounds because one's mind is free from accepting and rejecting, one's faculties are extremely pure and keen, and one's mind in its true nature, in great nirvāṇa, and in absolute emptiness, is motionless. The fifth step is relinquishment. Relinquishment means that one does not abide in emptiness because one's true wisdom is revealed. One's great compassion is an appearance of true suchness but does not abide in true suchness. Although one does not attain anuttara-samyak-saṁbodhi, one's mind is boundless, has no place, and has reached a Tathāgata's state. Good man, these five steps are the benefits of one's inherent awareness. When one transforms sentient beings, one should start from their own place [inherent awareness]."

Śāriputra asked, "What is meant by starting from their own place?"

The Buddha answered, "[One's inherent awareness] has no origin and no place. Realizing that it is emptiness, one enters the true reality of dharmas, activates the bodhi mind, and completes the holy path. Why? Because, good man, holding empty space in one's fist is neither attainment nor no attainment."

Śāriputra said, "As the World-Honored One says, before one does anything, one should use the benefits of one's inherent awareness to see that one's thoughts are in nirvāṇa, which is true suchness. It encompasses all virtues and all dharmas in a perfect fusion. It is inconceivable. Know that one's inherent awareness is mahā-prajñā-pāramitā [the great wisdom pāramitā], which is the great spiritual mantra, the great illumination mantra, the unsurpassed mantra, and the unequaled mantra.[7]"

The Buddha said, "Indeed, indeed. True suchness is the emptiness of dharma nature [dharmatā]. One's realization of this emptiness is the wisdom fire that burns away one's afflictions. Then one will realize that all dharmas are equal [in their emptiness]. And one will complete the three grounds of virtually perfect enlightenment[8] and acquire the three bodies of perfect enlightenment [three bodies of a Buddha], because one has entered one's ninth consciousness [amala consciousness], which is bright and pure, free from one's making mental projections.

"Good man, this dharma [one's inherent awareness] is neither a cause nor a condition because its wisdom naturally arises. It is neither moving nor motionless because its nature is emptiness. It is neither existent nor nonexistent because the appearance of emptiness is empty. Good man, when you transform sentient beings, have them study this meaning. Whoever fathoms this meaning sees a Tathāgata."

Śāriputra said, "To study this meaning revealed by the Tathāgata, one should not abide in the flows [of afflictions, wrong views, and ignorance],[9] but should leave the four dhyānas and transcend Akaniṣṭha Heaven, the top heaven in the form realm."

The Buddha said, "Indeed. Why? Because all dharmas, including the four dhyānas, are described by names and numbers. To see a Tathāgata is to realize that one's Tathāgata mind is hindrance free and constantly in nirvāṇa, neither entering nor exiting anything, because [one's mind] inside and [objects perceived as] outside are equal [in their emptiness].

"Good man, the four dhyānas are meditations on the appearance of emptiness, but observing true suchness is not like them. Why? Because if one uses true suchness to observe true suchness, one can find neither an observer nor an object observed, for the appearance of true suchness is in nirvāṇa. Nirvāṇa means true suchness.

"Meditations on the appearance of emptiness imply motion, which is not dhyāna. Why? Because the nature of dhyāna is no motion. It neither taints nor is tainted, is neither a mental object nor a mental projection, and is apart from making differentiations, because it is a benefit of one's inherent awareness. Good man, doing meditation according to this observation is called dhyāna."

Śāriputra asked, "Inconceivable! The Tathāgata always uses the meaning of true suchness to transform sentient beings, which contains many words and broad meanings. While those with a keen capacity can train accordingly, those with a dull capacity find it hard to comprehend. What skillful means can be used to enable them to enter this truth?"

The Buddha answered, "Have those with a dull capacity accept and uphold a four-line stanza, and they will enter the truth. The entire Buddha Dharma is encompassed in this stanza."

Śāriputra asked, "What is this four-line stanza? I pray that you will speak it."

Then the World-Honored One spoke in verse:

The statement that dharmas are born through causes and conditions
Means that they are in nirvāṇa and have no birth.
Ending [one's perception of] a dharma's birth and death
Means [that one's realization of its true reality] arises and never ends.

When the multitude heard this stanza, all greatly rejoiced, ended [their perception of] a dharma's birth and death, and entered the ocean of wisdom, realizing that dharma nature is emptiness.

Chapter 7 – The Tathāgata Store

Then Brahma Way the Elder rose from [his meditation on] the true reality of dharmas and asked the Buddha, "World-Honored One, a dharma's birth [through conditions] is no birth; a dharma's death [through conditions] is no death. Mastering the meaning of true suchness is attaining Buddha bodhi, and bodhi is by nature free from differentiation. One's differentiation-free wisdom-knowledge[10] can differentiate countless appearances and end one's making differentiations. Dharma appearances and the meaning of true suchness are inconceivable, and whatever is inconceivable is free from differentiation. World-Honored One, the entire Dharma encompasses countless names and appearances. However, they have only one true meaning and abide in only one nature. What does this mean?"

The Buddha answered, "Inconceivable! Elder, I expound the Dharma to the confused and use skillful means to guide them. All dharma appearances have only one true meaning. Why? Because it is like a city with four gates, each providing an entrance to the city. Multitudes can enter the city through any gate at will. Likewise various Dharma flavors come down to only one flavor."

Brahma Way said, "If the Dharma is like this, I can abide in one Dharma flavor to taste all flavors."

The Buddha said, "Indeed, indeed. Why? Because the true meaning in one flavor is like a vast ocean, into which all streams flow. Elder, all Dharma flavors are like streams. Although all streams have different names, their waters are no different. If one abides in the vast ocean, one accesses all streams. Likewise if one abides in one Dharma flavor, one tastes all flavors."

Brahma Way asked, "If all Dharmas have one flavor, why do riders of the Three Vehicles have different wisdoms?"

The Buddha answered, "Elder, as an analogy, a creek, a stream, a river, and an ocean[11] have different sizes, depths, and names. Water in a creek is called creek water; water in a stream is called stream water; water in a river is called river water. When these waters are in the ocean, they all are called ocean water.

Likewise all teachings arise from true suchness and are called the path to Buddhahood. Elder, whoever walks this path should understand three actions."

Brahma Way asked, "What are the three actions?"

The Buddha answered, "The three actions are actions that (1) follow things, (2) follow one's consciousnesses, and (3) accord with true suchness. These three actions encompass all Dharma Doors [dharma-paryāya] without exception. Whoever takes these actions does not fabricate the appearance of emptiness but enters his Tathāgata store, though entering is no entering."

Brahma Way asked, "Inconceivable! Entering one's Tathāgata store is like a seedling coming to bear fruit without entering any place. When one uses the power of the benefits of one's inherent awareness to realize one's inherent awareness, how much wisdom does one acquire?"

The Buddha answered, "One acquires limitless wisdom. In brief, one acquires four wisdoms: (1) absolute wisdom, which accords with true suchness; (2) applied wisdom, which provides skillful means to eliminate faults; (3) nirvāṇa wisdom, which halts one's lightning-speed consciousnesses; (4) ultimate wisdom, which reveals the true reality of dharmas when one completes the path to Buddhahood. Elder, past Buddhas have already expounded the use of these wisdoms. They are a great bridge and a great ferry. Whoever transforms sentient beings should use these wisdoms.

"Elder, to put these four great wisdoms to great use, one must do three great things: (1) attain the three samādhis and abide in neither [one's mind] inside nor [objects perceived as] outside; (2) use one's body-mind structure to choose to follow the principle and end one's afflictions; (3) use one's wisdom and samādhi that accord with true suchness, to benefit oneself and others with great compassion. One must do these three things to attain bodhi. Without doing them, one's mind cannot flow into the ocean of those four wisdoms, but will allow māras to gain the upper hand. Elder, until each of you in this multitude attains Buddhahood, each of you should train to do these three things without lapsing even temporarily."

Brahma Way asked, "What are the three samādhis?"

The Buddha answered, "The three samādhis are (1) emptiness samādhi, (2) no-appearance samādhi, and (3) no-action samādhi. These are the three samādhis.[12]"

Brahma Way asked, "[In one's body-mind structure], what are the great domains, the three sets of components, and the foundation?"

The Buddha answered, "The great domains [which make up one's body] are earth, water, fire, and wind. The three sets of components are one's five aggregates, twelve fields, and eighteen spheres. The foundation is one's root consciousness [ālaya consciousness]. These are a sentient being's body-mind structure."

Brahma Way said, "Inconceivable! As one does these three things to put the four wisdoms to great use, one benefits oneself and others, enters the Bodhisattva Way, transcends the Three Realms of Existence, and does not abide in nirvāṇa. However, one may perceive the births and deaths of dharma appearances because of one's differentiation. If one stays away from making differentiation, [one will realize that] dharmas have neither birth nor death."

Then, to restate this meaning, the Buddha spoke in verse:

Dharmas are born from differentiation
And die from differentiation.
If one ends making differentiations,
[One will realize that] dharmas have neither birth nor death.

When Brahma Way heard this stanza, he found great joy in his heart and affirmed its meaning in verse:

Dharmas have always been in nirvāṇa,
Which has no birth.
Dharmas perceived as undergoing birth and death
Do not reveal the meaning of no birth.

Birth and death are not the same as nirvāṇa
If one holds the view of a dharma's perpetuity or cessation.
Nirvāṇa is apart from these two opposites
And does not abide in the middle.

If someone holds that dharmas are existent,
[He does not know that] their appearances are false,
Like a wheel of swirling hair
Or water in a mirage.

If someone holds that dharmas are nonexistent
Like the open sky,
He is like a blind man who claims that there is no sun,
A claim that is like the hair of a turtle.

I now have heard the Buddha's words
And learned that dharmas are apart from opposite views,
Do not abide in the middle,
But abide nowhere.

As the Tathāgata's teachings
Abide nowhere,
So I abide nowhere
To make obeisance to the Tathāgata.

I make obeisance to the appearance of the Tathāgata,
Whose immovable wisdom equals the sky.
With no attachment and no place,
I make obeisance to His [dharma] body, which abides nowhere.

Wherever I am,
I constantly see Tathāgatas.
I pray that Tathāgatas
Will expound to me what is eternal.

Then the Tathāgata said, "Good men, all of you hearken. I will expound to you what is eternal. Good men, what is eternal cannot be described by words. It is not perpetuity [as the opposite of cessation] because it is apart from the view of perpetuity or cessation. It has no time frames [past, present, and future], and is not a truth, not a liberation, not a mental object, not nonexistence, and not impermanence. One clearly sees that one's root consciousness [ālaya consciousness] is eternal because it is constantly in nirvāṇa, which is beyond description.

"Good men, one's mind that knows that dharmas are in nirvāṇa is not the mind in nirvāṇa, because the mind constantly in nirvāṇa is one's true awareness [which is free from knowing and not knowing an object]. The mind in one's name and form [mind and body][13] is one's deluded mind, which differentiates dharmas by means of words. Nothing else is done by one's name and form. Knowing that they are like this, one should not follow words. If one's mind accords with the true reality of dharmas and does not differentiate between self and no self because one knows that "self" is but a false name, one attains nirvāṇa. Attaining nirvāṇa is attaining anuttara-samyak-saṁbodhi."

When Brahma Way heard these words, he spoke in verse:

Name, appearance, and differentiation
Are the three dharmas [embraced by ordinary beings].
True wisdom-knowledge [samyag-jñāna] and true suchness,
Together with the preceding three, constitute the five dharmas.[14]

I now know that these dharmas
Are connected with [the opposite views:] perpetuity and cessation.
Entering the path of birth and death
Is entering [the cycle of] impermanence.
The emptiness of dharmas expounded by the Tathāgata
Is far apart from perpetuity and cessation.

Causes and conditions have no birth,
And whatever has no birth has no death.
Taking causes and condition as truly existent
Is like trying to pluck a flower in the sky
Or looking for a barren woman's child,
Because neither object can be grasped.

One should not take a dharma's birth and death as real,
Because they arise from causes and conditions.
One should stay away from the four domains and one's three sets of components,
Because one relies on true suchness to enter the true reality of dharmas.

While true suchness
Is always changeless and hindrance free,
All myriad dharmas
Are manifested by one's consciousness.

Without one's consciousness, dharmas are nonexistent.
Therefore, emptiness is their true reality.
By discarding the view that dharmas have birth and death,
One can abide in nirvāṇa.

However, driven by great compassion,
One does not abide in the quietness of nirvāṇa.
Turning away from perceiving a grasper and an object grasped,
One enters one's Tathāgata store.

When the multitude heard this meaning, all began to live a righteous life and acquired a Tathāgata's wisdom in the ocean of the Tathāgata store.

Chapter 8 – Total Retention of Teachings

Then, in the midst of the multitude, Earth Store [Kṣitigarbha] Bodhisattva rose from his seat and came before the Buddha. Kneeling with joined palms, he said to the Buddha, "World-Honored One, I observe that all in this multitude have unresolved doubts and that the Tathāgata wants to resolve their doubts. I would like to ask questions according to their doubts and pray that the Buddha, out of lovingkindness and compassion, will give me permission."

The Buddha said, "Bodhisattva-Mahāsattva, you can rescue and deliver sentient beings in this way because your great compassion is inconceivable. You should ask questions widely. I will explain to you."

Earth Store Bodhisattva asked, "Why are dharmas not born from conditions?"

Then the Tathāgata answered in verse:

If dharmas were born from conditions,
Without conditions, there would be no dharmas.
As dharma nature is emptiness,
How can any condition give birth to a dharma?[15]

Earth Store Bodhisattva asked, "If dharmas have no birth, why is it said that they are born from one's mind?"

Then the World-Honored One answered in verse:

To say that dharmas are born from one's mind
Is to imply subject [one's mind] and object [dharmas],
Like a drunkard's eye seeing a flower in the sky,
Though dharmas [in true reality] have no birth.

Earth Store Bodhisattva said, "If a dharma is like this, it is not relative [to other dharmas]. A dharma that is not relative must be formed by itself."

The World-Honored One spoke in verse:

A dharma is neither existent nor nonexistent,
Nor does it have a self versus others.
It has neither a beginning nor an end,
Neither formation nor destruction.

Earth Store Bodhisattva said, "As all dharma appearances are in nirvāṇa, so too are nirvāṇa and the appearance of emptiness. As nirvāṇa and emptiness cannot be grasped, they accord with true suchness."

The Buddha agreed, "As nirvāṇa and emptiness cannot be grasped, they are true suchness."

Earth Store Bodhisattva said, "Inconceivable! The appearance of true suchness is neither together with nor apart from [dharmas perceived as undergoing birth and death]. It cannot be grasped by means of one's mind or actions. Likewise one's mind cannot be grasped, because it is empty, quiet, and in nirvāṇa."

Then the World-Honored One spoke in verse:

Although all dharmas are empty and quiet,
They are quiet but not empty [because they vividly appear in one's perception].
While one's mind is not empty,
It is not existent.[16]

Earth Store Bodhisattva said, "One's mind is not encompassed in the three truths [emptiness, form, and one's mind].[17] When one realizes that form is emptiness, one's mind is in nirvāṇa. As dharmas have always been in nirvāṇa, so too one's mind has always been in nirvāṇa."

Then the World-Honored One spoke in verse:

Dharmas have no self-essence
And are born from one's differentiation.
One cannot use differentiation
To realize their true nature.

Earth Store Bodhisattva asked, "If dharmas have neither birth nor death, why are they not the same?"

Then the World-Honored One answered in verse:

As dharmas abide nowhere,
They are nonexistent because their appearances and numbers are empty.
Their names and descriptions
Are established by using subject and object.

Earth Store Bodhisattva asked, "All dharma appearances abide on neither of the two opposite shores [such as subject and object, existence and nonexistence, saṁsāra and nirvāṇa], nor in the stream between them. Likewise one's consciousness does not abide in any of these three places. Then why are objects of perception born from one's consciousness? If they are born from one's consciousness, one's consciousness is also born from its perceived objects. Why can one's consciousness, which has no birth, have subject and object?"

Then the World-Honored One answered in verse:

Birth and what is born
Are one's perception and perceived objects,
And neither has self-essence.
However, one takes an illusory flower in the sky as real.

Before one's consciousness arises
There is no object of perception.
Before an object is perceived,
One's consciousness is nonexistent.

One's consciousness and its objects of perception are nonexistent,
And nonexistence is not a state that can be grasped.
As one's consciousness, which has no birth, is nonexistent,
How can it give birth to objects of perception?

Earth Store Bodhisattva said, "Such are dharma appearances. [One's consciousness] inside and [objects perceived as] outside are both empty because they have always been in nirvāṇa. The true reality of dharmas revealed by the Tathāgata is absolute emptiness, which never collects [things].[18]"

The Buddha said, "Indeed. The true reality of dharmas has no form, abides nowhere, is neither a collector nor things collected, and is neither the four domains nor one's five aggregates, twelve fields, or eighteen spheres. It is encompassed in one's inherent awareness, which has a mass of profound virtues."

Earth Store Bodhisattva said, "Inconceivable! One acquires its mass of inconceivable virtues when one's seventh and sixth consciousnesses halt and one's eighth and first five consciousnesses become quiet,[19] because one's ninth consciousness [amala consciousness] is revealed, which is neither empty nor not empty. As the World-Honored One says, dharmas and their meanings are empty. As one enters the liberation door of emptiness without taking action, one never stops doing karmas [to deliver sentient beings]. Then one realizes that one has no self and its belongings, and discards one's perception of subject and object, and the view that one has an embodied self. When one's faculties inside and objects perceived as outside become quiet, one is freed from their fetters and achieves the no-wish liberation.[20] As one makes observations in accordance with the principle, one's wisdom and samādhi accord with true suchness. As the World-Honored One often says, realizing that dharmas are empty is good medicine [for eliminating one's afflictions]."

The Buddha said, "Indeed. Why? Because dharma nature is emptiness. As emptiness has no birth, so too one's mind has no birth. As emptiness has no death, so too one's mind has no death. As emptiness abides nowhere, so too one's mind abides nowhere. As emptiness is free from causes and conditions, so too one's mind is free from causes and conditions. As emptiness neither enters nor exits, is apart from gain and loss, and has no five aggregates, twelve fields, or eighteen spheres, so too one's mind has no attachment to anything. Bodhisattva, I expound the emptiness [of dharmas] to shatter [one's perception of their] existence."

Earth Store Bodhisattva said, "World-Honored One, one should know that existence is unreal, like water in a mirage, and that true reality is existent, like the nature of fire hidden in wood. Whoever can make this observation is a wise person."

The Buddha said, "Indeed. Why? Because he makes observations in accord with true suchness. As he observes his mind in nirvāṇa, he sees that appearance and no appearance are equally empty. Because he cultivates [his understanding of] emptiness, he never fails to see a Buddha. Because he sees a Buddha, he rides the Mahāyāna to go against the flow of afflictions in the Three Realms of Existence. Walking the path of the three liberations, he realizes that dharmas are in unity because they have no self-essence. Because they have no self-essence, they are empty. Because they are empty, they have no appearance. Because they have no appearance, one takes no action [to grasp them]. Because one takes no action, one has no wish [to be reborn in the Three Realms of existence]. Because one has no wish, one knows one's karmas and purifies one's mind. Because one's mind is pure, one sees a Buddha. Because one sees a Buddha, one will be reborn in a Pure Land. Bodhisattva, one should diligently train through the Three Liberation Doors to master the profound Dharma. When one's wisdom and samādhi are perfected, one transcends the Three Realms of Existence."

Earth Store Bodhisattva asked, "As the Tathāgata says, birth and death mean impermanence. When one ends [one's perception of a dharma's] birth and death, one realizes the eternality of nirvāṇa, which never ends and is apart from motion and no motion in the Three Realms of Existence. Therefore, one should avoid dharmas subject to causes and conditions, like avoiding a fire pit. World-Honored One, because of what things should one reprove oneself in order to enter the one door [to Buddhahood]?"

The Buddha answered, "Bodhisattva, one should reprove one's mind because of three grave things and should follow three great truths to train to attain bodhi."

Earth Store Bodhisattva asked, "Because of what three grave things should one reprove one's mind? What three great truths should one follow in order to train to attain bodhi?"

The Buddha answered, "The three grave things are (1) cause [such as one's ignorance of the truth and one's karmas], (2) effect [such as one's karmic requitals], and (3) one's consciousness [which perceives subject and object]. These three things have always been empty and are not one's true self. Why should one be attached to them? One should observe these three things and know that they are one's fetters as one drifts in the ocean of suffering. Because of these things, one should constantly reprove one's mind.

"The three great truths are as follows: (1) the bodhi path leads to the truth of the equality, not inequality, of dharmas; (2) great enlightenment is attained through true wisdom-knowledge, not false wisdom-knowledge; (3) equal training in wisdom and samādhi, not other trainings, brings one bodhi. If one follows these three truths to train to attain Buddha bodhi, one will never fail to attain true enlightenment. One will acquire a Buddha's wisdom-knowledge, exude great compassion, benefit oneself and others, and attain Buddha bodhi."

Earth Store Bodhisattva said, "World-Honored One, the truth that dharmas are equal means that they are free from causes and conditions. Without conditions, causes will not arise. How can one use motionless dharmas to enter a Tathāgata's state?"

Then, to explain this meaning, the Tathāgata spoke in verse:

As dharmas appear,
Their nature is emptiness, free from motion [and no motion].
Then a dharma at any given time
Does not arise.

A dharma has no time frames [past, present, and future]
And does not arise at such various times.
It neither moves nor does not move,
And is in nirvāṇa, because its nature is emptiness.

However, because dharma nature is emptiness,
A dharma appears at any given time.
Apart from its appearance, it abides in nirvāṇa.
Abiding in nirvāṇa, it does not follow conditions.

Although dharmas depend on conditions to appear,
They are empty and not born from conditions.
Causes and conditions have neither birth nor death
Because the nature of birth and death is emptiness.

A condition perceived as a subject or an object
Also arises from conditions.[21]
[In true reality] a dharma does not arise from conditions,
Because conditions do not arise.

Dharmas born from causes and conditions
Are causes and conditions [for other dharmas].
They have the appearances of birth and death,
But their nature has neither birth nor death.

In true reality
Dharmas neither appear nor disappear,
Although they appear and disappear
At any given time.

Their extremely pure root [true suchness]
Never depends on the power of conditions.
When one eventually attains bodhi,
One's enlightenment is but realizing one's inherent awareness.

When Earth Store Bodhisattva heard the Buddha's words, he found great joy in his heart and knew that all in the multitude no longer had any doubts in their minds. Then he spoke in verse:

Knowing that all in this multitude had doubts in their minds,
I eagerly asked questions.
With great lovingkindness,
The Tathāgata explained in detail without reservation.

The two groups [monastics and laity][22]
Have understood His teachings.
I will use my understanding
To transform all sentient beings.

As the Tathāgata, out of great compassion,
Never abandons his original vows,
I should regard sentient beings as an only son
And deliver them as I abide in my afflictions.

Then the Tathāgata told the multitude, "This Bodhisattva is inconceivable. He constantly uses great lovingkindness to remove sentient beings' suffering. Whoever upholds this sūtra and this Bodhisattva's name will never go down any evil life-paths, and his hindrances and difficulties will be eliminated. If someone intently thinks of this sūtra without distracting thoughts, and trains accordingly, this Bodhisattva will manifest a body to expound the Dharma to him. He will support and protect him, never abandon him even temporarily, and enable him to quickly attain anuttara-samyak-saṁbodhi. To transform sentient beings, you Bodhisattvas should have them study this Mahāyāna sūtra of absolutely definitive meaning."

Chapter 9 – Entrusting This Sūtra

Then Ānanda rose from his seat, came forward, and asked the Buddha, "This sūtra pronounced by the Buddha is a mass of Mahāyāna virtues. It definitely enables one to end one's afflictions and acquire the benefits of one's inherent awareness. Its teachings are inconceivable. What is the name of this sūtra? How much merit will one acquire by upholding his sūtra? I pray that the Buddha, out of lovingkindness and compassion, will tell me."

The Buddha answered, "Good man, the name of this sūtra is inconceivable. It is protected and remembered by all Buddhas and can enable one to enter the ocean of a Tathāgata's wisdom-knowledge. Whoever upholds this sūtra will not seek other sūtras. This sūtra retains all teachings of Buddhas and encompasses the essentials of all sūtras. It is the hub of the teachings in all sūtras. This sūtra is called *Adopting the Mahāyāna,* also called *Vajra Samādhi,* also called *Tenet of Immeasurable Meaning.* Accepting and upholding this sūtra is accepting and upholding [the teachings of] 100,000 Buddhas. The merit acquired in this way is inconceivable and boundless, like the open sky. I entrust to you this sūtra."

Ānanda asked, "What mental actions should be taken by whoever can accept and uphold this sūtra?"

The Buddha answered, "Good man, whoever accepts and upholds this sūtra should take five mental actions: (1) have no concern for gain or loss; (2) always practice the Brahma way of life; (3) always delight in quietness even when hearing ludicrous statements; (4) always abide in samādhi even when in the midst of a crowd; (5) have no attachment to the Three Realms of existence while living a family life.

"Because he accepts and upholds this sūtra, in his present life he enjoys five benefits: (1) he is respected by multitudes; (2) he will not die an untimely death; (3) he can refute wrong theories; (4) he delights in delivering sentient beings; (5) he can enter the holy path. Such benefits are enjoyed by a person who accepts and upholds this sūtra."

Ānanda asked, "If that person delivers sentient beings, can he accept their offerings?"

The Buddha answered, "That person can serve as a great fortune field to sentient beings. He uses great wisdom to give provisional and definitive teachings because he relies upon four dharmas.[23] He can accept even such offerings as head, eyes, brain, and bone marrow, not to mention food and clothing. Good man, that person is your beneficent learned friend and your bridge [to cross over to the opposite shore[24]]. How can ordinary beings not make offerings to him?"

Ānanda asked, "If one accepts and upholds this sūtra under that person and makes offerings to him, how much merit will one acquire?"

The Buddha answered, "Suppose that one takes gold and silver that fill a city and gives them away as alms. This act is not as meritorious as accepting and upholding under that person one four-line stanza from this sūtra. The merit acquired by making offerings to that person is inconceivable.

"Good man, one who has sentient beings uphold this sūtra should constantly be in samādhi and never forget one's true mind [Buddha mind]. If one forgets it, one should immediately repent because repentance brings tranquility."

Ānanda said, "Repenting of past sins does not mean entering the past."

The Buddha said, "Indeed. As an analogy, if a bright lamp is placed in a dark room, darkness is expelled. Good man, do not say that repenting of past sins is entering the past."

Ānanda asked, "What is meant by repentance?"

The Buddha answered, "Repentance means following the teachings in this sūtra to observe the true reality of dharmas. As soon as one makes this observation, one's sins are expunged, and one leaves all evil life-paths, and will be reborn in a Pure Land and quickly attain anuttara-samyak-saṁbodhi."

After the Buddha pronounced this sūtra, Ānanda, the Bodhisattvas, and the Buddha's four groups of disciples acquired a resolute mind and greatly rejoiced. They prostrated themselves at the Buddha's feet and joyfully carried out His teachings.

Notes

1. Here, the four conditions that encompass the three clusters of Bodhisattva precepts are a special case, unrelated to the "four conditions" in the glossary.

2. In different fascicles of text 374 (T12n0374), the 40-fascicle Chinese version of the *Mahāparinirvāṇa Sūtra,* these four virtues variously belong to nirvāṇa, Buddha nature, a Tathāgata, or His dharma body.

3. See Thirty-seven Elements of Bodhi in the glossary.

4. The "three kinds of suffering" are (1) pain brought by a cause, (2) deterioration of pleasure, and (3) continuous change in every process. For comparison, see "eight kinds of suffering" listed in the glossary's "suffering."

5. It is also possible to interpret the three appearances as opposite edges and the middle, or as emptiness, existence, and the middle.

6. For "mental coverings," see "five coverings" in the glossary.

7. These four mantra names also appear in the text 251 (T08n0251, 0848c18–20), a Chinese version of the *Heart Sūtra,* translated from Sanskrit in the Tang Dynasty (618–907) by Xuanzang (玄奘, 600– or 602–64) from China. An English translation of text 251 appears in *Teachings of the Buddha* (Rulu 2012a, 121). The last three of these four mantra names also appear in fascicle 2 of text 227 (T08n0227, 0543b28–29), the Chinese version of the *Small Prajñā-Pāramitā Sūtra,* translated from Sanskrit in the Later Qin Dynasty (384–417) by Kumārajīva (鳩摩羅什, 344–413) from Kucha.

8. These three grounds might be the three timelines mentioned in text 1485, the Chinese version of the *Sūtra of the Garland of a Bodhisattva's Primary Karmas,* for the development of a holy Bodhisattva on the eleventh Bodhisattva ground, whose enlightenment is virtually perfect. According to text 1485, fascicle 1, chapter 3, he lives for a hundred kalpas to attain a thousand samādhis and enter the Vajra Samādhi, lives for a thousand kalpas to learn the deportment of a Buddha, and lives for ten thousand kalpas to acquire inconceivable spiritual powers and sit in the bodhimaṇḍa of a Buddha. Then he manifests as a Buddha and enters the Great Silent Samādhi. An English translation of text 1485 in 2 fascicles appears in *The Bodhisattva Way* (Rulu 2013, 33–88).

9. For details of the flows, see "four torrential flows" in the glossary.

10. Differentiation-free wisdom-knowledge is root wisdom-knowledge of the true reality of dharmas, which is emptiness. See "two kinds of wisdom-knowledge" in the glossary.

11. In text 273, the Chinese word *hai* 海 means ocean, and the three Chinese words *huai* 淮, *he* 河, and *jiang* 江 are used to suggest that three rivers are of small, medium, and large sizes. These three words also appear in other sūtras, such as text 985 (T19n0985, 0473b2–3), text 1045b (T20n1045b, 0042a7–8), and text 1332 (T21n01332, 0548a24–25). Here, they are translated as a creek, a stream, and a river, which may be likened to the Voice-Hearer Vehicle, the

Pratyekabuddha Vehicle, and the Mahāyāna, respectively. An ocean may be likened to the One Vehicle, the Buddha Vehicle.

12. The "three samādhis" are defined in the glossary's Three Liberation Doors.

13. See "name and form" defined in the glossary's "five aggregates."

14. The five dharmas also appear in fascicle 7 of text 671, the 10-fascicle Chinese version of the *Laṅkāvatāra Sūtra* (T16n0671, 0557b6–12).

15. In chapter 5, the Buddha explains that "the appearances of conditions are by nature empty. As each condition also arises through conditions, in true reality there is no dependent arising of dharmas."

16. One's mind is not empty because it gives birth to dharmas. It is not existent because it cannot be grasped.

17. In text 245, the Chinese version of *Buddha Pronounces to the Benevolent King the Sūtra of Prajñā-Pāramitā,* the Buddha says, "Great King, existence or nonexistence is a worldly truth. All dharmas are encompassed in three truths: emptiness, form, and one's mind" (T08n0245, 0829b27–29). Here, one's mind is not encompassed in these three truths because it is both empty and not empty.

18. In fascicle 3 of text 670, the 4-fascicle Chinese version of the *Laṅkāvatāra Sūtra* (T16n0670), the Buddha says, "While one's [ālaya] consciousness collects [seeds], one's wisdom does not" (T16n0670, 0501a6).

19. Text 273 states, ". . . when one's seventh and first five consciousnesses halt and one's eighth and sixth consciousnesses become quiet, ..." Here, the English translation pairs one's consciousnesses in a different way. One reason is that, in chapter 5, one's seventh and sixth consciousnesses are paired. Another reason is that, according to the Consciousness-Only School, on the Bodhisattva grounds one's seventh and sixth consciousnesses are gradually purified to possess the equality wisdom-knowledge and the discernment wisdom-knowledge, respectively; on the Buddha Ground, one's eighth and first five consciousnesses come to possess the great mirror-like wisdom-knowledge and the accomplishment wisdom-knowledge, respectively.

20. See "no wish" in the glossary's Three Liberation Doors.

21. Each of the Twelve Links of Dependent Arising is the main condition for the next one to arise. For example, as ignorance is the condition for karmic actions, ignorance is the subject and karmic actions are the object. As karmic actions are the condition for consciousness to arise, karmic actions are the subject and consciousness is the object. See Twelve Links of Dependent Arising in the glossary.

22. The two groups can also refer to riders of the Two Vehicles and riders of the Mahāyāna.

23. See Four Dharmas to Rely Upon in the glossary.

24. The opposite shore is that shore of nirvāṇa, opposite this shore of saṁsāra.

PART II

Ancient Translators Prayers

Ancient Translators

Buddhabhadra

Buddhabhadra (佛馱跋陀羅, 359–429) means enlightenment worthy. Born in northern India, he was a descendent of King Amṛtodana, who was the youngest of the three uncles of Śākyamuni Buddha (circa 563–483 BCE). He renounced family life at age seventeen and became a monk. Studying hard, he mastered meditation and the Vinaya.

In 408, the tenth year of the Hongshi (弘始) years of the Later Qin Dynasty (384–417), one of the Sixteen Kingdoms (304–439), he went to its capital, Chang-an. The illustrious translator Kumārajīva (鳩摩羅什, 344–413) had arrived there in 401. However, Buddhabhadra did not like Kumārajīva's students. Together with his own forty-some students, he went to the Lu Mountain (廬山, in present-day Jiangxi Province) and stayed with Master Huiyuan (慧遠, 334–416), the first patriarch of the Pure Land School of China.

In 415, the eleventh year of the Yixi (義熙) years of the Eastern Jin Dynasty (317–420), Buddhabhadra went south to its capital, Jiankong (建康), present-day Nanjing, Jiangsu Province. He stayed at the Daochang Temple (道場寺) and began his translation work. Altogether, he translated from Sanskrit into Chinese thirteen texts in 125 fascicles. For example, texts 376 and 1425 were translated jointly by him and Faxian (法顯, circa 337–422). Text 376 (T12n0376) in 6 fascicles is the earliest of the three Chinese versions of the *Mahāparinirvāṇa Sūtra;* text 1425 (T22n1425) in 40 fascicles is the Chinese version of the Mahāsaṅghika Vinaya. Texts 278 and 666 were translated by him alone probably between 418 and 421. Text 278 (T09n0278) is the 60-fascicle Chinese version of the *Mahāvaipulya Sūtra of Buddha Adornment* (Buddhāvataṁsaka-mahāvaipulya-sūtra); text 666 (T16n0666) in one fascicle is the earlier of the two extant Chinese versions of the *Mahāvaipulya Sūtra of the Tathāgata Store.*

In 429, the sixth year of the Yuanjia (元嘉) years of the Liu Song Dynasty (420–79), Buddhabhadra died, at age seventy-one. People called him the Indian Meditation Master. He is one of the eighteen exalted ones of the Lu Mountain.

Guṇabhadra

Guṇabhadra (求那跋陀羅, 394–468) means merit worthy (功德賢). He was from central India. Being in the Brahmin caste, he started the five studies as a child, and learned astrology, literature, medicine, and mantra practices. After studying *A Heart Treatise on the Abhidharma*, he turned to the teachings of the Buddha, renounced family life, and became a fully ordained monk.

Guṇabhadra first studied the Tripiṭaka of the Small Vehicle, then Mahāyāna teachings. With profound understanding of the *Mahā-Prajñā-Pāramitā Sūtra* and the *Mahāvaipulya Sūtra of Buddha Adornment*, he began to teach. He even converted his father to Buddhism.

In 435, the twelfth year of the Yuanjia (元嘉) years of the Liu Song Dynasty (420–79), Guṇabhadra went to China by sea. Emperor Wen (文帝) sent an emissary to welcome and take him to the Qihuan Temple (祇洹寺) in Jiankang (

建康), present-day Nanjing, Jiangsu Province. With the help of Huiyan (慧嚴), Huiguan (慧觀), and student monks, he translated the Saṁyukta Āgama (T02n0099) in 50 fascicles.

Guṇabhadra's life in China spanned the reigns of three emperors—Wen, Xiaowu, and Ming (文帝、孝武帝、明帝)—and he was highly revered by all of them. Because of his contribution to the Mahāyāna teachings, people called him Mahāyāna. Altogether, he translated, from Sanskrit into Chinese, fifty-two sūtras in 134 fascicles, including the *Sūtra of the Great Dharma Drum* (T09n0270) in 2 fascicles, the *Sūtra of Śrīmālā's Lion's Roar* (T12n0353) in one fascicle, the *Sūtra of Aṅgulimālika* (T02n0120) in 4 fascicles, the 4-fascicle version of *Laṅkāvatāra Sūtra* (T16n0670), and the mantra for rebirth in Amitābha Buddha's Pure Land. Guṇabhadra died in 468, at the age of seventy-five. On the day he died, he saw celestial flowers and the holy images of Amitābha Buddha and His retinue.

Bodhiruci

Bodhiruci (菩提留支, 5th–6th centuries) means bodhi splendor. A Buddhist master from northern India, he was versed in mantra practices and the Tripiṭaka. Aspiring to propagate the Dharma, in 508, the first year of the Yongping (永平) years of the Northern Wei Dynasty (386–534, the first of the five successive Northern Dynasties), he arrived in its capital, Luoyang (洛陽). Emperor Xuanwu (宣武帝) valued him highly and commanded him to stay in the Yongning Temple (永寧寺) to translate Sanskrit texts into Chinese, and he translated thirty-nine texts in 127 fascicles. The sūtras he translated include the *Diamond Sūtra* (T08n0236) in one fascicle, the *Sūtra Pronounced by Mahāsatya, a Nirgranthaputra Master* (T09n0272) in 10 fascicles, the *Sūtra of Buddha Names* (T14n0440) in 12 fascicles, the *Sūtra of Neither Increase Nor Decrease* (T16n0668) in one fascicle, the 10-fascicle version of the *Laṅkāvatāra Sūtra* (T16n0671), the *Sūtra of the Profound Secret Liberation* (T16n0675) in 5 fascicles, and the *Dharma Collection Sūtra* (T17n0761) in 6 fascicles. The treatises he translated include *A Treatise on the Sūtra of the Ten Grounds* (T26n1522) in 12 fascicles, *A Treatise on the Great Treasure Pile Sūtra* (T26n1523) in 4 fascicles, and the *Upadeśa on the Sūtra of Amitāyus Buddha* (T26n1524) in one fascicle. After 537, Bodhiruci was not seen again.

Bodhiruci expressed his unique view on classification of the Buddha's teachings. Based on the *Mahāparinirvāṇa Sūtra* (T12n0374), he said that, for the first twelve years, the Buddha gave only half-worded teachings, followed afterward by fully-worded teachings. Bodhiruci proposed the one-tone theory, saying that the Buddha pronounces teachings in one tone, and sentient beings come to a variety of understandings according to their capacities. Moreover, based on the *Laṅkāvatāra Sūtra,* he held that one's enlightenment can be immediate or gradual.

Bodhiruci and Ratnamati (勒那摩提, 5th–6th centuries) from central India jointly translated from Sanskrit into Chinese *A Treatise on the Sūtra of the Ten Grounds* (Daśa-bhūmika-sūtra-śāstra), written by Vasubandhu (世親, circa 320–80). Then Bodhiruci's students in northern China established the Ground Treatise School (地論宗), and Ratnamati's students in southern China established their school with the same name. Although both paths of this school were founded on Vasubandhu's treatise, they differed in their views of the nature of ālaya consciousness (ālaya-vijñāna). The northern path viewed ālaya consciousness as an impure consciousness and upheld dependent arising of dharmas from ālaya consciousness, while the southern path viewed ālaya consciousness as one's inherent pure mind, one's Tathāgata store (Tathāgata-garbha), and upheld dependent arising of dharmas from dharma nature (dharmatā), which is true suchness. Then the northern path merged into the Parigraha Treatise School (攝論宗, see this school in Paramārtha's biography). The southern path stood as the orthodox Ground Treatise School for some time, and then merged into the Huayan School.

Because Bodhiruci gave Tanluan (曇鸞, 476–542 or after 554) a copy of the Chinese version of the *Sūtra of Visualization of Amitāyus Buddha* (T12n0365), Tanluan dedicated the rest of his life to the study, practice, and dissemination of Pure Land teachings. Therefore, Bodhiruci is also revered as a patriarch of the Pure Land School.

Paramārtha

Paramārtha (真諦, 499–569) means the highest truth. He was from Ujayana, the capital of Avanti, in northwestern India. He belonged in the Brahmin caste, and his family name was Bhārata. Intelligent and eloquent, in his youth he visited many kingdoms, studied under various teachers, and became versed in the four Vedas. He also studied the Tripiṭaka and mastered the Mahāyāna doctrine.

In 546, the first year of the Zhongdatong (中大同) years of Emperor Wu (梁武帝) of the Southern Liang Dynasty (502–57, the third of the four successive Southern Dynasties), Paramārtha arrived in Nanhai County (南海郡), in present-day southern Guangdong Province, bringing with him 240 folios of Sanskrit texts. To see the emperor in his capital city, Jianye (建業), present-day Nanjing, Jiangsu Province, Paramārtha traveled intermittently for two years. Upon his arrival in 548, Emperor Wu, a devout Buddhist, revered him and settled him in the palace to do translation work. However, in 549, a rebellion broke out, Jianye fell, and Emperor Wu starved to death in prison.

Then Paramārtha went south, moving from province to province. Wherever he stayed, he continued to translate Sanskrit texts into Chinese. In the twenty-three years between his arrival in China in 546 during the Southern Liang Dynasty and his death in 569 during the Southern Chen Dynasty (557–89, the fourth and last of the Southern Dynasties), Paramārtha translated into Chinese sixty-four texts in 278 fascicles, which were only a portion of the Sanskrit texts he brought to China. Of the sixty-four Chinese texts, only thirty are extant. Paramārtha, Kumārajīva (鳩摩羅什, 344–413), Xuanzang (玄奘, 600– or 602–64), and Yijing (義淨, 635–713) are known in China as the four great translators.

Paramārtha translated many sūtras from Sanskrit into Chinese. For example, in 557, he translated the *Sūtra of the Unsurpassed Reliance* (T16n0669) in 2 fascicles; in 562, he translated the *Diamond Sūtra* (T08n0237) in one fascicle; in 563, he translated the *Sūtra of the Dharma Door with a Broad Meaning* (T01n0097) in one fascicle. However, his translation of the *Sūtra of the Golden Radiance* has been lost.

Paramārtha also translated from Sanskrit into Chinese many treatises, among which the most significant are texts 1559, 1593, 1595, 1610, and 1666. He is revered as the founding patriarch of two Chinese schools. The Abhidharma School (毗曇宗) was founded on text 1559 (T29n1559) in 22 fascicles, which is the Chinese version of Vasubandhu's (世親, circa 320–80) *A Commentary on the Treasury of the Abhidharma* (Abhidharma-kośa-bhāṣya). The Parigraha Treatise School (攝論宗) was founded on texts 1593 and 1595. Text 1593 (T31n1593) in 3 fascicles is one of the three Chinese versions of Asaṅga's (無著, circa 310–90) *A Treatise on Adopting the Mahāyāna* (Mahāyāna-saṁparigraha-śāstra); text 1595 (T31n1595) in 15 fascicles is one of the three Chinese versions of Vasubandhu's *Mahāyāna-saṅgraha-bhāṣya,* his commentary on Asaṅga's treatise. This school held that one has nine consciousnesses, of which the eighth consciousness, ālaya consciousness, is false, and the ninth consciousness, amala consciousness, is true and eternal. Then in the Tang Dynasty (618–907), the Abhidharma School merged into the Kośa School (俱舍宗), founded on text 1558 (T29n1558) in 30 fascicles, which is the Chinese version of Vasubandhu's *A Treatise on the Treasury of the Abhidharma* (Abhidharma-kośa-śāstra), translated from Sanskrit by Xuanzang (玄奘, 600– or 602–64); the Parigraha Treatise School merged into the Dharma-Appearance School (法相宗), also called the Consciousness-Only School.

Text 1610 (T31n1610) in 4 fascicles is the Chinese version of Vasubandhu's *A Treatise on Buddha Nature* (Buddhagotra-śāstra). Text 1666 (T32n1666) in one fascicle is the earlier of the two Chinese versions of *A Treatise on Eliciting Faith in the Mahāyāna* (Mahāyāna-śraddhotpāda-śāstra), attributed to Aśvaghoṣa (馬鳴, circa 100–60) from central India. These two treatises, which discuss Buddha nature, true mind, inherent awareness, ālaya consciousness, and the Tathāgata store (Tathāgata-garbha), are highly valued by all Buddhist schools of China.

Prayers

1 Opening the Sūtra 開經偈

The unsurpassed, profound true Dharma
無上甚深微妙法
Is hard to encounter in billions of kalpas.
百千萬劫難遭遇
This I now have seen and heard, and have come to accept and uphold,
我今見聞得受持
Hoping to understand the true meaning of the Tathāgatas.
願解如來真實義

2 Transferring Merit 回向偈

May the merit of my practice
願以此功德
Adorn Buddhas' Pure Lands,
莊嚴佛淨土
Requite the fourfold kindness from above,
上報四重恩
And relieve the suffering of the three life-paths below.
下濟三途苦
Universally wishing sentient beings,
普願諸眾生
Friends, foes, and karmic creditors,
冤親諸債主
All to activate the bodhi mind,
悉發菩提心
And all to be reborn in the Land of Ultimate Bliss.
同生極樂國

3 The Four Vast Vows 四弘誓願

Sentient beings are countless; I vow to deliver them all.
眾生無邊誓願度
Afflictions are endless; I vow to eradicate them all.
煩惱無盡誓願斷
Dharma Doors are measureless; I vow to learn them all.
法門無量誓願學
Buddha bodhi is unsurpassed; I vow to attain it.
佛道無上誓願成

4 The Universally Worthy Vow of the Ten Great Actions
普賢十大行願

First, make obeisance to Buddhas.
一者禮敬諸佛
Second, praise Tathāgatas.
二者稱讚如來
Third, make expansive offerings.
三者廣修供養
Fourth, repent of karma, the cause of hindrances.
四者懺悔業障
Fifth, express sympathetic joy over others' merits.
五者隨喜功德
Sixth, request Buddhas to turn the Dharma wheel.
六者請轉法輪
Seventh, beseech Buddhas to abide in the world.
七者請佛住世
Eighth, always follow Buddhas to learn.
八者常隨佛學
Ninth, forever support sentient beings.
九者恒順眾生
Tenth, universally transfer all merits to others.
十者普皆迴向

5 Always Walking the Bodhisattva Way 常行菩薩道

May the three kinds of hindrances and all afflictions be eliminated.
願消三障諸煩惱
May I gain wisdom and true understanding.
願得智慧真明了
May all hindrances caused by sin be removed.
普願罪障悉消除
May I always walk the Bodhisattva Way, life after life.
世世常行菩薩道

6 Repenting of All Sins 懺悔偈

The evil karmas I have done with my body, voice, and mind are caused by greed, anger, and delusion, which are without a beginning. Before Buddhas I now supplicate for my repentance.
往昔所造諸惡業，皆由無始貪瞋癡，從身語意之所生。今對佛前求懺悔。
The evil karmas I have done with my body, voice, and mind are caused by greed, anger, and delusion, which are without a beginning. I repent of all sins, the cause of hindrances.
往昔所造諸惡業，皆由無始貪瞋癡，從身語意之所生。一切罪障皆懺悔。

The evil karmas I have done with my body, voice, and mind are caused by greed, anger, and delusion, which are without a beginning. I repent of all the roots of sin.
往昔所造諸惡業，皆由無始貪瞋癡，從身語意之所生。一切罪根皆懺悔。

7 Wishing to Be Reborn in the Pure Land 願生淨土

I wish to be reborn in the Western Pure Land.
願生西方淨土中
I wish to have as my parents a lotus flower in nine grades.
九品蓮花爲父母
When the flower opens, I will see that Buddha and realize that dharmas have no birth,
花開見佛悟無生
And I will have as my companions the Bodhisattvas who never regress.
不退菩薩爲伴侶

8 Supplicating to Be Reborn in the Pure Land 求生淨土

I single-mindedly take refuge in Amitābha Buddha in the World of Ultimate Bliss. I pray that He will illuminate me with pure light and draw me in with His loving-kind vows. With right mindfulness, I now say this Tathāgata's name. To walk the Bodhi Way, I supplicate to be reborn in His Pure Land.
一心皈命極樂世界阿彌陀佛。願以淨光照我、慈誓攝我。我今正念稱如來名，爲菩提道求生淨土。
Before this Buddha attained Buddhahood in the past, he made a vow: "Suppose there are sentient beings who, with earnest faith and delight, wish to be reborn in my land, even if by only thinking ten thoughts. If they should fail to be reborn there, I would not attain the perfect enlightenment."
佛昔本誓：若有眾生欲生我國，志心信樂乃至十念，若不生者不取正覺。
Through my thinking of this Buddha as the cause and condition, I have gained entrance into this Tathāgata's ocean of great vows. By the power of this Buddha's lovingkindness, my sins will be expunged and my roots of goodness will expand. At the end of my life, I will know the coming of my time. My body will have no illness or suffering. My heart will have no greed or attachments. My mind will not be demented but will be peaceful as if in meditative concentration. This Buddha, holding a lotus-borne golden platform in His hands, together with a holy multitude, will come to receive me. In the instant of a thought, I will be reborn in the Land of Ultimate Bliss. When the lotus flower opens, I will see this Buddha and hear the Buddha Vehicle, and my Buddha wisdom will immediately unfold. I will widely deliver sentient beings, fulfilling my bodhi vow.
以此念佛因緣，得入如來大誓海中。承佛慈力，眾罪消滅、善根增長。若臨命終，自知時至。身無病苦、心不貪戀、意不顛倒，如入禪定。佛及聖眾手執金臺來迎接我。於一念頃，生極樂國。華開見佛，即聞佛乘、頓開佛慧、廣度眾生滿菩提願。

Homage to all Buddhas of the past, present, and future, in worlds in the ten directions!
Homage to all Bodhisattva-Mahāsattvas!
Homage to mahā-prajñā-pāramitā!
十方三世一切佛。一切菩薩摩訶薩。摩訶般若波羅蜜。

9 Ascending the Golden Steps 上金階

In the ocean-like lotus pond assembly, seated on lotus-borne platforms are Amitābha Tathāgata and Bodhisattvas Avalokiteśvara and Great Might Arrived, who welcome me to ascend the golden steps. I majestically declare my great vows, wishing to leave all afflictions behind.
蓮池海會，彌陀如來觀音勢至坐蓮臺，接引上金階。大誓弘開，普願離塵埃。

Homage to Buddhas and Bodhisattvas in the ocean-like lotus pond assembly! (Repeat three times.)
蓮池海會佛菩薩 (三稱)

10 Praising Amitābha Buddha 讚阿彌陀佛

Amitābha Buddha in a golden body is
阿彌陀佛身金色
Unsurpassed in His excellent appearance and radiance.
相好光明無等倫
The curling white hair between His eyebrows is like five Sumeru Mountains.
白毫宛轉五須彌
His blue eyes are as clear as four great oceans.
紺目澄清四大海
Present in His radiance are innumerable koṭis of magically manifested Buddhas
光中化佛無數億
And countless magically manifested Bodhisattvas.
化菩薩眾亦無邊
He has made forty-eight vows to deliver sentient beings,
四十八願度眾生
Enabling them to arrive in nine grades at the opposite shore.
九品咸令登彼岸

Namo Amitābha Buddha of great lovingkindness and great compassion, in the Western Land of Ultimate Bliss!
Namo Amitābha Buddha! (Say these words or "namo amituo fo" as many times as one wishes.)
南無西方極樂世界。大慈大悲阿彌陀佛。
南無阿彌陀佛 (多稱)

Appendix

Table A. The Sanskrit Alphabet

	33 Consonants							13 Vowels			
	Unvoiced			Voiced				Voiced			
	Un aspirate	Aspirate	Sibilant (aspirate)	Un aspirate	Aspirate	Nasal	Semi-vowel	Simple		Diphthong	
								Short	Long	Long	
1 Velar	ka	kha	ha	ga	gha	ṅa		a	ā	a+i	ā+i
2 Palatal	ca	cha	śa	ja	jha	ña	ya	i	ī	=e	=ai
3 Cerebral	ṭa	ṭha	ṣa	ḍa	ḍha	ṇa	ra	ṛ	ṝ		
4 Dental	ta	tha	sa	da	dha	na	la	ḷ		a+u	ā+u
5 Labial	pa	pha		ba	bha	ma	va	u	ū	=o	=au
Anusvāra						ṁ					
Visarga			ḥ								

Note:

1. The sounds of the twenty-five consonants are formed by *complete* contact of the tongue with the palate.
2. The four semi-vowels are voiced and unaspirated, and their sounds are formed by *slight* contact.
3. Three of the four sibilants (excepting *ha*) are unvoiced and aspirated, and their sounds are formed by *half* contact. Note that *ha* is a voiced velar sound but classified as a sibilant.
4. Voiced consonants are low and soft; unvoiced consonants are crisp and sharp. To feel the difference between a voiced and an unvoiced sound, hold the front of your throat with your hand and pronounce a syllable. It is a voiced sound if your hand detects a vibration in your throat, an unvoiced sound if no vibration. To know the difference between an aspirated and an unaspirated sound, place your palm in front of your mouth and pronounce a syllable. It is an aspirated sound if your breath hits your palm, an unaspirated sound if there is no hit. Native English speakers may find it difficult to pronounce the five unvoiced, unaspirated syllables in column one. This difficulty can be overcome once you understand the difference.
5. In table A, each consonant is followed by the short vowel *a* to facilitate pronunciation. To learn the Sanskrit alphabet, follow the pronunciation guideline in table B and table C. Recite the thirteen vowels in table B row by row. Recite the thirty-three consonants in the first column of table C, also adding the short vowel *a* to each. Unlike the consonants, the sounds of anusvāra and visarga in the last two rows of table A or table C depend on the vowel preceding them. Textbooks include them with the vowels.

Table B. Pronunciation of the 13 Vowels

5 short vowels (Each lasts one count)		8 long vowels (Each lasts two counts)	
a	atra (here), like ***a***bout or ***a***like	ā	mahā (great), like f***a***ther
i	iva (as if, like), like ***ea***sy but not like ***i*** t or ***i*** s	ī	kīrti (fame), like ***ea***se
u	guru (heavy), like p**u**ll	ū	bhūta (reality, being), like p**oo**l
ṛ	amṛta (nectar for immortality), like p***re***tty but not like p**ri**ck	ṝ	pitṝn (fathers, accusative case), like p***re***tty lengthened
ḷ	kḷpta (arranged), like app***le*** or kett***le***		
		e = a+i	ehi (come near!), like s***a***fe
		ai = ā+i	maitreya (benevolent), like ***ai***sle
		o = a+u	namo (homage), like **o**cean without bunching the lips as if to pronounce the word *woe*
		au = ā+u	kauśalya (skillfulness), like l**ou**d

Table C. Pronunciation of the 33 Consonants

1. Velar or guttural sounds are produced by touching the rear of the tongue to the soft palate near the throat.	
k	kāya (body), like s**k**ill or s**k**in
kh	sukha (happiness), like **k**ill or **k**in
g	gagana (sky), like **g**azelle or **g**o
gh	gharma (heat), like do**gh**ouse
ṅ	gaṅgā (the Ganges), like mi**n**gle or hu**n**ger
2. Palatal sounds are produced by touching the blade of the tongue to the front palate.	
c	cakra (wheel), like **ch**uck or **ch**oke, but without aspiration
ch	chāya (shadow), like **ch**uck or **ch**oke
j	jaya (victory), like **j**ug or **j**oke
jh	nirjhara (waterfall), like **j-h**ug or fu**dge-h**ome
ñ	jñāna (wisdom), like ca**ny**on. Some people change the sound of *j* and pronounce this word like g**ny**āna, or like d**ny**āna.
3. Cerebral sounds are produced by retroflexing the tongue to touch the hard palate.	
ṭ	koṭi (ten million, the edge), like s**t**ar or s**t**ow, with the tongue retroflexed
ṭh	adhiṣṭhāna (rule over), like **t**ar or **t**ow, with the tongue retroflexed
ḍ	vaiḍūrya (aquamarine), like **d**ouse or **d**ead, with the tongue retroflexed
ḍh	mūḍha (perplexed), like ma**dh**ouse or re**dh**ead, with the tongue retroflexed
ṇ	maṇi (jewel), like **n**ativity or **n**ote, with the tongue retroflexed
4. Dental sounds are produced by touching the tip of the tongue to the back of the front teeth near their roots.	
t	tad (he, she, or it), like s**t**ar or s**t**ow
th	tathāgata (the thus-come one), like **t**ar or **t**ow
da	dāna (the act of giving), like **d**ouse or **d**ead
dh	dhāranī (retention), like ma**dh**ouse or re**dh**ead
n	nāga (dragon), like **n**ativity or **n**ote
5. Labial sounds are produced by closing and opening the lips.	
p	padma (red lotus), like s**p**in or s**p**oke
ph	phala (fruit), like **p**in or **p**oke
b	bodhi (enlightenment), like **b**ore or **b**out
bh	bhagavān (the world-honored one), like a**bh**or or ho**bh**ouse
m	mudrā (seal), like **m**agenta or **m**ode

Table C Continued

6. Four semi-vowels, the sounds of which are formed by slight contact	
y	hṛdaya (heart, mind), like **y**east or **y**oga
r	ratna (jewel), like **r**ite or **r**ote, with the tongue slightly tapping the front palate. Avoid bunching the lips for the implicit *w* before the r-syllable as in English, which causes **r**ite to be pronounced as write, **r**ote as wrote.
l	loka (world), like **l**agoon or **l**otus
v	If not preceded by a consonant, it is pronounced as *v;* e.g., avidyā (ignorance). If preceded by a constant, it may be pronounced as *w*. Thus, sattva (being, creature) may be pronounced as sa-ttwa, sarva (all) as sar-wa, adhvan (time) as a-dhwan, and svāhā (hail) as swā-hā.
7. Four sibilants, the sounds of which are formed by half contact	
ś	śuddha (pure), like ***sh***ip or ***sh***ow
ṣ	uṣṇīṣa (crown of the head), like ***sh***ip or ***sh***ow, with the tongue retroflexed
s	sama (equal), like **s**alute or **s**olo
h	sahasra (thousand), like **h**abituate or **h**oly
8. Other sounds	
Anusvāra (ṁ)	The preceding verb is nasalized; e.g., saṁskāra (formation) is pronounced as sa***ng***-skā-ra, and hūṁ (a mantra syllable) as hū***ng***.
Visarga (ḥ)	The preceding verb is faintly echoed; e.g., namaḥ (homage) is pronounced as nama***ha***, narayoḥ (of the two men) as narayo***ho***, naraiḥ (with the men) as narai***hi***, and duḥkha (sorrow) as du***hu***kha.

Note:

1. A vowel as the first letter of a word, or a consonant followed by a vowel, forms a syllable, which is short or long, depending upon the vowel. All consonants are pronounced. For example, tadyathā is pronounced as tad-ya-thā, ratna as rat-na, and sattva as satt-va or sa-ttwa.
2. The stressed syllable, or guru syllable, in a multi-syllable word is the penultimate syllable if (1) it has a long vowel, or (2) it has a short vowel followed by two or more consonants. For example, the stressed syllable in bālābhyām (with, for, or from the two boys) is *lā* because it meets the first condition, and in saṁyukta (complex) is *yu* because it meets the second condition. If the penultimate syllable meets neither condition, then check the anti-penultimate syllable, and so on. For example, the stressed syllable in udbhavakara (productive) is *u*, the fifth syllable from the last.
3. The nasal sound of anusvāra (ṁ) may extend a count or two. For example, the mantra syllable hūṁ or oṁ can last two to four counts.

Glossary

ācārya (阿闍梨). A teacher, or an eminent monk who guides his students in conduct and sets an example. To receive the complete monastic precepts, three ācāryas must be present: (1) a preceptor ācārya (得戒和尚), who imparts the precepts; (2) a karma ācārya (羯磨阿闍梨), who directs the precept recipients in the ceremony; (3) an instructor ācārya (教授阿闍梨), who teaches them the right conduct and procedures.

affliction (kleśa, 煩惱). Something that agitates one's mind, resulting in evil karmas done with one's body and/or voice. The three root afflictions, called the three poisons, are (1) greed, (2) anger, and (3) delusion. Derived from these three are (4) arrogance, (5) doubt, and (6) wrong views. The list can be extended to ten by distinguishing five kinds of wrong views: (6) the self-view that an embodied self exists in a person composed of the five aggregates and that this self owns the five aggregates and things perceived as external; (7) the opposite view of perpetuity or cessation; (8) the evil view of no causality; (9) the preceding three wrong views, plus certain inferior views; (10) the view in favor of observing useless precepts, such as staying naked, smearing oneself with ashes, imitating cows or dogs, and self harm, futilely hoping to achieve a better rebirth. These ten afflictions drive sentient beings. The first five are called the chronic drivers (鈍使), which can be removed gradually; they are also called thinking confusions (思惑) because they arise from one's thinking of self, others, or both. The last five are called the acute drivers (利使), which can be removed quickly; they are also called view confusions (見惑). Ignorance of the truth is the root of all afflictions.

agalloch (沉水). The fragrant, resinous wood of an East Indian tree, aquilaria agallocha, also called agarwood, used as incense in the Orient. It is called in China the sink-in-water fragrant wood.

Akaniṣṭha Heaven (阿迦尼吒天), or Ultimate Form Heaven (色究竟天). It is the top heaven (有頂天) of the eighteen heavens in the form realm.

ālaya-vijñāna (阿賴耶識). Storehouse consciousness (藏識), the eighth consciousness, which stores the pure, impure, and neutral seeds of one's experience without a beginning. These seeds manifest as causes and conditions that lead to karmic events in one's life, which in turn become seeds. Maintaining the physical and mental life of a sentient being, ālaya is neither different from nor the same as the physical body. As the source of the other seven consciousnesses (see eighteen spheres), ālaya is the root consciousness (mūla-vijñāna). After one's death, ālaya may either immediately manifest a rebirth according to karmic forces and conditions or first manifest an ethereal interim body, which can last up to forty-nine days, pending the right karmic conditions for rebirth. When one attains Buddhahood, all seeds stored in ālaya consciousness become pure seeds that will neither change nor manifest any karmic rebirth. Then it sheds its name "ālaya-vijñāna" and takes a new name "amala-vijñāna," stainless consciousness, which is one's inherent pure awareness and possesses the great mirror-like wisdom-knowledge.

Anāthapiṇḍika (給孤獨). Provider for the Deprived, a name given to Sudatta the Elder for his generosity to the poor and forlorn. He bought a garden from Prince Jeta as an offering to the Buddha.

anuttara-samyak-saṁbodhi (阿耨多羅三藐三菩提). The unsurpassed, equally perfect enlightenment (無上正等正覺). *Anuttara* means unsurpassed; *samyak* is derived from the stem *samyañc*, which means same or identical; *saṁbodhi* means perfect enlightenment. *Equally* means that the perfect enlightenment of all Buddhas is the same. The third epithet of a Buddha is Samyak-Saṁbuddha, the Equally, Perfectly Enlightened One.

anuttara-samyak-saṁbodhi mind (阿耨多羅三藐三菩提心). The resolve to attain the unsurpassed, equally perfect enlightenment, to benefit self and others.

araṇya (阿蘭若). A forest, or a quiet remote place for spiritual training. One who stays in such a place is called an āraṇyaka (阿蘭若迦). Such a way of life is called the araṇya way, which is one of the twelve dhūta practices. A temple in an area away from urban noise is also called an araṇya.

Arhat (阿羅漢). A voice-hearer who has attained the fourth and highest fruit on the Liberation Way (see voice-hearer fruits) by shattering his fixation on having an autonomous self and eradicating all his afflictions. A Buddha is also an Arhat, but not vice versa (see bodhi). As the second of a Buddha's ten epithets, Arhat means worthy of offerings.

arrogance (慢). Arrogance has seven types: (1) arrogance (慢) is vaunting one's superiority over inferiors; (2) over-arrogance (過慢) is asserting one's superiority over equals; (3) arrogant over-arrogance (慢過慢) is alleging one's superiority over superiors; (4) self-arrogance (我慢) is the root of all other arrogances, considering oneself by definition to be superior to others; (5) exceeding arrogance (增上慢) is alleging realization of truth one has not realized; (6) humility-camouflaged arrogance (卑慢) is admitting slight inferiority to those who are much superior; and (7) evil arrogance (邪慢) is boasting of virtues one does not have.

asaṁkhyeya (阿僧祇). Innumerable, or an exceedingly large number.

asaṁskṛta (無爲). Not formed or made through causes and conditions. Although *asaṁskṛta* is an antonym of *saṁskṛta* (有爲), the asaṁskṛta dharma is the true reality of saṁskṛta dharmas, not their opposite.

asura (阿修羅). A sub-god or non-god. An asura may assume the form of god, human, animal, or hungry ghost. Given to anger and jealousy, an asura is considered more an evil life-path than a good one.

Avīci Hell (阿鼻地獄). The last of the eight hot hells. It is a hell of uninterrupted suffering for those who have committed grave sins, such as the five rebellious sins.

avinivartanīya (阿鞞跋致). The spiritual level from which a Bodhisattva will never regress (不退). Bodhisattvas with the first six or more of the ten faithful minds will never regress from faith; Bodhisattvas at the seventh and higher levels of abiding will never abandon the Mahāyāna; Bodhisattvas on the first and higher Bodhisattva grounds will never lose their spiritual realization; Bodhisattvas on the eighth and higher Bodhisattva grounds will never lose their mindfulness, and their progress will be effortless (see stages of the Bodhisattva Way).

Ayodhyā (阿踰陀). An ancient kingdom in central India, in the present-day Indian state of Uttar Pradesh. The Sanskrit word *ayodhyā* means unconquerable by war.

Bhagavān (薄伽梵). The tenth epithet of a Buddha is Buddha-Bhagavān, or Buddha the World-Honored One.

bhikṣu (比丘). A fully ordained monk in the Buddha's Order, who observes, in the Mahāyāna tradition, 250 monastic precepts.

bhikṣuṇī (比丘尼). A fully ordained nun in the Buddha's Order, who observes, in the Mahāyāna tradition, 500 monastic precepts.

birth-death (jāti-maraṇa, 生死). See saṁsāra.

bodhi (菩提). Enlightenment or unsurpassed wisdom. Corresponding to the enlightenment of holy beings who ride the Three Vehicles, there are three kinds of bodhi: (1) voice-hearer bodhi, the bodhi of a voice-hearer who has attained Arhatship; (2) Pratyekabuddha bodhi, the greater bodhi of a Pratyekabuddha; (3) Buddha bodhi, the greatest bodhi of a Buddha, which is anuttara-samyak-saṁbodhi, the unsurpassed, equally perfect enlightenment, attained only by a Buddha. In old translations, *bodhi* is translated into Chinese as the Way (道), which should be distinguished from the path (mārga).

bodhi mind (bodhi-citta, 菩提心). See anuttara-samyak-saṁbodhi mind.

bodhimaṇḍa (道場). The bodhi place, which refers to the vajra seat of a Buddha sitting under the bodhi tree where He attains Buddhahood. In a general sense, it is a place for spiritual learning and practice, such as a temple or one's home. In a profound sense, since the Way to Buddhahood is one's mind, all sentient beings are bodhi places.

Bodhisattva (菩薩). A bodhi being who is resolved to attain anuttara-samyak-saṁbodhi, to benefit himself and others. Riding the Great Vehicle (Mahāyāna) on the Bodhisattva Way, he accumulates merits by helping and teaching others, and develops wisdom by hearing and pondering the Dharma, and training accordingly.

Bodhisattva-Mahāsattva (菩薩摩訶薩). A holy Bodhisattva who is a mahāsattva (great being) because of his great vows, great actions, and the great number of sentient beings he delivers.

Bodhisattva precepts (菩薩戒). Precepts for both lay and monastic Buddhists who ride the Mahāyāna. They are called the three clusters of pure precepts (tri-vidhāni śīlāni, 三聚淨戒), consisting of (1) restraining precepts, (2) precepts for doing good dharmas, and (3) precepts for benefiting sentient beings. The first cluster is to prevent negative actions, and the other two are to cultivate the positive qualities essential to the development of a Bodhisattva. Bodhisattva precepts vary with their sources. In the *Brahma Net Sūtra* (T24n1484), there are ten major and forty-eight minor precepts; in the *Sūtra of the Upāsaka Precepts* (T24n1488), there are six major and twenty-eight minor precepts. Chinese monastic Buddhists observe the former set of Bodhisattva precepts. Lay Buddhists may choose to accept either set of Bodhisattva precepts.

Brahmā (梵). Purity, or freedom from desire. It is deified in Hinduism as the Creator. The Brahma way of life in the desire realm is celibacy.

Brahmin (婆羅門). A member of the highest of the four Indian castes. As a priest, a Brahmin officiates at religious rites and teaches Vedic literature.

Buddha (佛). The Enlightened One. According to the Mahāyāna tradition, Śākyamuni Buddha (circa 563–483 BCE) is the present one in a line of past and future Buddhas. Each Buddha has a particular name, such as Śākyamuni, to suit the needs of sentient beings of His time. The ten epithets common to all Buddhas are (1) Tathāgata (Thus-Come One or Thus-Gone One), (2) Arhat (Worthy of Offerings), (3) Samyak-Saṁbuddha (Equally, Perfectly Enlightened One), (4) Vidyācaraṇa-Sampanna (Knowledge and Conduct Perfected), (5) Sugata (Well-Arrived One or Well-Gone One), (6) Lokavid (Understanding the World), (7) Anuttara (Unsurpassed One), (8) Puruṣa-Damya-Sārathi (Tamer of Men), (9) Śāstā Deva-Manuṣyāṇām (Teacher of Gods and Humans), and (10) Buddha-Bhagavān (Buddha the World-Honored One).

Buddha Vehicle (Buddha-yāna, 佛乘). The Great Vehicle (Mahāyāna) is also called the Buddha Vehicle because its destination is Buddhahood. In the *Lotus Sūtra* (T09n0262), the Buddha introduces the One Vehicle (eka-yāna, 一乘), declaring that not only riders of the Two Vehicles but all sentient beings will eventually attain Buddhahood.

Cause Ground (因地). It means the training ground of a Bodhisattva before attaining Buddhahood, the Fruit (Result) Ground, or the Buddha Ground. It may also refer to the training ground of a Bodhisattva before ascending to the first Bodhisattva ground (see stages of the Bodhisattva Way).

character-type (gotra, 種姓 or 種性). The Sanskrit word *gotra* means family, family name, or species. According to the *Sūtra of the Garland of a Bodhisattva's Primary Karmas* (T24n1485), Bodhisattvas are classified into five character-types, corresponding to the middle five of the seven stages of the Bodhisattva Way: (1) the learning character-type (習種性) is developed through the ten levels of abiding; (2) the nature character-type (性種性) is developed through the ten levels of action; (3) the bodhi character-type (道種性) is developed through the ten levels of transference of merit; (4) the holy character-type (聖種性) is developed through the Ten Grounds; (5) the virtually perfect enlightenment nature (等覺性) is developed when a Bodhisattva attains enlightenment that nearly equals a Buddha's. At the seventh stage, a Bodhisattva becomes a Buddha, whose perfect enlightenment nature (妙覺性) is fully revealed. Besides, those with affinity for the Voice-Hearer Vehicle are called the voice-hearer character-type; those with affinity for the Pratyekabuddha Vehicle are called the Pratyekabuddha character-type (see Two Vehicles).

Command of the Eight Great Displays (八大自在). According to the *Mahāparinirvāṇa Sūtra* (T12n0374), fascicle 23, the vast self (dharma body) of a Buddha has command of the eight great displays: (1) it can manifest copies of a physical body as numerous as dust particles to fill countless worlds; (2) it can display a physical body that fills a Large Thousandfold World; (3) it can lift off and travel across countless Buddha Lands; (4) it can manifest innumerable varieties of forms, which have their own minds; it can display a physical body in one world, which can be seen by people in other worlds; (5) the functions of its six faculties can be interchangeable; (6) it can acquire all dharmas without any thought of attainment; (7) it can expound the meaning of one stanza for countless kalpas; (8) it can pervade everywhere, like space.

deliverance (度). Liberation achieved by crossing over to that shore of nirvāṇa from this shore of saṁsāra. Those who have achieved deliverance are Arhats, Pratyekabuddhas, and Buddhas. The first two have achieved the liberation fruit and the bodhi fruit for themselves. Buddhas have achieved not only the liberation fruit for themselves but also the great bodhi fruit of omniscience, for delivering sentient beings.

dhāraṇī (陀羅尼). Usually in the form of a long mantra, it means total retention (總持). With excellent memory, samādhi, and wisdom, A Bodhisattva has the inconceivable power to unite all dharmas and hold all meanings. He can not only retain all good dharmas but also stop the rise of evil dharmas.

dharma (法). (1) The teachings of a Buddha (the word dharma in this meaning is capitalized in English); (2) law; (3) anything (mental, physical, event); (4) a mental object of consciousness, such as a thought.

dharma eye (法眼). The spiritual eye that not only penetrates the true reality of all things but also discriminates all things. Bodhisattvas who have realized that dharmas have no birth ascend to the first Bodhisattva ground and acquire the pure dharma eye, with which they continue to help sentient beings according to their natures and preferences (see five eyes).

dharma realm (dharma-dhātu, 法界). It includes all saṁskṛta and asaṁskṛta dharmas. The Huayan School of China classifies the dharma realm into five dharma realms: (1) saṁskṛta, (2) asaṁskṛta, (3) both saṁskṛta and asaṁskṛta, (4) neither saṁskṛta nor asaṁskṛta, and (5) hindrance free. The Tiantai School of China, basing on different minds, recognizes ten dharma realms: (1) hell-dwellers, (2) hungry ghosts, (3) animals, (4) humans, (5) asuras, (6) gods, (7) voice-hearers, (8) Pratyekabuddhas, (9) Bodhisattvas, and (10) Buddhas. All dharma realms are encompassed in the one true dharma realm, one's true mind, which is hindrance free and beyond purity and impurity.

Dharma Seal (dharma-mudrā, 法印). Buddhist teachings are summarized in Dharma Seals, against which other doctrines should be measured. The Four Dharma Seals are as follows: (1) processes are impermanent; (2) experiences boil down to suffering; (3) dharmas have no self; (4) nirvāṇa is silence and stillness. Because suffering is the consequence of the impermanence of a sentient being and everything in its life, the second Dharma Seal can be omitted from the list to make the Three Dharma Seals. Five Dharma Seals can be established by adding a fifth Dharma Seal: (5) dharmas are empty. In the Mahāyāna doctrine, all these seals are integrated into one, the one true reality.

Dharma vessel (法器). (1) A person capable of accepting and learning the Buddha Dharma. (2) A Buddhist ritual object, such a drum, a bell, or a wooden fish.

dhūta (頭陀). Shaken off. To shake off one's desire for creature comfort in food, clothing, and shelter, one follows these twelve rules as a way of life: (1) beg for food; (2) beg for food from one door to the next without discrimination; (3) eat only one meal a day, at noon; (4) eat with moderation in quantity; (5) do not drink liquids after lunch; (6) wear clothes made of cast-away rags; (7) keep only three garments; (8) live in a quiet remote area; (9) live among graves; (10) live under a tree; (11) sit on open ground under the open sky; (12) sit, without reclining.

dhyāna (禪). Meditation. Meditation above the desire-realm level is generally classified into four levels, called the four dhyānas (四禪) of the form realm. In the first dhyāna, one's mind is undisturbed by the pleasures of the desire realm, but it has coarse and subtle perception. In the second dhyāna, there is bliss in meditation. In the third dhyāna, there is subtle joy after abandoning the bliss of the second dhyāna. In the fourth dhyāna, one's mind is in pure meditation, free from any subtle feelings or movements. Each level of dhyāna is also called the Root Samādhi, from which will grow virtues, such as the Four Immeasurable Minds and the eight liberations (see the four samādhis of the formless realm).

dhyāna with appearance (有相禪). Meditation supported by the appearance of a mental object. One can focus one's attention on a point of the body, count the breaths, recite mantra syllables silently, gaze at an object, or visualize an object.

dhyāna without appearance (無相禪). Meditation unsupported by the appearance of any mental object. One can ponder true suchness without thoughts or think of a Buddha without saying His name or visualizing His body.

discharge (āsrava, 漏). Outflow of afflictions, characteristic of sentient beings in their cycles of birth and death. For example, anger is an affliction in one's mind, which is discharged through one's body and voice. Any discharge is a display of one's affliction and does not decrease it.

dragon (nāga, 龍). (1) A serpent-like sea creature, which can take a little water and pour down rains. (2) A symbol of one's true mind in the statement that the great nāga is always in samādhi, never moving. An Arhat is likened to the great dragon.

duṣkṛta (突吉羅). A wrongdoing, considered a minor sin. If one commits a duṣkṛta intentionally, one must repent to only one person in private. If unintentional, one needs only to repent to oneself.

eight classes of Dharma protectors (八部護法). The nonhuman protectors of the Dharma are gods, dragons, gandharvas, asuras, yakṣas, garuḍas, kiṁnaras, and mahoragas.

eight evil ways (八邪行). The opposite of the Eightfold Right Path. They are (1) evil views, (2) evil thinking, (3) evil speech, (4) evil actions, (5) evil livelihood, (6) evil endeavor, (7) evil mindfulness, and (8) evil samādhi.

eight holy ranks (八聖). See voice-hearer fruits.

eight precepts (aṣṭa-śīla, 八關齋戒). Besides the five precepts, which are observed for life at all times, lay Buddhists may accept and observe the eight precepts regularly each lunar month on the six purification days. The eight precepts are (1) no killing; (2) no stealing; (3) no sex; (4) no lying; (5) no drinking alcohol; (6) no wearing perfumes or adornments, and no singing, dancing, or watching song-dance entertainments; (7) no sleeping on a luxurious bed; and (8) no eating after lunch, until morning. Note that the third of the eight precepts is no sex whereas the third of the five precepts is no sexual misconduct. Observing these eight prohibitions (關) for 24 hours at a time, one abstains (齋) not only from sins prohibited by the five precepts but also from sensory gratification.

eight winds (八風). One's love or hate is fanned by the eight winds: (1) advantage, (2) disadvantage, (3) fame, (4) infamy, (5) praise, (6) scorn, (7) pleasure, and (8) pain.

eighteen emptinesses (十八空). Given in the *Mahā-prajñā-pāramitā Sūtra* (T08n0223, 0218c17) is the emptiness of (1) the insides of the body; (2) anything outside of the body; (3) the appearance of inside or outside; (4) the preceding three emptinesses; (5) the four domains; (6) the highest truth [nirvāṇa]; (7) that which is saṁskṛta; (8) that which is asaṁskṛta; (9) the preceding eight emptinesses; (10) sentient beings without a beginning; (11) a composite thing disassembled; (12) self-essence of anything; (13) general and particular appearances of anything; (14) dharmas that make up a sentient being, such as the five aggregates, the twelve fields, and the eighteen spheres; (15) dharmas, which can never be captured; (16) existence; (17) nonexistence; and (18) the appearance of existence or nonexistence (see two emptinesses).

Eighteen Exclusive Dharmas (aṣṭādaśa-āveṇika-dharma, 十八不共法). Only a Buddha has these eighteen attainments, which Arhats, Pratyekabuddhas, and Bodhisattvas do not have. They are (1–3) faultless body, voice, and mind karmas; (4) impartiality to all; (5) abiding in constant meditation; (6) equability toward pleasure or pain; (7) never-diminishing desire to deliver sentient beings; (8) never-diminishing energy for delivering sentient beings; (9) never-diminishing memory of the Buddha Dharma; (10) never-diminishing wisdom; (11) never-diminishing liberation from afflictions and habits; (12) never-diminishing knowledge and views of liberation; (13–15) all body karmas, voice karmas, and mind karmas, led by wisdom; (16–18) perfect knowledge of the past, present, and future. Another set of eighteen comprises the Ten Powers, the Four Fearlessnesses, the three abidings of mindfulness, and great compassion. The three abidings of mindfulness means that a Buddha's mind abides in right mindfulness and wisdom, free from joy and woe in regard to (1) the group that believes in the Dharma and trains accordingly, (2) the group that neither believes in the Dharma nor trains accordingly, and (3) the group that comprises believers and nonbelievers.

eighteen heavens in the form realm (色界十八天), or eighteen Brahma heavens. Gods with pure desires reside in the form realm, in eighteen heavens, classified into four dhyāna heavens (四禪天), or four levels of meditation. The first dhyāna heaven comprises three heavens: Brahma Multitude (Brahma-pāriṣadya), Brahma Minister (Brahma-purohita), and Great Brahmā (Mahābrahmā). The second dhyāna heaven comprises three heavens: Limited Light (Parīttābha), Infinite Light (Apramāṇābha), and Pure Radiance (Ābhāsvara). The third dhyāna heaven comprises three heavens: Limited Splendor (Parīttaśubha), Infinite Splendor (Apramāṇaśubha), and Pervasive Splendor (Śubhakṛtsna). The fourth dhyāna heaven comprises nine heavens: Cloudless (Anabhraka), Merit Arising (Puṇyaprasava), Massive Fruition (Bṛhatphala), No Perception (Asaṁjña), No Vexation (Avṛha), No Heat (Atapa), Good Appearance (Sudṛśa), Good Vision (Sudarśana), Ultimate (Akaniṣṭha). The top five are the five pure-abode heavens (see Three Realms of Existence).

eighteen spheres (aṣṭādaśa-dhātu, 十八界). A sentient being is composed of the eighteen spheres: the six faculties (eye, ear, nose, tongue, body, and mental faculty [manas]), the six sense objects (sights, sounds, scents, flavors, tactile sensations, and mental objects), and the six consciousnesses (eye consciousness, ear consciousness, nose consciousness, tongue consciousness, body consciousness, and mental consciousness). Mental consciousness, the sixth consciousness, functions by itself as well as together with the first five consciousnesses. As the eye is the physical base from which eye consciousness arises, likewise manas (mental faculty) is the mental base from which mental consciousness arises. In the Mahāyāna doctrine, manas is also designated as the seventh consciousness, which has four innate defilements: (1) self-delusion (我癡), (2) self-love (我愛), (3) self-view (我見), and (4) self-arrogance (我慢). Ālaya, the eighth consciousness, though not explicitly included in the eighteen spheres, is the root of them all.

Eightfold Right Path (āryāṣṭāṅga-mārga, 八正道), or Noble Eightfold Path. The right path to one's liberation from one's cycle of birth and death includes (1) right views, (2) right thinking, (3) right speech, (4) right actions, (5) right livelihood, (6) right effort, (7) right mindfulness, and (8) right meditative absorption (samādhi). Paths 1–2 educate one with understanding, paths 3–5 establish one on the ground of morality, paths 7–8 develop one's mental power and wisdom through meditation, and path 6 is applied to the other seven paths of training.

emptiness (śūnyatā, 空). The lack of self-essence (independent inherent existence) of any dharma that arises and perishes through causes and conditions. Emptiness is not nothingness because it does not deny the illusory existence of all things. The non-duality of emptiness and existence and of nirvāṇa and saṁsāra, is the Middle View of the Mahāyāna doctrine (see two emptinesses).

Endurance of Dharmas (法忍). It includes endurance of persecution and suffering, and continued acceptance of the truth that dharmas are never born.

Endurance in the Realization That Dharmas Have No Birth (無生法忍). The lasting realization of the truth that dharmas have neither birth nor death as they appear and disappear through causes and conditions (see Three Endurances in the Dharma).

Five Āgamas (五阿含). An Āgama is a collection of early Buddhist scriptures. The Five Āgamas in the Chinese Canon are the Dīrgha Āgama (Long Discourses), the Madhyama Āgama (Middle-Length Discourses), the Saṁyukta Āgama (Connected Discourses), the Ekottarika Āgama (Numbered Discourses), and the Kṣudraka Āgama (Minor Discourses). They are parallel but not identical to the Five Nikāyas in the Pāli Canon, which are the Dīgha Nikāya, the Majjhima Nikāya, the Saṁyutta Nikāya, the Aṅguttara Nikāya, and the Khuddaka Nikāya.

five aggregates (pañca-skandha, 五蘊, 五陰). A sentient being is composed of the five aggregates: rūpa (form), vedanā (sensory reception), saṁjñā (perception), saṁskāra (mental processing), and vijñāna (consciousness). The first one is material and the other four are mental. Since these four are non-form (非色), thus present in name only, the five aggregates are summarized as name and form (名色). *Skandha* (蘊) in Sanskrit also means that which covers or conceals (陰), and the regular working of the five skandhas conceals true reality from a sentient being.

five coverings (pañca-āvaraṇa, 五蓋). One's true mind is covered by (1) greed, (2) anger, (3) stupor, (4) restlessness, and (5) doubt.

five desires (五欲). One's desires for pleasures in the five sense objects are (1) sights, (2) sounds, (3) scents, (4) flavors, and (5) tactile sensations. One also has the desire for pleasure in (6) mental objects, verbal or nonverbal, coarse or fine. Humans are driven especially by their desires for (1) riches, (2) sex, (3) reputation, (4) food and drink, and (5) sleep. These are impure desires in the desire realm, and there are pure desires in the form and formless realms.

five eyes (pañca-cakṣu, 五眼). These are (1) the physical eye, which a sentient being is born with; (2) the god eye, which can see anything anywhere; (3) the wisdom eye, which can see the emptiness of dharmas; (4) the dharma eye, which can differentiate all dharmas; and (5) the Buddha eye of omniscience, which includes the preceding four at the highest level (see three kinds of wisdom-knowledge).

five faculties (pañca-indrya, 五根). The first five of the six faculties.

five kinds of wisdom-knowledge (pañca-jñāna, 五智). According to esoteric teachings, a Buddha has acquired (1) the nature-of-the-dharma-realm wisdom-knowledge [dharma-dhātu-svabhāva-jñāna], (2) the mirror-like wisdom-knowledge [ādarśa-jñāna], (3) the equality wisdom-knowledge [samatā-jñāna], (4) the discernment wisdom-knowledge [pratyavekṣaṇā-jñāna], and (5) the accomplishment wisdom-knowledge [kṛtyānuṣṭhāna-jñāna]. According to the Consciousness-Only School, the last four kinds of wisdom-knowledge are transformed from the eighth, seventh, sixth, and the first five consciousnesses, respectively.

five precepts (pañca-śīla, 五戒). For lay Buddhists, the five precepts are (1) no killing, (2) no stealing, (3) no sexual misconduct, (4) no lying, and (5) no drinking alcohol.

five rebellious acts or sins (五逆). These are (1) patricide, (2) matricide, (3) killing an Arhat, (4) shedding the blood of a Buddha (including maligning His Dharma), and (5) destroying the harmony of a Saṅgha. They are also called the karma of the five no interruptions because any of them drives one into Avīci Hell, the hell of the five no interruptions.

five studies (pañca-vidyā, 五明). These are (1) language and composition, (2) science and technology, (3) medical arts, (4) logic, and (5) inner knowledge in a certain discipline.

five transcendental powers (五通). Through meditation, one can develop these powers: (1) the god eye to see anything anywhere; (2) the god ear to hear any sound anywhere; (3) the ability to know the past lives of self and others; (4) the ability to know the thoughts of others; (5) the ability to transform one's body and to travel instantly to any place.

five turbidities (pañca-kaṣāya, 五濁). The five kinds of degeneracy in a decreasing kalpa. They begin when human lifespan has decreased from 80,000 years to 20,000 years, and become more severe as human lifespan decreases to 10 years. They are (1) the turbidity of a kalpa in decay, which is characterized by the next four turbidities; (2) the turbidity of views, such as the five wrong views; (3) the turbidity of afflictions, including greed, anger, delusion, arrogance, and doubt; (4) the turbidity of sentient beings that live a wicked life and are in increasing suffering; (5) the turbidity of human lifespan as it decreases to 10 years. The wrong views in (2) and the afflictions in (3) are turbidity itself, which leads to the results in (4) and (5).

Four Abidings of Mindfulness (四念住, 四念處). One practices śamatha and vipaśyanā with one's mindfulness abiding in four places: body, sensory experiences, mind, and dharmas.

A. According to the Pāli Canon of the Theravāda School, one practices (1) mindfulness of one's body in stillness and in motion; (2) mindfulness of one's sensory experiences as pleasant, unpleasant, or neither; (3) mindfulness of one's mind, from which arises greed, anger, and delusion; (4) mindfulness of one's mental objects, including the teachings of the Buddha. Through vigilant mindfulness, one realizes that all dharmas are impermanent and that there is no self in command.

B. According to the Mahāyāna doctrine, one needs to observe that (1) the body is impure, (2) all experiences boil down to suffering, (3) the mind is constantly changing, and (4) all dharmas have no self (see right mindfulness).

four appearances (四相).

A. The four appearances of any saṁskṛta dharma are the four stages of a process: (1) arising, (2) continuing, (3) changing, and (4) ending. In the case of a sentient being, these four are (1) birth, (2) aging, (3) illness, and (4) death (see ten appearances). In the case of a world, these four are (1) formation, (2) continuation, (3) destruction, and (4) void.

B. The four appearances in the *Diamond Sūtra* are the four false self-images: (1) an autonomous self, (2) a person, (3) a sentient being, and (4) an everlasting soul (T080235, 0749a10–11). An autonomous self relates to everything conceived or perceived as non-self; a person has something in common with or different from other people; a sentient being has something in common with or different from other sentient beings; an everlasting soul remains the same as it assumes different bodies for different lives. The last three self-images are derived from the first. The four appearances are also called the four views (四見). In the *Buddha Store Sūtra,* a fifth self-image is given: (5) a living being with a lifespan (T15n0653, 0799b22–23) to terminate, preserve, or prolong.

four conditions (catuḥ-pratyaya, 四緣). These are (1) a causal condition (因緣), e.g., a seed is the direct cause of a sprout; (2) uninterrupted successive conditions (等無間緣), e.g., a sequence of mental activities forms one's perception; (3) an object as a condition (所緣緣), e.g., a thought or a sprout is an object of perception; (4) supporting conditions (增上緣), e.g., soil, water, and sunlight support a seed's ability to sprout. A mental event requires all four conditions; a physical event requires only the first and fourth conditions.

four continents (catur-dvīpa, 四洲). In the center of a small world in the Three Realms of Existence is Mount Sumeru. It is encircled by eight concentric mountain ranges, and these nine mountains are separated by eight oceans. Rising above the salty ocean between the outermost mountain range and the seventh inner mountain range are four large continents aligned with the four sides of Mount Sumeru. In the east is Pūrvavideha; in the south is Jambudvīpa; in the west is Aparagodānīya; in the north is Uttarakuru, where life is too pleasant for its inhabitants to seek the Dharma. Between every two large continents are two medium-sized continents and five hundred uninhabited small continents.

Four Dharmas to Rely Upon (四依法). In fascicle 6 of the *Mahāparinirvāṇa Sūtra* (T12n0375 [different from the *Mahāparinibbāna Sutta* in the Pāli Canon]), the Buddha teaches us to rely upon (1) the Dharma, not an individual; (2) sūtras of definitive meaning, not provisional meaning; (3) the true meaning, not just the words; (4) one's wisdom-knowledge, not consciousness. In summary, dharma means dharma nature (dharmatā); definitive meaning refers to Mahāyāna sūtras; true meaning refers to the eternal abiding and changelessness of a Tathāgata; wisdom-knowledge means the understanding that all sentient beings have Buddha nature.

four domains (catur-dhātu, 四界). According to ancient Indian philosophy, matter is made of the four domains—earth, water, fire, and wind—which have four corresponding appearances: solid, liquid, heat, and motion. Hence they are also called the great seeds (mahābhūta, 大種) with the four appearances as their self-essence, or changeless qualities. In fact, these appearances are the states of matter under prevailing conditions (see six domains).

Four Drawing-in Dharmas (四攝法). To draw sentient beings into the Dharma, one should use these four skillful ways: (1) almsgiving, (2) loving words, (3) beneficial actions, and (4) collaborative work.

Four Fearlessnesses (四無畏). Only a Buddha has (1) fearlessness because He has acquired the knowledge of all wisdom-knowledge [sarvajña-jñāna]; (2) fearlessness because He has eradicated all His afflictions; (3) fearlessness in explaining hindrances to one's attaining bodhi; (4) fearlessness in explaining the right path to end one's suffering.

four god-kings (四天王). They reside halfway up Mount Sumeru, in the first of the six desire heavens. As protectors of the world, they ward off the attacks of asuras. On the east side is Dhṛtarsaṣtra, the god-king Upholding the Kingdom; on the south side is Virūḍhaka, the god-king Increase and Growth; on the west side is Virūpākṣa, the god-king Broad Eye; and on the north side is Vaiśravaṇa, the god-king Hearing Much.

four grave prohibitions (四重禁). These are the prohibitions against committing the four grave root sins: (1) killing, (2) stealing, (3) sexual misconduct, and (4) lying, especially alleging spiritual attainment one does not have. The third root sin for monastic Buddhists is having sex.

four groups of disciples (四眾). See Saṅgha.

Four Immeasurable Minds (四無量心). These are (1) lovingkindness, (2) compassion, (3) sympathetic joy, and (4) equability.

four Indian castes (四姓). These are (1) Brahmin (priest), (2) kṣatriya (royalty and warrior), (3) vaiśya (farmer and merchant), and (4) śūdra (serf). The Buddha ruled that all from the four castes would be allowed to become Buddhist śramaṇas as the fifth caste, the highest of all castes.

four kinds of unimpeded wisdom-knowledge (catur-pratisaṁvid, 四無礙智, 四無礙解, 四無礙辯), also called four kinds of unimpeded understanding, and four kinds of unimpeded eloquence. A Bodhisattva has unimpeded wisdom-knowledge of (1) all dharmas; (2) their meanings; (3) all forms of expression, e.g., sounds, gestures, and words, in any language; (4) eloquent teaching of dharmas and their meanings, using apt expressions, according to sentient beings' capacities and preferences.

four kinds of wisdom-knowledge (catur-jñāna, 四智). A Buddha has the virtue of complete wisdom-knowledge, which includes (1) teacher-free or innate wisdom-knowledge [svayambhū-jñāna], (2) overall wisdom-knowledge [sarvajña], (3) knowledge of all wisdom-knowledge [sarvajña-jñāna], and (4) effortless wisdom-knowledge. Also, the last four of the "five kinds of wisdom-knowledge" are also called "four kinds of wisdom-knowledge."

four modes of birth (四生). Sentient beings are born through (1) the womb, such as humans and other mammals; (2) the egg, such as birds and reptiles; (3) moisture, such as fishes and insects; (4) miraculous formation, such as gods, ghosts, and hell-dwellers.

four necessities (四事供養). Offerings to a monk or nun, usually including (1) food and drink, (2) clothing, (3) bedding, and (4) medicine.

Four Noble Truths (catur-āryasatya, 四聖諦). In His first turning of the Dharma wheel, the Buddha taught the Four Noble Truths: (1) suffering (duḥkha), (2) accumulation (samudaya), (3) cessation (nirodha), and (4) the path (mārga). Suffering is the essence of repeated birth and death through the six life-paths; accumulation of afflictions, especially thirsty love of being (tṛṣṇā), is the cause of suffering; cessation of suffering comes with attainment of nirvāṇa; and the Eightfold Right Path is the path to nirvāṇa. As a condensed version of the Twelve Links of Dependent Arising, the first two truths reveal that, for continuing the flow of saṁsāra, the cause is accumulation of afflictions and the effect is suffering; the last two truths reveal that, for ending the flow of saṁsāra, the cause is taking the Eightfold Right Path and the effect is cessation of suffering upon realizing nirvāṇa.

four torrential flows (catur-ogha, 四暴流). One's afflictions that can wash away one's goodness. They are also called the four yokes (catur-yoga, 四軛) because sentient beings live under these yokes. They are (1) twenty-nine afflictions in the desire realm; (2) twenty-eight afflictions, such as greed, arrogance, and doubt, in the form realm and the formless realm; (3) thirty-six wrong views, such as permanence or impermanence of the world, existence or nonexistence of a Tathāgata after His parinirvāṇa, etc., in the Three Realms of Existence; (4) ignorance of the truth, of which there are five kinds in each of the three realms, totaling fifteen. They total 108 afflictions (Buddha's Light Dictionary 1988, 1831).

four types of troops (四種兵). They are (1) cavalry, (2) elephants, (3) chariots, and (4) infantry.

gandharva (乾闥婆). A fragrance eater who is also a celestial musician playing in the court of gods.

garuḍa (迦樓羅). A large bird-like being that eats dragons.

general appearance and particular appearance (總相別相). A general appearance, such as impermanence or no self, is common to all saṁskṛta dharmas. A particular appearance is a distinctive feature of a dharma; for example, earth has the appearance of solidity, and fire has the appearance of heat. A horse as a whole is the general appearance of all horses, while the black mane and white legs are the particular appearances of a particular horse.

god (deva, 天). The highest life form in the Three Realms of Existence. According to their merits and mental states, gods reside in six desire heavens, eighteen form heavens, and four formless heavens.

Gṛdhrakūṭa Mountain (耆闍崛山). The Vulture Peak Mountain (靈鷲山), northeast of the city of Rājagṛha. There the Buddha pronounced the *Lotus Sūtra* (T09n0262) and many other sūtras.

hell of the five no interruptions (五無間獄). In Avīci Hell, sentient beings undergo suffering with no interruption in five aspects: (1) no interruption in time; (2) no unoccupied space because one or many hell-dwellers fill up the hell; (3) no interruption in torture; (4) no exception for any sentient being; and (5) no interruption from life to life until their requital is done.

Hīnayāna (小乘). The Small Vehicle (see Two Vehicles).

icchantika (一闡提迦). One who has cut off one's roots of goodness and has no desire to attain Buddhahood. However, Buddhas never abandon any sentient beings and, through their spiritual power, an icchantika may replant his roots of goodness through causes and conditions in a future life and eventually attain Buddhahood. A Bodhisattva who has made a vow not to become a Buddha until all sentient beings have been delivered is called an icchantika of great compassion.

inversion (顛倒). The seven inversions are (1) taking the impermanence of dharmas as permanence; (2) taking suffering as happiness; (3) taking a nonexistent self as a self; (4) taking impurity as purity; (5) inverted perceptions, which refer to the inverted differentiations in the first four inversions; (6) inverted views, which refer to the establishment of, attachment to, and delight in the first four inversions; and (7) inverted mind, which refers to afflictions arising from the first four inversions. According to fascicle 7 of text 374, the 40-fascicle Chinese version of the *Mahāparinirvāṇa Sūtra*, the first four inversions also include (1) taking the eternity of a Tathāgata as impermanence, (2) taking the bliss of a Tathāgata as suffering, (3) taking the true self, which symbolizes a Tathāgata, as no self, and (4) taking the purity of a Tathāgata as impurity (T12n0374, 0407a14–b5).

Jambudvīpa (贍部洲). One of the four continents surrounding Mount Sumeru in a small world. Located south of Mount Sumeru and identified by the huge jambū (rose apple) tree, Jambudvīpa, the southern continent, is where humans and animals reside.

Jetavana (祇樹園). The Jeta Grove, a garden near Śrāvastī, presented to the Buddha by Sudatta the Elder, who purchased it from Prince Jeta, with gold covering its ground. In honor of the two benefactors, the estate was henceforth known as the Garden of Jeta and Anāthapiṇḍika (祇樹給孤獨園). The Buddha spent nineteen rainy seasons with His 1,250 monks in the monastery built in this garden. There he gave many of His teachings.

kalaviṅka (迦陵頻伽). A bird with a melodious voice, found in the Himalayas. It has beautiful black plumage and a red beak. It starts singing in the eggshell before it is hatched. Its beautiful voice surpasses that of humans, gods, kiṁnaras, and other birds, and is likened to the wondrous tones of Buddhas and holy Bodhisattvas.

kalpa (劫). An eon. A large kalpa is the long period of formation, continuation, destruction, and void of a world. It is divided into eighty small kalpas, each lasting 16,800,000 years.

karma (業).

A. An action, a work, or a deed done with one's body, voice, or mind. Good and evil karmas bring corresponding requitals in one's present and/or future lives. Neutral karmas (無記業) are actions that cannot be accounted as good or evil.

B. Karma (羯磨) is also the work in a ceremony for imparting Buddhist precepts or for repentance. It includes four requirements: (1) the dharma, i.e., the procedure; (2) the purpose; (3) people meeting the quorum; (4) the designated place.

Kauśala (憍薩羅國), or Kośala. Situated in central India, it is one of the sixteen ancient kingdoms of India.

kiṁnara (緊那羅). A celestial musician that resembles human, but with horns on his head.

koṭi (俱胝). The edge, the highest point. As a numeral, koṭi means one hundred thousand, one million, or ten million.

Licchavi (離車). An Indian clan in the kṣatriya caste, which was a ruling dynasty of the ancient kingdom of Vaiśālī in central India. After the Buddha's parinirvāṇa, the Licchavi people received one eighth of His relics.

life-journey (gati, 趣), or life-path (道). The life experience of a life form in its cycle of birth and death. According to past karmas, a sentient being continues to transmigrate through the six life-paths in corresponding life forms: god, asura, human, animal, hungry ghost, and hell-dweller. The first three life-paths are considered the good (fortunate) ones; the last three, the evil (unfortunate) ones. Given to anger and jealousy, asuras may be considered the fourth evil life-path. Sometimes, only five life-paths are mentioned in the sūtras because asuras may assume any of the first four life forms and live among sentient beings in these forms. In comparison with life in the Pure Land of Ultimate Bliss, all life-paths in this world are evil.

ludicrous statement (prapañca, 戲論). All wrong views are ludicrous statements. Furthermore, any statement is composed of words, which are empty names and appearances employed to make differentiations. It is ludicrous because in true reality it is empty.

Magadha (摩竭陀). A kingdom in central India, the headquarters of Buddhism up to year 400 CE.

mahāvaipulya sūtra (大方廣經). An extensive Mahāyāna sūtra that is great in explaining the right principles and great in its vast scope.

Mahāyāna (大乘). The Great Vehicle that can carry many people to Buddhahood. It is also called the Bodhisattva Vehicle because its riders are Bodhisattvas, who are resolved to attain Buddhahood, to benefit themselves and others (see Buddha Vehicle). The Mahāyāna doctrine, widely followed in Northeast Asia (China, Korea, and Japan), refers to the Theravāda School in Southeast Asia (Sri Lanka, Burma, Thailand, Laos, and Cambodia) as the Small Vehicle (Hīnayāna, 小乘), which can be either or both of the Two Vehicles (二乘).

Maheśvara (大自在天). In Hinduism, Maheśvara evolved from Śiva, his predecessor, into the highest god, creator and ruler of the universe. He is later admitted into Buddhism. According to fascicle 39 of text 279 (T10n0279), the 80-fascicle Chinese version of the *Mahāvaipulya Sūtra of Buddha Adornment* (Buddhāvataṁsaka-mahāvaipulya-sūtra), Maheśvara is the Brahma-king of the fourth dhyāna heaven, and rules a small world's Three Realms of Existence.

mahoraga (摩呼洛迦). A serpent or land dragon.

mantra (咒). An esoteric incantation. Buddhist mantras are imparted by Buddhas, sometimes through holy Bodhisattvas or Dharma protectors.

māra (魔). Killer, destroyer, evil one, or devil. The four kinds of māras are (1) the celestial māra, a god named Pāpīyān, residing with legions of subordinates in Paranirmita-vaśa-vartin Heaven, the sixth desire heaven; (2) māra of the five aggregates, which conceals one's Buddha mind; (3) māra of afflictions, which drives one to do evil karma; and (4) māra of death, which ends one's life.

namo (南無). Reverential homage, salutation, adoration, or obeisance. Based on the Sanskrit rule of pronunciation, this word may be spelled as namo, nama, namaḥ, namas, or namaś, according to the initial letter of the next word.

Nārāyaṇa (那羅延天). A Hindu god who has great strength. He is identified as Viṣṇu in the desire realm, and is included in the trinity of Brahmā, Nārāyaṇa, and Maheśvara (Śiva, in Hinduism).

nayuta (那由他), or niyuta. A numeral, meaning one hundred thousand, one million, or ten million.

Nirgranthaputra (尼乾子). One of the six non-Buddhist groups in ancient India. Nirgrantha means untied, which is the former name of the devotees of Jainism, who wander naked, untied to possessions. Nirgrantha-Jñātaputra (尼乾陀若提子), named after his mother, Jñātī, was the 24th and last patriarch of the Jain School, and he is now revered as the Mahāvīra (great hero). Their doctrine is fatalistic, stating that no spiritual practice can change one's good or evil karma and that all sentient beings would be automatically liberated after 80,000 kalpas of birth and death.

nirvāṇa (涅槃). By taking the Eightfold Right Path, one eradicates one's afflictions and attains nirvāṇa, liberating oneself from one's cycle of birth and death. The four nirvāṇas are (1) inherent nirvāṇa (自性涅槃), which means the true reality that all dharmas have neither birth nor death; (2) nirvāṇa with remnants (有餘依涅槃), which means the enlightenment of an Arhat or a Pratyekabuddha who is still living in his body, the remnants of his karmic existence; (3) nirvāṇa without remnants (無餘依涅槃), which means the death of an Arhat or a Pratyekabuddha, who has abandoned his body, the remnants of his karmic existence; and (4) nirvāṇa that abides nowhere (無住處涅槃), which means the supreme enlightenment of a Buddha. The great nirvāṇa of a Buddha includes the realization of the eternity, bliss, true self, and purity of a Tathāgata, and the attainment of powers unavailable to an Arhat or a Pratyekabuddha. Beyond the duality of existence and nonexistence, saṁsāra and nirvāṇa, a Buddha continues to manifest in most suitable ways in response to the needs of sentient beings, thus abiding nowhere.

no regress. See avinivartanīya.

one appearance (eka-lakṣaṇa, 一相). All dharmas are in the one appearance of true suchness, which is beyond differentiation of appearances and beyond differentiation between appearance and no appearance. However, the one appearance is often referred to as the one appearance of no appearance.

one flavor (eka-rasa, 一味). (1) All dharmas are in the one flavor of true suchness. (2) The Buddha's teachings of the Three Vehicles are all in the one flavor of the One Vehicle. As the one appearance of dharmas is likened to the earth, the one flavor of the Buddha's teachings is likened to the rain nourishing all the plants on earth.

parājika (波羅夷). The Sanskrit word *parāji* means succumb to or overcome by. Because one succumbs to one's afflictions, one commits a grave sin. A parājika is an extreme evil, the consequence of which is likened to having one's head severed, never to be recovered. The four parājikas a Buddhist monk should not commit are the four root sins: killing, stealing, having sex, and lying about his spiritual attainment. Because of any of these four, he will be expelled from the Saṅgha and, after death, will fall into hell. A Buddhist nun should not commit any of the eight parājikas: the listed four for monks and four more.

parinirvāṇa (般涅槃). It means beyond nirvāṇa, the death of an Arhat or a Buddha by entering profound samādhi. Whether or not He has abandoned His body in demonstrating parinirvāṇa, a Buddha is in the nirvāṇa that abides nowhere, beyond the duality of existence and nonexistence. A Buddha's parinirvāṇa is called mahāparinirvāṇa.

piśāca (畢舍遮). A demonic ghost that eats human flesh and sucks human vitality.

poṣadha (布薩). Nurturing purity, a mandatory system for monastic Buddhists to convene twice each lunar month on poṣadha days (布薩日), new-moon and full-moon days, in designated places for different groups, to disclose their transgressions, repent of them, and listen to a qualified member recite the precepts. When lay Buddhists choose to accept and observe the eight precepts on one or more of the six purification days during a lunar month, it is also called poṣadha.

prātimokṣa (波羅提木叉). The Sanskrit word *prati* means toward or severally, and *mokṣa* means liberation. The term *prātimokṣa* is translated into Chinese as "liberation achieved severally" (別解脫). It is also referred to as prātimokṣa-saṁvara, where *saṁvara* means restraint (律儀), or more commonly as prātimokṣa-śīla, where *śīla* means precept (戒), because observance of different precepts leads to liberation severally from corresponding evils of one's body, voice, and mind. Moreover, prātimokṣa precepts instituted by the Buddha for His seven groups of disciples in the desire realm are separate from meditation precepts (定共戒) that naturally arise in one's mind from one's meditation at the form-realm level, and separate from affliction-free precepts (無漏戒) that naturally arise in one's mind upon attaining bodhi.

Pratyekabuddha (緣覺佛). One who is enlightened through pondering the Twelve Links of Dependent Arising. He is also called a solitary Buddha (獨覺佛) because, living in solitude, he has realized the truth without receiving teachings from a Buddha.

preceptor (upādhyāya, 和尚). A monk qualified to teach other monks. However, the Chinese title *heshang* was phonetically translated from *khosha,* a word used in the kingdom of Yütian (于闐), or Khotan, present-day Hetian (和田), in Xinjiang, China. It has become an honorific address to an exalted monk.

pure-abode heavens (淨居天). The top five of the nine heavens that constitute the fourth dhyāna heaven in the form realm (see Three Realms of Existence and "eighteen heavens in the form realm").

Rājagṛha (王舍城). The capital city of Magadha in central India, near the Vulture Peak Mountain.

rākṣasa (羅刹). A demonic ghost that eats human flesh. Rākṣasas are said to be the original inhabitants of Sri Lanka.

right mindfulness (samyak-smṛti, 正念). The seventh in the Eightfold Right Path. A few examples of right mindfulness include (1) practice of the Four Abidings of Mindfulness; (2) memory of the Dharma, such as the teaching that all dharmas have no birth; (3) memory of a Buddha; and (4) the inconceivable mindfulness of a Buddha.

roots of goodness (kuśala-mūla, 善根). These are (1) no greed, (2) no anger, and (3) no delusion. The Five Roots included in Thirty-seven Elements of Bodhi are goodness in themselves and can grow other good dharmas.

ṛṣi (仙人). An ascetic hermit considered to be an immortal or a godlike human. Śākyamuni Buddha is also revered as the Great Ṛṣi. In the *Śūraṅgama Sūtra* (T19n0945), the Buddha describes ten kinds of ṛṣis, who live thousands or tens of thousands of years, with the five transcendental powers, such as traveling across the sky, changing themselves into any form, etc.

Sahā World (sahā-lokadhātu, 娑婆世界). The endurance world. It refers to Jambudvīpa or the Three-Thousand Large Thousandfold World, where sentient beings are able to endure their suffering and may even find their lives enjoyable.

Śakro-Devānām-Indra (釋提桓因). The title of the god-king of Trayastriṁśa Heaven, often abbreviated as Śakra or Indra. The Buddha calls the incumbent Śakra by his family name, Kauśika.

samādhi (定). A state of mental absorption in meditation. Above the level of the desire realm, there are eight levels of worldly samādhi (八定). The first four levels are the four dhyānas (四禪) of the form realm. The next four levels are the four samādhis of the formless realm (四空定): Boundless Space (空無邊), Boundless Consciousness (識無邊), Nothingness (無所有), and Neither with Nor without Perception (非有想非無想). A Buddhist or non-Buddhist who has attained any of the eight levels of meditation can be reborn in a corresponding heaven in the form or formless realm. Only an Arhat can attain the ninth level called the Samādhi of Total Halt (滅盡定), also more appropriately called the Samādhi of Total Suspension of Sensory Reception and Perception (滅受想定). To enter the Samādhi Door of Buddhas is to attain innumerable samādhis.

samāpatti (三摩鉢底). The right experience in equilibrium (正受), which is samādhi in a balanced and stable state.

śamatha (奢摩他). It means stillness, a mental state in which one's mind is in single-minded concentration (see vipaśyanā).

saṁsāra (輪迴), or jāti-maraṇa (生死). The cycle of birth and death, in which every sentient being transmigrates through the six life-paths in the Three Realms of Existence. This endless cycle is called the hard-to-cross ocean, also called the ocean of suffering (see two kinds of birth and death).

saṁskṛta (有爲). Formed or made through causes and conditions. Each saṁskṛta dharma is a process with the four appearances. Sentient beings and all the things they perceive or conceive are saṁskṛta dharmas (see asaṁskṛta).

Saṅgha (僧伽). A community comprising a Buddha's four groups of disciples (四眾): monks (bhikṣu), nuns (bhikṣuṇī), laymen (upāsaka), and laywomen (upāsikā).

sarvajña. See three kinds of wisdom-knowledge.

sarvajña-jñāna. See three kinds of wisdom-knowledge.

self-essence (svabhāva, 自性). An inherent state of being, self-made, self-determined, and changeless. This is a false perception of a dharma. In truth, nothing has self-essence because everything is constantly changing through causes and conditions. That a dharma has no self-essence is the true reality defined as emptiness.

Seven Bodhi Factors (sapta-bodhyaṅga, 七覺分). These are (1) critical examination of theories [dharma-vicaya], (2) energetic progress [vīrya], (3) joyful mentality [prīti], (4) lightness and peacefulness in body and mind [praśrabdhi], (5) mindfulness in all activities and memory of the Dharma [smṛti], (6) meditative absorption [samādhi], and (7) equability under favorable or unfavorable circumstances [upekṣa].

seven noble treasures (七聖財). They are (1) faith, (2) almsgiving, (3) observing the precepts, (4) having a sense of shame, (5) having a sense of dishonor, (6) hearing the Dharma, and (7) wisdom.

seven treasures (七寶). These are (1) suvarṇa (金, gold); (2) rūpya (銀, silver); (3) vaiḍūrya (琉璃, aquamarine); (4) sphaṭika (頗梨, crystal); (5) musāragalva (硨磲, conch shell or white coral); (6) lohita-muktikā (赤珠, ruby); and (7) aśmagarbha (瑪瑙, emerald). Sometimes coral and amber are included in place of crystal and ruby. F. Max Müller cites a reference in *Buddhist Mahāyāna Texts* (Cowell et al. [1894] 1969, part 2, 92), in which *vaiḍūrya* is matched with lapis lazuli, and *aśmagarbha* with diamond. According to the online dictionary spokensanskrit.de, *vaiḍūrya* means beryl; *abhraroha* means lapis lazuli; *aśmagarbha* means emerald; *vajra* (金剛) means diamond. Contexts of *vaiḍūrya* mentioned in Buddhist sūtras indicate that it should be a pale blue variety of beryl, i.e., aquamarine, not lapis lazuli, an opaque deep blue stone.

siddhi (悉地). Achievement through spiritual training using one's body, voice, and mind. The ultimate siddhi is Buddhahood.

six causes (ṣad-hetu, 六因). A saṁskṛta dharma may be one of the six causes: (1) a working cause 能作因, e.g., empty space can accommodate objects, and the earth can support life; (2) a concurrent cause 俱有因, e.g., three sticks together support something; (3) a corresponding-effect cause 同類因, e.g., a good thought leads to a corresponding good action; (4) an interactive cause 相應因, e.g., mental functions interact with one another; (5) an all-affecting cause 遍行因, e.g., a wrong view affects all one's actions; (6) a ripening cause 異熟因, or requital cause, e.g., the karma of killing a sentient being brings the killer a requital, his rebirth in hell, like a ripened fruit.

six desire heavens (六欲天). (1) Heaven of the Four God-Kings (Cātur-mahārāja-kāyika-deva, 四天王天); (2) Trayastriṁśa Heaven (忉利天), or Thirty-three Heavens (三十三天), ruled by Śakra-Devānām-Indra; (3) Yāma Heaven (夜摩天), ruled by Suyāma-devarāja; (4) Tuṣita Heaven (兜率天), ruled by

Saṁtuṣita-devarāja; (5) Nirmāṇa-rati Heaven (化自在天), ruled by Sunirmita-devarāja; (6) Paranirmita-vaśa-vartin Heaven (他化自在天), ruled by Vaśavartti-devarāja. The first two heavens are earth-abode heavens; all other heavens are sky-abode heavens.

six domains (ṣad-dhātu, 六界, 六大). A sentient being is made of the six domains—earth, water, fire, wind, space, and consciousness—and appears to have these features: solid substance, fluid, heat, motion, space within the body, and consciousness. A non-sentient thing (plant or nonliving thing) is made of the first five domains (see four domains).

six faculties (ṣaḍ-indriya, 六根, 六入). These are eye, ear, nose, tongue, body, and mental faculty (manas). The first five are physical, and the last is mental. They are also called six entrances or six internal fields (see twelve fields).

six pāramitās (六度, 六波羅蜜). The Sanskrit word *pāramita* means gone across to the opposite shore. To cross over to that shore of nirvāṇa, opposite this shore of saṁsāra, a Bodhisattva must practice the six pāramitās: (1) dāna (almsgiving), (2) śīla (observance of precepts), (3) kṣānti (endurance of adversity), (4) vīrya (energetic progress), (5) dhyāna (meditation), and (6) prajñā (development of wisdom). See ten pāramitās.

six periods (六時). The day is divided into morning (6–10 a.m.), midday (10 a.m.–2 p.m.), and afternoon (2–6 p.m.); the night into evening (6–10 p.m.), midnight (10 p.m.–2 a.m.), and post-midnight (2–6 a.m.). Each period has four hours.

six transcendental powers (六通). With no more afflictions to discharge, an Arhat has liberated himself from his cycle of birth and death. Hence complete eradication of afflictions (漏盡通) is called the sixth transcendental power of an Arhat, which is unavailable to those who have not attained Arhatship. It also makes his achievement in the first five transcendental powers superior to that of those others (see five transcendental powers).

sixty-two views (六十二見). The wrong views held by ancient Indian philosophers. One set of 62 views argues about each of the five aggregates of a sentient being: in the past it is permanent, impermanent, both, or neither; in the present it is with boundary, without boundary, both, or neither; in the future it is going, not going, both, or neither. To these 60 views, two opposites, perpetuity and cessation of existence, are added to make a total of 62. Another set of 62 views includes 56 views of a self and 6 views of existence. They hold that each of the five aggregates of a sentient being in the desire realm and the form realm, and each of the four aggregates of a god in the formless realm, is a self, not a self, both, or neither, totaling 56 views. In addition, a sentient being's perpetuity and cessation of existence in the Three Realms come to 6 views.

śramaṇa (沙門). An ascetic or a monk, one who has renounced family life and lives a life of purity, poverty, and diligent training, seeking the truth.

Śrāvastī (舍衛國). The capital city of the ancient kingdom of Kauśala.

stages of the Bodhisattva Way (菩薩階位). The spiritual levels of a Bodhisattva on the Way to Buddhahood. According to the 80-fascicle Chinese version of the *Mahāvaipulya Sūtra of Buddha Adornment* (T10n0279), a Bodhisattva progresses through fifty-two levels, which are classified into seven stages:

(1) ten faithful minds, (2) ten levels of abiding, (3) ten levels of action, (4) ten levels of transference of merit, (5) Ten Grounds, (6) virtually perfect enlightenment, and (7) perfect enlightenment. A Bodhisattva will continue to be an ordinary being as he cultivates the ten faithful minds; he will be a sage as he practices the ten pāramitās, progressing through the ten levels of abiding, ten levels of action, and ten levels of transference of merit; and he will be a holy being as he progresses through the Ten Grounds. A Bodhisattva will ascend to the first ground when he realizes that all dharmas have no birth. As he progresses from the first ground to the tenth ground, he will achieve the ten pāramitās one after another, in one-to-one correspondence with the Ten Grounds. At the fifty-first level, his enlightenment being virtually perfect, he will be in the holy position of waiting to become a Buddha in his next life. At the fifty-second level, he attains perfect enlightenment, achieving the ultimate fruit of the aspiration and training of a Bodhisattva.

store (藏). An interpretation of the Sanskrit word *garbha,* which means embryo or womb. The store of all teachings is the Dharma store; the store of all precepts is the precept store. The Tathāgata store (tathāgata-garbha) is equated to one's true mind, sheathed in one's afflictions. It is likened to the space store (ākāśa-garbha) in its vastness and to the earth store (kṣiti-garbha) in its supportiveness and hidden treasures.

stūpa (窣堵婆). A memorial tower for the remains of a holy being, whether scriptures or relics of bones.

suffering (duḥkha, 苦). The first of the Four Noble Truths.

A. The eight kinds of suffering are (1) birth, (2) old age, (3) illness, (4) death, (5) inability to get what one wants, (6) loss of what one loves, (7) encounter with what one hates, and (8) the driving force of the five aggregates. Driven by the five aggregates, one experiences impermanence, pain, and sorrow in the preceding seven situations.

B. The three kinds of suffering are (1) pain brought by a cause (苦苦), (2) deterioration of pleasure (壞苦), and (3) continuous change in every process (行苦).

sūtras in the twelve categories (十二部經). The teachings of the Buddha are classified by content and form into the twelve categories: (1) sūtra, discourses in prose; (2) geya, songs that repeat the teachings; (3) vyākaraṇa, prophecies; (4) gāthā, stanzas; (5) udāna, self-initiated utterances; (6) nidāna, causes of the discourses; (7) avadāna, parables; (8) itivṛttaka, sūtras that begin with "so it has been said"; (9) jātaka, past lives of the Buddha; (10) vaipulya, extensive teachings; (11) adbhuta-dharma, marvelous events; and (12) upadeśa, pointing-out instructions.

Tathāgata (如來). The Thus-Come One, the first of the ten epithets of a Buddha, which signifies true suchness. Although a Tathāgata never moves, He appears in the world as if He has come, and enters parinirvāṇa as if He has gone, in the same way as did past Buddhas.

ten appearances (十相).

A. According to fascicle 25 of the 40-fascicle Chinese version of the *Mahāparinirvāṇa Sūtra* (T12n0374), "no appearance" means freedom from these ten appearances: (1) sights, (2) sounds, (3) scents, (4) flavors, (5) tactile sensations, (6) birth, (7) existence, (8) death, (9) maleness, and (10) femaleness.

B. According to fascicle 27, nirvāṇa is free from these ten appearances: (1) birth, (2) old age, (3) illness, (4) death, (5) sights, (6) sounds, (7) scents, (8) flavors, (9) tactile sensations, and (10) impermanence.

ten directions (十方). The spatial directions of east, southeast, south, southwest, west, northwest, north, northeast, the nadir, and the zenith.

ten evil karmas (十惡). These are (1) killing, (2) stealing, (3) sexual misconduct, (4) false speech, (5) divisive speech, (6) abusive speech, (7) suggestive speech, (8) greed, (9) anger, and (10) the wrong views.

ten good karmas (十善). The opposites of the ten evil karmas are (1) no killing, (2) no stealing, (3) no sexual misconduct, (4) no false speech, (5) no divisive speech, (6) no abusive speech, (7) no suggestive speech, (8) no greed, (9) no anger, and (10) no wrong views.

ten kinds of wisdom-knowledge (daśa-jñānāni, 十智). An Arhat has acquired ten kinds of wisdom-knowledge: (1) worldly wisdom-knowledge, (2) dharma wisdom-knowledge, (3) ensuing wisdom-knowledge, (4) wisdom-knowledge of suffering, (5) wisdom-knowledge of accumulation of afflictions, (6) wisdom-knowledge of cessation of suffering, (7) wisdom-knowledge of the path, (8) wisdom-knowledge of others' minds, (9) wisdom-knowledge that his afflictions have ended forever, (10) wisdom-knowledge that dharmas have no birth.

ten pāramitās (十度, 十波羅蜜). In parallel with the Ten Grounds for Bodhisattva development (see stages of the Bodhisattva Way), added to the list of six pāramitās are four more pāramitās: (7) upāya (skillful means), (8) praṇidhāna (earnest wishing), (9) bala (power), and (10) jñāna (wisdom-knowledge).

Ten Powers (daśa-bala, 十力). Because a Buddha's wisdom-knowledge is indestructible and unsurpassed, it is called powers. He has perfect wisdom-knowledge of (1) everyone's right or wrong action in every situation, and its corresponding karmic consequences; (2) the karmic requitals of every sentient being in the past, present, and future; (3) all stages of dhyāna, liberation, and samādhi; (4) the capacity of every sentient being; (5) the desires and preferences of every sentient being; (6) the nature and kind of every sentient being; (7) the consequences of all actions, with or without afflictions; (8) all past lives of every sentient being and their karmic reasons; (9) all future rebirths of every sentient being and their karmic reasons; (10) the permanent ending of all His afflictions and habits upon attainment of Buddhahood.

ten precepts (daśa-śīla, 十戒). Observed by novice monks and nuns, the ten precepts include the eight precepts, but precepts 7 and 8 are renumbered 8 and 9, because precept 6 is divided into two: (6) no wearing perfumes or adornments, and (7) no singing, dancing, or watching song-dance entertainments. A tenth precept is added: (10) no touching or hoarding money or treasures.

Thirty-seven Elements of Bodhi (三十七道品). Also called Thirty-seven Aids to Attain Bodhi, these trainings are classified into seven categories:

A. Four Abidings of Mindfulness;

B. Four Right Endeavors: (1) end forever the existing evil, (2) do not allow new evil to arise, (3) cause new goodness to arise, and (4) expand existing goodness;
C. Four Ways to Attain Samādhi: (1) aspiration, (2) energetic progress, (3) memory, and (4) contemplation;
D. Five Roots: (1) root of faith, (2) root of energetic progress, (3) root of memory, (4) root of samādhi, and (5) root of wisdom;
E. Five Powers: (1) power of faith, (2) power of energetic progress, (3) power of memory, (4) power of samādhi, and (5) power of wisdom;
F. Seven Bodhi Factors;
G. Eightfold Right Path.

three ages of the Dharma (正像末期). The Dharma of Śākyamuni Buddha will end after these three ages: (1) The true Dharma age (正法) lasted 500 to 1,000 years after His passing. During this age, there were teachings, carrying out of the teachings, and attaining of fruits. (2) The Dharma-likeness age (像法) lasted 500 to 1,000 years. During this age, there were teachings and carrying out of the teachings, but no attaining of fruits. (3) The Dharma-ending age (末法) will last 10,000 years. During this age, the teachings will gradually vanish, and there will be neither carrying out of the teachings nor attaining of fruits. Because people will no longer be receptive, the Dharma will be gone for a long time until the advent of the next Buddha. In the *Sūtra of the Bodhisattva in Mother's Womb* (T12n0384, 1025c15–19), fascicle 2, the Buddha prophesies that, after 56 koṭi and 70 million years, which means 630 million years (if a koṭi is 10 million), Maitreya Bodhisattva will descend from Tuṣita Heaven and become the next Buddha, bringing the Dharma to a renewed world.

three bodies of a Buddha (三身). These are (1) dharmakāya (dharma body or truth body), which is emptiness, the true reality of all dharmas; (2) saṁbhogakāya (reward body or enjoyment body, in a sublime ethereal form), which personifies a Buddha's immeasurable merit; (3) nirmāṇakāya (response body through birth or miraculous manifestation), which is a Buddha's response to sentient beings ready to accept the Dharma. The reward body and response body are the appearances of the dharma body, and these three bodies are inseparable. According to the Tiantai School of China, of the latest Buddha, Vairocana is the dharmakāya, Rocana is the saṁbhogakāya, and Śākyamuni is the nirmāṇakāya.

three Buddha natures (三佛性). These are (1) Buddha nature inherent in all sentient beings but unknown to them, (2) Buddha nature gradually revealed through one's spiritual training, and (3) Buddha nature fully revealed in a Buddha.

three fortune fields (三福田). These are (1) the reverence field (敬田), which means the Three Jewels; (2) the kindness field (恩田), which means one's parents and teachers; and (3) the compassion field (悲田), which means the poor, the sick, and animals. By making offerings to any of these three fortune fields, one plants seeds that will yield harvests of fortune in one's present and future lives.

three groups (三聚). Sentient beings are divided into three groups: (1) the group that definitely progresses on the right path to bodhi (正定聚); (2) the group that definitely is on the wrong path (邪定聚); (3) the group that is indecisive about its path (不定聚). Some members of the third group, through causes and conditions, may come to join one of the other two groups.

Three Jewels (三寶). These are (1) the Buddha, the unsurpassed perfectly enlightened teacher; (2) the Dharma, His teachings; and (3) the Saṅgha, the Buddhist community.

three kinds of hindrances (三障). Hindrances to realization of one's true mind are (1) afflictions, such as greed, anger, and delusion, which agitate one's mind and lead to negative karmas; (2) karmas, done with one's body, voice, and mind, which lead to requitals; and (3) requitals, such as an unfortunate rebirth in human form with incomplete faculties, or in the form of animal, hungry ghost, or hell-dweller.

three kinds of wisdom-knowledge (三智). These are (1) overall wisdom-knowledge (sarvajña, 一切智), which is the emptiness of everything, acquired by an Arhat, a Pratyekabuddha, and a holy Bodhisattva; (2) discriminative wisdom-knowledge (道種智), which is a holy Bodhisattva's growing wisdom-knowledge of the differences of all things; (3) knowledge of all wisdom-knowledge (sarvajña-jñāna, 一切種智), or omniscience, which is a Buddha's perfect wisdom-knowledge of all beings and all things in their general and particular aspects, and of the non-duality of emptiness and myriad displays of illusory existence.

Three Liberation Doors (trīṇi vimokṣa-mokha, 三解脫門), or Three Samādhis. These are (1) emptiness, (2) no appearance, and (3) no wish or no action. Through samādhi, one realizes emptiness, verifying that all dharmas have no birth. One also realizes that the illusory appearances of dharmas conceived or perceived are no appearance. One makes no wish and does nothing for future rebirths in the Three Realms of Existence.

Three Realms of Existence (trayo-dhātu, 三界, 三有). The world of illusory existence, in which sentient beings transmigrate, comprises (1) the desire realm (欲界), where reside sentient beings with the full range of afflictions, such as hell-dwellers, ghosts, animals, humans, asuras, and some gods; (2) the form realm (色界), where Brahma gods, who have only pure desires, reside in eighteen form heavens classified into the four dhyāna heavens (四禪天), or four levels of meditation; and (3) the formless realm (無色界), where formless gods are in mental existence in four formless heavens, or at four levels of long, deep meditative absorption (see samādhi).

Three Refuges (三皈依). One becomes a Buddhist by taking refuge, for protection and guidance, in the Three Jewels: the Buddha, the Dharma, and the Saṅgha. According to the *Sūtra of the Garland of a Bodhisattva's Primary Karmas,* with the four indestructible faiths one should take the Four Refuges, and the fourth refuge is the precepts (T24n1485, 1020c22–24).

Three Samādhis (三三昧). See Three Liberation Doors.

Three Vehicles (三乘). The Great Vehicle (Mahāyāna) and the Two Vehicles.

Three-Thousand Large Thousandfold World (三千大千世界). A galaxy, the educational district of a Buddha. It consists of a billion small worlds, each including a Mount Sumeru surrounded by four continents and interlaying circles of eight oceans and eight mountain ranges. One thousand such small worlds constitute a Small Thousandfold World. One thousand Small Thousandfold Worlds constitute a Medium Thousandfold World. Finally, one thousand Medium Thousandfold Worlds constitute a Large Thousandfold World. Therefore, *Three-Thousand* does not mean 3,000, but 1,000 raised to the power of 3, as just described. It can also mean that there are three kinds of Thousandfold World: small, medium, and large.

total retention (總持). See dhāraṇī.

Trayastriṁśa Heaven (忉利天). The second of the six desire heavens. It is on the top of Mount Sumeru, and the first desire heaven is halfway up Mount Sumeru, while all other heavens are up in the sky. Trayastriṁśa Heaven means Thirty-three Heavens, all ruled by the god-king Śakro-Devānām-Indra, who is commonly called Śakra or Indra.

Tripiṭaka (三藏). The three collections of texts of the Buddhist Canon: (1) the Sūtra-piṭaka, discourses of the Buddha; (2) the Vinaya-piṭaka, rules of conduct; and (3) the Abhidharma-piṭaka, treatises on the Dharma. A Tripiṭaka master is accomplished in all three areas.

true suchness (bhūta-tathātā, 真如). The changeless true reality of all dharmas, the absolute truth that dharmas have neither birth nor death. It has other names, including emptiness, true emptiness, ultimate emptiness, one appearance, one flavor, ultimate reality, true reality (bhūta-koṭi), true state, primal state, Buddha mind, true mind, inherent pure mind, the Thus-Come One (Tathāgata), the thus-come store (tathāgata-garbha), vajra store, Buddha nature, dharma nature, dharma body (dharmakāya), dharma realm, the one true dharma realm, the highest truth (paramārtha), the great seal, and the great perfection. One's body and mental states, and objects perceived as external, are all manifestations of one's true mind, projected through causes and conditions from the pure, impure, and neutral seeds stored in ālaya consciousness.

twelve fields (dvādaśa-āyatana, 十二處, 十二入), or twelve places. A sentient being is composed of the twelve fields: the six faculties (eye, ear, nose, tongue, body, and mental faculty [manas]) and their six objects (sights, sounds, scents, flavors, tactile sensations, and mental objects). The six faculties are also called the six internal fields, and their objects are called the six external fields. The Consciousness-Only School calls the latter "projected appearances" (影像相分). And modern neurologists recognize that percepts are "brain representations" (see eighteen spheres).

Twelve Links of Dependent Arising (十二因緣法). The principle that explains why and how a sentient being continues to be reborn according to karma. Each link is the main condition for the next one to arise. These twelve links are (1) ignorance, (2) karmic actions, (3) consciousness, (4) name and form, (5) six faculties, (6) contact with sense objects, (7) sensory reception, (8) love, (9) grasping, (10) karmic force for being, (11) birth, and (12) old age and death. Links 1–2 refer to the afflictions and karmic seeds from previous lives, links 3–7 refer to the karmic fruit in the present life, links 8–10 refer to karmas in the present life, and links 11–12 refer to the karmic fruit in the next life. In this sequence, the twelve links connect one's lives from the past to the present, continuing to the future. With ignorance, one goes from affliction to karma to suffering, continuing the endless spiral of birth and death. By ending ignorance one will disengage the remaining eleven links and end one's cycle of birth and death.

two emptinesses (二空). (1) The emptiness of a sentient being (人空) composed of dharmas, such as the five aggregates, and dependent on causes and conditions; (2) the emptiness of a dharma (法空), such as any of the five aggregates, dependent on causes and conditions (see eighteen emptinesses).

two kinds of hindrances (二障).

A. (1) Affliction hindrances (kleśāvaraṇa, 煩惱障), which lead to another two kinds of hindrances: evil karmas and corresponding requitals (see three kinds of hindrances); (2) hindrances to wisdom-knowledge (jñeyāvaraṇa, 智障), which are one's ground-abiding ignorance (住地無明), the root ignorance (根本無明).

B. (1) Affliction hindrances as in A (1); (2) hindrances to liberation, which prevent one from attaining the Samādhi of Total Suspension of Sensory Reception and Perception.

two kinds of wisdom-knowledge (二智). There are several pairs, such as true wisdom-knowledge (實智) and applied wisdom-knowledge (權智); root wisdom-knowledge (根本智) and consequent wisdom-knowledge (後得智); overall wisdom-knowledge (一切智) and knowledge of all wisdom-knowledge (一切種智). True wisdom-knowledge, root wisdom-knowledge, and overall wisdom-knowledge are synonyms, all pertaining to knowledge of the true reality of dharmas, which is emptiness. Applied wisdom-knowledge, also called facilitation wisdom-knowledge (方便智), pertains to knowledge of skillful means to train oneself and deliver sentient beings. True wisdom-knowledge is the essence, and applied wisdom-knowledge is its usage. Consequent wisdom-knowledge pertains to knowledge of all varieties of dharmas, consequent to acquiring the root wisdom-knowledge (see "knowledge of all wisdom-knowledge" in "three kinds of wisdom-knowledge").

two kinds of birth and death (二種生死). (1) An ordinary being, whose lifespan and life form are governed by the law of karma, repeatedly undergoes karmic birth and death through successive lifespans (分段生死). (2) A holy Bodhisattva on any of the Ten Grounds, whose lifespan and mind-created body (意生身) are changeable at will, undergoes changeable birth and death (變易生死). Only a Buddha has ended both kinds of birth and death.

Two Vehicles (二乘). The Voice-Hearer Vehicle that leads to Arhatship and the Pratyekabuddha Vehicle that leads to Pratyekabuddhahood, for one's own liberation only. The Mahāyāna doctrine refers to the Theravāda School in Southeast Asia (Sri Lanka, Burma, Thailand, Laos, and Cambodia) as the Small Vehicle (Hīnayāna), which can be either or both of these Two Vehicles.

Two-Footed Honored One (dvipadottama, 兩足尊). A Buddha is the most honored one among sentient beings standing on two feet, i.e., gods and humans. Moreover, the two feet of a Buddha are compared to meditation and moral conduct, merit and wisdom, knowledge in the relative and absolute truth, knowledge and action, or vow and action. A Buddha has perfected both.

unimpeded eloquence (無礙辯). This term can mean a Bodhisattva's four kinds of unimpeded wisdom-knowledge or only the fourth kind (see four kinds of unimpeded wisdom-knowledge).

upadeśa (優波提舍). A pointing-out instruction, usually interpreted as a treatise (see sūtras in the twelve categories).

upaniṣad (優波尼薩曇). Sitting down at the feet of another to listen to his words. It suggests secret knowledge given in this manner. It may be an esoteric unit of measure.

upāsaka (優婆塞). A Buddhist layman (see Saṅgha).

upāsikā (優婆夷). A Buddhist laywoman (see Saṅgha).

Vairocana (毘盧遮那). The name of the dharmakāya or saṁbhogakāya of a Buddha (see three bodies of a Buddha). Vairocana means pervasive radiance, and signifies the universal equality of everything in true suchness as well as the all-encompassing wisdom of a Buddha. According to the *Mahāvaipulya Sūtra of Buddha Adornment* (T09n0278) in 60 fascicles, Vairocana is the name for a Buddha's dharmakāya. According to the *Brahma Net Sūtra* (T24n1484), Rocana is the name for a Buddha's saṁbhogakāya. Śākyamuni Buddha, in His nirmāṇakāya, is sometimes referred to as Vairocana Buddha or Rocana Buddha.

Vaiśālī (毘舍離). The domicile of the Licchavi clan, one of the sixteen great city kingdoms of ancient India. One hundred years after the Buddha's parinirvāṇa, in this city, 700 sages gathered in the second assembly for the compilation and revision of the Buddhist Canon.

vajra (伐折羅, 金剛). (1) Adamantine and indestructible, a description of the true suchness of all dharmas. (2) Diamond, considered to be as hard as a thunderbolt. (3) A ritual object, as a symbol of skillful means to deliver oneself and others from the cycle of birth and death.

Vārāṇasī (波羅奈國). An ancient city state on the Ganges, the present-day city of Benares. Nearby is Deer Park, where the Buddha gave His first teachings to five monks.

Veda (吠陀). Sacred knowledge, the general name of the Hindu canonical sacred texts. The four Vedas are the Ṛg-veda, Sāma-veda, Yajur-veda, and Athara-veda. They include mantras, prayers, hymns, and rituals. The Ṛg-veda is the only original work of the first three Vedas. Its texts are assigned to a period between 1400 and 1000 BCE. The fourth Veda, Athara-veda, emerged later.

view of void (空見). The wrong view that the emptiness of dharmas means nothingness and that therefore causality can be ignored.

vipaśyanā (毗婆舍那). Correct observation or clear seeing, which leads to insight. Śamatha-vipaśyanā has been translated as stillness and observation (止觀), or as silent illumination (默照). When śamatha and vipaśyanā are balanced in power, one may realize the non-dual state of one's mind.

voice-hearer (śrāvaka, 聲聞). One who has received oral teachings from the Buddha. Those who follow only His teachings preserved in the Hīnayāna Canon recognized by the Theravāda School are present-day voice-hearers. Listed below are a few disciples of the Buddha:

Ājñātakauṇḍinya (阿若憍陳如) was one of the first five disciples of the Buddha. He is well regarded as an Elder.

Ānanda (阿難) was the younger brother of Devadatta. As the Buddha's attendant, he is noted for hearing and remembering all the teachings of the Buddha. Ānanda became an Arhat after the Buddha's parinirvāṇa. In the first assembly of Arhats, he recited from memory all the teachings for the compilation of the sūtras. Succeeding Mahākāśyapa, he is recognized as the second patriarch of the Buddhist lineage.

Aniruddha (阿那律) became a disciple soon after the Buddha's enlightenment. He used to fall asleep when the Buddha was teaching and was reproved by the Buddha. Ashamed, he practiced day and night without sleep and lost his eyesight. However, he was able to see with his god eye.

Aśvajit (阿說示) was one of the first five disciples of the Buddha. He had comely features and majestic deportment. Śāriputra was impressed and asked him about his teacher. Aśvajit explained to Śāriputra the dependent arising of dharmas. Then Śāriputra joined the Buddha's order.

Devadatta (提婆達多) was a cousin of the Buddha, with whom he had competed since childhood. He became a disciple after the Buddha had attained perfect enlightenment. He trained hard for twelve years but did not attain Arhatship. Disgusted, he studied magic and formed his own group. Devadatta beat a nun named Utpalavarṇā to death and made several attempts to murder the Buddha and destroy the Saṅgha. He fell into hell after his death. However, in a previous life he had given the Buddha Mahāyāna teachings. Despite the wicked deeds in his life, the Buddha prophesies in the *Lotus Sūtra* (T09n0262) that Devadatta will become a Buddha called Devarāja.

Kapphiṇa (劫賓那) was born under the constellation Scorpio. He is said to have understood astronomy, been the king of Southern Kauśala, and then become a disciple of the Buddha, receiving his monastic name Mahākapphiṇa. In the *Lotus Sūtra* (T09n0262), the Buddha prophesies that Kapphiṇa will become a Buddha called Samanta-prabhāsa.

Kāśyapa brothers (三迦葉) were Uruvilvākāśyapa (優樓頻螺迦葉), Nadīkāśyapa (那提迦葉), and Gayākāśyapa (伽耶迦葉). Initially fire-worshippers, they joined the Buddha's Order together with their 1,000 followers.

Mahākāśyapa (摩訶迦葉) was initially a Brahmin in Magadha. He became a disciple three years after the Buddha had attained enlightenment. In eight days, Mahākāśyapa attained Arhatship. He is considered foremost in ascetic practices. When the Buddha held up a flower, only Mahākāśyapa in the huge assembly understood the meaning and responded with a smile (X01n0027, 0442c16–21). Then the Buddha entrusted him with the continuation of the lineage, and he became the first patriarch after the Buddha's parinirvāṇa. After entrusting the lineage to Ānanda, Mahākāśyapa went to the Vulture Peak (Gṛdhrakūṭa) Mountain. There he has remained in samādhi. He will enter parinirvāṇa after the advent of the next Buddha, Maitreya.

Mahākauṣṭhila (摩訶拘絺羅) joined the Buddha's Order after his nephew Śāriputra did. He soon attained Arhatship and acquired unimpeded eloquence. The Buddha praised him as foremost in eloquence.

Mahāmaudgalyāyana (大目揵連), together with his own disciples, following his good friend Śāriputra, became a disciple of the Buddha and attained Arhatship in a month. Śāriputra is portrayed as standing on the Buddha's right, with Maudgalyāyana on His left. Maudgalyāyana was stoned to death by Brahmins shortly before the Buddha's parinirvāṇa. He is considered foremost in transcendental powers.

Mahānāma (摩訶那摩 or 摩訶男) means great name. He was one of the first five disciples of the Buddha.

Nanda (難陀). (1) Nanda was the half brother of the Buddha. He was also called Sundara-Nanda (孫陀羅難陀), with his wife's name Sundarī added to differentiate him from Nanda the Cattle Herder. He was tall and handsome, with thirty marks of a great man. After becoming a monk under the Buddha, he was still attached to his wife. Through the Buddha's skillful teachings, he ended his love and desire and attained Arhatship. (2) Nanda was the Cattle Herder who offered milk every day to the Buddha and His disciples during their three-month summer retreat. Assuming that the Buddha knew nothing about cattle herding, he asked Him questions. After the Buddha told him eleven things about cattle herding, Nanda was deeply moved and joined the Buddha's Order.

Pilindavatsa (畢陵伽婆蹉) had been a Brahmin accomplished in mantra practice. After he encountered the Buddha, his mantras lost their power. He then joined the Buddha's order.

Pūrṇa (富樓那) is also called Pūrṇa-Maitrāyaṇīputra, under his mother's family name Maitrāyaṇī. He was the son of a minister of King Śuddhodana of the kingdom of Kapilavastu. He was very intelligent, and studied the Vedas at a young age. On the night Prince Siddhārtha left the palace to seek the truth, he too left with thirty friends to practice asceticism in the snow mountain. He attained the four dhyānas and the five transcendental powers. After Siddhārtha attained Buddhahood and did the first turning of the Dharma wheel in Deer Park, he became a monk in the Buddha's Order and soon attained Arhatship. He is considered foremost in expounding the Dharma because some 99,000 people were delivered through his teachings.

Rāhula (羅睺羅) was the only son of Śākyamuni Buddha and Yaśodharā. He had been in gestation for six years and was born on the lunar eclipse after the Buddha had attained perfect enlightenment. Rāhula was six years old when the Buddha returned to the city kingdom of Kapilavastu, and he became a novice monk at the command of the Buddha. Foremost in secret training, he is to be reborn as the eldest son of every future Buddha.

Revata (離婆多) is the younger brother of Śāriputra. In his meditation at a temple, he saw two ghosts fighting to eat a corpse. Realizing the illusoriness of the body, he renounced family life and became a disciple of the Buddha. Traveling barefoot in a snow country, his feet were frostbitten. The Buddha praised him for his contentment with few material things and allowed him to wear shoes.

Śāriputra (舍利弗), together with his own disciples, joined the Buddha's Order soon after the Buddha's enlightenment. After being a principal disciple for forty-four years, to avoid his grief over the Buddha's parinirvāṇa, he requested and received the Buddha's permission to enter parinirvāṇa sooner than the Buddha. He is considered foremost in wisdom among the disciples.

Subhūti (須菩提) is the foremost among the disciples in understanding the meaning of emptiness. He is the principal interlocutor in the *Prajñā-Pāramitā Sūtra*.

Upāli (優波離) had been a barber in the royal court. He became a disciple, together with Ānanda, six years after the Buddha had attained perfect enlightenment. Foremost in observing the precepts, he contributed to the compilation of the Vinaya in the first assembly of the Arhats after the Buddha's parinirvāṇa.

Vāṣpa (婆師波) was one of the first five disciples of the Buddha. After the Buddha's parinirvāṇa, while Mahākāśyapa became the leader of elders who formed the Sthaviravāda sect, which survives to this day as the Theravāda School, Vāṣpa became the leader of the multitude that formed the Mahāsaṅghika sect, which laid the foundation for the rise of the Mahāyāna.

Yaśoda (耶舍 or 耶輸陀) was from Vārāṇasī in central India, son of a wealthy elder. He saw the Buddha in Deer Park with His first five disciples, and became His sixth one.

voice-hearer fruits (聲聞果).

A. The four holy fruits achieved by voice-hearers on the Liberation Way are (1) Srotāpanna, the Stream Enterer, who will attain Arhatship after at most seven times being reborn as a god then a human; (2) Sakṛdāgāmin, the Once Returner, who will be reborn as a human only once more before attaining Arhatship; (3) Anāgāmin, the Never Returner, who will not be reborn as a human but will attain Arhatship in a pure-abode heaven in the form realm; (4) Arhat, the Foe Destroyer, who has attained nirvāṇa with remnants by annihilating his fixation on having an autonomous self and eradicating all his afflictions.

B. These four holy fruits and the corresponding nearness to them are called the eight holy ranks (八聖). Actually, one who is in the first rank, nearing the first holy fruit, is only a sage, and those in the higher seven ranks are holy beings. Those who are still learning (śaikṣa, 有學) are in the first seven ranks. Only Arhats, in the eight rank, are those who have nothing more to learn (aśaikṣa, 無學).

Vulture Peak Mountain. See Gṛdhrakūṭa Mountain.

Way (道). The Way in the Mahāyāna doctrine is to find the ultimate truth within one's own mind. Those who see objects as existing outside their minds are considered not on the Way. The word *Way* (Dao or Tao) in Chinese Daoism means the natural order of things in the world, contrary to its meaning in Buddhist doctrine.

Wheel-Turning King (cakra-vartī-rāja, 轉輪王). A ruler, the wheels of whose chariot roll everywhere unimpeded. The wheel (cakra), one of the seven precious things he owns, comes in four ranks: iron, copper, silver, and gold. The iron wheel king rules one continent, the south; the copper wheel king rules two, east and south; the silver wheel king rules three: east, west, and south; the gold wheel king rules all four continents. A Buddha, the universal Dharma King, turns the Dharma wheel, giving teachings to sentient beings.

yakṣa (夜叉). A demonic ghost that eats human flesh.

Yama (夜摩). The king of the underworld and superintendent of the karmic punishment of hell-dwellers.

yojana (由旬). The distance covered by one day's march of an army or by one day's walk of a yoked bull. One yojana may equal 4 or 8 krośas, each krośa being the distance at which a bull's bellow can be heard. The estimated distance of a yojana varies from 8 to 19 kilometers.

Reference

In English

Anacker, Stefan, trans. 1998. *Seven Works of Vasubandhu.* Delhi: Motilal Banarsidass Publishers. (Org. pub. 1984)

Buswell, Robert E., Jr. 1989. *The Formation of Ch'an Ideology in China and Korea: The Vajrasamadhi-Sutra, a Buddhist Apocryphon.* Princeton, NJ: Princeton University Press.

———, ed. 1990. *Chinese Buddhist Apocrypha.* Honolulu: University of Hawaii Press.

———, trans. 2007. *Cultivating Original Enlightenment: Wŏnhyo's Exposition of the Vajrasamādhi-Sūtra (Kŭmgang Sammaegyŏng Non).* Honolulu: University of Hawaii Press.

Chang, Garma C. C., ed. 1983. *The True Lion's Roar of Śrīmālā.* In *A Treasury of Mahāyāna Sūtras: Selections from the Mahāratnakūṭa Sūtra* (Translated from Chinese by the Buddhist Association of the United States). University Park, PA: Pennsylvania State University Press.

Grosnick, William H., trans. 1995. *Tathagata-garbha Sutra.* In *Buddhism in Practice,* edited by Donald S. Lopez Jr. Princeton, NJ: Princeton University Press.

Johnston, E. H., ed. 1950. *The Ratnagotravibhāga Mahāyānottaratantraśāstra* (in Sanskrit). Seen through the press and furnished with indexes by T. Chowdhury. Patna, India: Bihar Research Society.

King, Sallie B. 1991. *Buddha Nature.* Albany, NY: State University of New York Press.

Obermiller, E., trans. 1931. "The sublime science of the great vehicle to salvation: Being a manual of Buddhist monism." *Acta Orientalia* IX: 81–306. Reprinted in 1991 in *The Uttaratantra of Maitreya,* compiled by H. S. Prasad. Delhi: Sri Satguru Publications.

Olivelle, Patrick, trans. 2008. *Upaniṣads.* New York: Oxford University Press. (Orig. pub. 1996)

Paul, Diana Y. 1980. *The Buddhist Feminine Ideal: Queen Srimala and the Tathagatagarbha.* Missoula, MT: Scholars Press. (Orig. published as the author's thesis, University of Wisconsin—Madison, 1974)

———, trans. 2004. *The Sutra of Queen Srimala of the Lion's Roar.* Berkeley, CA: Numata Center for Buddhist Translation and Research. PDF file online at http://www.bdk.or.jp/pdf/bdk/digitaldl/dBET_Srimala_Vimalakirti_2004.pdf

Prasad, H. S., comp. 1991. *The Uttaratantra of Maitreya* (Containing Introduction, E. H. Johnston's Sanskrit Text, and E. Obermiller's English Translation). Delhi: Sri Satguru Publications.

Radich, Michael. 2015. *The Mahāparinirvāṇa-mahāsūtra and the Emergence of Tathāgatagarbha Doctrine.* Hamburg, Germany: Hamburg University Press. PDF file online at http://hup.sub.uni-hamburg.de/volltexte/2015/153/pdf/HamburgUP_HBS05_Radich.pdf

Rulu, trans. 2012a. *Teachings of the Buddha.* Bloomington, IN: AuthorHouse. (Orig. pub. 2009)

———, trans. 2012b. *Thinking of Amitābha Buddha*. Bloomington, IN: AuthorHouse. (Orig. pub. 2011)
———, trans. 2012c. *Bodhisattva Precepts*. Bloomington, IN: AuthorHouse.
———, trans. 2013. *The Bodhisattva Way*. Bloomington, IN: AuthorHouse.
———, trans. 2014. *Two Holy Grounds*. Bloomington, IN: AuthorHouse.
———, trans. 2015. *Transcending the World*. Bloomington, IN: AuthorHouse.
Shih Heng-Ching 釋恆清. "The Significance of Tabhagatagarbha – A Positive Expression of Sunyata." *Philosophical Review*, vol. 2 (1988): 227–46. Also available online at http://web.archive.org/web/20050215202318/http://zencomp.com/greatwisdom/ebud/ebdha191.htm
Silk, Jonathan A. 2015. *Buddhist Cosmic Unity: An Edition, Translation and Study of the "Anūnatvāpūrṇatvanirdeśaparivarta."* Hamburg, Germany: Hamburg University Press. PDF file online at http://hup.sub.uni-hamburg.de/volltexte/2015/154/pdf/HamburgUP_HBS4_Silk_Unity.pdf
Suzuki, Daisetz Teitaro, trans. 1999. *The Lankavatara Sutra: A Mahayana Text*. Delhi: Motilal Banarsidass Publishers. (Orig. pub. 1932)
Takasaki, Jikido 高崎直道. 2014a. *A Study on the Ratnagotravibhāga (Uttaratantra): Being a Treatise on the Tathāgatagarbha Theory of Mahāyāna Buddhism*. Delhi: Motilal Banarsidass Publishers. (Org. pub. 1966)
———. 2014b. *Collected Papers on the Tathāgatagarbha Doctrin e*. Delhi: Motilal Banarsidass Publishers.
Tāranātha. 1990. *Tāranātha's History of Buddhism in India*. Translated from Tibetan by Lama Chimpa [and] Alaka Chattopadhyaya. Edited by Debiprasad Chattopadhyaya. Delhi: Motilal Banarsidass Publishers. (Orig. Pub. 1970) PDF file online at http://www.ahandfulofleaves.org/documents/Taranatha's%20History%20of%20Buddhism%20in%20India.pdf
Thera, Nyanaponika, and Hellmuth Hecker. 2003. *Great Disciples of the Buddha: Their Lives, Their Works, Their Legacy*. Edited by Bikkhu Bodhi. Somerville, MA: Wisdom Publications.
Wayman, Alex, and Hideko Wayman, trans. 1974. *The Lion's Roar of Queen Srimala: A Buddhist Scripture on the Tathagatagabha Theory*. New York: Columbia University Press. Also available online at http://www.purifymind.com/SrimalaDeviSutra.htm

In Chinese

Chinese Electronic Tripiṭaka Collection 電子佛典集成. DVD-ROM, 2014 version. Containing the Taishō Tripiṭaka 大正藏, vols. 1–55, 85, and the Shinsan Zokuzōkyō 卍續藏, vols. 1–88. Taipei, Taiwan: Chinese Buddhist Electronic Text Association. Also available online at http://cbeta.org/
Du Zhengmin 杜正民. Rulai zangxue yanjiu xiaoshi—Rulai zangxue shumu jianjie yü daodu (shang) 如來藏學研究小史—如來藏學書目簡介與導讀（上） [A concise history of studies of the Tathagata store: A brief introduction and guide to a catalog of texts on the Tathagata store (part 1)]. *Buddhist Library Newsletter* 佛教圖書館館訊 10/11 (1997.9): 32–52. Also available online at http://ccbs.ntu.edu.tw/FULLTEXT/BM/bm83070.htm

———. Rulai zangxue yanjiu xiaoshi—Rulai zangxue shumu jianjie yü daodu (xia) 如來藏學研究小史—如來藏學書目簡介與導讀（下） [A concise history of studies of the Tathagata store: A brief introduction and guide to a catalog of texts on the Tathagata store (part 2)]. *Buddhist Library Newsletter* 佛教圖書館館訊 12 (1997.12): 37–63. Also available online at http://ccbs.ntu.edu.tw/FULLTEXT/BM/bm83529.htm

Foguang Dacidian 佛光大辭典 [Buddha's light dictionary]. 7 vols. 1988. Kaoshiung, Taiwan: Buddha's Light Publishing. Also available online at http://etext.fgs.org.tw/etext6/search-1.htm

Mizuno, Kōgen 水野弘元. "Bodaidaruma no Ninyūshigyō setsu to Kongōzammaikyō 菩提達摩の二入四行說と金剛三昧經" (in Japanese) [The Vajra Samadhi Sutra and Bodhidharma's teaching on the two entrances and four actions]. *Komazawa University Proceedings of Buddhist Studies* 駒澤大学佛教学部研究紀要 13 (1955): 33–57.

Nakamura, Zuiryū 中村瑞隆. 1988. *Fanhan Duizhao Jiujing Yisheng Baoxinglun Yanjiu* 梵漢對照究竟一乘寶性論研究 [A study of the Ratnagotravibhāga Mahāyānottaratantra-śāstra in Sanskrit and Chinese]. Taipei, Taiwan: Huayü Publishing 華宇出版社. Translated into Chinese by Yicong Bianweihui 譯叢編委會 from the Japanese original published in 1961 in Tokyo by Shanxifang Buddhist Books 山喜房仏書林. PDF file online at http://www.baohuasi.org/e_book/xz-3977.pdf

Shi Sheng-yen 釋聖嚴, trans. 2001. *Zijia Baozang: Rulai Zangjing Yüti Yishi* 自家寶藏: 如來藏經語體譯釋 [One's own treasure store: the Tathagata Store Sutra rendered into modern Chinese]. Taipei, Taiwan: Fagu Wenhua Shiye 法鼓文化事業. Also available online at http://ddc.shengyen.org/mobile/toc/07/index.php

Shi Yinshun 釋印順. 1985. *Chengfo Zhidao* 成佛之道 [The way to Buddhahood]. Taipei, Taiwan: Zhengwen Publishing 正聞出版社. Also available online at http://www.mahabodhi.org/files/yinshun/10/yinshun10-00.html

———. 1992. *Rulai Zangzhi Yanjiu* 如來藏之研究 [A study of the Tathagata store]. Taipei, Taiwan: Zhengwen Publishing 正聞出版社. (orig. pub. 1981). Also available online at http://www.mahabodhi.org/files/yinshun/34/yinshun34-00.html

———. 2011. *Shengmanjing Jiangji* 勝鬘經講記 [A talk on the Shrimala Sutra (given in 1951)]. Taipei, Taiwan: Zhonghua Bookstore 中華書局. Also available online at http://www.mahabodhi.org/files/yinshun/06/yinshun06-00.html

Shi Zhiyü 釋智諭. 2002. *Jingang Sanmeijing Yiboji* 金剛三昧經一波記 [A wave of the Vajra Samadhi Sutra]. Taipei County, Taiwan: Xilian Jingyuan Publishing 西蓮淨苑出版社. Also available online at http://www.seeland.org.tw/zhiyu/seeland_taida_old/fahua/016.htm

Shih Heng-Ching 釋恆清. "Pipan fojiao boyi" 「批判佛教」駁議 [A rebuttal of "critical Buddhism"]. *National Taiwan University Philosophical Review* 國立台灣大學哲學論評 24 (2001): 1–46. Also available online at http://ccbs.ntu.edu.tw/FULLTEXT/JR-NX020/nx99885.htm

Soothill, William Edward, and Lewis Hodous., comps. 1962. *A Dictionary of Chinese Buddhist Terms* 中英佛學辭典. Kaohsiung, Taiwan: Buddhist Culture Service. Also available online at http://mahajana.net/texts/kopia_lokalna/soothill-hodous.html

Reference

Xü Wenming 徐文明. "Jingang sanmei jing zozhe bian" 《金剛三昧經》作者辨 [Identifying the author of the Vajra Samadhi Sutra]. *Chinese Culture Research* 中国文化研究 1997/4. Also available online at http://www.guoxue.com/discord/xwm/jgsm.htm

Yang Weizhong 杨维中. 2012. *Rulai Zang Jingdian Yü Zhongguo Fojiao* 如来藏经典与中国佛教 [Tathagata-store scriptures and Chinese Buddhism]. Nanjing, China: Jiangsu People's Publishing.

Yü Delong 于德隆. "Jingang sanmei jing zhenwei kao" 《金剛三昧經》真僞考 [On the authenticity of the Vajrasamadhi Sutra]. *Yuan Kuang Journal of Buddhist Studies* 圓光佛學學報 20 (2012): 135–92. PDF file online at http://enlight.lib.ntu.edu.tw/FULLTEXT/JR-BJ010/bj010395613.pdf

On the Internet

Bhikkhu Thanissaro, trans. 2003. *Angulimala Sutta*. http://www.freedharma.com/text/canonical/angulimala_sutta/14a29efd9ef0b29e5a4905caa66f11e2/

Hamburg Buddhist Studies. http://blogs.sub.uni-hamburg.de/hup/reihen/hamburg-buddhist-studies/

Hecker, Hellmuth, trans. 2007. "Angulimala: A Murderer's Road to Sainthood." *Access to Insight* (Legacy Edition) 30 November 2013. http://www.accesstoinsight.org/lib/authors/hecker/wheel312.html

Hodge, Stephen. 2006. "On the Eschatology of the Mahaparinirvana Sutra and Related Matters" (A lecture delivered at the University of London). http://www.nirvanasutra.net/historicalbackground2.htm

Nirvana Sutra. http://www.nirvanasutra.net/

Online Buddhist Dictionary 在線佛學辭典. http://www.baus-ebs.org/fodict%5Fonline/

Online Buddhist Sutras. http://fodian.net/world/

Rulu. Mahayana Buddhist Sutras and Mantras. http://www.sutrasmantras.info/

Sanskrit, Tamil and Pahlavi Dictionaries. http://webapps.uni-koeln.de/tamil/

Shi Taixü 釋太虛. "Fofa zongjueze tan" 佛法總抉擇談 [A summary critical examination of Buddhist teachings] (written in 1922). http://read.goodweb.cn/news/news_view.asp?newsid=62450

University of the West. Digital Sanskrit Buddhist Canon. http://www.uwest.edu/sanskritcanon/dp/

WIKIPEDIA: The Free Encyclopedia. http://en.wikipedia.org/